1709

War and Society

Series Editors

MICHAEL B. BARRETT *and* KYLE SINISI

The study of military history has evolved greatly over the past fifty years, and the "War and Society" series captures these changes with the publication of books on all aspects of war. The series examines not only traditional military history with its attention to battles and leaders, but it explores the broader impact of war upon the military and society. Affecting culture, politics, economies, and state power, wars have transformed societies since the ancient world. With books that cut across all time periods and geographical areas, this series reveals the history of both the conduct of war and its societal consequences.

Darryl Dee, *1709: The Twilight of the Sun King*
Marc Gallicchio, *The Scramble for Asia: U.S. Military Power in the Aftermath of the Pacific War*
Ear J. Hess, *Civil War Torpedoes and the Global Development of Landmine Warfare*
Brian D. Laslie, *Air Power's Lost Cause: The American Air Wars of Vietnam*
Geoffrey Megargee, *War of Annihilation: Combat and Genocide on the Eastern Front, 1941*
Lawrence Sondhaus, *German Submarine Warfare in World War I: The Ons et of Total War at Sea*
Haruo Tohmatsu and H. P. Willmott, *A Gathering Darkness: The Coming of War to the Far East and the Pacific, 1921–1942*
Alan Warren, *Slaughter and Stalemate in 1917: British Offensives from Messines Ridge to Cambrai*
H. P. Willmott, *The War with Japan: The Period of Balance, May 1942–October 1943*
Thomas W. Zeiler, *Unconditional Defeat: Japan, America, and the End of World War II*

1709

The Twilight of the Sun King

Darryl Dee

ROWMAN & LITTLEFIELD
Lanham • Boulder • New York • London

Published by Rowman & Littlefield
An imprint of The Rowman & Littlefield Publishing Group, Inc.
4501 Forbes Boulevard, Suite 200, Lanham, Maryland 20706
www.rowman.com

86-90 Paul Street, London EC2A 4NE

Copyright © 2025 by The Rowman & Littlefield Publishing Group, Inc.

All rights reserved. No part of this book may be reproduced in any form or by any electronic or mechanical means, including information storage and retrieval systems, without written permission from the publisher, except by a reviewer who may quote passages in a review.

British Library Cataloguing in Publication Information Available

Library of Congress Cataloging-in-Publication Data

Names: Dee, Darryl, 1972- author.
Title: 1709 : the twilight of the Sun King / Darryl Dee.
Other titles: Seventeen hundred and nine, the twilight of the Sun King
Description: Lanham : Rowman & Littlefield, 2025. | Series: War and society | Includes bibliographical references and index.
Identifiers: LCCN 2024042882 (print) | LCCN 2024042883 (ebook) | ISBN 9781538176658 (cloth) | ISBN 9781538176665 (paperback) | ISBN 9781538176672 (epub)
Subjects: LCSH: France—History, Military—1643-1715. | France—History—Louis XIV, 1643-1715. | Louis XIV, King of France, 1638-1715—Last years. | Spanish Succession, War of, 1701-1714. | Flanders—History, Military—18th century.
Classification: LCC DC127.6 .D44 2025 (print) | LCC DC127.6 (ebook) | DDC 940.2/526—dc23/eng/20241115
LC record available at https://lccn.loc.gov/2024042882
LC ebook record available at https://lccn.loc.gov/2024042883

∞™ The paper used in this publication meets the minimum requirements of American National Standard for Information Sciences—Permanence of Paper for Printed Library Materials, ANSI/NISO Z39.48-1992.

For Amy and Inès

Contents

Preface	ix
1 The New Year: January 1, 1709	1
2 The Winter: January–March, 1709	33
3 The Army: March–May, 1709	63
4 The Negotiations: May–June, 1709	95
5 The Campaign: June–August, 1709	131
6 The Battle: September–December, 1709	171
7 A New Year	219
Bibliography	241
Index	253
About the Author	265

Preface

At Versailles, in a corner of what were once the apartments of the princes of the blood, largely overlooked by the armies of tourists who tramp through the great palace every day, hangs my favorite picture of Louis XIV. It is a wax effigy done by the King's Painter Antoine Benoist around 1705. Even today, three and a half centuries after it was built, Versailles remains a shrine to Louis. Images of him, including the famous state portrait in his coronation robes by Hyacinthe Rigaud, are everywhere you look. Out of them all, Benoist's work is unique in portraying Louis not how he wanted to be seen but as he actually was. He was then about sixty-seven years old. His age shows in his face—in the sallowness of his skin, the droop of his cheek, the crow's feet at the corner of his eye, and the wrinkles around his mouth. Nevertheless, he has an expression of stern determination and looks out with a bright, piercing gaze. He possesses the commanding presence of a man who had been an absolute monarch since he was four years old and had known nothing else.

By the time Benoist made his effigy, Louis was entering the twilight of his reign (at seventy-two years, the longest in history and unlikely ever to be surpassed). This period has long fascinated me. When I wrote my first book on Louis' conquest and integration of Franche-Comté, I was struck by how the last thirty years of his reign were filled with overlapping crises in a way wholly unlike the glorious first half. The nadir was 1709, when France suffered foreign invasion, a financial crash, the coldest winter of the past five centuries, and its last great famine. I decided to make this year the subject of my next book. I had also become interested in the military history of the War of the Spanish Succession, the general conflict from 1702 to 1714 that pitted France against the other great powers of Western Europe. Histories of this war are still dominated by the mighty figure of John Churchill, Duke of Marlborough. The monumental—and monumentally influential—hagiography by his descendant Winston Churchill depicts him as a military genius, an outstanding statesman, and the prime mover of the Grand Alliance that opposed Louis XIV. I realized that an account of this war from the French perspective was sorely needed.

Not unlike Antoine Benoist's portrait, this book attempts to show Louis XIV and his kingdom as they actually were at their most perilous moment. It is a narrative history of a year, a campaign, and a battle. During 1709, the conjunction of catastrophes served as the ultimate trial of Louis and the French absolute monarchy he had perfected. Historians once neglected Louis' late reign, preferring instead its first quarter century when he established himself famously as the Sun King. After 1700, it was thought, the king and his regime both declined as Louis grew old and tired, government became ossified and torpid, and the court of Versailles lost its liveliness and luster. In recent years, groundbreaking research has completely overturned this long-standing view. The final period of the reign was, in fact, one of dynamic change and far-reaching reforms in which the absolute monarchy evolved into a seasoned state possessing a council of experienced ministers, an incipient bureaucracy of effective royal agents, and deep ties of collaboration with powerful social elites throughout France. Moreover, Louis remained determined to the end of his life to fully exercise the duties, powers, and prerogatives of kingship—what was called in his day the *métier de roi*. How the absolute monarchy and the king confronted and survived their greatest ordeal is one of the stories this book tells.

A second story is about the Flanders campaign. Flanders—today northern France and southern Belgium—was the most important theater of the War of the Spanish Succession. In 1709, Louis' foes were poised to advance on Paris and Versailles, while he set his last remaining major field army to stop them. This book gives the first full account in English of the French side of this crucial campaign. Moreover, it provides a total history of the campaign. It gives logistics their due, showing how the immense challenges of paying soldiers and feeding men and horses decisively shaped French designs and actions. It also merges diplomatic and military dimensions. Diplomacy and fighting were inextricably linked and worked hand in hand: events on the battlefield were meant to influence developments at the negotiating table and vice versa.

The last story this book tells is of the Battle of Malplaquet. On September 11, 180,000 French and Allied soldiers clashed in the largest and bloodiest engagement of the eighteenth century. For a long time, academic historians eschewed studying battles. They were largely relegated to amateurs who, though enthusiastic and energetic, often lacked the languages, the sources, and the intellectual formation required to extract full meaning from their subjects. Two generations ago, the academic study of battles began a remarkable revival. This is happening, surprisingly, even in France, where the historical profession has long devoted itself to investigating the deep structures of society, economy, and culture over the *longue durée* to the exclusion of supposedly ephemeral events like wars and battles. An important school of historians has fashioned a "new history of battle" (*la nouvelle histoire-bataille*). One of its chief arguments is that battles are moments of apocalyptic revelation that expose the nature and characteristics of the states and societies that fought them.

Such an approach is especially necessary for the battles of the eighteenth century. There remains a widely accepted stereotype that European warfare in this era was limited because it was driven by neither the religious furies of the seventeenth century nor the ideological passions of the nineteenth century. Wars were fought to achieve specific, defined objectives, such as the acquisition of morsels of territory or the upholding of dynastic prestige. Their violence was restrained by baroque conventions accepted and practiced by all combatants. The image of eighteenth-century wars as constrained and full of artifice is wonderfully captured by the French phrase *guerres en dentelles* or wars of lace. Perhaps, the most widely known incident from an eighteenth-century battle is from Fontenoy in 1745, in which the aristocratic officers of the British and French Guards exchanged courtesies, then politely invited each other to fire first.

Malplaquet explodes these stereotypes. It was intended to be a showdown that would decisively end the greatest war of its time. It was fought with great determination and utter ferocity—the leaders of both armies remarked that their troops both gave and expected no quarter. With at least 32,000 casualties, its carnage was enormous: it would not be matched until fifty years later at Kunersdorf and not surpassed until Austerlitz in 1805. This book recounts this battle in detail and in depth. It anatomizes it at the strategic, operational, and tactical levels. Finally, it delves into the expectations, motivations, and experiences of the combatants, from the generals in command to the common soldier trapped in its smoke-filled, clamorous, terrifying chaos.

In researching and writing this book, I have incurred debts of gratitude to many people. During years of archival work in France, the staffs of the Archives Nationales, the Service Historique de la Défense, and the

Archives du Ministère des Affaires Étrangères have been unfailingly kind and helpful. Bill and Millie Beik were cherished mentors, professionally and personally. I have had many illuminating chats with Greg Monahan and Mark Bryant about the late reign of Louis XIV. My great friend David Monod read the entire manuscript and gave me considerable valuable feedback. Steve Beckman, scholar and soldier, taught me much about Marshal Boufflers, the unjustly oft-overlooked French hero of 1709. Caleb Karges reminded me to always keep the Habsburgs in mind. Jonathan Abel and Jamel Ostwald were unfailingly generous in sharing with me their vast knowledge of the French army and French ways of warfare during the eighteenth century. During a memorable conversation in a Detroit casino, Julia Osman imparted numerous insights about French military culture. My department's faculty research colloquium offered useful critiques of an early draft. I am exceedingly fortunate and grateful to have such supportive colleagues. Matt Baker made maps worthy of the Marquis de Chamlay. My deepest and most heartfelt thanks go to my family. My parents, Dewey and Lily, made great sacrifices so that I could become what I am today. Rufino, Lana, Marcus, Duncan, Mary, Connor, Maggie, Dwight, Elaine, Evan, Derek, Larry, Jen, Rick, and Bob (hope it was worth the wait) provided constant support and much-needed distraction. I dedicate this book to my wife Amy and my daughter Inès. Thank you for your unstinting love, for making me smile and laugh in good times, for holding me up in bad ones, and for asking only twice or thrice why a book on a single year was taking so long to finish. I love you more than I can ever say or write.

1

The New Year
January 1, 1709

On the first morning of the new year, in his bedchamber in the château of Versailles, the old king's rising began at its usual hour.¹

As it had for nearly five decades, the machinery of the *lever du roi* sprang smoothly into action.² At six-thirty, the *premier valet de chambre* got up from the narrow cot on which he had spent the night at the foot of the king's bed and went into his nearby apartment to carefully dress himself in a blue justaucorps, the livery of the royal household. He then returned to the king's chamber and softly opened the door to admit a troop of servants. One laid fresh wood in the fireplace. The fire blazed up, filling the room with shadows and smoke, yet it could not entirely banish the damp winter chill. The other servants quietly took down the valet's cot, opened the shutters, replaced the candles, and cleared away the remains of the king's midnight collation. Meanwhile, in the Bull's Eye Antechamber (so named because of its great round window), the Antechamber of the Grand Couvert, and the Guard Room of the King's Apartments, the courtiers were already gathering to await the moment appointed for their entries into the royal presence. They greeted each other, exchanged the latest news, rumors, and gossip. Those furthest from the king's door talked so loudly that an usher had to call for order. His Majesty, he reminded them, would be rising presently.

Behind the heavy curtains screening his bed, Louis XIV would likely have been awake for some time. There was much on his mind. Above all was the great war for the throne of Spain, which was now in its eighth year. It had been a catastrophe for him and for France. His armies, invincible for so long, had suffered a series of crushing defeats and had been

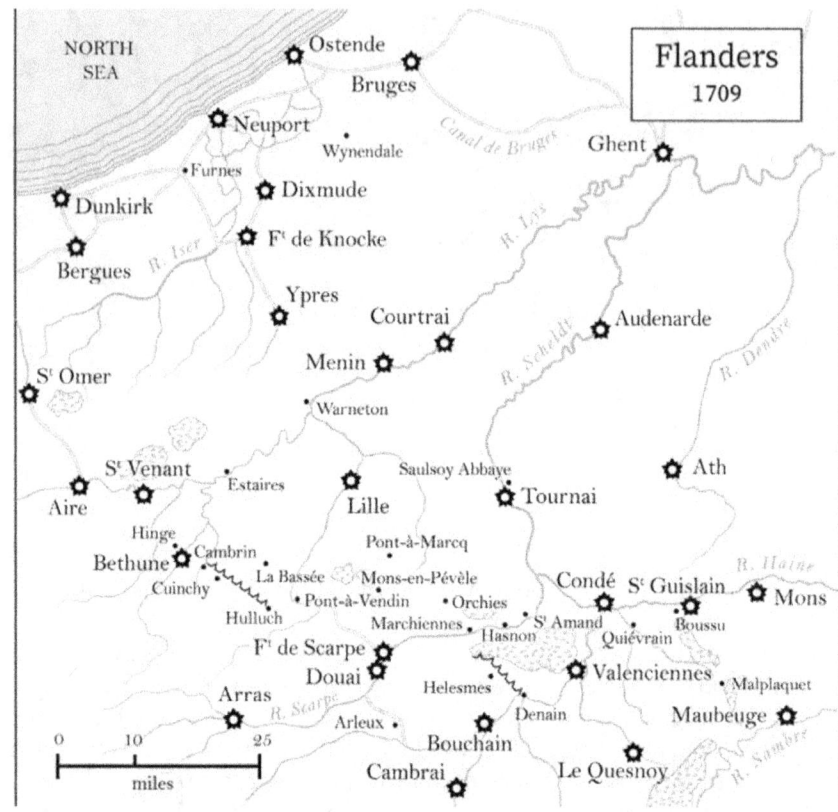

Map 1.1   Flanders 1709.

driven back to the frontiers of his kingdom. His treasury, having borne the costs of war against all Europe, was empty. In the spring, the enemy were threatening to invade and march on Versailles itself. If they succeeded, they would overturn the victories of all his previous wars.

Louis had loved war for most of his life. When he was a boy, among his first toys had been a miniature army, complete with infantry, cavalry, and artillery. At the age of five, he had banged endlessly on his drums, imitating the calls of his Cent Suisses bodyguards. He had mustered his playmates into a company uniformed in black velvet trimmed with gray. Madame de Salle, one of his mother's ladies, had served as their officer instructor. Dressed in a hat decorated with tall plumes, sword at her side, and half-pike in her hand, she had drilled the king and his companions in the manual of arms.[3] Louis had ordered a miniature fort built in the gardens of the Palais-Royal for them to attack and defend. Then, not even eight, he had gone for the first time to inspect his soldiers in the field. In the following years, he had made many more visits to his armies and acquired a taste for the life of the camps.

Having played at war for so long, Louis yearned to fight a real one after he began his personal rule in 1661. A victorious war of conquest would extend the frontiers of France and confirm that it was the greatest power in Christendom. It would enlarge the patrimony Louis would bequeath his heirs as well as add to the grandeur of his dynasty, the House of Bourbon. It would strengthen his authority at home, particularly among the French nobility, who expected their liege sovereign to be a true *roi de guerre*.[4] Not least, a great and successful war was the surest means to acquire *gloire*. In the French of the day, *gloire* meant glory, but even more honor, esteem, and reputation. From the distance of three centuries, *gloire* can seem scarcely different from megalomania. In fact, Louis' understanding of it was nuanced and complex. *Gloire* was an amalgam of personal renown—not least in posterity—dynastic prestige, and state interest. Nevertheless, his pursuit of it would be lifelong and unrelenting. He sought to make his *gloire* so immense that the princes of Europe would regard him as preeminent, and history would remember him as the greatest king in the world.[5]

Louis had a target for his first war: Spain. During the sixteenth century, Charles V and the Habsburg kings of Spain had created an empire upon which the sun never set, including vast territories in Europe and America along with outposts in North Africa and Asia. Then, in the seventeenth century, Spain had bled itself white trying to crush the revolt of the Dutch provinces of the Netherlands and uphold the Catholic cause in the Thirty Years' War. In 1635, Louis XIII and his prime minister, Cardinal Richelieu, entered France into the lists against King Philip IV and his kinsman, the Austrian Habsburg Holy Roman Emperor. The struggle against the Habsburgs was protracted and grueling.[6] It pushed France to the breaking point and provoked the great civil war called the Fronde. Only in 1659 was Spain finally defeated. Cardinal Mazarin, Louis XIV's political mentor, forced the Peace of the Pyrenees on Philip IV. France had eclipsed Spain as Europe's foremost power.

After the Pyrenees peace, Spain's still sprawling empire appeared ripe for the plucking. Louis set his sights on Flanders (map 1.1). Encompassing the three southern provinces of the Spanish Netherlands—Flanders itself, Hainault, and Brabant—it was a rich, populous country, full of fat villages and bustling towns. It was also the cockpit of Europe and a gateway into France for hostile armies. Conquering it would achieve a longstanding French goal of protecting Paris from invasion. The death of King Philip IV in 1665 handed Louis an opportunity. Philip's successor was a three-year-old boy, who became King Charles II. Monarchies were at their weakest and most irresolute when governed by the regencies of child rulers. All Louis needed now was a pretext; he soon had one made for him. As part of the Pyrenees treaty, Louis had married Philip's daughter, the Infanta Marie-Thérèse. Other clauses of the treaty called for her to renounce her rights to Spain and its empire in exchange for a dowry of 500,000 *écus*. The bankrupt Spanish Monarchy had never been able to pay this enormous sum; Louis therefore asserted that the infanta retained all her rights. In addition, French jurists ruled that according to the so-called Law of Devolution observed in the Netherlands, Marie-Thérèse, as a daughter of Philip's first wife, had a prior claim to her father's property over Charles, who was merely the son of his second wife. This legal reasoning was as fragile and full of holes as fine lace. Nevertheless, on May 8, 1667, Louis proclaimed that Flanders, Hainault, Brabant, Limburg, Namur, Luxembourg, Antwerp, and much else belonged to his queen.[7]

The ensuing War of Devolution was more parade than campaign. Three French armies overwhelmed feeble Spanish resistance. In Flanders, town after town either opened its gates to the invaders or fell quickly. But French success caused alarm among the Dutch. Their Republic of the United Netherlands was the greatest trading and maritime power in Europe.[8] Dutch merchants dominated the commerce of much of the world from the splendid entrepot of Amsterdam. The Dutch fleet had just humiliated its archrival, the Royal Navy, in the second of their three seventeenth-century wars. The Dutch Republic preferred to have on its borders a declining Spain rather than a rising France under a young, warlike king. Its diplomats concluded an alliance with Britain and Sweden, which were both also concerned about French aggression. The allies then approached the king of France with an offer to broker a peace with Spain; at the same time, they indicated they were willing to enter the war on the Spanish side if it continued. The Triple Alliance was the first anti-French coalition Louis faced. It would not be the last. In May 1668, he agreed to the Treaty of Aix-la-Chapelle, by which he gained valuable fortresses and towns in Flanders, including Lille, the province's capital.

For Louis, these gains were not enough, and he remained committed to waging a glorious war of conquest. Yet he now shifted targets to the Dutch Republic. During the first half of the seventeenth century, France and the Republic had been steadfast allies against Spain. Louis treated the Dutch intervention in his Flanders war as a personal betrayal that had to be avenged. With uncharacteristic patience, he prepared his assault methodically. French diplomats skillfully wooed away Britain and Sweden, breaking up the Triple Alliance and isolating the Dutch. Moreover, thanks to the sweeping economic and fiscal reforms of Jean-Baptiste Colbert, his brilliant controller general of finances, Louis was able to amass a formidable war chest. At the same time, the French army grew to 144,000 men.

When it struck in May 1672, it overran most of the Republic in a matter of weeks. The Dutch saved themselves by opening the sluices of their dikes and flooding the lowlands of Holland before the advancing French. Then other European states intervened, fearing that Louis would become too powerful if he was given a free hand to crush the Republic. The Holy Roman Emperor Leopold I and the German princes declared war on France.

The Dutch War had been intended to be short, sharp, and decisive. Instead, it lasted for seven years. Throughout, Louis devoted himself to waging it. He did not charge at the head of his cavalry as his grandfather Henry IV had done. Wars, armies, and states had changed too much for rulers to risk their lives in the smoke and chaos of a pitched battle. Louis was a strategist-king. Each winter, he and his advisers determined the dispositions and objectives of the French armies for the following year. These meetings were exhaustive and exhausting, for no detail was too minor to escape Louis' attention. A key assistant was Jules-Louis Bolé, Marquis de Chamlay, *maréchal général des logis*. A master of logistics, geography, and cartography, Chamlay became the king's favorite officer and de facto chief of staff.[9] But Louis' most important collaborator was François-Michel Le Tellier, Marquis de Louvois, minister and secretary of state for war. Scorned by court snobs for his corpulence, coarse manners, and allegedly common origins (in fact, his family, the Le Tellier, had been noble for at least two generations), Louvois was an administrative genius.[10] Tireless, cold, brutal, and domineering, he would, over his three-decade tenure as secretary of state for war, transform Louis XIV's army into the colossus of Europe. During the Dutch War, he became, in effect, co-commander-in-chief of the French armies. He helped fashion strategy and direct operations and wrote the orders and memoranda that poured from the council rooms of Saint-Germain or Versailles to the generals on the various fronts.[11]

Louis was no mere chateau general. At the opening of each campaigning season, he left court to join one of his armies. He immersed himself in the military life, spending hours on horseback and sharing the rigors of the campaign and the camp with his men. He developed a particular predilection for sieges. The predictable procedures and precision of these actions, especially when they were conducted by the master engineer Sebastien Le Prestre de Vauban, appealed to his love of order and control. Moreover, they allowed him to exercise and display his courage by exposing himself to enemy fire. He regularly toured the most advanced trenches of the siege works, where he made a conspicuous target thanks to his white horse, his sumptuous clothing, and his glittering suite of courtiers. On more than one occasion, members of his entourage were wounded or killed near him. Only once during the Dutch War was Louis tempted to fight a battle. On May 10, 1676, at Heurtebise near Valenciennes in the

Spanish Netherlands, the king wished to attack a far inferior enemy force. But his generals and, most vociferously, Louvois argued that he should not risk either his reputation or his safety by commanding a field action in person. Louis yielded to their collective experience. He would regret this decision for the rest of his life. Twenty-three years later, while strolling in the gardens of Versailles, he suddenly declared to his courtiers that he could not recall the day of Heurtebise without anger and how he blamed Louvois.[12]

French prowess at arms and skill at diplomacy brought the Dutch War to a successful conclusion in 1678. By the Peace of Nijmegen, France won an entire province, Franche-Comté, and more valuable towns and strongholds in Flanders. Louis thus considered Nijmegen a triumph. In France, prose, poetry, painting, and sculpture celebrated his *gloire*. During the first thirty years of his life, works of art and literature had portrayed him as Apollo, fashioning the image by which he is still best known: the Sun King. Now he became linked to Mars and victorious war.[13] Yet, beyond the borders of his kingdom, Louis' image could not have been more different. In the courts and chancelleries of Europe, he was cast as a tyrant seeking what statesmen and diplomats of the time called "universal monarchy": hegemony over all Christendom. Two princes now emerged as his staunchest opponents. The first was Leopold I, the head of the Austrian Habsburgs. As Holy Roman Emperor, he was the feudal overlord of a sprawling, dizzyingly diverse agglomeration of three hundred German states ranging from powerful principalities to ecclesiastical lordships to Imperial Free Cities. The 1648 Peace of Westphalia that ended the Thirty Years' War had greatly reduced the authority and power of the emperor over these states. Yet Leopold still personally ruled a considerable domain in Central Europe consisting of the Habsburg Hereditary Lands in Austria, Bohemia, Moravia, and Upper Hungary (the sliver of the medieval Magyar kingdom unconquered by the Ottoman Turks). Throughout his long reign, he would pursue the interests and claims of his dynasty with a dogged determination that exhausted his enemies and vexed his friends. The other prince was William of Orange. He had risen to leadership of the Dutch Republic in 1672, the *Rampjaar* or disaster year, when French armies had almost reached the gates of Amsterdam. A great aristocrat in a bourgeois society and a would-be monarch in a republic, he became captain general of the Dutch forces and *stadtholder*, or chief executive, of the major provinces. Until the end of his life in 1702, he would be the Sun King's most relentless enemy.

At exactly seven-thirty, the *premier valet de chambre* parted the curtains around the royal bed and murmured, "Sire, it's time." Louis' *lever* began. The *Premier Médecin* Guy Fagon and the *Premier Chirurgien* Georges

Mareschal entered and performed a quick examination of the king. Their charge was seventy, extraordinarily old for a time when life expectancy averaged less than thirty years. His face featured a prominent nose and a spray of tiny scars, the legacy of childhood smallpox. Nonetheless, until well into late middle age, he had been counted as handsome. His countenance had since become careworn and drawn. He had lost many of his teeth and, thanks to the clumsy ministrations of his surgeons, part of his jawbone, which left his cheeks sunken. His hair had been thinning for fifty years; just a few pale wisps remained to be concealed beneath his wigs. His once athletic body had grown ponderous with a pronounced belly.[14] But his legs were still slim and shapely, and he was inordinately proud of them—they were displayed prominently in Hyacinthe Rigaud's famous 1701 state portrait. As for his health, he had enjoyed a rude vigor for much of his adult life. This had begun to change in 1686 when he came down with an anal fistula. Its removal required a six-hour-long operation without anesthesia, which he had endured with impressive stoicism. Now, he suffered constantly from colds. His nose dripped unceasingly, and he was frequently doubled over by prolonged fits of coughing. Other chronic complaints resulted from his unrelenting gluttony—a few crusts of bread, a bowl of soup, and four roast chickens were, he lamented, a light supper. He was often attacked by gout, constipation, diarrhea, and flatulence. Lately, he suffered from more insidious ailments: bouts of insomnia and episodes of deep melancholy.[15]

After Mareschal and Fagon took their leave, the premier valet approached Louis with a flagon of *esprit de vin*. The king thoroughly washed his face and hands. At the same time, the first courtiers were being admitted. Some were high officers of the king's household who had a role to play in the *lever*. The *grand chambellan*, the Duc de Bouillon, assisted with the king's first prayers. The *grand maître de la garde-robe*, the Duc de la Rochfoucauld, helped prepare his clothing. The *gobelet* and the *bouche* brought in his breakfast of bread, soup, and wine in a special canteen. Others possessed the privilege of *grande entrée*, perhaps the most envied and sought-after distinction in the French court. Among them were Louis' legitimate son and grandchildren as well as his much-loved legitimated offspring. The rest were either his personal friends or men whom he wished to honor for particularly distinguished service. These fortunate few had precious moments to speak discreetly with him.

Toilette finished and first prayers said, Louis chose a wig from several presented to him by his barber, then got out of bed. Clad in a dressing gown and wearing slippers carefully warmed by the *premier valet*, he sat in an armchair by the fireplace. The barber combed his hair, a task which he finished himself while looking into a mirror. This was the signal for the next wave of courtiers to enter. It consisted of more household officers, such as the *grand-maitre de France*, who was always the Prince de Condé. It also included those who enjoyed the rare *brevets d'affaires*, which admitted their holders into the king's presence while he sat and exerted himself on his *chaise d'affaires*. They included one of the great chroniclers of the French court, Philippe de Courcillon, Marquis de Dangeau.

Once Louis was ready to dress, the final stages of his *lever* commenced. A royal usher had identified to the *premier gentilhomme de la chambre* the persons of quality who were waiting in the antechambers: cardinals, ambassadors, dukes and peers, marshals of France, governors of the provinces, presidents of the superior courts, ministers, and secretaries of state. They were fetched and admitted one by one in order of rank. Another usher arranged them along the gilded balustrade before the king's bed. After each entry, the bedroom door was shut again. Outside, the crowd of courtiers, knowing their own admission was imminent, began to talk loudly. When all was ready, the bedroom doors were flung wide open, and the courtiers flooded inside. Just a handful could find places in the room itself; most remained in the Bullseye Antechamber. They pushed, elbowed, and shoved in order to stand as close to the king as possible. Far from observing a respectful silence, they chattered, laughed, and even yelled. Elisabeth Charlotte, the German princess Palatine who was the widow of Louis' brother Philippe d'Orléans, caustically condemned this "insipid etiquette" as undignified and unworthy of the king.

Nevertheless, Louis placed great store by this moment of his rising. It was the first opportunity to see his nobles and to be seen by them. Yet, as he cast his eye over the milling throng, he could not help feeling disquieted. There were many familiar faces that had not been at his *lever* for many months. They belonged to the officers of his Army of Flanders. With the end of the fighting season, they had left their regiments in winter quarters and returned to court. The campaign they had just fought had been long, grueling, and a fiasco.

Following the triumph of Nijmegen, Louis rethought and redefined his *gloire*. The gains of his first two wars had satisfied his lust for conquest. Henceforth, he would tie his reputation and grandeur to preserving all that he had won and to passing down every inch of his enlarged kingdom to his heirs. French grand strategy shifted from aggression to a quest for security. This change brought Vauban to the fore. The master engineer had perfected the design of the bastioned artillery fortress and, more importantly, he thought of weaving individual strongpoints together to create complete defensive systems. France's most vulnerable frontier remained Flanders. Even after the gains of Aix-la-Chapelle and Nijmegen, still less than one hundred and fifty miles of open country separated Paris from enemy armies. In a famous letter to Louvois in 1673, Vauban proposed fortifying the Flanders frontier with what he called a *pré carré*—a dueling field.[16] Begun soon after the letter's writing, the *pré carré* would eventually consist of barriers of fortresses stretching across northern France from the North Sea coast to the Meuse. The key to the whole system was Lille. Vauban considered the Flemish capital's redesigned and renovated fortifications, especially its citadel, among his masterpieces.[17]

Louis XIV's shift to a quest for security did not mean that he had turned his back on war and armed might. Far from it: the success of the Dutch War emboldened him to regard force as an indispensable tool of his will. In this regard, he was encouraged by Louvois, who was now the dominant voice in his government. During the 1680s, the king and his favorite minister sought to further strengthen France's frontiers by unilateral annexations of strategically located towns and strongholds. In 1681, they gobbled up the Imperial Free City of Strasbourg, which controlled the most important bridge over the Rhine. Many other annexations took place on France's northern and eastern borders. Pushed to the breaking point by Louis' bullying, Spain declared war on October 26, 1683. In the ten-month War of the Reunions, French armies crushed the Spanish.[18] On August 15, 1684, Spain and the Empire agreed to the Truce of Ratisbon, which permitted Louis to keep his latest acquisitions.

The king wielded violence as an instrument of power not just abroad. He also used it on his own subjects. From the beginning of his reign, the French Protestants, the Huguenots, had suffered escalating persecution. To bolster his reputation as the Most Christian King, Louis sought to end the existence of Protestantism in his realm altogether. In 1685, he implemented the *dragonnades*: dragoons of the French army were lodged in Huguenot homes to intimidate and molest the inhabitants until they converted to Catholicism. Thousands did so. Many other Huguenots fled to the Dutch Republic, Britain, Brandenburg, and as far away as America and southern Africa. In August, the Edict of Nantes, which had granted religious toleration to French Protestants, was revoked. All over Protestant Europe, the persecution of the Huguenots further blackened Louis' reputation, adding the specter of religious despotism to the long-standing fears of universal monarchy.

In 1688, Louis' hubris brought forth nemesis. The king and his servants had been watching events to the east with mounting unease. Five years before, the Ottoman Turks invaded Central Europe. They reached and besieged Vienna, capital of the Holy Roman Emperor and the Austrian Habsburgs. A Christian coalition—one from which France was conspicuously absent—went to the rescue. On September 12, 1683, a German and Polish army charged down from the heights of the Kahlenberg and destroyed the Turkish host. Afterward, Austrian Habsburg and Imperial forces launched a great counteroffensive that led to the conquest of

Hungary and much of Serbia. Louis worried that a hugely strengthened and emboldened Emperor Leopold would turn on France as soon as he had finished with the Ottomans. France's gains from the Ratisbon truce, the king decided, had to be made permanent by a formal treaty. When an ultimatum to Leopold failed, he prepared to attack the Holy Roman Empire.

In October, the French army crossed the Rhine at Strasbourg and invaded western Germany. Louis, Louvois, and Chamlay hoped to fight a brief, triumphant action like the War of the Reunions. What unfolded was their worst strategic blunder. The French took the key fortress of Philippsburg and swiftly occupied the Palatinate, one of the most important states of the Empire. But far from being cowed, the *Reichstag*, the assembly of the Empire, declared a *Reichskrieg*, an Imperial war, against France. With this unprecedented move, the German states united against the Most Christian King as they had against the infidel Turks. Louis answered by commanding his generals to ravage the occupied territories with fire and sword. The goal was to make the right bank of the Rhine such a wasteland that the Imperial armies would not be able to use it as a base to attack France. The order backfired. The devastation of the Palatinate was regarded everywhere as an atrocity. Its infamy hardened resistance against the French in the Empire and beyond.[19]

An even more catastrophic consequence of the invasion of Germany was that it gave William of Orange a free hand in Britain. A group of prominent Englishmen, fearing that the birth of a son to King James II would lead to the establishment of a Catholic dynasty, invited the Prince of Orange to take the throne. As both James' nephew and his son-in-law by virtue of marriage to his eldest daughter Mary, William had a very strong claim. During the summer and fall, he readied his army and fleet. On November 15, blown across the North Sea by a so-called Protestant wind, William landed at Torbay with 21,000 troops. Louis immediately declared war on the Dutch Republic. But he counted on James resisting William fiercely and embroiling him in a civil war in Britain. This proved to be another serious blunder. The Dutch invasion—soon dubbed the Glorious Revolution by William's partisans—drove James from his kingdom. He took refuge with Louis, who installed him at the chateau of Saint-Germain.[20] The Prince of Orange became King William III of Great Britain.

James and his Jacobite followers were the only allies France had in the general war that now broke out. In 1689, a Grand Alliance took shape. It eventually comprised Spain, Portugal, Savoy, the Holy Roman Empire, and the Maritime Powers, Britain and the Dutch Republic, both now ruled by William III. Its aim was to restrain French power and put an end to Louis' pretensions to universal monarchy. What came to be called the Nine Years' War saw fighting in Western Europe, the British Isles, the

Americas, and the Indian Ocean. Louis mobilized truly vast forces. At sea, the French navy, *La Royale*, rivaled the Dutch and British fleets. On land, the French army mustered 420,000 men, its largest size during the Sun King's entire reign.[21]

Louis remained a *roi de guerre*. Yet, with advancing age, he could no longer bear the rigors of campaigning: 1693 was the last time he joined one of his armies in the field. Even more profound changes had followed the death of the Marquis de Louvois in 1691. For more than a decade, Louvois had been Louis' indispensable partner in command: he had administered the army, shared in the formulation of strategy, and communicated with the forces in the field. With him gone, the king believed that no one else could match his own knowledge and experience of military affairs. He took it upon himself to correspond personally with the commanders of his armies, initiating a dialogue that would last until the end of his reign. This role dramatically increased his labors. In 1696, the penultimate year of the war and one without major military operations on any front, he wrote 348 letters to his generals, and received and read even more.[22] Armed with the information and advice they provided and following consultations with a handful of trusted confidants, such as Vauban and Chamlay, Louis fashioned French strategy and oversaw operations. He had become the sole commander-in-chief of his armies.

The war at first favored France. As always, the most important theater was Flanders and the Spanish Netherlands. There, Louis' chief general was François-Henri de Montmorency-Boutteville, Marshal Luxembourg. A hunchback and a sybarite, he was also a commander of rare gifts, defeating the Allied armies at Fleurus, Leuze, Steenkerque, and Neerwinden. In the last, he captured so many flags from William III (a more dogged than skillful general) that when they were hung in the nave of Paris' cathedral, he earned the nickname the Tapestry Maker of Notre-Dame.[23] Moreover, Luxembourg's exploits in pitched battle were matched by Vauban's in sieges. He was not just a brilliant designer and builder of fortresses; he had developed a highly effective method for attacking them. Employing a painstaking combination of trenches that allowed French troops to safely approach enemy defenses and concentrated artillery bombardments to smash breaches in the walls, he took a whole series of strong places. His admirers claimed that once Vauban beleaguered a place, he always took it. His greatest conquest was Namur, an imposing citadel at the confluence of the Meuse and Sambre of great strategic value. It capitulated after a five-week siege in July 1692.

These victories led Louis to hope his foes would soon acknowledge his military dominance and make peace on his terms. Instead, in 1692 and 1693, his kingdom was brought to its knees. The weather, not the Grand Alliance, struck the fateful blows. During these years, torrential rains fell all over France. These deluges were combined with frigid temperatures that continued well into the summer.[24] Under such terrible conditions, French agriculture, primitive and unproductive even at the best of times, buckled, then broke. Despite the frantic efforts of nineteen million French peasants, the harvest failed nearly everywhere. Food prices soared. The well-to-do faced malnutrition, everyone else starvation. The royal government, its attention consumed by the war, proved completely unable to rise to the challenge of the famine. Left largely to their own devices, local authorities tried to extemporize relief. In many towns, the clergy organized soup kitchens. In Paris, the *lieutenant général de police*, Nicolas de La Reynie, had thirty ovens built in the courtyard of the Louvre to bake bread for the indigent. Yet even the most well-meaning efforts could barely plumb the depths of hunger and misery. Ordinary French men and women then tried to take matters into their own hands. Food riots roiled the poorer quarters of the capital until well into 1694. Similar uprisings swept the provinces down to the smallest villages. The starving also took to the roads. Armies of ragged, skeletal wretches tramped the highways and byways of France, wandering from place to place searching for something to eat. For too many, even the most desperate measures were unavailing. The famine killed 1.3 million people, more than one in twenty of the Sun King's subjects.[25]

Financial collapse followed hard on famine's heels. To mobilize the vast forces needed to fight all of Europe, France's resources had been pushed to their limits. After 1693, almost every source of revenue dried up. The royal treasury faced bankruptcy. Louis and his ministers embarked on a frantic search for more money. With the peasantry suffering and already exploited to the hilt, they had no choice but to turn to the nobility. Perhaps the most cherished privilege of French nobles was exemption from royal direct taxation. In 1695, the king promulgated the *capitation*, a new imposition that all his subjects, regardless of social rank, were obliged to pay. It brought in some badly needed cash. More importantly, it helped underwrite borrowing on an immense scale. The French war effort was kept going, barely.

The catastrophe turned the tide of the Nine Years' War. Louis realized that his subjects and his state badly needed peace. He therefore implemented a decisive shift in strategy. His armies went on the defensive, while his diplomats strove to negotiate an end to the war. In 1695, William III mustered a powerful army to retake Namur as a first step to undoing French gains in Flanders. Louis assigned the defense to Marshal Louis-Francois de Boufflers. William opened the siege on July 1. It only ended on September 5 when Boufflers and what remained of his garrison marched out of the battered citadel with flags flying and drums beating.

Taking Namur had cost the Allies 20,000 casualties and had immobilized their main field army for an entire campaigning season.

Diplomacy at last brought an end in 1697. The Peace of Ryswick awarded Strasbourg to Louis. In return, he gave up many of his most prized conquests: Mons, Tournai, Luxembourg, Philippsburg, Landau, Freiburg, and Breisach. Barcelona, captured during the last campaign of the war, was handed back to the Spanish. By a subsidiary agreement, the Dutch were permitted to garrison numerous fortresses across the Spanish Netherlands to create a so-called Barrier against future French aggression. In addition to these territorial concessions, Louis recognized William III as de facto king of England, Scotland, and Ireland. While James II could remain at Saint-Germain, he was to receive no aid to regain his throne. Given that French armies had won all the major battles and taken more fortresses than they lost, many in France regarded the peace as a humiliation. Writing to the great playwright and royal historiographer Racine, Vauban condemned Ryswick as a stain on the honor of the king and the French nation.[26] Yet, for Louis, his lost gains were the price he had to pay to bring tranquility to his long-suffering people. Moreover, he had at last fallen out of love with war. He now hoped to spend his last years restoring order and prosperity to his kingdom.

At Versailles, the first day of the year was devoted to one of the court's grandest rituals: the induction of new members into France's premier order of chivalry, the Holy Spirit. The king was its grandmaster. As soon as the *lever* was done, the knights gathered in his apartments. All were resplendently dressed in flowing black velvet mantles decorated with embroidered red and gold flames. All were wearing their order's eight-pointed white cross hanging from golden collars.[27]

Louis led out the Order of the Holy Spirit in a stately procession. He exited the Bullseye Antechamber and entered the Hall of Mirrors. There a crowd was waiting. It included many denizens of the great palace: courtiers, lackeys, servants, and soldiers. But many others were outsiders, visitors to Versailles. By ancient tradition, the court of France was open to all. Anyone could enter so long as one was dressed like a lady or gentleman. And if a man were missing that indispensable mark of gentility, a sword, enterprising entrepreneurs at the palace's gates could rent him one for a modest fee. Most in the crowd wished only to catch a glimpse of the king, no matter how fleeting or distant. A handful had a more serious purpose. They hoped to press a note into the hands of one of the royal confidants or even whisper a quick word in Louis' ear as he passed.

The crowd could not obscure the splendors of the Hall of Mirrors. Lining the eastern wall were the seventeen massive panels of polished glass that gave the hall its name. Reflected in them were the dancing lights from scores of candles set in gilded girandoles and tall torchières spaced as regularly as sentries along the parquet floor. Opposite the mirrors were seventeen wide windows. The architect Jean-François Blondel once rhapsodized that they gave on to "the most beautiful scene that one could possibly imagine by the view of the fountains and the gardens of this palace."[28] No one loved Versailles' exquisite gardens more than the king. He had written guides to them in his own hand and was accustomed to strolling in them every day.

The decorative highlight of the Hall of Mirrors was its ceiling. This entire immense surface—almost 240-feet long and 34-feet wide—was covered by thirty-six frescoes conceived and executed by Charles Le Brun. In 1678, during the building of the great gallery, Le Brun had proposed an iconography based on Hercules; the demigod had long served as a metaphor for French monarchs, including Louis' grandfather and father. This scheme was rejected; instead, the artist was to make his subject the king himself and the great achievements of the first thirty years of the reign.[29] Some paintings depict Louis seizing the reins of power and restoring good government to France: *The King Governs by Himself*, *Order Re-established in Finances*, and *The Reformation of Justice*. Many more extol the triumphs of the Dutch War: *The King Arms by Land and Sea*, *The Passage of the Rhine*, *The King Takes Maastricht in Thirteen Days*, and *Franche-Comté Conquered for the Second Time*. All have Louis at the center of tumultuous action—serene, majestic, commanding, in complete control of himself as well as everyone and everything around him.[30]

Louis' newfound commitment to peace was confounded by the dying king of Spain. Charles II was the product of generations of inbreeding between the Spanish and Austrian branches of the Habsburg family—his mother was his father's niece, and his grandmother was also his aunt. He suffered from so many physical and mental afflictions that his subjects dubbed him *El Hechizado*, the Bewitched. None had expected him to live long, so it was to universal amazement that he had survived into adulthood and had even married twice. As the eighteenth century approached, his health was in final decline, and he had failed to produce an heir. His imminent death raised the question of who would succeed to Spain and its still huge empire. As the son of one infanta and the husband of another, Louis XIV had arguably the strongest claim to the Spanish thrones, one further buttressed by the nonpayment of Marie-Thérèse's dowry. However, Leopold of Habsburg was sure to contest a Bourbon succession.

The king of France was determined both to press his claims to the Spanish Monarchy and avoid war. Vauban and his other advisors preferred the acquisition of choice pieces of Spanish territory to seeing a French prince ruling Spain. Louis therefore turned to an ingenious solution: a partition of the Spanish empire between the contending houses of France and Austria. He discovered he had a surprising partner in William III. The Stadholder-King, too, wished to prevent a new Europe-wide conflagration. As well, he calculated that if the Spanish Monarchy went in its entirety to either the Bourbons or the Habsburgs, the result would be the creation of an overmighty state able to assert universal monarchy over Europe. The ink had hardly dried on the Ryswick treaties when Louis' and William's representatives began intensive talks. The negotiations soon focused on a claimant to Spain who belonged to neither of the two great dynasties. Joseph Ferdinand was the six-year-old son of Maximilian Emmanuel, elector of Bavaria, and a Habsburg archduchess. In a treaty hammered out in the fall of 1698, the young Bavarian prince would receive Spain itself and its American dominions. The Archduke Charles, second son of the Emperor Leopold, would get Milan, and the Grand Dauphin Louis, heir to Louis XIV, Naples, and Sicily. This treaty represented the best hope of defusing the Spanish timebomb. Unfortunately, on February 3, 1699, Joseph Ferdinand suddenly died.

Even after this setback, Louis remained fixed on peacefully resolving the succession crisis through partition. As he wrote to his ambassador in London, the Comte de Tallard, "the division of the Spanish Monarchy is now reduced to two parts. The change it involves does not remove the resolution that I have taken to prefer the tranquility of Europe to my own advantages."[31] The diplomats went back to work. In June 1699, France and the Maritime Powers signed a second partition treaty. It awarded Spain and its overseas empire to the archduke while the Dauphin received Milan, Naples, and Sicily. Throughout the negotiations over partition, Leopold had not been consulted. The emperor would not be moved from his position that his second son should inherit the whole Spanish Monarchy. But Louis and William believed that, together, they could force their terms on the Habsburg ruler, if necessary by resorting to arms.

The other key party that had not been consulted was Spain. The Spanish grandees opposed any dismemberment of their empire. They agreed about nothing else. As Charles II lay dying, his court became bitterly divided between pro-Habsburg and pro-Bourbon factions. As news of the partition negotiations trickled into Madrid, the grandees who favored the Bourbons gained the upper hand by making it clear that only Louis XIV was powerful enough to preserve the unity of the Spanish Monarchy. In October, they convinced their king to sign a new will declaring that all his dominions would go to Philip, Duc d'Anjou, Louis' second grandson. Their triumph represented a remarkable reversal, for Spain had been France's historic enemy as well as the principal victim of Louis' ambitions. It was a tribute to the Sun King's political prestige and military prowess.

Charles the Bewitched died on All Saints' Day. A Spanish courier carrying the will arrived on November 9 at the French court, which had repaired to the chateau of Fontainebleau for its annual season of hunting in the vast forests east of Paris. Louis had been informed by his ambassador in Madrid of the Spanish grandees' choice, but he had not allowed himself to believe it until he read the testament itself. He now faced an agonizing dilemma: should he remain faithful to his agreement with William III or accept Charles II's will? He ordered the council of ministers, the *Conseil d'en haut*, to meet and offer him advice. It gathered in the apartment of Madame de Maintenon, Louis' last mistress and his secret wife since 1683. Jean-Baptiste Colbert, Marquis de Torcy, the secretary of state for foreign affairs, and Paul de Beauvilliers, Duc de Beauvilliers, the head of the council of finances, vehemently urged adhering to the partition treaty, warning that its rejection risked a long, hugely destructive war. Louis Phélypeaux, Comte de Pontchartrain, the chancellor, and the longest-serving minister, argued in favor of the king of Spain's will. Pontchartrain then received unexpected support from the Grand Dauphin. Louis' only surviving legitimate child was very different from him. He loved pleasure and had turned his principal residence, the chateau of Meudon, into a center of entertainments that rivaled Versailles. He matched his father's heroic reputation only at the table. In the work of government, he betrayed much less interest. Although a member since 1691 of the *Conseil d'en haut*, he had largely maintained a submissive silence during its deliberations. Now, he forcefully and articulately argued for accepting Charles the Bewitched's final testament:

> Turning toward the king with a respectful but firm air, he said to him that after having given his advice like the others, he was taking the liberty to demand from the king his patrimony because he was in a condition to accept it. The monarchy of Spain was the inheritance of his mother the queen and so it was his own and his second son's, to whom he ceded it with all his heart. He would abandon no inch of it to anyone else. His demand was just and accorded with the honor of the king and the greatness of his crown, and he hoped it would not be refused.[32]

The Grand Dauphin's intervention decided the debate. When the king asked her opinion, Madame de Maintenon agreed with the heir to the throne. At a second meeting on November 10, Beauvilliers and Torcy changed their minds. Six days later, after returning to Versailles, Louis presented his seventeen-year-old grandson Philip to his court and announced, "Here is the king of Spain."[33]

William III was incensed by what he regarded as Louis' betrayal. Yet, by themselves, the dramatic events of November 1700 did not make a general Europe-wide conflict inevitable. The English Parliament and the

Dutch States General were both willing to accept Philip as king of Spain. The British and Dutch had concluded that the partition treaty was unworkable. Furthermore, they were reassured by clauses of Charles' will which indicated that France and Spain would never be united under a single ruler. Emperor Leopold was certainly prepared to fight: in early 1701, he sent his army over the Alps into Italy. But in a contest against the combined forces of France and Spain, the Habsburgs would have found themselves overmatched.

It was Louis' towering arrogance that brought on a full-blown war. Over the course of 1701, he took a series of actions that, while seemingly prudent and even just from his perspective, were regarded by everyone else as highhanded and aggressive. In February, he declared that King Philip V of Spain retained his right to inherit the French throne, raising the possibility that a Bourbon superpower would be created that would unite France's might with Spain's enormous empire. Louis' next move alienated the Dutch: he sent his troops into the Spanish Netherlands to take over the Barrier fortresses. At a stroke, the Republic was stripped of the security it had striven for three decades to achieve. Then Louis angered both Maritime Powers by having his grandson award the *Asiento de negros*, the contract to supply Spain's American colonies with African slaves, much coveted by the merchants of London and Amsterdam, to the French Guinea Company. His final misstep roused the fears and fury of the British. In September, following the death of James II, Louis recognized his son as King James III of England, Scotland, and Ireland. On the other side of the Channel, the recognition of a Stuart pretender was regarded as a violation of the Ryswick Peace and a threat to overturn the Glorious Revolution in favor of the restoration of a Catholic dynasty. The last and greatest anti-French coalition of Louis' reign formed quickly. Already on September 7, 1701, the Dutch Republic, Great Britain, and the Holy Roman Empire had signed a treaty at The Hague recreating the Grand Alliance. The death of William III, Louis' bitterest foe, following a fall from his horse in February 1702 did not slow the march to war. It was declared a month later. Louis had blundered into a conflict he did not want. Nonetheless, he resolved to fight it with all his old energy and determination. To his grandson Philip, he advised "if you must make war, place yourself at the head of your armies."[34]

The War of the Spanish Succession began in the Bourbons' favor. Unlike in 1688, France had allies. There was, of course, Spain. Louis then persuaded two powerful German princes of the House of Wittelsbach to cast their lot with him: Maximilian Emmanuel, elector of Bavaria, and Joseph Clemens, archbishop of Cologne. Other allies were the splendidly vulpine Victor Amadeus, Duke of Savoy, and the dashing Ferenc Rakozci, prince of Transylvania, who, with Louis' encouragement and assistance, raised the Hungarian nobility against the Habsburgs. Furthermore, the French war machine was still able to field formidable forces. In 1702, Louis mobilized one hundred new regiments of infantry. He reinforced his cavalry by adding troopers to existing companies and mobilizing 120 new ones. Finally, he created a royal militia, which conscripted peasants, then fed them as new recruits and replacements to frontline units. By 1707, the French army reached a paper strength of 373,000 men; perhaps 255,000 were actually serving in the ranks.[35]

Yet dangerous weaknesses in the French war effort appeared almost at once. As the Spanish grandees had hoped when they chose Philip as their new king, Louis devoted the power of France to holding Spain's empire together. French armies marched into the Spanish Netherlands, Italy, and Spain itself. He was also determined to support his allies: other armies went into Germany to succor the Wittelsbachs. The scale and geographical extent of these commitments imposed terrible strains on France's resources. Supplying food, small arms, cannon, powder, and horses to so many far-flung forces overburdened the French logistical apparatus.[36] Even worse was the toll on French finances. The five years between the Peace of Ryswick and the beginning of the struggle for the throne of Spain were hardly enough of a respite for Louis XIV's exhausted treasury. Already in 1702, military spending was outstripping revenues. Debt began piling up with terrifying speed.[37]

Even as Louis' power waned, that of his enemies waxed. Thirty years of confronting the Sun King had pushed the Empire, the Dutch Republic, and Britain to build up their military and financial capabilities. The Grand Alliance's initial mobilization saw Great Britain pledge 40,000 troops, the Republic 102,000, and the Empire 90,000.[38] Moreover, the Dutch and the British had implemented far-reaching changes to their states' finances that amounted to nothing less than revolutions.[39] The Maritime Powers could raise revenues and underwrite loans on a truly imposing scale. They used this money to field large forces of their own and to act as the paymasters of Europe, subsidizing the armies of the emperor and the German princes, and hiring mercenaries from across the continent. For the first time in his long reign, Louis would find his armies outnumbered.

The Grand Alliance did not just possess an edge in quantity but also in quality. One of William of Orange's most significant achievements was the reform of the Dutch States Army. After 1672, he turned it from an ill-assorted collection of mercenary bands into a cohesive, regular force trained in the most advanced military methods.[40] William's other army, the British, underwent a similar transformation.[41] During the War of the Spanish Succession, British and Dutch infantry earned an enviable reputation for discipline, steadiness, and firepower. If not quite as advanced in techniques and tactics, the army of Emperor Leopold also became more potent. After twenty years of victorious campaigning against the Turks, the Habsburgs possessed a corps of doughty veteran regiments.[42]

Not the least advantage enjoyed by the Allies was superior generalship. The captain general of the Dutch-British Confederate Army was John Churchill, Duke of Marlborough, while the emperor's principal commander was Prince Eugene of Savoy. In appearance and bearing, the contrast between the two was striking. Marlborough was, according to all contemporary accounts, a handsome man with pleasant, courtly manners. Already fifty-two, he was commanding an army for the first time. He owed his prominence and position in large measure to his wife Sarah, who was the favorite of Queen Anne, William III's sister-in-law and successor.[43] Eugene was often described as ugly, and he could be difficult and haughty. Not yet thirty, he had been a paladin of the Great Turkish War and had already won victories over the French in Italy in 1701.[44] But the two had more in common than met the eye. Both men proved to be among history's great captains. Both were energetic and aggressive, apostles of battle, practitioners of swift, surprise movements, and masters of devastating offensive tactics. Both also worked well together. In 1706, Marlborough told Sarah that "I not only esteem, but really love that prince."[45]

The middle years of the War of the Spanish Succession saw France suffer a crescendo of defeats. In 1704, two French armies under Marshals Marsin and Tallard joined the Bavarians of Elector Max Emmanuel for an offensive against the Habsburgs and the German princes. In response, Marlborough brought his army from the Netherlands into Germany and linked up with Eugene. On August 13, at the village of Blenheim, they destroyed the French and Bavarian forces. Blenheim ended fifty years of French battlefield invincibility. Its strategic and political consequences were even greater. The Allies routed the French from Germany and occupied Bavaria. The Wittelsbachs were compelled to seek refuge with Louis.[46]

The turn of the tide against France pushed Louis and his ministers to make their first serious effort to negotiate an end to the war. Their diplomacy focused on the Dutch. They perceived that certain Dutch powerholders were growing weary of the war, chafing at its costs and the overweening ambitions of their British allies. They calculated they could detach the burgher Republic from the Grand Alliance by offering advantageous terms for a separate peace. A captured French general, the Marquis d'Alègre, presented Louis' offer. In exchange for recognizing his grandson as king of Spain, he promised favorable commercial relations and the re-establishment of the fortress Barrier in the Spanish Netherlands. Most importantly, he declared he was willing to partition the Spanish Monarchy in order to compensate the emperor and Archduke

Charles. The Dutch were not satisfied, and Alègre's mission came to nothing. Nevertheless, peace talks would henceforth be virtually continuous for the rest of the war.[47]

The *annus horribilis* of French arms was 1706. The main seat of war had shifted to Flanders. Louis sent Francois de Neufville, Duc et Maréchal de Villeroy, to take command of his principal field army. Villeroy was a childhood friend of the king; unfortunately, he was also a terrible general. Ordered by Louis to act aggressively, he marched out to challenge Marlborough, who set upon him at Ramillies on May 23. The French army was shattered. Worse still, because the battle had taken place at the beginning of the campaigning season, Marlborough had ample time to exploit his victory. In three months, he overran almost the entire Spanish Netherlands and pushed the French back to the *pré carré*, Vauban's great belt of frontier fortresses.[48] Louis treated Ramillies as a divine judgment that he had to humbly accept. "Monsieur le Maréchal," he greeted Villeroy upon his return to court, "at our age, we are no longer lucky."[49]

The divinity was not done with France. The defeat in Flanders was soon matched by another in Italy. Three years previously, Victor Amadeus had changed sides. Louis punished his treachery by carrying out a systematic conquest of his lands of Piedmont and Savoy. By the summer of 1706, the turncoat duke's capital of Turin was besieged by French armies commanded by the Duc de La Feuillade and Louis' nephew, Philippe, Duc d'Orléans. In a brilliant series of marches, Eugene of Savoy managed to approach Turin from the west. On September 7, he swept down on the French armies and scattered them. The results of Turin were as far-reaching as Ramillies. The French were forced over the Alps and out of Italy. The next year, Eugene and Victor Amadeus advanced along the Mediterranean coast into Provence, aiming to capture the port of Toulon.[50] Though this attempt failed, it drove home to Louis that his kingdom now lay open to invasion.

From the Hall of Mirrors, the king led the Order of the Holy Spirit into the Salon of War. This room was dominated by a huge bas relief portraying Louis on horseback trampling his enemies while being crowned by glory. Then the procession made its way through the long enfilade of the State Apartments. First was the throne room. The ceiling here was painted with the most famous metaphor for Louis: shining Apollo driving the chariot of the sun across the sky. A magnificent silver-covered throne once had pride of place. During the nadir of the Nine Years' War, it had been removed, its precious metal stripped, melted down, and sent to help replenish the royal treasury. It had been replaced by a much less impressive gilded chair. Next was the old royal bedchamber, where, almost nine years before, Louis had introduced his grandson Philip to his assembled court as the new king of Spain. Three more rooms followed, all richly decorated with painted ceilings, marble walls, and luxurious furnishings. At the enfilade's end, the procession came to the Great Staircase: two broad flights of steps, splendidly ornamented with colored marbles, gilded bronze sculptures, and paintings depicting victories from the Dutch War. It was designed to impress and awe, especially foreign emissaries newly come to Versailles,—hence its other name: the Staircase of the Ambassadors.

The king and the knights of the Holy Spirit proceeded down the steps. Once they reached the palace's ground floor, they only had a short way to go before they reached their destination: the Royal Chapel. Installed in 1681 at the junction of the central body of the palace and its north wing, this chapel had been intended to be only temporary. A new, permanent chapel, a magnificent, soaring, Gothic-style building, was at last nearing completion nearby. Many criticized the great expense of its construction during a time of deepening crisis. Even the devout Madame de Maintenon thought it was an indulgence that Louis ought to forsake.[51] He would, however, brook no delay to this final embellishment to his beloved Versailles. Throughout the war, an army of workers and artists labored to finish the work.

In the chapel, the Abbé d'Estrées celebrated mass. Then the initiation ceremony began. As grandmaster of the Holy Spirit, Louis took his place before the altar, seated in a tall armchair. Only one novice was being presented, but he was of exalted rank and personally close to the king. The sixteen-year-old Louis Henri de Bourbon-Condé, Duc d'Enghien, was heir to the Prince de Condé. He was also the son of Louise-Françoise de Bourbon, formerly Mademoiselle de Nantes, oldest legitimated daughter of Louis and Madame de Montespan. The youthful aspirant was dressed in a magnificent habit made personally by his mother. As the king's grandson, he was given an unusual and unprecedented honor by being escorted to his oathtaking by the Grand Dauphin and his eldest son, Louis, Duc de Bourgogne. He knelt and pressed his hands together as if in prayer. The king leaned forward and took them between his own.

Yet, to Louis, the presence of the Duc de Bourgogne served as an uncomfortable reminder of the debacle of the latest campaign. The past year's defeats were especially galling because the king and his ministers had once again made a serious bid for peace with the Dutch.[52] In December 1707, Louis and his foreign minister Torcy sent Nicolas Mesnager, a merchant of Rouen with extensive experience as a diplomatic envoy, to The Hague with instructions to negotiate a new partition treaty while at the same time offering the Republic advantageous commercial terms and a substantial Barrier.[53] But the Dutch leaders were convinced that the balance of the war was tilting so heavily in the Allies' favor that the Sun King would soon be forced to accept peace on their terms. Their counterproposals proved so intolerable that Mesnager immediately broke off discussions and returned to France.[54]

The failure of Mesnager's mission persuaded Louis and Torcy that they needed a stronger hand at the negotiating table. They therefore aimed to win victories in Flanders to show their enemies that France was still full of fight. According to a strategic appreciation produced by Chamlay, the French could advance along the Scheldt or the Meuse and retake much of the ground lost after Ramillies.[55] To conduct this crucial campaign, the king turned to Louis-Joseph de Bourbon, Duc de Vendôme. Bold, aggressive, enormously courageous, and wildly popular with the troops, Vendôme had won several victories in Italy, including one over Eugene at Cassano in 1705. Furthermore, as a descendant of a legitimated son of Henry IV, he was among the grandest of aristocrats. No expense was spared to furnish him with a powerful Army of Flanders. But by now, France's resources were almost completely spent. This offensive, Louis realized, would likely be the last his forces would be able to undertake. As he warned Vendôme, "you know the state of my finances well enough to understand that it is no longer possible to sustain for long expenses so disproportionate to my revenues."[56]

Then Louis made a decision that would have fatal and far-reaching consequences. He had always believed that the prestige of his dynasty depended in large measure on the military achievements of its members, and so he conscientiously prepared his heirs to lead armies themselves. In addition, the king was convinced that having a Bourbon at their head inspired the troops and boosted their morale.[57] During his last two wars, he often appointed the Grand Dauphin and the Duc de Bourgogne to command in key theaters. In 1708, Louis named Bourgogne as commander-in-chief in Flanders. In the field, the princes were always corseted by experienced generals. The twenty-six-year-old Bourgogne was to listen closely to Vendôme and follow his counsels. At first, Vendôme treated this command arrangement as an exceptional honor: he would be directing the operation that would save France and mentoring a future king. Yet the two men could not have been more different in temperament and character. Vendôme alternated between bouts of extreme lassitude and bursts of furious action. He was famously libertine and did little to conceal his homosexuality. Bourgogne had been heavily influenced by his tutor, François Fénelon, Archbishop of Cambrai, and one of the leading savants of the age. He was mild-mannered, reserved, profoundly pious, and austere in his personal habits. Above all, he betrayed little inclination, much less liking, for war. This mismatched pair was sent to face the partnership of Marlborough and Eugene.

The Flanders campaign of 1708 opened with a significant French success. Disaffected elements in Allied-occupied Ghent and Bruges offered to help the French seize their towns. Vendôme leaped at this opportunity. On July 5, a party of French soldiers disguised as deserters begged entry into Ghent. When the Dutch garrison admitted them, the French captured and opened one of the gates. Vendôme's army swept inside. Upon learning of Ghent's fall, Bruges surrendered. The loss of the two most important towns in western Flanders galvanized Marlborough and Eugene into action. From its initial positions near Brussels, the Dutch-British army executed a forced march that at one point covered fifty miles in sixty hours. On July 9, Eugene joined with his cavalry; the prince had hurried ahead of his army, which was still coming up to Brussels from the Moselle. The next day, the Allies reached Lessines on the River Dender. From there, they could thrust to the River Scheldt and sever the Army of Flanders' lines of supply running back to its base at Lille. To forestall this threat, Vendôme and Bourgogne marched from near Ghent to the vicinity of Oudenarde.

On July 11, the French commanders fell into the first of what would be many hugely destructive quarrels. Vendôme wanted to immediately engage the enemy. Bourgogne wished to avoid battle. Before the argument could be resolved, Marlborough and Eugene struck. At 1:00 p.m., the French vanguard was attacked by Allied infantry and cavalry. "If they are there, the Devil must have carried them," Vendôme exclaimed in disbelief, "such marching is impossible."[58] The battle of Oudenarde pitted 85,000 French against 80,000 Allies.[59] In military parlance, it was a meeting engagement. This meant that it was a chaotic affair in which the armies, instead of being fully deployed before combat, arrived in battalions and squadrons that were then flung piecemeal into the fray. Vendôme quickly recovered from his initial shock. Acting with his inimitable blend of aggression and courage, he led the right wing of the Army of Flanders in a furious assault that drove the Allies back. The crisis of the battle came in the early evening when Vendôme, half-pike in hand in the thick of the fighting, ordered Bourgogne to launch an attack with his still largely unengaged left wing. But the young prince believed the ground in front of his troops was too marshy for an advance and countermanded the order. Marlborough and Eugene were allowed to concentrate their forces against Vendôme. At 9:00 p.m., the French right wing disintegrated. It had suffered 15,000 dead, wounded, and taken prisoner. Allied casualties numbered 3,000.

The defeated French army retreated to Ghent. There, the simmering quarrel between Vendôme and Bourgogne exploded into vicious, open conflict. Each blamed the other for the Oudenarde debacle. Even more seriously, each enlisted his supporters in the army and at court to press his case with the king. Far from acting as the *Grand Monarque* and imposing order, Louis was drawn into mediating between the feuding dukes. With its commanders tearing at each other, the Army of Flanders was paralyzed. Marlborough and Eugene hurried to exploit their victory. On August 14, they opened a siege of Lille. Louis had anticipated this possibility. He had bolstered the city's garrison to nine thousand men and placed it under the command of Marshal Boufflers.

The siege of Lille was the greatest of the war.[60] While Marlborough and his army guarded against any intervention by the French, Eugene's Imperial troops beleaguered the city. Boufflers resisted with ingenuity, determination, and energy, outdoing even his performance at Namur fourteen years before. The Allies' progress was slow and costly. But even Boufflers could only delay Lille's fall. To save it, the French would have to give battle. The army of Vendôme and Bourgogne was reinforced by another under James Fitz-James, Duc et Maréchal de Berwick. The bastard son of James II and Arabella Churchill, Marlborough's sister, Berwick was a fine general: he had saved Spain for Philip V by defeating a British-Dutch-Huguenot-Portuguese force at the Battle of Almanza in April 1707. His arrival, though, only worsened the infighting among the French generals, as he refused to subordinate himself to Vendôme, claiming that he, too, was a duke and a royal bastard. It took a direct order from the king for him to yield. Even then, he refused to speak to Vendôme and dealt exclusively with Bourgogne.

In early September, the Army of Flanders, now 110,000 strong, lunged toward Lille. Marlborough interposed his army between the French and their target. Badly outnumbered, he instructed his troops to dig in. At this critical moment, the French generals fell into a fresh round of bickering. Vendôme wished to attack; Berwick did not. Bourgogne agreed with the Jacobite duke but also knew that his grandfather wanted the army to fight to rescue Lille. A fortnight passed with the armies facing each other. In the meantime, the Allied entrenchments became proof against assault; Marlborough told his wife that he was so well entrenched that "I no ways fear their forcing us."[61] Eventually, even Vendôme had to agree. On September 17, the Army of Flanders and its still squabbling generals slunk away to Tournai.

The failure of the French to attack sealed Lille's fate. Boufflers continued his valiant defense for a further three months. At last, on December 8, he capitulated with the 2,500 survivors of the garrison. His performance was the sole bright spot in a year of unrelieved gloom. The 1708 Flanders campaign had begun with high hopes, descended into tragedy, then ended in farce. The loss of Lille was a devastating blow. Vauban's *pré carré* had been breached.

After the ceremony of the Holy Spirit, much of the rest of Louis' day was taken up by other rituals of the court. The last had him returning to the chapel at sunset to hear Vespers with members of the royal family. Only when it was done could he turn to the problem that had been weighing on him since even before his rising: the war, particularly the Flanders front. As well as being a *roi de guerre*, Louis had always been a *roi-bureaucrate*. He presided personally over his government, working closely every day with his ministers and secretaries of state on all major and many minor matters. For most of his reign, this work had mainly taken place in the state councils, particularly the *Conseil d'en haut*, the council of ministers. But after the death of the Marquis de Louvois, Louis began to prefer a more informal and personal practice involving one-on-one meetings with his officials. These were called *liasses* after the bundles of dossiers and working papers that a minister or secretary brought and laid before the king. Often, important decisions were reached at a *liasse*, then presented to the rest of the ministers. So, early in the evening, in the hours before his supper, Louis summoned Michel Chamillart, secretary of state for war, to a meeting in the bedchamber of Madame de Maintenon.

The choice of venue was not incidental. *Liasses* always took place in the apartment of the king's consort, for Maintenon had become Louis' most trusted advisor and veritable partner in government. This role was one she had never imagined fulfilling. The daughter of a minor noble family, Françoise d'Aubigné had been introduced to the French court as the widow of the writer Paul Scarron. In 1669, she had been appointed the governess of Louis' children with Madame de Montespan. In this capacity, she had frequent interactions with the king. Affection, attraction, then love had grown between them. Louis saw in her, a woman two years his senior, an indispensable companion for his mature years. In 1675, he made her the Marquise de Maintenon. Eight years later, following the death of Queen Marie-Thérèse, they wedded. The morganatic nature of the marriage meant that it had to be clandestine and that Maintenon could never be queen.

Maintenon's position in power evolved gradually. After the loss of Louvois, his favorite minister, Louis had taken on even more of the business of government, particularly the direction of war. Finding this burden increasingly onerous, he first depended on Maintenon for emotional and moral support. During *liasses*, she sat in a chair or in her bed and knitted while her husband and his collaborators worked at a table. Soon, her proximity to Louis prompted officials and officers to seek out her protection and patronage. By the War of the Spanish Succession, many of her protégés were well-placed in the government and the army. At last, Louis, valuing her good sense and judgment, came to consult her on even the weightiest matters. Whenever he sought her opinion, he would turn to her and address her solemnly as "Votre Solidité." Initially reluctant and reticent, Maintenon came to accept and even embrace her role. By 1709, her friend Madame Dangeau, wife of the diarist, could playfully—and truthfully—address her as "La Ministresse."[62]

The minister who joined the king and his consort was well-liked by them both. Michel Chamillart was affable, intelligent, conscientious, and modest. The scion of a legal family, he had entered public life as a judge in the Parlement of Paris, the highest superior law court. He came to the king's notice because of his sublime skill at billiards. Louis was a keen player: he had tables installed in the State Apartments at Versailles and regularly took part in games. One night in December 1684, Chamillart partnered with the king. Afterward, he enjoyed a rapid rise. He was made a master of requests, the traditional steppingstone to high government office. Appointments as intendant of Rouen and intendant of finances (one of the chief subordinates of the finance minister, the controller general) followed. His performance in both posts was impressive. More importantly, Louis liked working with him. As did Maintenon: in 1690, he became the financial advisor for her cherished school for noble girls at Saint-Cyr.[63]

In 1699, Chamillart was promoted to controller general of finances. Two years later, he completed his dizzying ascent when he was named secretary of state for war. The concentration of the royal government's two most important offices in the hands of one man, particularly on the eve of a great war, was unprecedented. Demonstrating admirable self-awareness, Chamillart warned Louis that he could not be compared to the great men who had held these posts before him. Unfortunately, he was right. As war minister, he proved mediocre. On the one hand, he did well enough at advising the king on strategy, corresponding with the commanding generals, and managing the officials of the war department. On the other hand, he did too little to prevent the breakdown of the army's logistical machinery. Then, during the 1708 fiasco in Flanders, despite traveling personally to the front, he failed to resolve the quarrel between Vendôme and Bourgogne. As finance minister, he was a disaster. He allowed revenues to stagnate, spending to spiral out of control, payment orders to become hopelessly confused, debts to pile up, and financiers and bankers to exert excessive influence over royal financial policy.[64] In 1707, overwhelmed by his duties, depressed by his failures, and pushed to the brink of exhaustion, he begged the king to be allowed to resign the controller generalship. But Louis prized continuity in his government. Throughout his personal rule, he remained stubbornly loyal to his chief servants even when their performance left something to be desired: he only ever dismissed three of them. He therefore turned down the request and instead did his best to boost his minister's flagging morale with words of encouragement. Then, in February 1708, Chamillart's health collapsed, and he missed several sessions of the *Conseil d'en haut*. Louis finally had to admit he needed relief. Chamillart resigned as controller general in favor of his second-in-command, Nicolas Desmaretz. He soldiered on as secretary of state for war.

Ensconced in the comfort and privacy of Madame de Maintenon's apartment, the trio pondered what to do in Flanders. There, the situation had become even more grave since the fall of Lille. After the surrender of its citadel on December 8, Louis and his advisers had been convinced that the campaign was over. Surely, the enemy, exhausted by a long, costly siege, would have to cease operations. The Army of Flanders had been stood down, its battalions and squadrons dispersed to their winter quarters, its commanders—Vendôme, Bourgogne, and Berwick—recalled to court. But the French had underestimated Marlborough and Eugene. Noticing that the opposing army had left the field, they had resolved to retake Bruges and Ghent. Both sat squarely on the Allies' lines of communication. In particular, Ghent controlled the rivers and canals indispensable for moving supplies to Lille. By December 13, Marlborough's army had the town surrounded. Five days later, Eugene and his troops had invested it.[65]

News of the Allied move surprised and alarmed Louis and Chamillart. Although Ghent was defended by a powerful garrison, its fortifications were in a poor state of repair and could not long withstand a siege. The Army of Flanders would have to be reconstituted and sent to its relief. Yet, who was to command posed a quandary. The conflict between Bourgogne and Vendôme raged on unabated. In early December, Bourgogne had returned to court and, with the help of his popular wife, Marie-Adélaide de Savoie, wasted no time in publicly savaging Vendôme's reputation. Louis had no choice except to take his grandson's side. He had ordered Vendôme to retire to his château at Anet; two months later, he would be stripped of his army commission.[66] The only general at Versailles untouched by the feud was the hero of the siege of Lille, Marshal Boufflers. The king had appointed him to take command in Flanders.

The indefatigable Boufflers had left Paris on December 27. His carriage had raced through the night, through the hushed winter countryside of the Ile-de-France, Picardy, Artois, and the Cambresis, and arrived at Douai the next day. After making a swift appraisal of the situation and consulting with Louis de Bernières, intendant of Flanders, who would play a crucial role in provisioning his army, Boufflers had drawn up a plan and sent it off to Versailles. He would assemble 86 battalions and 135 squadrons, then march on Lille.[67] The siege had wrecked its walls and the Allies had not had enough time to repair them. In addition, they had left a garrison of just twenty battalions. Nevertheless, even with a considerable

28   Chapter 1

superiority of force, Boufflers doubted he could recapture Lille. Rather, his thrust would be a feint designed to lure Marlborough and Eugene down from Ghent. He could then slip his army up either the Lys or the Scheldt and relieve the town.[68]

Louis, Chamillart, and Maintenon approved this scheme. A letter from the king ordered the marshal to put it into motion.[69] A mounted courier immediately galloped off for Douai. At the same time, through Versailles' halls, galleries, antechambers, and apartments, a rumor flew that the officers of the Army of Flanders would soon be going back to their regiments.

NOTES

1. This account of January 1, 1709, is based on Philippe de Courcillon, marquis de Dangeau, *Journal du marquis de Dangeau avec les additions inédite du duc de Saint-Simon*, eds. E. Soulié and L. Dussieux, vol. 12 (Paris: Fermin Didot, 1857), 299, and Louis François du Bouchet, marquis de Sourches, *Mémoires du marquis de Sourches sur le règne de Louis XIV*, eds. G. Cosnac and E. Pontal, vol. 11 (Paris: Hachette, 1891), 246.

2. Good descriptions of the *lever du roi* are found in Jean-François Solnon, *La Cour de France* (Paris: Perrin, 2014), 321–325, and Mathieu Da Vinha, *Les valets de chambre de Louis XIV* (Paris: Perrin, 2004), 57–67.

3. Louis-Henri de Loménie, comte de Brienne, *Mémoires*, ed. F Barrière, vol. 1 (Paris: Ponthieu, 1828), 217–219.

4. Joel Cornette, *Le roi de guerre; Essai sur la souveraineté dans la France du Grand Siècle* (Paris: Payot, 1993), 152–153.

5. Olivier Chaline, *Le règne de Louis XIV*, vol. 1 (Paris: Champs histoire, 2009), 156–161.

6. On France's war against the Habsburgs, see David Parrott, *Richelieu's Army: War, Government, and Society in France, 1624–1642* (Cambridge: Cambridge University Press, 2001).

7. Andrew Lossky, *Louis XIV and the French Monarchy* (New Brunswick: Rutgers University Press, 1994), 132.

8. Good introductions to the Dutch Republic include Jonathan Israel, *The Dutch Republic: Its Rise, Greatness, and Fall, 1477–1806* (Oxford: Clarendon Press, 1995), Maarten Prak, *The Dutch Republic in the Seventeenth Century: the Golden Age* (Cambridge: Cambridge University Press, 2015), and Simon Schama, *An Embarrassment of Riches: An Interpretation of Dutch Culture in the Golden Age* (New York: Knopf, 1987).

9. On Chamlay, see Jean-Philippe Cénat, *Chamlay. Le stratège secret de Louis XIV* (Paris: Belin, 2011).

10. On Louvois, the standard works are Camille Rousset, *Histoire de Louvois*, 4 vols. (Paris: Didier, 1862), and André Corvisier, *Louvois* (Paris: Fayard, 1983).

11. Jean-Philippe Cénat, *Le roi stratège: Louis XIV et la direction de la guerre, 1661–1715* (Rennes: Presses universitaires de Rennes, 2010); Guy Rowlands, *The Dynastic State and the Army under Louis XIV: Royal Service and Private Interest, 1661–1701* (Cambridge: Cambridge University Press, 2002), 286–295.

12. Dangeau, *Journal*, vol. 7, 66.
13. Peter Burke, *The Fabrication of Louis XIV* (New Haven and London: Yale University Press, 1992), 78.
14. Thierry Sarmant, *Louis XIV. Homme et roi* (Paris: Tallandier, 2012), 419–421.
15. C. D. O'Malley, "The Medical History of Louis XIV: Intimations of Mortality," in *Louis XIV and the Craft of Kingship*, ed. J. Rule (Columbus: Ohio State University Press, 1969), 150–152, and Chaline, *Le règne de Louis XIV*, vol. 1, 60–62.
16. Service historique de la Défense (hereafter SHD), AG GR A^1 337/111, Vauban to Louvois, 20 January 1673.
17. Christopher Duffy, *The Fortress in the Age of Vauban and Frederick the Great* (London: Routledge and Kegan Paul, 1979), 85–87.
18. John A. Lynn, *Wars of Louis XIV* (London: Routledge, 1999), 174.
19. Jean-Philippe Cénat, "Le ravage du Palatinat: politique de destruction, stratégie de cabinet et propaganda au début de la guerre de la Ligue d'Augsbourg," *Revue historique* 633 (2005/1), 97–132.
20. Useful overviews of the Glorious Revolution include Eveline Cruickshanks, *The Glorious Revolution* (New York: St. Martin's, 2000), Tim Harris, *Revolution: The Great Crisis of the British Monarchy, 1685–1720* (London and New York: Allen Lane, 2006) and Steven Pincus, *1688: The First Modern Revolution* (London and New Haven: Yale University Press, 2009).
21. Olivier Chaline, *Les armées du Roi. Le grand chantier. XVIIe-XVIIIe siècle* (Paris: Armand Colin, 2016), 23–30.
22. Thierry Sarmant and Pierre Waksman, "The King and His Generals: The Military Correspondence of Louis XIV in 1696," *French History* 22/2 (2008), 159.
23. Bertrand Fonck, *Le maréchal général de Luxembourg et le commandement des armées sous Louis XIV* (Paris: Champ Vallon, 2014), 488–538.
24. Marcel Lachiver, *Les années de misère: la famine au temps du Grand Roi* (Paris: Fayard, 1991), 116–117.
25. Ibid., 203.
26. Philip Mansel, *King of the World: The Life of Louis XIV* (Chicago: University of Chicago Press, 2019), 359.
27. On the Order of the Holy Spirit under Louis XIV, see Lenaig Roumegou, "L'ordre du Saint-Esprit sous Louis XIV: un instrument au service du pouvoir (1643–1715)" (Thesis, École nationale des chartes, 2017).
28. Jean-François Blondel, *L'Architecture française*, quoted in Guy Walton, *Louis XIV's Versailles* (Chicago: University of Chicago Press, 1986), 105.
29. Walton, *Versailles*, 98–100.
30. The Musée national du château de Versailles and the Réunion des musées nationaux have produced an excellent website on the Hall of Mirrors, complete with high-resolution images of the ceiling frescoes: http://www.galeriedesglaces-versailles.fr/html/11/accueil/index.html.
31. Letter from Louis XIV to Tallard, quoted in John B. Wolf, *Louis XIV* (New York: Norton, 1968), 499.
32. Louis de Rouvroy, Duc de Saint-Simon, *Mémoires complets et authentiques du duc de Saint-Simon sur le siècle de Louis XIV et la Régence*, ed. Adolphe Chéruel, vol. 3 (Paris: Hachette, 1856), 28–29.
33. Ibid., 34.

34. Chaline, *Le règne de Louis XIV*, vol. 1, 94.

35. John A. Lynn, *Giant of the Grand Siècle: The French Army, 1610–1715* (Cambridge: Cambridge University Press, 1997), ch. 2.

36. Guy Rowlands, "Moving Mars: The Logistical Geography of Louis XIV's France," *French History* 25/4 (2011), 492–514.

37. Guy Rowlands, *The Financial Decline of a Great Power: War, Influence and Money in Louis XIV's France* (Oxford: Oxford University Press, 2012), ch. 1.

38. Julian Hoppit, *A Land of Liberty? England, 1689–1727* (Oxford: Oxford University Press, 2000), 115.

39. On the transformation of England into a fiscal-military state, see the classic study by John Brewer, *The Sinews of Power: War, Money, and the English State, 1688–1783* (Cambridge, MA: Harvard University Press, 1990). On the origins of the Dutch fiscal-military state, see Jan Glete, *War and the State in Early Modern Europe: Spain, the Dutch Republic and Sweden as Fiscal-Military States, 1500–1660* (New York: Routledge, 2002), ch. 4.

40. The reform of the Dutch States Army is discussed in Olaf van Nimwegen, *The Dutch Army and the Military Revolutions, 1588–1688*, trans. Andrew May (Woodbridge: Boydell, 2010). John M. Stapleton, "Forging a Coalition Army: William III, the Grand Alliance, and the Confederate Army in the Spanish Netherlands, 1688–1697" (PhD diss., The Ohio State University, 2003) demonstrates the crucial role of Dutch military practice in the reform of the British Army.

41. On the British army, see John Childs, *The British Army of William III, 1689–1702* (Manchester: Manchester University Press, 1987), Roger B. Manning, *An Apprenticeship in Arms: The Origins of the British Army, 1585–1702* (Oxford: Oxford University Press, 2006), and R. E. Scouller, *The Armies of Queen Anne* (Oxford: Clarendon Press, 1966).

42. The Habsburg army is described in Michael Hochedlinger, *Austria's Wars of National Emergence, 1683–1797* (New York and London: Longman, 2003), 98–150.

43. The literature on the Duke of Marlborough is vast. His descendant Winston Churchill's hagiography is *Marlborough: His Life and Times*, 2 vols. (Chicago: University of Chicago Press, 2002). More recent biographies include J. R. Jones, *Marlborough* (Cambridge: Cambridge University Press, 1993) and Richard Holmes, *Marlborough: England's Fragile Genius* (London and New York: Harper, 2008). The newest biography is in French, Clément Oury, *Le Duc de Marlborough. John Churchill, le plus redoutable ennemi de Louis XIV* (Paris: Perrin, 2022). A study focused on Marlborough's generalship is David Chandler, *Marlborough as Military Commander* (New York: Charles Scribner's Sons, 1973).

44. The standard biographies in English of Eugene of Savoy are Nicholas Henderson, *Prince Eugene of Savoy* (New York: Frederick Praeger, 1964) and Derek McKay, *Prince Eugene of Savoy* (London: Thames and Hudson, 1977).

45. Letter from Marlborough to Sarah, quoted in Chandler, *Marlborough as Military Commander*, 183.

46. Good accounts of Blenheim and its aftermath include Chandler, *Marlborough as Military Commander*, 139–150 and Clément Oury, *La Guerre de Succesion d'Espagne: la fin tragique du Grand Siècle* (Paris: Tallandier, 2020), 131–137.

47. Arsène Legrelle, *La diplomatie française et la succession d'Espagne*, vol. 4, *La Solution (1700–1725)* (Paris: Cotillon, 1892), 364–376.

48. Jamel Ostwald, "The 'Decisive' Battle of Ramillies, 1706: Prerequisites of Decisiveness in Early Modern Warfare," *Journal of Military History* 64/3 (2000), 649–677.

49. Sarmant, *Louis XIV*, 456.

50. Ciro Paoletti, "Prince Eugene of Savoy, the Toulon Expedition of 1707, and the English Historians—A Dissenting View," *Journal of Military History* 70/4 (2006), 939–962.

51. Walton, *Versailles*, 195.

52. John C. Rule and Ben S. Trotter, *A World of Paper: Louis XIV, Colbert de Torcy, and the Rise of the Information State* (Montreal and Toronto: McGill-Queens University Press, 2014), 401–417.

53. Lucien Bély, *Espions et ambassadeurs au temps de Louis XIV* (Paris: Fayard, 1990), 576.

54. Oury, *La Guerre de Succession d'Espagne*, 255.

55. SHD AG GR A^1 2486/3, "Mémoire de Chamlay sur la campagne prochaine aux Pays Bas," 13 April 1708.

56. SHD AG GR A^1 2080/186, Louis XIV to Vendôme, 20 May 1708.

57. Rowlands, *The Dynastic State and the Army*, 303.

58. Churchill, *Marlborough*, vol. 2, 360.

59. The following account of the Battle of Oudenarde is based on Chandler, *Marlborough as Military Commander*, 215–222, Lynn, *Wars of Louis XIV*, 318–320, and Oury, *La Guerre de Succession d'Espagne*, 265–268.

60. The fullest account of the siege of Lille remains Maurice Sautai, *Le siège de la ville et de la citadelle de Lille en 1708* (Lille: Lefebvre-Ducrocq, 1899).

61. 1098. Marlborough to Sarah, 6/17 September 1708 in *The Marlborough-Godolphin Correspondence*, ed. Henry L. Snyder, vol. 2 (Oxford: Clarendon Press, 1975), 1098.

62. Mark Bryant, *Queen of Versailles: Madame de Maintenon, First Lady of Louis XIV's France* (Montréal and Kingston: McGill-Queen's University Press, 2020), 214–269.

63. Emmanuel Pénicaut, *Faveur et pouvoir au tournant du Grand Siècle. Michel Chamillart, Ministre et secretaire d'État de la guerre de Louis XIV* (Paris: École des Chartres, 2004), 55–78.

64. Rowlands, *Financial Decline*.

65. Oury, *La Guerre de Succession d'Espagne*, 275–276.

66. Bryant, *Queen of Versailles*, 266–267.

67. In 1709, a French battalion had a theoretical strength of 585 men, a squadron 140. Real strengths were invariably lower. Lynn, *Wars of Louis XIV*, 61.

68. SHD AG GR A^1 2084/313, Boufflers to Louis XIV, 29 December 1708.

69. SHD AG GR A^1 2149/2, Louis XIV to Boufflers, 1 January 1709.

2

The Winter
January–March, 1709

Louis XIV's orders were sent too late to save Ghent. Even as the courier carrying them was galloping on the road north from Versailles, word reached Marshal Boufflers at Douai that it had surrendered; even worse, Bruges soon followed suit. The news stunned the marshal. Both towns had been strongly garrisoned, and he had expected them to hold out for some time.[1] But the French commander at Ghent, the Comte de La Mothe-Houdancourt, had chosen to save his troops rather than sacrifice them defending places he deemed badly fortified and poorly provisioned. According to the terms of the capitulation he negotiated with the Allies, thirty-four battalions and twenty squadrons evacuated western Flanders and received safe conduct back to French lines. La Mothe's consideration for his men incurred the royal wrath: Louis stripped him of his commission and commanded him to retire to his estates.[2]

For the French, the loss of Ghent and Bruges crowned the disastrous defeats of 1708. The enemies were now masters of the lower reaches of the Lys and the Scheldt and had reopened the main lines of communication and supply to Lille. Boufflers feared that the Allies were still not done. Credible rumors reached him that they were planning to attack Charleroi, Mons, or Douai. For several anxious days, he threw himself into dispatching reinforcements to the threatened fortresses.[3] Fortunately, even Marlborough and Eugene could not indefinitely continue a winter campaign. On January 6, Boufflers learned to his immense relief they were standing down their armies and sending them to winter quarters.[4]

With the emergency at last over, Boufflers could turn to his own priorities and plans. Short and stout, he radiated a vigor and alertness that belied his sixty-five years. A scion of the minor nobility of Picardy, he was a true warrior who had spent his entire life in the army of the Sun King.[5] He had first come to prominence as a young dragoon officer waging the *petite guerre*, the skirmishing and raiding in which armies were constantly engaged beyond the great clashes of sieges and battles.[6] By the Nine Years' War, he was a lieutenant general in Flanders. He captured the fortress-city of Mons, then assisted Marshal Luxembourg in his great victory at Steenkerque. These and other feats of arms won him elevation to the marshalate in 1693. Two years later, Namur made him a French hero. For eight weeks, he defended the walled town and the citadel with enormous skill, resourcefulness, tenacity, and courage: at the siege's climax, he had plunged into a breach, sword in hand at the head of his bodyguards, to drive back an English storming column.[7] As a reward, Louis made him a duke. Boufflers proved almost as redoubtable at court as on the battlefield. He befriended the Duc du Maine, legitimated and favorite son of the king. Through Maine, he grew close to Madame de Maintenon. On the same day he became a marshal, he asked Maintenon for her niece's hand in marriage. Though she graciously declined, she continued to conspicuously favor him. Boufflers became a key military protégé of the powerful royal consort.[8]

At the outbreak of the War of the Spanish Succession, Boufflers was one of France's leading generals. In 1702 and 1703, he commanded the Army of Flanders and faced Marlborough for the first time. He never met the captain general in pitched battle, and his record in these campaigns was mixed. He successfully defended the Spanish Netherlands and won a tidy little victory over the Dutch at Eckeren. But he could not prevent Marlborough from capturing important outposts along the Moselle and overrunning Cologne and Liège, the territories of France's Wittelsbach allies.[9] At court, critics accused Boufflers of excessive caution. Some even whispered he had lost his earlier drive. In 1704, the king appointed him captain of the second company of the Gardes du Corps, his elite mounted lifeguards. It was at once a key military post, a high social honor, and an exalted place in the court hierarchy.[10] It also removed Boufflers from active service with the armies. For the next four years, he cooled his heels in the royal palaces, performing ceremonial duties and serving as a military adviser to the king. He longed to return to the field. The siege of Lille was his chance. Approaching Louis directly, he volunteered to defend the beleaguered city. His performance, the finest ever of any commander of a besieged fortress, silenced his critics, raised his reputation to new heights, and demonstrated his prowess was undiminished. After it, Boufflers was the only marshal who could command the Army of Flanders in what might be the most important campaign of the war. As Maintenon declared to her confidant, the princesse des Ursins, he "can neither be too much praised nor too highly recompensed."[11]

Boufflers first took stock of his army. "I will be setting out on a tour of this frontier," he announced to the king on January 9. "I will inspect the troops in all the places where I am going in order to discover their condition for myself, and to speak to them, and to try to impress in them the sentiments that each man must have to serve Your Majesty well."[12] The Army of Flanders had been in winter quarters since early December. Eighteenth-century warfare had a strict seasonal rhythm because of the limited capacity of the subsistence agriculture of the day to feed great masses of men and horses. At the end of September or the beginning of October—the 1708 campaign had been unusually long—food supplies ran low and grass disappeared from the meadows. Large-scale operations then had to cease. Armies broke up and went to ground, their units dispersing over a wide area so they could be more easily provisioned. The Army of Flanders' infantry regiments were lodged in cities, towns, and villages across Artois, Hainault, and Picardy. The cavalry and dragoons had gone deeper into France to find more abundant forage. Eighteen battalions and thirty-one squadrons had been left behind to cover the frontier. When foodstuffs became more plentiful and grass reappeared, which might occur as early as April, the armies could once again reassemble and take the field.

Winter quarters, however, were more than just an operational pause.[13] They were also indispensable for rebuilding and readying armies for the renewal of fighting. Captains led recruiting parties to find men to refill the ranks of their companies. Troops were issued new arms, uniforms, and shoes to replace worn-out gear. Remounts were furnished to the cavalry and dragoons. Magazines were refilled with grain and fodder, armories with ammunition and gunpowder. The long period of rest allowed men and horses to recover their health and strength. It was also indispensable for restoring soldiers' morale as well as reestablishing order and discipline. Good winter quarters contributed immeasurably to fighting power. Poor winter quarters could wreck an army.

Even as he was inspecting his troops, Boufflers was also pondering what to do for the next campaign. He was acutely aware of the importance of the Flanders frontier. Spanning one hundred and twenty-five miles from the River Meuse to the English Channel, it was where enemy armies stood closest to Paris. In addition, the Lys, Scarpe, Scheldt, Sambre, and Meuse rivers were like highways leading deep into France. Protecting his kingdom's heartlands by pushing this frontier northward had been a preoccupation—even an obsession—of Louis XIV from the earliest days of his reign. To this end, he had employed his most powerful armies led by his finest generals. Until he grew too old, he had personally campaigned in Flanders in every war.

It was to safeguard the king's gains that Vauban had built the *pré carré*. After 1678, across Flanders, massive fortresses rose. Each had walls of stone and packed earth forty feet thick. Angling out from them were arrow-shaped bastions mounting artillery that could bring down a withering crossfire on an attacking force. Around this main body of curtain walls and bastions—the enceinte—were detached outworks: ravelins, demilunes, lunettes, and hornworks, each a strongpoint on its own. To complete the defenses, the surrounding terrain was landscaped into a maze of moats, ditches, and infantry entrenchments. Together, enceinte, outworks, and earthworks gave a Vauban fortress its distinctive shape, resembling a many-pointed star. As long as its fortifications were in good repair, and it was properly garrisoned, provisioned, and armed, it could defy a besieging army for weeks or months.[14] The *pré carré* comprised two lines of these fortresses arranged, as Vauban himself described, like an army arrayed for battle. The first line included Dunkirk, Bergues, Furnes, Fort Knocke, Ypres, Menin, Lille, Tournai, Mortagne, Condé, Valenciennes, Le Quesnoy, Maubeuge, Philippeville, and Dinant; the second, Gravelines, Saint-Omer, Aire, Béthune, Arras, Douai, Bouchain, Cambrai, Landrecies, Avesnes, Mariembourg, Rocroi, and Charleville.[15] Over the years, scores of secondary strongholds had been integrated into the barriers. By the time Vauban died in 1707, the *pré carré* was an immensely strong fortified frontier. It sealed off the entrances into France. It barred the rivers and waterways—water transport was indispensable for the supply of large armies. Above all, it afforded defense in depth. Its fortresses were mutually supporting so that if one was lost, others would still block the enemy's way.

The Allies' capture of Lille was nevertheless a serious blow. The capital of Flanders was like the keystone of an arch: its fall threatened the integrity of the entire defensive structure. From there, an Allied field army could dominate a great swathe of the country from Boufflers' headquarters at Douai to the upper Lys fortress of Saint-Venant. The enemy would be able to cut off Ypres, Dunkirk, and the Channel coast, isolate Artois, and penetrate Picardy. Then the road to Paris would be open.[16] Furthermore, Boufflers was receiving a steady stream of intelligence that the Allies intended to press their advantage. They had already issued their troops new uniforms and shoes. They had also not sent their German contingents home for the winter as usual. Instead, they had billeted them in the Low Countries and had paid them a double wage. All were signs that the Allies were planning to begin operations as soon as possible in the spring.[17]

Boufflers conceived of an audacious plan to thwart the enemy: the Army of Flanders would seize the strategic initiative and begin the 1709 campaign by quickly mobilizing, besieging, and recapturing Lille. On January 12, he drew up a long letter describing his scheme to the king and War Minister Michel Chamillart.[18] There were, he stressed, two requirements for success. First, the French had to strike in March, before the Allies could themselves take the field. Second, they must make meticulous preparations. They would have to assemble and bring to bear a siege train of unprecedented power and size: twenty 33-pounder cannons, one hundred and fifty 24-pounders, thirty 12-inch mortars, ten 8-inch mortars, and ten stone-firing perriers. These guns would need enormous quantities of ammunition—30,000 shot for the 33-pounders alone—gunpowder, and other equipment.[19] Once in position around Lille, the 100,000-strong Army of Flanders would consume 140,000 rations of bread per day. Another 40,000 rations would go to the 20,000 peasant pioneers who would dig the trenches and build the siege works.[20] To satisfy these demands as well as all the others that would arise during the 1709 campaign, 216,000 sacks of grain would have to be amassed and stored in the magazines of twenty-one fortresses across Flanders from Givet on the Meuse to Dunkirk on the Channel coast. Each sack weighed 200 pounds and could provide 180 days of bread rations for a common infantryman.[21] And not only men had to be fed, but horses too. This burden was the most onerous of all. Since the siege would take place well before the appearance of the spring grass, the army's tens of thousands of animals would have to subsist entirely on dry fodder. At least four million rations, each amounting to about twenty-two pounds of hay, straw, and oats, would have to be stockpiled.[22]

Completing all these preparations in just six weeks posed a daunting challenge. Yet it was one the French had successfully met before. Under the Marquis de Louvois, Louis XIV's great minister of war, the French had time and again filled fortress magazines over the winter months with everything needed by a campaign army. They were then able to steal a march on their foes as soon as the weather broke. Boufflers had given one of the most striking demonstrations of this priceless French advantage in 1691 when he had captured Mons. Bringing his army of 40,000 troops swiftly out of winter quarters, he had surrounded his target on March 15. Louvois had painstakingly prepared the siege down to the last detail: the horses had been fed by 900,000 rations of dry fodder, while the troops had eaten their bread with 220,000 red-skinned Dutch cheeses that had been stored in the citadel of Tournai. Taken by surprise, the Allied commander, William III, had been unable to intervene. Mons had surrendered on April 8.[23] Lille would be Mons writ large. Though the French logistical machine had deteriorated badly since, Boufflers had reasons to hope it could still play its part in his plan. Having been pushed back to their own frontiers, the French armies were now much closer to their sources of supply. French officials and officers could gather resources from across northern France and even further afield. Finally, the *pré carré* offered the Army of Flanders an ideal position from which to beleaguer Lille. Vauban had designed his fortresses not just as defensive bulwarks. They were also forward bases and springboards for attack.[24] The army could be supported and sustained from a ring of nearby French strongholds from Tournai to Ypres.

Recapturing Lille promised to restore France's fortunes in Flanders. It would repair the breach in the *pré carré* and stop the Allied invasion of the kingdom in its tracks. Just embarking on the preparations, Boufflers argued, would offer great strategic and diplomatic benefits. They would cause Marlborough and Eugene to fear for the safety of Lille as well as Oudernarde and Ath, forcing them to delay the beginning of their own offensive in the spring. They would bolster Louis' efforts to negotiate an end to the war by demonstrating that France still had the military strength, resources, and, above all, the will to hold its own.[25] Louis and Chamillart needed little convincing. Both enthusiastically endorsed the marshal's scheme.[26] But all their plans would be wrecked and their hopes dashed by the unfolding of two crises: the Great Winter and the collapse of France's finances.

During the opening years of the eighteenth century, the weather was beautiful. After the cold, wet, and dismal 1690s, the winters turned mild, the summers hot. Rains fell at the right times and in the right measures. These conditions were perfect for French agriculture: wheat and grapes, olives and chestnuts grew in easy abundance. Bread, then as now the staple of the French diet, could be afforded even by the most indigent. Beset by the many hardships of a great war, the Sun King's subjects were fortunate not to also face scarcity and hunger. The famine of 1693 became just an awful memory.

The weather held fair at the beginning of 1708. "We have not had winter," rejoiced a vigneron of Chanteloup-les-Vignes near Paris. "Little snow, very little ice, a humid season, ideal for work." But the spring was chilly and icy, the summer sunless and rainy. Only in the middle of August could the peasants take in their crops. They had barely begun when strong hailstorms swept across northern France, beating down the wheat still standing in the fields. Unsurprisingly, the harvest was mediocre. The price of bread climbed steadily, disquieting the poorest French. To make matters worse, the cold arrived early. Temperatures in October were as low as in January, and there was heavy snow for several days in November. Then, unexpectedly, the last month of the year was warm and pleasant. All over France, spirits soared. Joseph Sevin, Chevalier de Quincy and an infantry captain in the régiment de Bourgogne, was billeted in Meaux. In his memoirs, he remembered that "toward Saint Andrew's Day, we had seven or eight very cold days. Afterward the weather softened so much we allowed ourselves to believe the winter was over."[27] On December 24, the temperature in the capital was eleven degrees Celsius. Parisians celebrated Christmas in conditions more resembling Easter. And the warmth lingered into the new year. At Versailles, Louis sought to distract himself from his many cares by hunting in the great park and promenading in his beloved gardens.

Yet disaster was on the wing. Over Scandinavia, an anticyclone had formed, drawing in great masses of Siberian air. On the eve of the Feast of Kings, January 5, it bore down on France from the northeast, its vanguard a freezing wind. By nine that night, it reached Lille, and the citadel's battered ramparts were cloaked in glittering ice. Toward midnight, it arrived in Paris. At the Abbey of Saint-Victor on the eastern edge of the city, the physician and savant Louis Morin was keeping a remarkable daily record of temperature, barometric pressure, and weather conditions that he had begun in 1676 and would continue until 1712. He carefully observed the dramatic changes the cold wrought. On January 5, he noted that the temperature was 10.7 degrees. By the next morning, it was −3.1. The rain, which had been falling steadily for days, turned into snow. Within just a few hours, icicles wreathed the spires and bell towers, while deep white drifts completely covered the ground.[28]

The cold advanced relentlessly. In the little town of Château-Porcien on the banks of the River Aisne in the Ardennes, the clerk and chronicler Jean Taté interpreted its advent as a sort of divine retribution:

> But our iniquities brought on us the wrath of God such that He sent the angel which is spoken of in the Apocalypse, with his sharp and cruel scythe, to reap this fair country and to harvest its vines and gardens; on the sixth of January of the year 1709, there fell in the night such a quantity of rain that the ground became full of water, and as soon as it ceased the sharp scythe began to be felt, that is to say a terrible cold, with such a great frost that all the earth became ice.[29]

At the other end of France, in the bustling port of Bordeaux, an equally vivid if less eschatological description was set down in the diary of Joseph-François-Ignace de Labat de Savignac, a judge in the city's Parlement: "on the night of the ninth it snowed double the preceding night, and the thermometer was at twelve degrees. Water coming off the fire froze in half an hour and cold water was freezing as it fell from the jug into the glass."[30]

By the time Savignac was writing, the cold had engulfed all of France. According to Morin's meticulous measurements, in Paris, the temperature was −10 or below for all save one day between January 7 and 24 and reached a nadir of −18.1. It was nearer to −25 in the rich grainlands of the Ile-de-France and the Beauce. The other provinces were just as frigid. The intensity and length of the cold were what made the Great Winter. There were extraordinary scenes rarely seen before or since in France. The whole country was covered by snow. In most places it was a foot deep; in Angoumois and Saintonge in the southwest, where it usually never fell at all, three. The Seine, the Somme, the Rhone, the Loire, and the Garonne froze solid for all or much of their lengths. In Alsace, the king's officers called out the peasant militia to guard against German raiders crossing over the Rhine, which was covered by a sheet of ice so thick it could bear the weight of a heavily laden wain. Even the sea was affected. In Marseilles, the Vieux Port became icebound, trapping numerous ships, barges, and fishing boats.[31]

In the face of this onslaught, Louis was at first determined to maintain his routine of outdoor pursuits. Dangeau marveled that the ferocious cold did not seem to bother the king. Others, unfortunately, were made of less stern stuff. On January 8, Louis was forced to cancel a trip to the Trianon because his guardsmen and officers were suffering so badly from the frigid temperatures. Afterward, even he had to seek shelter indoors, sequestering himself for nine days in the apartments of Madame de Maintenon and the Duchesse de Bourgogne.[32] At the same time, the Grand Dauphin had to abandon his chilly château of Meudon for Versailles. Inside the great palace, servants and lackeys fed a forest's worth of firewood into hundreds of fireplaces, stoves, and braziers. Despite their best efforts, it was hardly a comfortable refuge. On January 10, Elisabeth Charlotte, the king's sister-in-law, complained to her kinswoman, the Electress Sophia of Hanover:

> The cold here is so fierce that it fairly defies description. I am sitting by a roaring fire, have a screen before the door, which is closed, so that I can sit here with a sable fur piece around my neck and my feet in a bearskin sack, and I am still shivering with cold and can barely hold the pen. Never in my life have I seen a winter such as this one; the wine freezes in bottles.[33]

For too many of Louis' subjects, the cold was not merely a source of discomfort; it was a deadly threat. Vagabonds, beggars, and the homeless poor swarmed into cities and towns, desperately seeking help. They found little. The only measure taken by the authorities in Bordeaux, Montpelier, Nimes, and scores of other places was to set bonfires burning in public squares for the wretches to huddle around as best they could. Otherwise exposed to the full harshness of the elements, they perished in droves. Only a little more fortunate were those who had houses in which to take shelter. Their dwellings, badly insulated and meagerly heated by open fires, were scarcely proof against the Arctic conditions. For most, the warmest sanctuary was their beds. Even there, the lethal cold stalked them. Men and women, especially the old and infirm, froze to death in their sleep. Most vulnerable of all were the very youngest. In Civry in Burgundy, the curé wrote, "many children died shortly after they were born, so cold has it been in the humble cottages." Across France, other village priests recorded similar heartbreaking scenes. By the end of January, the Great Winter had killed 45,000 people.[34]

As painful as these deaths were, a more far-reaching and consequential tragedy was the destruction of French agriculture. Everywhere, fruit trees were devastated. Among the hardest losses were the chestnut orchards and olive groves, which provided food, fuel, and animal feed for the peoples of the Massif Central and the Midi. But France's most important crops were grapes and wheat, and there was, at first, hope they would survive the season's unprecedented rigors. The grapevine was an exceptionally hardy plant, able to withstand bitter cold and lashings of ice. The wheat had been sown in October. Once in the ground, its seeds lay dormant through the winter before germinating in the spring. The thick blanket of snow helped to insulate and protect them.

What happened next doomed both. On January 24, beginning in the south, the temperature climbed. The next day, according to Louis Morin, it reached 1.5 degrees in Paris. The snow turned into rain, the ice melted, the earth became a waterlogged morass. The respite, however, lasted less than a week. Then the mercury plunged again, snow returned, and ice covered everything. During February and March, there were two more intervals of warmth, followed by prolonged periods of cold. Only after March 16 did temperatures lastingly remain above zero, signaling that the Great Winter had finally ended.

The cycle of thawing and freezing killed the grapevines. Many succumbed at last to the repeated assaults of ice and snow. Most drowned in the inundations caused by the rain and meltwaters. Skillful vignerons managed to save a few plants by cutting them down to their roots. But French winegrowing—the most important and productive in Europe—was ruined; it would not fully recover until 1711. The lucrative export trade to England, the Netherlands, and Scandinavia withered away. At home, the well-to-do were forced to drink unfamiliar, inferior vintages bought at exorbitant prices. In western France, some priests resorted to Breton cider in place of wine for the Eucharist. Most French had to make do with water, which they normally avoided because it was notoriously unsanitary and a dangerous carrier of disease.

Far worse still, the same cycle destroyed the wheat. During the thaws, water seeping into the ground saturated the wheat seeds. With the freezes, they became entombed in ice. The annihilation of the winter wheat made a famine inevitable throughout the land. France might have been extraordinarily diverse in its landscapes and climates, encompassing the cool, rainy grasslands and forests of the north, the temperate coastal plains and marshes of the west, and the sunbaked uplands and valleys of the south, but because it yielded an incomparably high number of calories per acre, wheat was cultivated everywhere and to the exclusion of almost all other crops, even in places where growing conditions were far from ideal. When the peasants emerged from the shelter of their cottages in March, they feared the worst. All they could do, however, was anxiously wait and watch their fields for the appearance of the first shoots of wheat. They would wait in vain.

The fate of the harvest did not just concern France's peasants. Subsistence was a fundamental concern of eighteenth-century government. It touched on every area of public life: political stability, social order, military effectiveness, economic prosperity, and fiscal revenue. It therefore involved all powerholders in society, church, and state. At the very highest level of the monarchy, it formed an important part of the brief of one of Louis XIV's chief ministers: Nicolas Desmaretz, controller general of finances. He was determined to avoid a repetition of the terrible starvation of 1693. In September 1708, he ordered that grain should circulate around the kingdom free of the innumerable duties and tolls charged on all other goods. In doing so, he sought to encourage it to flow from places of plenty to places of scarcity. At the same time, he instituted a comprehensive system for monitoring wheat prices. He charged the intendants, the key royal agents in the provinces, with informing him each month of prices in their *généralités*, or administrative districts. He supplemented this data with a stream of information from correspondents all over France.

Unfortunately, in the early months of 1709, Desmaretz became convinced that France was not facing famine. The first intendants' reports on grain prices in October showed they were moderate, suggesting that the 1708 harvest had filled the granaries in most parts of the kingdom. A steady rise in prices from November to March failed to puncture this belief. The controller general's informants rang no alarm bells either. For instance, in February, Louis Ravat, *prévot des marchands* or head of the municipality of Lyon, informed him that local supplies were adequate, and no special measures needed to be taken.[35] Perhaps most importantly, while Desmaretz understood how snow could protect wheat seedlings, he completely failed to grasp the destructive effects of the thaw-freeze cycle. As a result, he was sure that the bulk of the grain had survived the Great Winter. In March, when peasants began raising the alarm about the absence of any sign of their crops, he condemned their warnings as either ignorant hysteria or deliberate disinformation to drive up food prices. At the beginning of April, he told the intendants they could expect a fine harvest.[36]

Desmaretz's attention and energies were instead consumed by France's collapsing finances. No one was better prepared to understand the full depth and extent of this crisis. He had been born in 1648 in Soissons. His father had been a tax officer, a treasurer of France. His mother had been the sister of Jean-Baptiste Colbert, controller general of finances from 1665 to 1683 and the most important minister of the first two decades of Louis XIV's personal reign. At sixteen, Desmaretz had gone to serve his uncle as his assistant. His intelligence, resourcefulness, and loyalty immediately impressed the Great Colbert. Over the next twenty years, he enjoyed a rapid ascent of the state hierarchy. He also gained an unmatched knowledge of the French financial system. Many came to regard him as Colbert's successor. Even Louis de Rouvroy, Duc de Saint-Simon, the most famous memoirist of the court of Louis XIV and an implacable and ferocious enemy of Desmaretz, had to admit that he was "mentored and educated by Colbert in all the maxims and arts of the finances."[37]

In 1683, shortly after the death of his patron and protector, Desmaretz's career was suddenly and unexpectedly cut short. He had been involved in a contract for the minting of sous, small-denomination silver coins. The contractors had done such shoddy work and reaped such immense profits that suspicions of corruption fell on him. Although his guilt was never conclusively proven, he hardly helped himself by making expensive renovations to his newly acquired lands and château at Maillebois in Normandy. The king forced him to leave the court and retire to his estates. Disgraced, stripped of his offices, and exiled, his public life should have been over. But he then engineered a stunning and unprecedented rehabilitation. At Maillebois, he established himself as an expert on the royal finances, producing a stream of reports and memoranda. So great became his reputation for financial sagacity and skill that he was sought out by Louis Phélypeaux de Pontchartrain, controller general during the Nine Years' War. As Pontchartrain's secret advisor, he shaped key policies, most notably the *capitation*, the new universal tax imposed on nobles and commoners alike. When Michel Chamillart was appointed minister of both war and finances, he concluded that he could not do without Desmaretz's expertise. He brought him out into the open and named him a director general of finances, one of his chief lieutenants. The diarist Dangeau recorded Desmaretz's return to court on September 19, 1703: "After dinner, M. Chamillart brought M. Desmaretz into the cabinet of the king at Versailles; he had last seen the king twenty years ago."[38] On

February 21, 1708, he capped his tour de force when Louis XIV appointed him controller general in the wake of Chamillart's resignation. Years later, to Philippe d'Orléans, regent of Louis XV, Desmaretz described his interview with the old king during the *lever du roi*:

> He warned me and explained the situation clearly, saying to me he knew well the state of the finances, that he was not demanding the impossible of me; that if I should succeed, I would be doing him a great service, for which he would not be able to thank me too much; if I should fail, he would not blame me for the outcome.[39]

When 1709 began, failure was looming large. During the War of the Spanish Succession, France's fundamental financial problem was the complete inadequacy of its ordinary forms of revenue to meet massive and ever-mounting military expenses. Louis XIV imposed two direct taxes on his subjects. The ancient hearth tax, the *taille*, was paid by the peasantry. Nobles, clergy, and high-status commoners—in other words, all except the poorest members of French society—enjoyed the privilege of being exempt from it. In 1695, the royal government created the *capitation*, a poll tax payable by all French subjects. It was a significant breach in the bastion of privilege protecting elites. Yet further assaults on privilege were ruled out as too politically risky. Extracting more from payers of the *taille* seemed almost equally dangerous. At the height of the Thirty Years' War, tax increases had provoked peasant resistance ranging from nonpayment to rebellions that had blazed across whole regions of the kingdom. A similarly volatile situation now appeared to be developing. By 1708, the *taille* had been in arrears for years in many provinces; in others, tax officers could only collect it with the backing of royal troops.[40]

In addition to direct taxes, the monarchy also levied customs duties, sales imposts on basic commodities such as wine, and a range of dues from its monopolies on tobacco and salt (the much-loathed *gabelle*). These indirect taxes were paid by both the privileged and the peasantry. As a result, beginning with Colbert, controllers general steadily raised the take from them, making them an ever more significant share of the overall royal revenues. Unlike the *taille* and *capitation*, which were administered by royal officers, they were contracted out to tax farmers. In 1691, all the indirect taxes were definitively integrated into a General Farm. It was the largest single economic enterprise in Europe: the Farm's 1697 contract had an annual lease price of 58,750,000 livres.[41] But the advent of the great war badly disrupted economic activity, and the proceeds from indirect taxation dropped precipitously. So low did they fall that the royal government, instead of enjoying a lucrative and reliable income stream, ended up indemnifying the tax farmers year after year.

With ordinary revenues from taxation languishing or collapsing, Controller General Chamillart was forced to raise the money the French monarchy needed by resorting to an array of expedients: extraordinary affairs in contemporary parlance. Some of these were old tricks long familiar from earlier wars. *Rentes* were bonds issued by the city hall of Paris on behalf of the king. A staggering volume of them was launched: by 1715, their total value reached around 1.4 billion livres.[42] Other long-standing extraordinary affairs involved the system of venal officeholding. To an extent unmatched elsewhere in Europe, the French monarchy sold its administrative, judicial, and financial offices to private individuals, who then owned them as a form of property. Chamillart put every conceivable public function up for sale and devised ingenious new ways to extort more money from existing officeholders.[43]

A lucrative, though risky, extraordinary affair was currency manipulation. French money took the form of coins such as the gold louis and the silver écu. The royal government set their values in a unit of account, the livre tournois. By declaring a reformation of the currency, it unilaterally rerated the coins in livres. People were required to bring their coins to the royal mints, where, for a processing fee or seigniorage, they were stamped with symbols denoting their new values. Once the stamping was complete, the mints returned the coins to their owners. Chamillart resorted to reformations in 1701 and 1704: the former raked in 29.2 million livres in seigniorage profits, the latter 29 million.[44] These windfalls, however, came at great cost, for currency manipulation wrecked public confidence in the stability of French money. At the slightest hint that a reformation was in the offing, people hoarded coins, sent them abroad, or even handed them over to counterfeiters who, for a smaller fee than charged by the mints, marked them with copies of the new symbols.

Yet even pushed to their limits, these tried-and-true extraordinary affairs could not come close to meeting the unprecedented costs of the struggle for the throne of Spain. Chamillart therefore turned to new expedients. Many were untested and not well understood, and the controller general often had little appreciation of their full implications. The most consequential was France's first large-scale experiment with paper money. During a reformation of the currency, the Paris Mint issued receipts for the coins deposited with it for rerating. Its work often took months or even years to complete and, in the meantime, France suffered from a serious shortage of ready cash. To remedy this problem, Chamillart declared in 1703 that the coin receipts, which were called mint bills, would henceforth circulate as a sort of supplementary money. Then his desperation for more funds drove him the next year to order the Paris Mint to issue new bills completely unbacked by coins. Until 1707, mint bills were printed in huge quantities. They proved highly unstable; public confidence in them fluctuated wildly. All too often, they were accepted as payment only at steep discounts from their face value. This, in turn, provoked costs to soar because transactions had to build in hefty premiums to compensate for monetary turbulence.

The most important financial expedient of all was borrowing. Here, France was at a grave disadvantage against its greatest enemies, the Maritime Powers of Great Britain and the Dutch Republic. A financial revolution begun during the Nine Years' War had created the Bank of England and the other classic institutions of the City of London. They enabled the government of Queen Anne to borrow enormous sums at favorable rates of interest. Holland, by far the largest and richest of the seven Dutch provinces, could draw upon the vast commercial wealth of the great global entrepot of Amsterdam and a well-established tradition of government borrowing to float public loans on an unprecedented scale.[45]

By comparison, French borrowing was ad hoc, inefficient, and expensive. One source was the royal government's own financial officers. Receivers and tax farmers collected taxes and other income. Bourbon kings and their finance ministers had always expected these officers to raise short-term loans from their own fortunes and credit to make up for delays or shortfalls in these revenues. Chamillart systematized and vastly expanded this practice by authorizing these financial officers to issue interest-paying negotiable bearer bills. After 1701, the state debt represented by this paper rose vertiginously. But Chamillart went even further. During wartime, almost all the monarchy's available funds and other resources were spent by the treasurers-general of the *Extraordinaire des Guerres*, the army's principal paymasters. Chamillart transformed them into another source of borrowing by allowing them to make payments with their own credit devices, the so-called War Bills. A huge quantity of these IOUs was issued; even worse, most were allowed to go unpaid for too long. The result was that the military paymasters were soon buckling badly under an increasingly unsupportable burden of debt.

Then, during the early years of the war, a further source of borrowing developed, one that would directly and devastatingly contribute to the crisis of 1709. The French government needed to supply money to Bourbon and Allied armies fighting all over Western Europe. To handle these massive and complex remittance operations, Chamillart enlisted the services of international merchant bankers. Their financial instrument of choice was the negotiable bill of exchange. By 1704, one banker had come to the fore: Samuel Bernard. In one of history's great ironies, Bernard was originally a Huguenot of Paris. The son of an artist, he had been a trader of luxury fabrics and jewelry before shifting into merchant banking. In 1685, following the Revocation of the Edict of Nantes, he had converted to Catholicism. But he continued to maintain close links with kith and kin in the Huguenot diaspora. Thanks to the cash and credit furnished by this Europe-wide network, Bernard became the chief international banking agent of the *Extraordinaire des Guerres*. Moreover, gambling that he could realize immense profits, he used his bills of exchange to borrow huge sums on behalf of the French monarchy. Between 1702 and 1708, he remitted 30 million livres per year to Louis XIV's armies at a time when France's annual income was just 40–60 million livres.[46]

Just how indispensable Bernard became to the French war effort is revealed in a famous story told by Saint-Simon. On March 6, 1708, Desmaretz invited him to the château of Marly, Louis XIV's private retreat, for dinner and a conference. At five in the evening, as Desmaretz was working with Bernard and Jean de Brouchoven, Comte de Bergeyck, Spain's principal minister in the Netherlands, Louis happened by:

> The king told Desmaretz that he was very happy to see him with M. Bernard, and then immediately said to the latter: You are a man who has never seen Marly. Come and see it on my walk, and I will return you to Desmaretz afterwards. Bernard followed, and, while it lasted, the king spoke only to Bergeyck and to him, and as much to him as to the other, leading them everywhere and showing them everything equally with the graces that he knew how to employ so well when there was something he wished to accomplish.

The king and his finance minister had contrived this affair because they desperately needed the banker to provide a new, massive loan for the Army of Flanders. "I admired, and not alone," Saint-Simon commented acidly, "this sort of prostitution by the king, who, usually so stingy with his words, nonetheless chose to speak with the likes of Bernard." Yet the contrivance worked. For, as the memoirist further observed, Bernard was "a man of incalculable vanity, capable of opening his purse if the king deigned to flatter him." After returning to Desmaretz from his promenade, he was "so enchanted . . . he said he would prefer ruin rather than leave in difficulties a prince who had shown him so much honor."[47] He immediately pledged 900,000 livres.[48]

That Desmaretz had to stoop to such subterfuge was to be blamed on the failings of his predecessor. Chamillart could have prevented—or more likely postponed—the crash of France's financial house of cards if only he had carefully organized, marshaled, and channeled the available resources to support the growing weight of debt. Instead, he had done the opposite. Appropriations and disbursement of funds descended into utter chaos. The finance ministry made payments late or not at all, spent anticipated funds in advance, too often assigned a single income source to several different expenses, and, worst of all, failed to shore up the main pillars of the war effort, the treasurers-general of the *Extraordinaire des Guerres* and Samuel Bernard, with good, reliable revenues.

An affable personality and superlative skill at billiards had turned out to be inadequate qualities for a finance and war minister waging the greatest conflict of Louis XIV's reign. By the time Desmaretz assumed office in February 1708, the situation was, as the king himself had bluntly described it, calamitous. The monarchy's debts amounted to 482,884,661 livres and expenses to 202,788,354 livres. The available revenues were just 20,388,338 livres.[49] Desmaretz was compelled to concentrate his initial efforts on safeguarding the remaining sound sources of revenue, imposing some order on the flow of payments, and eking out the available credit.

Unknown to him, Samuel Bernard was in dire straits. The banker was carrying an enormous load of outstanding loans, somewhere between 14 and 20 million livres. In July 1708, following the disastrous battle of Oudenarde, he had provided another emergency loan of 1 million livres for the Army of Flanders.[50] He was now seriously overextended. Moreover, Chamillart had been handing him, for the servicing and retiring of his debts, a vast amount of mint bills; their value was in free fall. Once appointed controller general, Desmaretz had assigned Bernard some more solid revenues, including coin. But these were not enough to stabilize his increasingly shaky financial operations.

These operations were based in Lyon. Located at the nexus of important trade routes and the historic seat of the silk industry, France's second city had evolved into a major financial center and money market. In particular, it had important ties to banking houses based in nearby Protestant Geneva. Financial business was transacted at four seasonal fairs—Kings, Easter, August, and All-Saints—held three months apart. Bernard had been using these fairs to contract new bills of exchange and settle outstanding ones. In December 1708, at the end of the All-Saints Fair, he realized that he would not be able to meet his obligations. In a desperate bid to remain solvent, he somehow convinced the Lyon authorities to postpone payments until the 1709 Fair of Kings. He then "rolled over" or rescheduled his loans by borrowing a further 36 million livres in bills of exchange. He was only able to do so by furnishing his lenders with extra security in the form of 28 million livres of mint bills. These lenders, primarily the bank Lullin Frères of Geneva, promised to return the mint bills to Bernard once he had liquidated the bills of exchange. But Lullins soon came to believe that France was in such a parlous condition that Bernard was unlikely to receive the money he needed to settle his bills of exchange. To protect themselves against this possibility, they began to sell their mint bills without Bernard's knowledge or approval. The Genevans had lit a gunpowder trail to a bomb. When it exploded, it would bring down the entire rickety edifice of French finances.[51]

Even before this crash, the exhaustion of French money and credit was already having grave consequences in Flanders. Immediately after taking command, Marshal Boufflers was alarmed to learn that the *Extraordinaire des Guerres* had failed to pay his army for more than a month. On January 4, the marshal warned the king:

> Everything on this frontier is in such prodigious chaos and disorder and most of the troops so embittered and badly disposed by the lack of wages, clothes, shoes, and other necessities that until some order is restored and a little tranquility and confidence re-established by the payment of the men, nothing can be done. I humbly beg Your Majesty not to believe I am exaggerating and doing more harm than good, for he knows that is neither my spirit nor my character.[52]

During the War of the Spanish Succession, French cavalry received 7 sous 4 deniers per day, dragoons 6 sous, and infantry 5 sous.[53] These wages were derisory—a skilled artisan such as a weaver could make 12 sous a day. Nevertheless, they posed a considerable challenge for the royal paymasters because, unlike other expenses, which could be reimbursed by paper credit instruments, they could only be paid in hard cash. Under urgent orders from Louis and Chamillart, Romain Dru de Mongelas, treasurer-general of the *Extraordinaire des Guerres*, scraped together 20,000 louis d'or and 100,000 écus. Mounted couriers rushed the gold coins to Douai, while the silver followed more slowly by cart.[54] However, this emergency measure came too late to stop unrest from breaking out. On January 4 and 5, in Arras, the fortress-capital of Artois, troops assembled in front of their barracks. Banging out a wild cacophony on their breastplates, pots, and pans, and yelling "baccara, baccara," they demanded their pay.[55] Similar seditious acts struck Namur, Le Quesnoy, and many other garrison towns. Though Boufflers commanded his colonels and captains to do their utmost to restrain their men, only the arrival of Mongelas' money brought back calm.[56]

The respite would be brief. On January 11, Chamillart told Boufflers that he had prevailed upon the *Extraordinaire des Guerres* to dispatch another 700,000 livres to the Army of Flanders. Yet the king himself cautioned the marshal that he could not expect much more:

> I was pained to see the disorders that the absence of wages had caused in many places. The first money which will arrive after the 20,000 louis will quell these movements. But the times have become so difficult that I cannot promise you that payments will be made with the desired regularity for the restoration of discipline, the subsistence of the troops, and to give to captains the money to reestablish their companies. I know only too well the sums that are due and which mount from day to day.[57]

The royal fears proved well founded. At first, news that more money was on the way pleased the troops. Their pleasure quickly soured into disappointment and worse after Treasurer-General Mongelas ended up sending just 580,000 livres, then very little thereafter.[58] Again and again, the soldiers' wages went unpaid so that, by the end of February, they were 506,800 livres and up to eighty days in arrears.[59] Mutinies flared across the Flanders frontier. In Namur, hundreds of soldiers assembled on the fortress' parade ground to demand their pay. In Aire, troops pillaged the town's market. In Arras, deserters distributed seditious pamphlets. In Tournai, infantrymen and cavalrymen plundered two bakeries. When guards arrested six of the looters, their comrades broke into the guardhouse and rescued them. Barricading themselves in their barracks, they fired musket and pistol shots from the windows at anyone who dared approach; it was a miracle that no one was killed or seriously hurt. The soldiers were only appeased after their officers promised they would be paid and pleaded with them for patience. Similar tumults and disorders erupted in Mons, Le Quesnoy, Valenciennes, Cambrai, Béthune, and Saint-Omer.[60]

And little further help would be forthcoming from the *Extraordinaire des Guerres*. It was almost completely spent. Mongelas himself was so deeply in debt that his creditors even tried to seize and sell his office of treasurer-general.[61] The incapacity of the military paymasters forced Louis and his ministers to improvise to provide the troops with at least a modicum of pay. On February 22, royal orders went out to the municipal authorities of Flanders, Artois, and Picardy—mayors, aldermen, and councilors—to furnish wages to the troops billeted in their cities and towns. They were to find the money from their own pockets on promise of future reimbursement from the war treasury.[62] As this promise would never be fulfilled, this makeshift amounted to a special tax on these wealthy, privileged subjects. Many more such measures would be taken in the months to come.

France's collapsing finances also prevented the troops from being adequately reequipped. During winter quarters, soldiers' worn-out uniforms, boots, and weapons were supposed to have been repaired or replaced. For this purpose, captains received a significant supplementary allowance, the *ustencile*. An infantry captain could expect 750 livres for himself and an additional 750 to be distributed to his subaltern officers; his counterparts in the cavalry and dragoons got much more. Boufflers pressed the king and Chamillart to pay the *ustencile*, arguing that it was second in importance only to the troops' wages; they agreed and vowed to do all they could.[63] Yet almost no funds were sent to the officers. What did reach them were not coins and other sound money but credit instruments they could trade only at steep discounts. By March, they had to accept just thirty to 40 percent of the face value of the War Bills that the

Extraordinaire des Guerres was passing on to them.[64] Other paper could be worth even less. The Chevalier de Quincy, captain in the régiment de Bourgogne-infanterie, was convinced this was the result of unrestrained greed by the military paymasters and their agents:

> The usurers, who always sought to profit from public misfortune, pushed their peculation to the utmost. Officers were only given bills for their pay, which we called subsistence bills, on which we lost 83 livres out of 100, leaving us only 17 francs. One day (this was some time before I departed for the army), I came across one of these gentlemen usurers. I asked him at how much of a loss were the subsistence bills. "I know nothing of it, Monsieur," he said to me. "And why do you not know?" I replied. "Monsieur," he answered, "it is Sunday today. I never work on holidays and Sundays." Such a tender conscience, the good apostle! He was one of the biggest scoundrels in Paris.[65]

With his officers unable to refurbish their units, Marshal Boufflers lamented that his troops were becoming ever more ragtag just as the English, Dutch, and Germans were being reinforced and rearmed.[66]

The Army of Flanders was not just short of wages and basic equipment. It was also in danger of lacking food. An army marches on its stomach; the Sun King's army filled its stomach with bread. A French common infantryman's daily ration consisted of one-and-a-half pounds of *pain de munition* or munition bread. Producing and distributing this essential foodstuff involved a complicated, labor- and capital-intensive process. Wheat had to be acquired and stockpiled in magazines. It had to be milled into flour, which was then formed into loaves that were baked in ovens.[67] Finally, the finished bread had to be brought and given out to the troops. Each of these stages required considerable skilled and unskilled labor as well as large trains of horse-drawn carts. The entire process was in the hands of specialist provisioners called *munitionnaires*. They were not soldiers, but civilian entrepreneurs who were organized into companies that supplied bread to a campaign army for a year. The contracts they entered with the royal government were both very demanding and highly lucrative. *Munitionnaires* were invariably ambitious businessmen with excellent connections at court and in high finance.[68]

Boufflers' plans to besiege Lille had called for amassing an enormous amount of wheat—216,000 sacks, each weighing 200 pounds—and the processing of much of it into munition bread before the fighting season began. On January 15, the marshal stressed to the court that the *munitionnaires* needed to begin their work at once, "for there is not a moment to lose to buy grain and to turn it into flour." Louis responded that he had ordered Chamillart and Desmaretz to work closely with the provisioners, and they had promised to have 100,000 sacks of wheat and flour in the

Flanders fortresses by the end of February.[69] The king turned out to be far too optimistic. Since the beginning of the war, the bread supply of the Army of Flanders had been handled by a company under François Mauricet de La Cour, an important financier and a close associate of Chamillart. The company had been caught up in the collapse of French finances. The fisc failed to pay its 6.9 million-livre contract and, by the end of 1708, La Cour claimed that it was owed 8 million livres. On January 21, Chamillart warned Boufflers that "the *munitionnaire*'s credit is entirely exhausted and his goodwill, I fear, will not suffice to fill the magazines as promptly as desired." Shortly after, the minister went even further. Mauricet's company was failing. Not only did it appear incapable of carrying out the preparations for the Lille operation. It was having great difficulty just feeding the troops in their winter quarters. A new company would likely have to be organized to take over the supplying of bread during the campaign. In the meantime, other *munitionnaires*, notably François Raffy and François-Marie Fargès, would do all they could to provide provisions to the men. The intendants had been ordered to assist their efforts by mobilizing money and resources locally in the frontier provinces.[70] Chamillart was admitting that the supply system of the Army of Flanders was falling apart. And famine was looming just over the horizon.

Since assuming command of the Army of Flanders, Marshal Boufflers had been resolved to retake Lille. Convinced it was the best hope to restore France's fading fortunes in Flanders, he had doggedly pursued preparations for this operation. But the tumultuous developments of the opening weeks of 1709 forced him to consider alternatives. On January 23, he came to the little fortress-town of La Bassée. Located fifteen miles southwest of Lille at the end of a great plain and flanked by vast marshes, it struck Boufflers as "the key and gate of the country." During the Allies' siege of Lille, the Duc de Bourgogne had occupied it to check enemy incursions and raids into French territory. The marshal revived and expanded on this idea by proposing to construct fortified lines running from the town westward to the upper reaches of the River Lys. Marshal Vauban had drawn up detailed plans for such a system of fieldworks following the Battle of Ramillies. If the siege of Lille could not be attempted or if it failed, the Army of Flanders should go on the defensive and make a stand in these La Bassée lines. They would then be "the sole means to cover Artois and Picardy and to preserve communications from the sea to the Sambre and Meuse."[71]

Boufflers had come to La Bassée as part of his inspection tour of Flanders. He had wanted to familiarize himself with the terrain and to survey the state of the fortresses of the *pré carré*. Above all, he had sought to calm his restive troops and buttress their morale. For weeks, he indefatigably crisscrossed the frontier, traveling in his carriage through the cold, darkness, wind, ice, snow, and rain. Late in January, he began to feel a pain in his chest. It became so severe that he had to halt at Ypres to rest and recuperate for a fortnight. He then tried to soldier on, yet his ailment would not go away. The king was solicitous, telling the marshal he had to take good care of himself so that he would be able to lead the Army of Flanders in the upcoming campaign.[72] More surprisingly, the Duke of Marlborough also showed great concern. He and Boufflers had once been comrades in arms, having served together as young officers under the great French hero Turenne during the Dutch War. He now offered to send a physician from Brussels who had successfully treated the marshal for a similar illness during the siege of Lille; the offer was gratefully accepted. Despite this doctor's best efforts, Boufflers' health continued to deteriorate. On February 27, he departed Arras for the court. Shortly after, he was compelled to give up his command.[73]

With the withdrawal of Boufflers, Louis once again faced the problem of who was to command the war's most crucial front. He had to send to Flanders a marshal of high reputation, proven ability, and a record of victories. There was almost no one available who fit the bill. The Duc de Vendôme was in disgrace, sulking in his château at Anet. Marshal Berwick was still tainted by his part in the disastrous 1708 campaign. He was also needed in Dauphiné, where an invasion by the forces of the Duke of Savoy was imminent. A third marshal, Henri d'Harcourt, was a competent, solid professional but no match for the genius of Marlborough and Eugene. He would go to the Army of Germany. In the end, Louis had only one possible choice: Claude-Louis-Hector, Duc et Maréchal de Villars. It was, nevertheless, not an easy choice to make. Many—not least Villars himself—believed he was the finest fighting general in the Sun King's army. Just as many thought him shamelessly vainglorious, insufferably arrogant, and insatiably ambitious.

Villars was then fifty-five years old. In the 1705 letters patent making him a duke and in his *Mémoires*, he claimed descent from an ancient line of warriors and prelates. In actuality, his pedigree was more recent and less illustrious. His family had been merchants and aldermen in Lyon and had been ennobled only in 1586. His father, Pierre, had been the first Villars to take up the profession of arms. His mother, Marie Gigaut de Bellefonds, was a woman of letters, a habituée of the salons of Paris as well as a correspondent of Madame de Sévigné and Madame de Scudery. It was through her literary network that Pierre de Villars met and gained the friendship of Françoise d'Aubigné, then the impoverished widow of the poet Paul Scarron. She would always remember his gallantry and generosity. As Madame de Maintenon, she would become his son's indispensable patron and protector.[74]

Louis-Hector de Villars' military career had a good beginning. At the age of eighteen, he was commissioned as a coronet in the elite Gendarmes and underwent his baptism of fire in the opening actions of the Dutch War. During the siege of Maastricht in June 1673, he offered one of the first demonstrations of the audacity that would become one of his trademarks when he led six of his troopers on an unauthorized raid on the enemy fortifications. Villars was then brought before the king:

> As soon as His Majesty saw him, he assumed a severe air, and said to him: "But do you not know that I have prohibited even volunteers to attack without my permission, let alone officers who must not leave their troops and still less cavalry troops?"
>
> "I believed," answered the marquis de Villars, "that Your Majesty will pardon me for wishing to learn the trade of the infantry, especially when the cavalry has nothing to do."
>
> This excuse could not but have its effect. It succeeded, and the reprimand ended on the king's part with very flattering praise for the marquis de Villars.[75]

Later in the siege, Louis remarked: "It seems that as soon as we shoot at some place, we find this little fellow springing up from the ground there." During the remainder of the war, Villars compiled an enviable combat record. Afterward, he expected to be promoted to brigadier, the first general officer rank. To his surprise and outrage, he was passed over again and again. In his *Mémoires*, he blamed the sudden stalling of his career on the enmity of the Marquis de Louvois, the powerful minister of war. Another, more plausible reason was that his impetuosity and aggressiveness, while sought-after qualities in a junior cavalry officer, were much less valued in an army commander. Both Louvois and the king deemed Villars not yet ready. He languished for almost a decade as a mere cavalry *maître de camp*.

He was rescued by Madame de Maintenon. In April 1687, thanks to her influence, he was chosen as an envoy to Maximilian Emmanuel, the able and ambitious elector of Bavaria, who was already regarded by the French king and his ministers as a potential ally. Finding they shared tastes in war, wine, and women, the two became fast friends. Villars followed Max Emmanuel on campaign against the Turks in Hungary. On August 12, 1687, he fought at the Battle of Mohacs. There he met and befriended Eugene of Savoy, a fast-rising star in the imperial army. Having successfully completed his diplomatic mission, he returned to France in the summer of 1688. A meteoric ascent followed. He was made a brigadier in the same year, a *maréchal de camp* in 1690, and, finally, a lieutenant general in 1693. In the Nine Years' War, he led troops on every front. His generalship was characterized by boldness, a preference for swift offensive action, and what eighteenth-century soldiers called *coup d'oeil*: the ability to recognize and exploit advantageous situations, no matter how fleeting.

At the beginning of the War of the Spanish Succession, Villars was convinced he would be taking the final step to the summit of the French military hierarchy: the marshalate. When he was not included among the marshals created by the king in 1702, he was so bitterly disappointed that he considered resigning from the royal service. Instead, he agreed to join the Army of Germany commanded by Marshal Catinat. He soon spotted an opportunity to seize the marshal's baton himself. Old and tired, Catinat conducted the campaign too timidly and allowed the Imperial army of Louis of Baden to capture the important fortress of Landau. Villars' loud denunciations of his superior's dilatoriness led to his recall. Invested with command of the army, Villars crossed the Rhine and entered southern Germany. Baden anticipated this move and marched to meet him. The two armies clashed at Friedlingen on October 18. The battle was long and ferociously hard fought. After initial success, the French infantry were put to flight by the enemy troops. The Imperial advance was then stopped by French cavalry charges personally led by Villars. Friedlingen's casualties favored the French: they suffered 2,000 dead against 3,000 for the Germans. Its outcome, however, was so inconclusive and ambiguous that *Te Deums* celebrating victory were sung in both France and the Empire.[76]

The undisputed victor of Friedlingen was Villars himself. He shamelessly and relentlessly promoted the battle, especially his own role in it. In his *Mémoires*, he described how his cavalrymen, after driving off the Imperial infantry, acclaimed him by chanting "marshal, marshal!" The story was then taken up and popularized by Voltaire, a friend and frequent guest of Villars and his wife. It was a complete fabrication. Louis XIV would never have tolerated such a large-scale show of indiscipline by his troops, nor would he ever have allowed them to interfere so blatantly in his relationships with his commanders. But another act of self-promotion by Villars had a much more immediate, important, and, for him, gratifying effect. On October 17, he wrote a dispatch to the king exaggerating Friedlingen's results: he claimed to have captured numerous flags and cannons and a great quantity of booty. These details at last convinced Louis—no doubt with his consort's encouragement—that the battle was indeed a great victory. On October 20, he sent his reply. The letter was addressed to the Marquis de Villars. Inside was another to the maréchal de Villars.[77]

At last acknowledged as one of Louis XIV's leading generals, Villars was entrusted with the key campaign for 1703: a linkup of the French Army of

Germany with the Bavarians of Max Emmanuel. After besieging and taking the Rhenish stronghold of Kehl, Villars marched deep into Germany and effected the junction in May. But no sooner was he reunited with his old friend and comrade that they fell into a heated quarrel about what to do next with their formidable forces. Villars' approach to war was always marked by optimism and confidence. He therefore proposed launching a wide-ranging offensive against the Habsburg Hereditary Lands, possibly including a march on Vienna itself. More prudent because he had much more to lose, Max Emmanuel wanted to focus on defending Bavaria. The differences between these two headstrong, excessively proud men soon caused their relationship to break down completely. Both appealed to Louis for support. The king chose to side with his most important ally. Deciding that he could not share command, Villars asked for and received permission to leave his post.

The Bavarian imbroglio did not keep Villars out of action for long. Louis needed his talents too badly. In southern France, in the rugged and remote hill country of the Cevennes, Huguenot peasants, fired by the millenarian visions of self-proclaimed prophets, had revolted against the king and the Catholic Church. The so-called Camisards waged a tenacious guerilla war against royal forces. In March 1704, the king ordered Villars to end the rebellion. He revealed impressive—and unexpected—flexibility and imagination by implementing a counterinsurgency strategy based on conciliation and compromise. He carefully controlled the conduct of the royal troops while offering amnesty to rebels who agreed to surrender. This approach quickly produced results. Within a month of Villars' arrival, Jean Cavalier, the most important Camisard chieftain, came to terms. Many others followed suit. Although a handful of guerilla bands would continue low-level resistance for years, by December, the Cevennes had been largely pacified.[78]

After his triumph with the Camisards, Villars was appointed to a command on France's eastern frontier. As he described to Maintenon, he was thrilled by his return to the front:

> As for me, Madame, I expect much of the army which the king is pleased to give me the honor of commanding. The cavalry will arrive and will be good. The consideration I have for our troops means I will not risk them lightly, but if the enemy make some false move, I hope that God will grant me the grace to defeat them.[79]

In the spring of 1705, he faced Marlborough for the first time. Though badly outnumbered, he used a skillful combination of maneuver and defensive lines to block the captain general's attempts to invade France through the Moselle Valley. Subsequently, with all his usual optimism and confidence, Villars proposed ambitious offensives into Germany.

But the court treated the eastern frontier as a subordinate theater to Flanders and Italy. Villars never received the reinforcements and resources he needed; indeed, he was often called upon to detach troops to bolster other armies. In 1707, he at last received authorization to attack across the Rhine. Yet, as Louis and Chamillart made clear, the goal of this operation was more financial than strategic: by having his army live off enemy territory, Villars would spare the treasury the burden of having to pay for it. On May 23, he broke through the Lines of Stollhofen, the Empire's most formidable defensive barrier. For two months, his army extorted from much of southwestern Germany what were euphemistically called contributions—protection money paid by communities to escape destruction at French hands. "Sire, I have divided the booty into three parts," Villars announced. "The first is for Your Majesty; the second is for the wages of my troops; and the third is for fattening my Vaux." The last referred to the domain he had bought when he became a duke. Its splendid chateau had been built by Nicolas Fouquet, a disgraced controller general of finances, and had served as a model for Versailles. It had also been the setting for the most infamous party in French history, one so opulent it had enraged Louis and helped lead to Fouquet's downfall.[80]

As the War of the Spanish Succession approached its climax, Villars was alone among France's generals in never having suffered defeat. Yet he had also never fought in Flanders. The reason was the conflict with Max Emmanuel. After being driven out of Bavaria, the elector had been named governor-general of the Spanish Netherlands. Out of consideration for his ally's feelings and the honor of a fellow prince, Louis had declined to send Villars there. After the Battle of Oudernarde, he fiercely lobbied Maintenon for the command. "I am," he boasted, "the sole general in Europe for whom the good fortune of war has never changed."[81] The withdrawal of Marshal Boufflers finally gave him his opportunity. On March 4, 1709, the king appointed this outrageously vain, tiresomely arrogant, irrepressibly optimistic, prodigiously gifted soldier as the new commander of the Army of Flanders.

NOTES

1. SHD AG A¹ 2149/6, Boufflers to Louis XIV, 1 January 1709.
2. Dangeau, *Journal*, book 12, 301.
3. SHD AG A¹ 2149/42, Boufflers to Louis XIV, 4 January 1709.
4. SHD AG A¹ 2149/51, Boufflers to Louis XIV, 6 January 1709 and SHD A¹ 2149/64, 7 January 1709.
5. Despite his prominence and importance, Boufflers has inexplicably lacked a modern biography. This gap has now been superbly filled by Steven A.

Beckman, "Sword of the Sun: Marshal Boufflers and the Experience of War in the Grand Siècle" (PhD diss., The Ohio State University, 2022).

6. A valuable study of the dynamics and importance of *petite guerre* is George Satterfield, *Princes, Posts, and Partisans: The Army of Louis XIV and Partisan Warfare in the Netherlands, 1673–1678* (Leiden: Brill, 2003).

7. Pádraig Lenihan, "Namur Citadel, 1695: A Case Study in Allied Siege Tactics," *War in History* 18/3 (2011), 299–399.

8. Bryant, *Queen of Versailles*, 116–117.

9. Oury, *La Guerre de Succession d'Espagne*, 92–94 and 103–104.

10. On the captaincies of the *Gardes du Corps*, see Guy Rowlands, "Louis XIV, Aristocratic Power, and the Elite Units of the French Army," *French History* 13/3 (1999), 308–309.

11. 353, Maintenon to des Ursins, 14 January 1709, *Lettres de Madame de Maintenon*, vol. 4, *1707–1710*, ed. Marcel Loyau (Paris: Honoré Champion, 2011), 484.

12. SHD AG A^1 2149/79, Boufflers to Louis XIV, 9 January 1709.

13. On the importance of winter quarters, see Francois Royal, "Les quartiers d'hiver des armées: pause et continuité dans la guerre. L'exemple de l'armée de Flandre entre les campagnes de 1711 et 1712," in *Combattre et gouverner. Dynamiques de l'histoire militaire de l'epoque moderne (XVIIe-XVIIIe siècles)*, eds. Bertrand Fonck and Nathalie Genet-Rouffiac (Rennes: Presses Universitaires de Rennes, 2015), 75–89, and "À l'aube de la campagne: l'impact du quartier d'hiver dans la campagne de Flandre de 1712," in *Les dernières guerres de Louis XIV, 1688–1715*, eds. Hervé Drévillon, Bertrand Fonck, and Jean-Philippe Cénat (Rennes: Presses Universitaires de Rennes, 2017), 205–226.

14. On Vauban and his fortresses, see Duffy, *The Fortress in the Age of Vauban and Frederick the Great*, 70–84, and John A. Lynn, "The *trace italienne* and the Growth of Armies: The French Case," *Journal of Military History* 55/3 (1991), 5–8.

15. Vauban, "Mémoire des places frontières de Flandres qu'il faudrait fortifier pour la sureté des pays de l'obéissance du Roy," in *Vauban. Sa famille et ses écrits, ses "Oisivetés" et sa Correspondance*, ed. Eugène Auguste Albert de Rochas d'Aiglun, book 1 (Paris: Berger-Levrault, 1910), 189–192.

16. SHD AG A^{1}2149/6, Boufflers to Louis XIV, 1 January 1709.

17. SHD AG A^{1}2149/51, Boufflers to Louis XIV, 6 January 1709.

18. SHD AG A^{1}2149/94, Boufflers to Louis XIV, 12 January 1709. Attached to the letter were three memoranda (items 95, 96, and 97) detailing the plan's logistical requirements.

19. SHD AG A^1 2149/95, "Artillerie et munitions de guerre pour l'Exécution d'un projet."

20. SHD AG A^{1}2149/97.

21. SHD AG A^1 2149/96, "Estat des bleds qu'il convient avoir en Flandres pour la campagne 1709." The fortresses and the number of sacks to be sent to each were: Tournai (20,000), Condé (10,000), Valenciennes (15,000), Douay (25,000), Arras (25,000), Cambrai (8,000), Mons (10,000), Maubeuge (10,000), Charleroi (10,000), Namur (10,000), Givet (10,000), Dunkirk (10,0000), Ypres (10,000), Nieuport (6,000), Furnes (4,000), Bergues (4,000), Gravelines (2,000), Calais (3,000), St. Omer (10,000), Aire (6,000) and Bethune (8,000). The weight of wheat sacks and the number of rations provided by each sack is taken from François Nodot's handbook

for military provisioners, *Le Munitionnaire des armées de France* (Paris: Imprimerie Royale, 1697), 4.
22. SHD AG A^1 2149/97.
23. Lynn, *Wars of Louis XIV*, 216–217.
24. Vauban, "Mémoire des places frontières," 189.
25. SHD AG A^1 2149/94, Boufflers to Louis XIV, 12 January 1709.
26. SHD AG A^1 2149/121, Louis XIV to Boufflers and Chamillart to Boufflers, 16 January 1709.
27. Joseph Sevin de Quincy, *Mémoires du Chevalier de Quincy*, vol. 2 (Paris: Leon Lecestre, 1899), 320–321.
28. Emmanuel Garnier, *Les Dérangements du Temps. 500 ans de chaud et de froid en Europe* (Paris: Plon, 2010), 141–143; Stephanie Pain, "The year that Europe Froze Solid," *New Scientist* (February 2009), 46–47.
29. Jean Taté, *Chronique de Jean Taté, greffier de l'hôtel-de-ville de Château-Porcien (1677–1748)*, ed. Henri Jadart (Arcis-sur-Aube: L. Frémont, 1890), 89.
30. Caroline Le Mao, *Chronique du Bordelais au crepuscule du Grand Siècle: Le Mémorial de Savignac* (Bordeaux: Presses Universitaires de Bordeaux, 2004), 58.
31. Lachiver, *Les années de misère*, 287–290
32. Dangeau, *Journal*, book 12, 302–306.
33. Elborg Forster, ed., *A Woman's Life in the Court of the Sun King: the Letters of Liselotte Von Der Pfalz, 1652–1722* (Baltimore: The Johns Hopkins University Press, 1984), 170.
34. Lachiver, *Les années de misère*, 290–296. The estimate of deaths is found on pages 351–352.
35. W. Gregory Monahan, *Year of Sorrows: The Great Famine of 1709 in Lyon* (Columbus: The Ohio State University Press, 1993), 75.
36. AN G^7 15, Desmaretz to the intendants, April 1709, fol. 237.
37. Saint-Simon, *Mémoires*, book 7, 132.
38. Dangeau, *Journal*, book 9, 296.
39. A. M. de Boislisle, ed., *Correspondence des Contrôleurs Généraux des Finances avec les intendants des provinces*, vol. 3, *1708 à 1715* (Paris: Imprimerie Nationale, 1897), "Compte Rendu de M. Desmaretz au Régent," 673–674.
40. Rowlands, *Financial Decline*, 62–63.
41. Gary B. McCollim, *Louis XIV's Assault on Privilege: Nicolas Desmaretz and the Tax on Wealth* (Rochester: University of Rochester Press, 2012), 22.
42. Guy Rowlands, "Royal Finances in the Third Reign of Louis XIV," in *The Third Reign of Louis XIV, c. 1682–1715*, eds. Julia Prest and Guy Rowlands (London: Routledge, 2017), 46.
43. William Doyle, *Venality: The Sale of Offices in Eighteenth-Century France* (Oxford: Oxford University Press, 1996), chs. 1 and 2.
44. Rowlands, *Financial Decline*, 98.
45. P. G. M. Dixon and John Sperling, "War Finance, 1689–1714," in *The New Cambridge Modern History*, vol. 6, *The Rise of Great Britain and Russia*, ed. J. S. Bromley (Cambridge: Cambridge University Press, 1970), 285–298.
46. Guy Rowlands, *Dangerous and Dishonest Men: The International Bankers of Louis XIV's France* (London: Palgrave, 2015), 41–44; Herbert Lüthy, *La Banque*

Protestante en France de la Révocation de l'Édit de Nantes à la Révolution, vol. 1 (Paris: SEVPEN), 120–125.

47. Saint-Simon, *Mémoires*, book 16, 34–36.
48. Jacques Saint-Germain, *Samuel Bernard, le banquier des rois* (Paris: Hachette, 1960), 162.
49. Boislisle, *Correspondence*, vol. 3, "Compte Rendu de M. Desmaretz au Régent," 673–674.
50. Rowlands, *Financial Decline*, 182.
51. Monahan, *Year of Sorrows*, 41–55; Rowlands, *Dangerous and Dishonest Men*, 144–165.
52. SHD AG GR A^1 2149/42A, Boufflers to Louis XIV, 4 January 1709.
53. Lynn, *Giant of the Grand Siècle*, 148–149.
54. SHD AG GR A^1 2149/24, Louis XIV to Boufflers, 2 January 1709.
55. SHD AG GR A^1 2149/48, Saint-Fremond to Chamillart, 5 January 1709.
56. SHD AG GR A^1 2149/51, Boufflers to Louis XIV, 6 January 1709.
57. SHD AG GR A^1 2149/91, Louis XIV to Boufflers, 11 January 1709.
58. SHD AG GR A^1 2149/121, Chamillart to Boufflers, 16 January 1709.
59. SHD AG GR A^1 2149/248, Mémoire sur les fonds et provisions pour la guerre dans les provinces d'Artois et de Picardie à la fin de fevrier 1709.
60. SHD GR A^1 2149/231, Comte de Salians to Boufflers, 16 February 1709; SHD GR A^1 2149/246, Boufflers to Louis XIV, 21 February 1709; SHD GR A^1 2149/253, Bernage to Chamillart, 17 February 1709.
61. Rowlands, *Financial Decline*, 161, 203.
62. SHD AG GR A^1 2149/266, Louis XIV to Boufflers, 25 February 1709.
63. SHD AG GR A^1 2149/119, Boufflers to Chamillart, 15 January 1709.
64. AN G^7 263/389, Bernières to Desmaretz, 5 March 1709.
65. Quincy, *Mémoires*, vol. 2, 321–322.
66. SHD AG GR A^1 2149/246, Boufflers to Louis XIV, 21 February 1709.
67. Geza Perjes, "Army Provisioning, Logistics, and Strategy in the Second Half of the Seventeenth Century," *Acta Academiae Scientiarum Hungarica* 16 (1970), 6–11.
68. Lynn, *Giant of the Grand Siècle*, 114–118.
69. SHD AG GR A^1 2149/119, Boufflers to Chamillart, 15 January 1709; SHD AG GR A^1 2149/121, Louis XIV and Chamillart to Boufflers, 16 January 1709.
70. Rowlands, *Financial Decline*, 221–225.
71. SHD AG GR A^1 2149/182, Boufflers to Louis XIV, 24 January 1709.
72. SHD AG GR A^1 2149/191, Louis XIV to Boufflers, 10 February 1709, 201.
73. Beckman, "Sword of the Sun," 282–283; 309, Maintenon to des Ursins, 4 March 1709, *Lettres de Madame de Maintenon*, vol. 4, 513–514.
74. The most recent biographies of Villars are Fadi El Hage, *Le maréchal de Villars. L'infatigable bonheur* (Paris: Belin, 2012) and François Ziegler, *Villars. Le centurion de Louis XIV* (Paris: Perrin, 1996). They largely supersede Claude C. Sturgill, *Marshal Villars and the War of the Spanish Succession* (Lexington: University of Kentucky Press, 1965). On Maintenon's support of Villars, see Bryant, *Queen of Versailles*, 249–250.
75. Claude Louis-Hector de Villars, *Mémoires du maréchal de Villars publiés d'après le manuscript original, pour la Société de l'histoire de France, et accompagnés de correspondances inédites*, ed. Melchior de Vogüé, vol. 1 (Paris: Renouard, 1884), 12.

76. Oury, *La Guerre de Succession d'Espagne*, 94–95.
77. El Hage, *Le maréchal de Villars*, 48–49.
78. W. Gregory Monahan, *Let God Arise: The War and Rebellion of the Camisards* (Oxford: Oxford University Press, 2014), 192–226.
79. Melchior de Vogüé, *Madame de Maintenon et le Maréchal de Villars. Correspondence inédite* (Paris: Jules Gervais, 1881), 21.
80. El Hage, *Le maréchal de Villars*, 73–80.
81. Vogüé, *Madame de Maintenon et le Maréchal de Villars*, 29–31. The quote is found in 30.

3

The Army
March–May, 1709

The day after Marshal Villars took charge of the Army of Flanders, Pierre Rouillé de Marbeuf, President of the Grand Conseil, a seasoned jurist, bureaucrat, and diplomat, left Versailles for Antwerp on a secret mission to make peace with the Allies.

Military defeat, financial exhaustion, and the Great Winter had driven the French king and his ministers to try to end the war through diplomacy. They continued to believe that their best chance of success was to draw the Dutch into a separate peace that would lead to the breakup of the Grand Alliance. They could offer the Republic of the United Netherlands valuable concessions, including favorable commercial relations with France and a restored or even enlarged fortress Barrier. They had also been maintaining several channels of communication with the Dutch. One ran through the intendant of Flanders, Charles-Étienne Maignart de Bernières, who kept in regular contact with Allied officials in charge of administering the conquered Spanish Netherlands. Another was the Comte de Bergeyck, Spain's chief minister in the Netherlands, who had cultivated numerous contacts in the Republic. A third channel was Hermann Petkum. Officially the emissary to The Hague of a German princeling, the Duke of Holstein-Gottorp, he was also a kind of mercenary diplomat who sold his services to other governments. He had long maintained a clandestine correspondence with Foreign Minister Torcy under the code name of the Sieur de Rivière.[1] But none of these channels had led to talks with important Dutch decisionmakers. Moreover, after the battle of Oudenarde and the fall of Lille, France's bargaining position appeared hopelessly weak. This dismal situation had dispirited the royal council.

Philippe, Duc d'Orléans and Louis' nephew, observed to the princesse des Ursins that while Louis remained firm in his resolve, Madame de Maintenon and the ministers were despondent and did not know where to turn.[2]

Then a diplomatic opening came from Spain. Throughout the war, the Allies were convinced that Philip V was merely a puppet of his grandfather, and that Spain was ruled from Versailles. The reality was much more nuanced. On the one hand, Philip surrounded himself with French advisors, including the Marquis de Bay, his best general, Jean Orry, his financial expert, Michel-Jean Amelot, Louis XIV's ambassador to the court of Madrid and Spain's de facto prime minister, and, above all, the princesse des Ursins, formally *camerara mayor* to the queen of Spain and informally the most influential voice in the Spanish government. French money, regiments, and men-of-war were indispensable for the defense of the sprawling dominions of the Catholic Monarchy, not least Spain itself. On the other hand, Philip's Castilian subjects had enthusiastically rallied to him, which had hastened his transformation from a French prince to a Spanish king.[3] He came to regard himself as a sovereign in his own right with his own aspirations, interests, and policies. In January 1709, he personally penned a letter to Bergeyck stating he was willing to concede expansive trading rights in Spain's empire to the Dutch Republic in exchange for peace. Bergeyck then made contact with Anthonie Heinsius, grand pensionary of Holland, and Bruno van der Dussen, burgomaster of Gouda and a leading Dutch diplomat. They declared they would consider peace negotiations only if Spain, the Indies, and Milan were ceded to the Habsburgs.[4]

At the beginning of February, Bergeyck came to Versailles to brief Louis and his ministers about this démarche.[5] The king immediately recognized the opportunity it presented to launch peace talks with the Allies in earnest. He decided to take it over. The Marquis de Torcy, minister for foreign affairs, dashed off a letter to van der Dussen declaring that his master was willing to negotiate a peace treaty based on the terms described to Bergeyck. Moreover, he was sending an envoy to open direct discussions.[6] The Dutch diplomat accepted this proposal. He also insisted on cutting off all further contact with Bergeyck, declaring that the Republic would only deal with the king of France.[7] Louis agreed to this condition; indeed, he did so with more than a little relief. For he had been forced to make a decisive change in his war aims. At the beginning of the war, he had fought to secure the entire Spanish Monarchy for his grandson. Now, to spare France further disasters, he was willing to abandon most of Philip's inheritance, including even the crown of Spain itself.

For the French envoy, the Marquis de Torcy initially chose Daniel Voysin, a well-regarded provincial intendant, councilor of state, and protégé of Madame de Maintenon. However, judging the mission's chances of success to be slim, he declined it. His replacement was Pierre Rouillé. He departed on March 5. Torcy imparted to him a sense of urgency: peace had to be made before the start of the campaigning season, now little more than two months away.[8]

"Marshal Villars left full of courage and confidence," Madame de Maintenon confided to the princesse des Ursins, "even though he knows the weight of the burden with which he is charged. Yet it seems to me that he finds himself more honored than burdened."[9] In fact, Villars' optimism and gifts were immediately put to the test. When he set out from Versailles for the Flanders front on March 16, he met a cold, unrelenting rain. His progress was slow and uncomfortable as his carriage struggled along roads transformed into a sodden morass.[10] His first order of business was to pay a call on Max Emmanuel. After the French defeat at Oudenarde, the exiled Bavarian prince had been confined to the walled town of Mons. There, he filled his days trysting with his mistresses, gambling at the card tables, and turning out exquisite pieces of jewelry on a little lathe. Having steeled himself for a frosty reception, Villars was surprised and gratified when Max Emmanuel greeted him with tears in his eyes and effusive expressions of regret for their past disagreements. His sojourn in Mons passed pleasantly in conversations with the elector in his workshop and intimate suppers with him and his favorite mistress.[11]

Flanders' other challenges proved more intractable. The king and War Minister Chamillart were still urging a pre-emptive strike on Lille.[12] Given his predilection for daring offensive action, Villars was in favor of it as well. But he soon realized that the paucity of supplies made it impossible. To besiege Lille, the Army of Flanders needed full magazines at Ypres, Douai, and Tournai. All remained largely empty. Furthermore, there was no dry fodder at all for the horses: the Army's contractor, François-Marie Fargès, had not been paid and was owed almost 5 million livres by the fisc. Villars had to lower his sights to an easier target. Located sixteen miles northeast of Lille was the town of Courtrai. Less strongly fortified and defended, it could be successfully stormed by a smaller force requiring more modest amounts of food, feed, and munitions. With Courtrai in their hands, the French would be able to cut the supply lines to the capital of Flanders, thereby forestalling an Allied advance deeper into France. Villars believed he could launch this operation as soon as the spring rains relented, and the ground became firm enough to bear the weight of heavy siege guns. In the meantime, he would send detachments to occupy the châteaux of Lannoy and Templeuve located between Lille and Tournai. From these posts, they could harass Allied convoys and work parties moving on the Lille-Menin highway.[13]

A few days later, the dangerously precarious state of the Army of Flanders' logistics was driven home to Villars by the *munitionnaire* François Raffy. After the failure of François Mauricet de La Cour's long-serving bread company, Raffy had stepped in to help with the provisioning of the Flanders forces. Now, he admitted to the marshal that most garrisons had just two weeks of supplies left. Many fortresses were down to four days. Almost no preparations had been made for the next campaign. Villars exploded:

> This terrible situation drove him to threaten to throw Raffy in a dungeon.
> "If you imprison me," he replied, "it will only be because my manner displeases you. I have done nothing wrong."
> "But your contract for bread is for the entire campaign," said Marshal Villars.
> "No, my lord," Raffy answered. "There is no contract and there will not be one."
> The marshal was astonished that not only was there no flour in the fortresses but there was no hope of having any for the field army and that on the first of April he should be in such distress.[14]

Not only were food and fodder lacking. Funds remained desperately scarce. Despite endless protestations that more money was on the way, the controller general and the treasurers of the *Extraordinaire des Guerres* had sent almost nothing to the northern frontier. In Artois, the province where much of the Army of Flanders was quartered, the troops should have received 1,188,300 livres from the military paymasters during the first three months of the year; instead, they got just 331,900 livres.[15] To make up for the shortfall, the royal government resorted to a whole series of makeshifts. Towns and villages paid the troops billeted on them. The provincial intendants channeled to the army their own money and loans they raised on their own credit. These stopgap measures were not nearly enough. Bereft of new uniforms, shoes, and equipment, the rank and file became ever more ragged and threadbare. The condition of the officers was worse still. The Flanders intendant Charles-Étienne Maignart de Bernières described captains and lieutenants lacking shoes and having to pawn their clothing for money to buy bread.[16] Villars painted a similarly pathetic picture to Chamillart:

> But, monsieur, I am obliged to represent to you what you already know too well: the extreme misery of the subaltern and reformed officers. They are paid only with great difficulty. Since many of these poor wretches have had nothing for a very long time, they have sold even their last shirt to live. However, it is necessary to put them in a condition to join the campaign. It would be deplorable to be forced to do without them. I speak to the officers and soldiers, listen to their complaints, appeal to their honor, and do not forget anything to encourage their patience.[17]

The great danger of unpaid and neglected troops was mutiny. On April 10, Louis de Bernage, intendant of Artois, warned Desmaretz that this was a very real possibility:

> It has been fifteen days since the troops have received any money in my department. I have exhausted my industry and my credit. I have redoubled my efforts with M. Chamillart and written several times to M. Poulletier and M. de Mongelas. I am on the verge of the most terrible disorders if this situation lasts a few more days.[18]

Two days after Bernage wrote, troops of the Swiss Greder regiment rampaged through Maubeuge. They pillaged numerous houses, stealing food and livestock. When an officer tried to put a halt to the plundering, he was bayonetted by a mutinous soldier. The Swiss were only brought back to order after strenuous efforts by their officers and the rest of the garrison.[19]

Villars was forced to further trim his plans. The breakdown of the Army of Flanders' logistics ruled out a surprise attack on Courtrai. At the same time, the marshal was receiving a steady stream of intelligence suggesting that the Allies were assembling formidable forces at Lille for an invasion of France. Prince Eugene was preparing to lead an Imperial corps from the Rhine to join the Duke of Marlborough's Anglo-Dutch Confederate Army. Flanders' rivers and canals were filling up with barges loaded with grain and fodder destined for Allied magazines. Troops from the minor German princely states, which made up substantial parts of both enemy field armies, were already marching to their mustering areas. Reluctantly, Villars concluded he had no choice except to shift from the offensive to the defensive. He now planned to deploy his army into fortified lines at La Bassée. If circumstances permitted, and more importantly, enough supplies could be assembled, he would sally out and seek battle with the enemy.[20] "We will have an army, madame," Villars declared to Maintenon with all his customary braggadocio. "And I flatter myself that we will find in our men an ardor which until now has not abandoned them in those actions where I have found myself." Yet, he could not help inserting a note of warning: "we must feed these troops and I cannot and must not conceal from you that there are still no magazines prepared for either the fortresses or the army."[21]

In the spring of 1709, another Frenchman was making his way to Flanders. Jean-Antoine Watteau had been painting in Paris for seven years. Perhaps to lick his wounds after failing to win the Prix de Rome or to help care for an aged relative or out of simple homesickness, he left the capital for his hometown, the gray, brooding fortress-city of Valenciennes. Watteau is celebrated as the master of the *fête galante*—luminous, charming depictions of amorous aristocrats at play in dream-like woods and parklands. But in the early years of his career, he was an artist of war. Between 1709 and 1715, he produced some fifteen military paintings as well as numerous drawings. Unlike the other great war artists of the time, such as Adam Frans van der Meulen or Jean-Baptiste Martin—nicknamed "Martin des Batailles"—he eschewed as his subjects great actions such as sieges and battles. Instead, he depicted what could be called the everyday life of war: sentries standing guard at one of the gates of Valenciennes, soldiers and camp followers at a halt during a march, a supply train at camp, or a company leaving its garrison at the end of winter quarters.[22]

One of these paintings was of recruits going to join their regiment. A mounted officer, his back to the viewer, leads eight newly enlisted men. They wear their freshly issued uniforms: black tricorn hats, cravats, knee-length white justaucorps coats over white waistcoats, shirts, breeches, stockings, and shoes. Their bearings and movements, though, are distinctly unsoldierly. They carry their flintlock muskets carelessly, cradled under their arms or slung over their shoulders, muzzles pointed at the ground. Some are bowed by the weight of their overstuffed haversacks. Others use their smallswords as improvised walking sticks. All have a bored, weary air. Only the officer's two little dogs are lively and alert as they follow their master's horse.[23]

Figure 3.1 Recruë allant joindre le Regiment (Engraving by Henri-Simon Thomassin after a painting by Jean-Antoine Watteau). *Source*: Art Institute of Chicago: The Amanda S. Johnson and Marion J. Livingston Endowment Fund.

Who were the recruits portrayed by Watteau? Long before he painted this picture, a belief had taken hold among the great and the learned in France that the men who joined its army were from society's margins: the propertyless poor, vagrants, ne'er-do-wells, and petty criminals. In reality, the Sun King's soldiers were rarely the Duke of Wellington's scum of the earth. They were mostly mature men in their twenties and early thirties from solidly respectable, if humble, backgrounds: traders, artisans, smallholding peasants, and vignerons. Most had joined the army out of a lack of economic opportunity; soldiering provided an honorable, though meager living. Surprisingly, in a country that was overwhelmingly rural, four out of ten were from cities and towns. They came from all parts and corners of the kingdom. Yet a disproportionate share originated from the long ribbon of frontier provinces running from Flanders on the Channel coast to Alsace on the Rhine, then south to Franche-Comté, Dauphiné, and Provence, then leaping over the Midi to Roussillon and Foix in the Pyrenees. These regions also happened to be where the army had the strongest, most visible presence. Recruitment itself took several forms. Some peasant lads were enlisted by noble officers from their estates. Many more recruits were enticed into the army by recruiting parties plying their trade in cities, towns, and villages all over France. Finally, as the War of the Spanish Succession wore on, an ever larger percentage of the rank and file consisted of conscripts levied through the royal militia.[24]

Watteau's recruits were on their way to one of the 239 French infantry regiments.[25] Each was commanded by a colonel and consisted of a number of companies under a captain and with a nominal strength of forty-five men. Louis' love of order had led him to organize his foot regiments into a hierarchy. At the top was the blue-coated Gardes francaises. Along with the red-coated Gardes suisses, it formed the infantry component of the Maison du Roi and was charged with the external security of the royal palaces. It was also the regiment of the city of Paris. After the guards came the six *vieux corps*—Picardie, Piémont, Champagne, Navarre, Normandie, and la Marine—then the six *petits vieux corps*—Feuquières, Bourbonnais, Auvergne, Sault, Baubecourt, and du Roi. The last was Louis' personal regiment, which he intended to serve as a model for the rest of the army as well as a school for promising future officers. After these twelve old regiments, the remainder were ranked according to the date of their creation. At the bottom were the many new formations mobilized for the war and fated for disbandment at its conclusion. The infantry made up by far the largest part of Louis XIV's army: 318,000 out of a total strength of 373,000 officers and common soldiers in 1707.[26]

When the recruits reached their regiment, their transformation into soldiers began. The key to this process was drill. Invented in its modern form by the great sixteenth-century Dutch military reformer Maurice of

Nassau, drill broke down the soldier's essential actions into their most basic components, which were then practiced again and again until they became second nature. It first taught a soldier how to use his weapon. By the War of the Spanish Succession, all French infantrymen were armed with the flintlock musket with bayonet. The military ordinance of March 2, 1703, which codified the fighting methods of the French infantry during the war, prescribed fifty-six separate steps for loading and firing the musket.[27] Drill also regulated a soldier's marching and movements. Above all, it instructed him how to handle his weapon and maneuver synchronously with all the other members of his unit. They were, in a crucial and very real sense, trained to fight as one.[28] A further effect of drill was to inculcate subordination and discipline. Drill drastically circumscribed individualism while expanding the scope of command. It required common soldiers to perform the smallest actions according to the orders of their superiors. In this way, obedience became ingrained, even conditioned. Ideally, it became so complete that soldiers would automatically, correctly, and precisely follow orders even under conditions of extreme peril to life and limb. Drill's final crucial result, one that French officers and soldiers themselves probably grasped only dimly if at all, was that moving together synchronously and in rhythm provoked atavistic feelings of camaraderie and solidarity among the members of a unit. What has been called muscular bonding helped weld these men drawn from across France and a wide variety of social backgrounds into a new community. It was therefore an important source of unit cohesion—or what was already being called at the time esprit de corps.[29]

No one was a keener proponent of drill than Louis XIV. In 1670, he advised the Dauphin that it was the foundation of fighting prowess:

> It is a maxim that the most experienced captains of this time hold for certain that many more battles are won by marching and by good order than by sword and musket blows. This good order makes one appear confident and it seems that it is enough to appear brave since most of the time our enemies do not wait for us closely enough to show if we are indeed brave.
>
> This habit of marching well and keeping in order can only be acquired by drill. The most valiant men in the world would fight very badly without training while the most mediocre courage finally hardens with constant exercise.[30]

Throughout his life, he took a special interest in the drilling of his household troops and the régiment du Roi. Until he grew too old, he often conducted their exercises in person. For the regular infantry units of the army, he and his war ministers required drill thrice a week. This requirement was understood to be the bare minimum. Troops garrisoning fortresses and lodging in winter quarters trained more frequently. Those on campaign exercised in quieter moments, such as while in encampments. Rigorous and uniform standards of training were enforced by the corps of inspectors. These high-ranking officers toured the field armies and garrisons, observing and assessing the performance of the troops. The name of the first inspector general of infantry, Martinet, has become a byword for strict discipline and punctilious attention to detail.[31]

Once the recruits had been sufficiently drilled, they were ready to go into action with their regiment. On campaign, each infantry regiment fielded one or more battalions, the basic tactical units of the French and all other Western European armies. The Gardes françaises deployed six battalions, a handful of prestigious regiments five, four, or three, and the majority two or only one. A battalion consisted of thirteen companies: twelve of line infantry and one of grenadiers—elite soldiers chosen for their impressive height and proven bravery.[32]

French infantry tactics were dictated by the properties of the flintlock musket. It was a weapon requiring an elaborate procedure to load and fire. Well-drilled, experienced troops could get off two or, at most, three shots a minute. Moreover, its range and accuracy were both limited. Maximum effective range—the distance that a shot had any possibility of hitting a target—was about 220 yards. Accurate fire was restricted to 100 yards or less.[33]

Given the musket's mediocre performance, the French sought to maximize firepower by bringing as many of their weapons to bear on an enemy as possible. The combat formation of the battalion was the line. The grenadier company was placed on the right, the traditional position of honor. A company of picked men drawn from the rest of the battalion was on the left. Between these two bodies of crack troops were ranged the twelve line companies. The March 1703 ordinance stipulated that the line was to have a depth of five ranks. The first three ranks were able to shoot: the first rank kneeling, the second crouching, and the third standing. A full-strength battalion could unleash 351 muskets in a single salvo.[34]

Such a blast of musketry, if well timed and judged, could cause fearful losses and shake an enemy's morale. But it also left a battalion effectively disarmed—the men of the fourth and fifth ranks were more or less spectators—until the firers had reloaded, a perilous situation on the battlefield. To avoid it, the French chose instead to have each rank shoot in turn. This meant they would usually have some of their fire in reserve. The battalion halted, and the first four ranks knelt. The fifth rank fired and began reloading. Then the fourth rank stood and fired, followed by the rest one by one. After the first rank shot, all but the fifth knelt and the cycle began again. If a particularly lethal volley was called for, the fifth and fourth ranks could fire together. Its invention credited to Martinet, this French system of *feu par rang*—fire by rank—was admired throughout Europe and was copied by many armies.[35]

During the War of the Spanish Succession, however, these French methods were outclassed by a new tactic developed by the Dutch and then adopted by the British: platoon fire.[36] A battalion formed up in a three-rank line. Its officers divided it into eighteen platoons, each of 30–40 men, that were then grouped into three firings. The six platoons of each firing were distributed across the whole length of the line. The first firing shot, then began reloading; the others followed in turn. After the third firing had shot, the first would be ready, and the pattern could be repeated. Platoon fire was time-consuming to organize, demanded a high degree of efficient control by officers, and required superbly trained troops. But its advantages were many. It produced continuous fire with volleys rippling up and down the battalion front. It threw out greater firepower than *feu par rang*: 180 to 240 muskets in each firing compared to 117 in each rank in the French system. It exposed the entire opposing line to a barrage of shots, placing it under greater physical and psychological pressure. Finally, it always preserved a third of the battalion's weapons loaded and ready to deal with an unexpected development.[37]

The British and Dutch demonstrated the potency of platoon fire in innumerable actions. At the battles of Blenheim and Ramillies, their battalions handily outshot their French adversaries. The most striking demonstration of Allied firepower was at Wynendale. On September 28, 1708, a French force of 23,000 infantry, dragoons, and cavalry under the Comte de La Mothe-Houdancourt attacked a detachment of 7,000 Allied troops commanded by General John Webb, which was escorting a vital convoy bound for the siege of Lille. Intending to quickly brush aside the escorts and fall upon the lumbering supply wagons, La Mothe threw his infantry, then his dragoons, in frontal assaults against Webb's line. Both were shot to pieces by platoon volleys from the Dutch, British, and German battalions. La Mothe withdrew in confusion, having suffered 4,000 casualties. Webb's losses totaled 944.[38]

The French were painfully aware they had fallen behind their enemies. Four months before Wynendale, Louis had warned the Duc de Vendôme that his infantry "is less accustomed to shooting than those of the Allies."[39] Throughout the War of the Spanish Succession, the French experimented with various firing systems; none proved as effective as the Allies'. Only in 1739 did platoon fire become part of their infantry regulations. The French did not adopt new and better infantry tactics sooner because they simply could not afford to do so. Platoon fire required constant training with live ammunition. The small, lavishly funded Dutch and British armies could supply their troops with all the musket balls and gunpowder they needed. One French officer enviously described the results:

The Dutch do not let a day pass without exercising their soldiers and without firing gunpowder, and they are so firm in battle by this continual drilling that they are hardly affected by their enemies.

For the huge, cash-strapped army of Louis XIV, such an outlay of gunpowder was an unattainable luxury. According to a 1682 ordinance, each company received enough powder for each soldier to discharge his firearm three times a month. A quarter century later, the situation had not improved. This paltry arms practice seriously hampered French combat performance during the great war. On many occasions, French troops could not even manage an organized battalion salvo or fire by ranks. Their shooting then degenerated into an irregular running fire in which each soldier banged away at will and without waiting for orders from the officers.[40]

Yet, Louis and his generals did not consider the backwardness of their infantry's tactics to be a fatal weakness. The French infantry maintained its traditional excellence in sieges, by far the most common actions of the war. On the battlefield, they learned how to cope with Allied firepower. Realizing that platoon fire was most dangerous in open-field engagements, they took cover in entrenchments, breastworks, or rough ground. At the Battle of Oudenarde, Vendôme's battalions sheltered in hedges, marshes, and watercourses, from where their irregular fire inflicted galling losses on the Allies.[41]

More importantly, the French believed they had a simple and effective tactic that could counter platoon fire: the bayonet charge. The bayonet had been invented by Vauban around 1687. It was a blade sixteen inches long that fitted on the muzzle of the musket, creating a six-and-a-half-foot-long spear. Many officers and military writers thought *l'arme blanche*—cold steel—was the natural weapon of the French, making the most of their inherent elan and impetuosity. "The best method for the French infantry," wrote the anonymous author of a 1704 treatise on field warfare, "is to fix the bayonet on the end of the musket and take good care to keep the ranks of the battalion closed and well ordered."[42] The bayonet charge was combined with a tactical maxim embraced by all contemporary European armies: to hoard a battalion's first fire of an engagement until it could be used to maximum effect. The first volley was always the most effective because the officers and sergeants would have a unit under tight control; the rank and file would have their muskets carefully loaded; their view of the enemy would be unobscured by the pall of smoke created by their own fire; and they could all shoot together at the battalion commander's order.

A French infantry battalion would begin its charge at a walk. The troops would hold their muskets, bayonets fixed, *à chasseur*—hunter style—slanted across their chests, ready to shoot. The advance would be carried out in complete silence so that the officers' orders could be better heard. As the battalion would likely be traversing a battlefield swept by cannon shots, musket volleys, and cavalry charges, it was now, as Louis' advice to the Dauphin intimated, that exacting drill came into its own: it kept the French moving forward under fire and without succumbing to the temptation of prematurely throwing away their first volley. Upon reaching musket range of the enemy, the officers would order the battalion's ranks closed and its pace quickened to *à prest*, a fast closing speed to reduce exposure to the enemy's volleys—it meant, often, a run. Ideally, at point-blank range—thirty paces or even less—the battalion would momentarily halt and discharge its salvo. Then the French troops would rush through their own musket smoke and fall upon the enemy.[43]

Bayonet charges won the French some of their most celebrated feats of arms of the war. Amid the disaster of Blenheim, the régiment de Clare, a unit of Wild Geese, Irish Jacobites in French service, covered itself in glory and renown by charging and destroying a British battalion without firing a shot:

> My lord Clare at the head of his regiment advanced against an English regiment that had challenged him not to fire. The Irish kept their muskets on their shoulders and the English, having fired at twenty paces, were overthrown with the bayonet. Only four survived.

At the battle of Calcinato on April 19, 1706, the Duc de Vendôme's infantry climbed a hill and crossed three ditches under constant enemy fire while holding their own. They finally unleashed their volleys at pistol range, rushed the enemy line with the bayonet, and put the Allied troops to flight. These and similar incidents reassured Louis that discipline, determination, and courage could compensate for his infantry's inferior training and firepower.[44]

The king and his generals had no such doubts about the excellence of their cavalry. From the beginning of the war and for as long as it lasted, they considered the mounted arm to be the pride of their army and their premier strike force on the battlefield. As with the foot, Louis established a clear hierarchy for his horsed units. At its pinnacle was the Maison du Roi: the *Gardes du Corps* (four companies, called the "Maison Bleue" for the color of their uniforms), Gendarmes of the Guard, Light Cavalry of the Guard, Black Musketeers, Grey Musketeers, and Grenadiers of the Guard (five companies, the "Maison Rouge"). Closely associated with the household troops were the sixteen companies of the Gendarmes. The Maison du Roi and the Gendarmes represented the elite corps of the French cavalry. They were no mere ornamental palace guard. The king expected them to be the shock troops of the army, always present at the point of maximum danger and spearheading the decisive attacks. The regular regiments of cavalry were ranked according to their dates of creation, with the many units created for the war at the bottom of the order of precedence. At the height of the conflict, the French regular cavalry had a strength of 105 regiments. In the field, each regiment deployed two or three squadrons. The mounted arm's equivalent of the battalion, a squadron consisted of four companies, each with thirty-five officers and troopers.[45]

French cavalrymen were armed with a saber, which was straight bladed with a single cutting edge, a brace of pistols, and a musketoon, a shorter version of the infantry firearm. For protection, in 1703, the king mandated the iron cuirass (which consisted of a breast- and backplate) or the plastron (which protected only the front of the chest). However, many French cavalrymen disliked them because of their weight and discomfort and chose to ignore the order. During the War of the Spanish Succession, there was only one regiment always clad in body armor, the aptly named Royal Cuirassiers. The one piece of protective gear that found universal favor was a steel cap to ward off saber blows to the head. It was worn concealed beneath horsemen's tricorn hats.[46]

Cavalry's raison d'etre was the charge. To carry one out, a squadron formed up in a three-rank line, its best men placed at the front and on the flanks. In the wars of Louis XIV, the power of the charge was seen as depending not on speed and momentum but on good order and cohesion. French cavalry rarely galloped. They approached their target at a steady walk, careful to keep their ranks straight and serried. When they were fifty yards away, they spurred their horses into a fast trot. According to British soldiers—and their historians—the French primarily relied on their firearms, resorting to their sabers only after pistols and musketoons had severely damaged and demoralized their enemies. By contrast, the Duke of Marlborough eschewed firepower for much more effective shock tactics, ordering his cavalry to charge home without first firing. He favored cold steel to such an extent that he famously allotted the British cavalry only three shots for their pistols per campaign. The implication of this calumny was that the French were outclassed both in their methods and in their courage.[47] In fact, the Sun King's horsemen were ardent believers in *l'arme blanche*. Some, though, advocated firing pistols at point-blank range to soften up the enemy just prior to contact. Others, such as Villars, maintained, like Marlborough, that cavalry should charge with the saber alone. In the field, regiments employed different variations of these tactics according to circumstances and the preferences of their commanders.[48]

During Louis XIV's long reign, several new types of horsemen were added to his mounted arm. Carabineers were sharpshooters on horseback armed with a rifled carbine. Originally two picked men in each cavalry company, they were brought together into a single massive regiment of fifty squadrons in 1693. Perhaps the most exotic element in the French army was the hussars. They were Hungarian light cavalrymen, products of the endless frontier war against the Ottoman Turks in Eastern Europe and the Balkans. Three regiments were in French service by the end of the War of the Spanish Succession. They retained their distinctive curved saber and, above all, their outlandish costume of shako, pelisse, and dolman. All mustachioed swagger, they were masters of *petite guerre* and peerless plunderers. The most important new horsemen of all were the dragoons. At first, they were mounted infantry who rode to the battlefield but fought on foot. By the Nine Years' War, they had become a so-called "second cavalry" adapted to a very wide variety of missions, including reconnaissance, screening, raiding, escorting convoys, pursuing defeated enemies, guarding a retreating army, and even siege work. Their equipment reflected their versatility: saber, pistol, musket, bayonet, and entrenching tools. In 1709, there were thirty-four dragoon regiments.[49]

For all the high regard in which it was held by Louis and his generals, the French cavalry compiled a mixed battle record. At Blenheim, in an incident made infamous by Saint-Simon, the Gendarmes stopped their mounts and fired their carbines at onrushing British horsemen. The elite French troopers were overrun and scattered. In this battle, however, the French cavalry had been in exceptionally poor condition. Its horses had suffered severely during a nightmarish march through Germany, with a third dying from an outbreak of glanders, a deadly and highly contagious equine disease. At Ramillies, the French squadrons performed much better, charging repeatedly with the saber, and with the Maison du Roi breaking through the much more numerous Dutch horse.[50]

Engraved on all of the Sun King's great guns was the legend "Ultima ratio regum"—the last argument of kings. Over the years, this argument had grown louder and more powerful. Artillery was the key weapon for attacking as well as defending fortresses. It was also increasingly important on the battlefield. Cannons, by far the most common type of artillery, were rated according to the weight of the shot they fired. The French had 33-, 24-, 16-, 12-, 8-, and 4-pounders. They also had howitzers, which lobbed shot in high arcs, and mortars, which launched explosive bombs over fortress and town walls. All French guns were intended to serve in both sieges and the field. They were therefore strongly constructed, long-barrelled (to enable their muzzles to protrude beyond a fortress' embrasures) and very heavy. A twenty-four-pounder weighed 3,000 pounds for the barrel alone. A twelve-pounder was 1,000 pounds.[51]

The troops who served the guns were organized into two regiments, the régiment Royal-Artillerie for cannons and howitzers, and the régiment des Bombardiers du Roi for mortars. In their ranks were gunners, matrosses, sappers, and artificers who had the various skills needed to keep the artillery pieces in action. What they did not include were the drivers, horse teams, and wagons that did the critical work of hauling the guns, their ammunition, and stores. These were provided by civilians who were contracted for each campaign. The artillery trains were only fully militarized long after the reign of Louis XIV.[52]

In battle, the guns were grouped into batteries and placed in front of the armies. Because of their great weight, they could be moved again only with great difficulty and so usually fired from their initial positions throughout an action. The main cannon ammunition was solid shot. With a maximum effective range of around 2,500 yards, solid shot whirled and tumbled through infantry and cavalry formations, smashing torsos, crushing limbs, and removing heads. The deadliest shots of all landed on the ground, then bounded and bounced through several enemy units. At 200 yards or less, cannons could switch to canister: a wood or tin container filled with musket balls. When fired, the canister burst at the gun's muzzle, spraying its contents in a wide arc to gruesome effect. Against villages and large buildings, howitzers came into their own, lobbing shots to smash walls and roofs. Artillery was at its most effective and potent in a battle's first phases when the armies were deploying, then approaching each other. This opening bombardment could be prolonged and cause heavy losses. At Blenheim, French and Bavarian batteries emplaced on high ground inflicted over 2,000 casualties on Marlborough's army in three hours; the carnage continued even after the captain general ordered his troops to take cover by lying down. But artillery was time-consuming and labor-intensive to set up. In a scrambling fight such as Oudenarde, where the armies rushed piecemeal onto the field, it could play little part.[53]

Battered, bloodied, and battle scarred, Watteau's soldiers—infantry, cavalry, and artillery—were, as Villars had declared to Madame de Maintenon, still full of ardor and valor. Would they have the funds, food, and fodder they needed to fight?

As April began, a mood of tense anticipation gripped Lyon. The end of the Fair of Kings was approaching, and Samuel Bernard's many creditors were determined to force a reckoning. Bernard's agent, Bertrand Castan, had precise instructions about how to proceed. The banker had received some reliable royal revenues from Controller General Nicolas Desmaretz, including sound money. Yet these were not nearly enough to satisfy all his outstanding liabilities, which amounted to an astronomical 38 million livres in letters of exchange. To remain solvent, Bernard was depending on the 28 million livres in mint bills he had given as security to the

Genevan banking house of Lullin Frères and which he was expecting to be returned to him. He would then force these bills on his creditors on a take-it-or-leave-it basis. Besieged by holders of letters of exchange demanding immediate payment in coin, Castan declared he would make no transactions until Jean-Antoine Lullin reached Lyon. His words only stoked anxieties further.

The Genevan arrived on April 7. At their first interview, Castan discovered to his horror that Lullin Frères, having lost confidence in the French government's ability to back Bernard, had been selling off its mint bills since February. Without them, the banker was short at least 6.7 million livres in meeting his liabilities; he was insolvent. Castan immediately refused to accept any letters of exchange presented to him. Panic erupted. Many Lyonnais merchants were left holding Bernard's worthless paper, and they were now compelled to default on their own obligations. Commerce and industry in the city ground to a halt. Thousands of artisans were thrown out of work. Hounded relentlessly by furious creditors, Castan fled to sanctuary in Bern. Bernard himself conveniently fell ill in order to avoid going to Lyon. But the shockwaves from the crash were spreading far and fast. In Geneva, Lullins Frères suspended all payments. The municipal authorities then ordered a halt to all negotiations in order to prevent a tide of bankruptcies that would have overwhelmed the local economy.[54]

The shockwaves soon reached Versailles. Desmaretz was caught by surprise. "If I could have foreseen such unexpected and extraordinary events," he later lamented to Intendant Louis de Bernage, "I could have taken some measures in January."[55] Once over his initial alarm, he realized Bernard was too big to fail. If he was allowed to be ruined, then no one would ever risk lending money to Louis XIV again. The stream of credit feeding France's finances would dry up. The minister engineered a bail out of the banker. In Lyon, Charles Trudaine, the energetic and very capable intendant, imposed a two-month moratorium on legal actions on debt. Then Desmaretz funneled 14 million livres in royal revenue assignments to Bernard. These revenues were postdated by up to two years and nine months, which meant the banker's creditors would only accept them at steep discounts. Nevertheless, they helped begin the rebuilding of his credit. Another measure was royal pressure on Lullins Frères to cough up Bernard's letters of exchange and mint bills. In May, Trudaine even briefly arrested Jean-Antoine Lullin. The Genevans, though, proved exceedingly tough bargainers who were not so easily intimidated. They dragged negotiations out for months. At last, in October 1709, Lullins agreed to return 1.8 million livres worth of Bernard's letters of exchange.

Bernard's default and the operation to rescue him consumed all the resources Desmaretz had on hand. He had nothing left for anything else.

Not even the army: no funds could be sent to the fronts in the immediate aftermath of the Lyon crash. The whole French war effort was now in mortal peril. Somehow more money had to be found. Louis and Desmaretz hatched a desperate scheme. The controller general approached bankers in Geneva, Venice, and Livorno for new loans; as collateral, he offered nothing less than the French crown jewels. The bankers refused. The sums demanded were too large. Moreover, the still unfolding Bernard debacle made them wary of dealing with the French monarchy.[56]

Desmaretz, Louis, and France were saved by a windfall. Following the ascension of Philip V to the throne of Spain, French merchants had sent ships across the Atlantic to open up the Carrera de Indias, the hugely profitable trade with Spanish America. Then, in 1706, the Spanish Monarchy requested the help of the French navy in protecting its treasure fleets. One squadron under the command of the experienced captain Michel Chabert sailed to the Pacific coast of the Viceroyalty of Peru. On March 27, 1709, Chabert's frigate *L'Aimable* led seven French merchant ships into the roadstead of Port Louis in Brittany. A ninth vessel, the *Vierge-de-Grace*, arrived in La Rochelle two months later. Their holds were crammed with bullion and specie from the fabled silver mountain of Potosi. Word sped to Versailles. On March 31, during his *lever*, the king was able to announce the good news to his astonished courtiers. The first reports valued Chabert's cargo at 20–30 million livres.[57] With characteristic impetuosity, Marshal Villars argued to Madame de Maintenon that the crown should simply seize the lot and spend it on the army:

> You do me the honor of telling me about the twenty million that has arrived, and you say that you would like us to be able to put our hands on it; who can prevent it? This is the time, Madame, when one must not omit any kind of remedy, even the silver in the churches, if there is any left. For nothing is so precious as to feed the men who must fight for the salvation of the State.[58]

Controller General Desmaretz kept a cooler head. After the ships were unloaded, the Peruvian silver was found to amount to 17 million livres, just over half the most optimistic initial estimates. This sum, Desmaretz decided, would still be enough to carry out a complete reminting of the French currency, an ambitious measure he had long been contemplating. It would, he hoped, accomplish two goals: suppress the mint bills that were playing such havoc with the credit of the French monarchy and conjure up the hard cash so badly needed by the army. He promulgated it by royal edict on May 22. All existing French coins were to be deposited at the mints. There, instead of being restamped with symbols denoting new values, they would be completely melted down and remade. At the same time, the precious metal from South America would be added to the money supply. The coins would be rerated: the louis d'or would go from

16 livres 10 sous to 20 livres, the écu from 4 livres 8 sous to 5 livres. This change in value represented a dramatic debasement of the livre tournois against gold and silver. Finally, each deposit at the mints had to consist of five-sixths coin and one-sixths mint bills.

For the rest of his life, Desmaretz would claim that his actions in the spring of 1709 saved France from financial and military catastrophe. He had sound reasons to believe it. The great recoining removed from circulation 43 million livres' worth of the poisonous mint bills. Moreover, it produced a solid profit of 11,370,773 livres. The controller general earmarked most of this money for the army, particularly the wages of the troops. Unfortunately, little of it would be forthcoming quickly. Flooded by old currency and American silver, France's mints would need weeks or even months to produce new coins.[59]

Hard on the heels of financial calamity stalked famine. After the snow and ice of the Great Winter had finally retreated in the middle of March, French peasants watched their fields in hopes of sighting the first shoots of wheat. They did not know that the thaw-freeze cycles of the preceding months had destroyed the seedlings in the ground. "In the month of April, an astonishing thing," wrote the vigneron of Chanteloup in bewilderment, "no more greenery in the fields than on the roads." Soon, a dreadful realization set in: there would be no crops and no harvest that spring.[60]

Hope and bewilderment gave way to fear and desperation. All over France, grain prices began an inexorable rise. The poorest, most desperate folk were quickly driven to the brink of starvation, and they answered by rising up in protest and rebellion. In Amboise on the last day of March, three thousand people swarmed down to the quays along the Loire to block four barges loaded with wheat for Paris. While some demanded the cargo at a just price, others ripped up the cobblestones from the town's bridge to hurl at the boats. In Marseilles on April 7, women and children ran amok, pillaging storehouses and bakeries for bread. The rioters included many wives of the soldiers and officers of the galley squadrons based in the city; their husbands had not been paid in months. That night, two thousand people besieged the hôtel de ville, trapping the municipal authorities inside. They only dispersed after the city's royal governor, the Marquis de Forville, handed out grain that he had expropriated from the local army provisioner. At Reims on April 18, crowds of starving wretches surrounded the Dominican and Cordeliers convents, scaled their walls, and despoiled the foodstuffs the municipal authorities had stored within. In the chaos and confusion, one girl was suffocated, and two others were crushed to death. These were some of the 298 bread riots and popular uprisings that rocked France in 1709. Only 1789 would see more.⁶¹ In addition to these upheavals, hunger also provoked much everyday violence and disorder. In Artois, the Lyonnais, and many other provinces, troops of armed peasants roamed the countryside at night, breaking into the dwellings of prosperous farmers and stealing their stocks of grain.⁶²

On April 8, from her girls' school at Saint-Cyr, Madame de Maintenon wrote to the princesse des Ursins:

> Would you believe, Madame, that something would distress me more than the war? However, I am even more afraid of the famine that now threatens us. News of it comes from all sides. The price of wheat is going up every day. There is no longer any doubt that the frost has completely destroyed this year's harvest. Dearth is everywhere. God, it seems, wants to reduce us to the last extremity.⁶³

No one at the French court was better informed about the threat than Nicolas Desmaretz. His correspondents kept him apprised of the disturbances that were breaking out almost daily, while reports from the intendants revealed the rapidly escalating cost of bread. Nevertheless, the controller general remained unmoved, stubbornly holding on to his belief that the crops had survived and the harvest would still occur. At the end of March, he ordered the provincial intendants to prevent peasants from re-plowing their fields and replanting them with new crops. On April 18, he told Nicolas Lamoignon de Basville, the veteran intendant of Languedoc, that he would be the last person in the kingdom who would lose all hope for the winter wheat.⁶⁴

The peasants could not wait for the king's minister to see sense. Their brown and barren fields promised them only suffering and starvation. In a collective frenzy, all over the country, they tilled and seeded the soil anew. They chose fast-growing grains that could be sown in the spring and harvested in the fall. Buckwheat, the traditional crop of Brittany, was planted all over the west and the valley of the Loire. In the south, millet and corn proved popular. But the most important of all the new plantings was barley. In normal times, it was mainly regarded as the basic ingredient in beer and sold at half the price of wheat. Now it would be the salvation of the French people.⁶⁵

At court, Desmaretz's stance was shifting slowly. In the middle of April, Henri d'Aguesseau, the powerful chief royal prosecutor (*procureur général*) of the Parlement of Paris, visited his estates. He inspected the fields and had the furrows opened. To his horror, he discovered that the peasant outcries about the destruction of the harvest were true. Instantly, he wrote to the controller general urging the planting of barley everywhere and a ban on the brewing of beer. His plea, as well as the overwhelming accumulation of evidence, at last compelled

Desmaretz to act. On April 27, he promulgated a royal declaration on the famine. It permitted peasants to plow and plant their fields with buckwheat, barley, and similar crops. It would be months, however, before these could be harvested. In the meantime, food would have to be found. All holders of grain in France were required to declare the extent of their stocks and to make them available for sale. To verify the declarations and to ensure that supplies reached the markets, the controller general would appoint inspectors in every *généralité* or administrative district in the kingdom. Failure to comply or giving a false report to the inspectors was penalized by a fine of 3,000 livres, of which one-third went to the denouncer of an infraction. Egregious offenses would be punishable by a sentence of penal servitude as a rower in the royal galleys or even death.[66]

These measures came too late to calm the king's subjects. Through the open windows of his apartments, Louis could hear cries of hunger and shouts of anger rising up from the streets of the town of Versailles. On the last day of April, the Grand Dauphin Louis left his château of Meudon to attend the opera in Paris. In the countryside and on the Pont Royal in the city, famished women forced his carriage to stop. They crowded around and begged for bread. The prince flung fistfuls of coins at the throng before commanding his coachman to drive on. And some were beginning to blame the monarch and his ministers for their increasingly desperate plight. On walls all over the capital, placards appeared bearing a parody of the Lord's Prayer:

Our father who art in Versailles
Your name is no longer glorified.
Your kingdom is no longer great.
Your will is no longer done on earth or sea.
Give us our daily bread which we completely lack.
Forgive our enemies who have beaten us.
But not our generals who let them do so.
Do not succumb to the temptations of Maintenon.
But deliver us from Chamillart.[67]

Even before Desmaretz finally acted on the famine, the royal ministers and generals were struggling to feed the Army of Flanders. The failures of the *munitionnaires* had left the magazines of the *pré carré* fortresses empty. Not only had grain not been stockpiled for the field army for the fighting season; there was almost none to feed the troops in winter quarters in Flanders, Artois, Picardy, and Hainault. On April 10, Chamillart warned Desmaretz that the lack of supplies represented an even greater danger than the shortage of money.[68]

A frantic search for food now began. One source was great landowners in northern France. François Fénelon, the archbishop of Cambrai and former preceptor to the Duc de Bourgogne, had generously promised the army 8,000 sacks of wheat from his estates at Le Cateau. In late April, with widespread hunger in his diocese, he tried to renege. But Chamillart insisted and the prelate managed to gather 4,000 sacks that went to the garrison of Tournai.[69] More promising was a deal struck by the war minister with the Marquise de Mailly for 12,000 sacks from her domain near Nesle on the Somme. Soon after, another noblewoman, the Marquise de Sailly, agreed to supply 7,000 sacks of wheat. In the end, neither was able to fully deliver, with Mailly providing just 7,000 sacks and Sailly 3,500.[70] Another source was regions and provinces far from the Flanders front. In early April, Dominique-Claude Barberie de Saint-Contest, intendant at Metz, declared that he had been able to purchase 30,000 sacks of wheat and flour in the neutral Duchy of Lorraine. Encouraged by this success, Desmaretz instructed the intendants of the Soissonais and Champagne to acquire similar quantities.[71]

The most important source of food was the frontier provinces themselves. On April 10, Chamillart informed Villars of a proposal to requisition grain from Flanders, Artois, Picardy, and the Soissonais on the promise of payment from the *munitionnaires*. The marshal enthusiastically endorsed this scheme.[72] The intendants, however, would confront considerable challenges in carrying it out. Flanders, Artois, and Hainault were already under immense strain because not only were they heavily taxed by their own government; they also owed substantial contributions to the Allies. Contributions had been developed over the course of the seventeenth century to limit the destructiveness of warfare: they were essentially protection money paid to a hostile army to spare a territory from the depredations of marauders and raiding parties. In August 1708, Artois agreed to contribute 1,800,000 livres to the Dutch States General, Flanders 542,236 livres.[73]

But the greatest obstacle to the requisitions was the opposition of the people of the frontier. Suffering badly from the famine, they were enraged by the removal of food from their cities, towns, and villages, particularly as this policy worked at cross purposes with Controller General Desmaretz's April 27 declaration. On May 7, in Abbeville, the capital of the ancient county of Ponthieu and a key garrison town in Picardy, a placard appeared:

> Gentlemen of the police, you are warned on behalf of all the common people, who number six thousand five hundred sixty-four individuals working day and night. We are dying of hunger, and we are obliged to absolutely command you to set the price of wheat and bread at such a reasonable level that

we can live. You must also force the wheat merchants to supply the markets with everything we need. If you fail to do so, we will emerge from our homes like enraged lions, arms in one hand and fire in the other, reducing you all to dust in such a way that no living person will have ever spoken of such a slaughter.[74]

Yet, in spite of such threats, the intendants had no choice except to follow through. Unless peace was made, their masters insisted the army must have priority. So that the king's soldiers could be fed, some of his subjects would have to starve.

What to do with the army exercised Marshal Villars during the last weeks of April. He toured the front between the Scarpe and the Lys, visiting the troops, inspecting the fortresses, and studying the ground. On May 1, he wrote a long letter to the king detailing his plans for the impending campaign. Lacking sufficient supplies, the Army of Flanders had to rule out any offensive operations against either Lille or Courtrai. Instead, it would have to stand on the defensive. The Allies would likely attack from Lille with the aim of overrunning Artois. Then they could either sweep westwards to the Boulonnais and the Channel coast or thrust south into Picardy, opening the road to Paris. To thwart this design, Villars proposed deploying the Army of Flanders at La Bassée. There, it could protect the vital strongholds of Douai, Béthune, and Aire as well as prevent the Allies from penetrating deeper into France. Marooned beyond the La Bassée position would be Ypres and Tournai, powerful *pré carré* fortresses flanking Lille and likely initial targets for the enemy. Both needed to be strongly garrisoned and adequately provisioned to withstand a siege. The king and War Minister Chamillart were assigning 150 battalions and 220 squadrons to Flanders, almost 90,000 men. Villars would reinforce the garrisons of Ypres and Tournai with twelve battalions each. He also had to bolster the forces of France's Wittelsbach allies, the electors of Bavaria and Cologne. After these detachments, his field army would consist of 110 battalions and 200 squadrons.

The position chosen by Villars was tactically strong and strategically advantageous. The Army of Flanders' right flank would protect the great stronghold of Douai. It would run along the canal joining the Deûle to the Scarpe; the ground was formidably rugged, alternately boggy or steep with escarpments. The Army's center would be just south of La Bassée between the vast marshes of Hulluch and Cuinchy, both impassable to troops. Its left would extend to the Lys. The shortest trace was to the town of Estaires. But this area, replete with ditches and streams, was unsuitable for cavalry, and Villars considered his mounted arm to be his trump card against the Allies. The marshal instead proposed building the lines just to the north of Béthune along ridges and behind swamps. From there, they would run westward to the heights of Hinge, then to Mont-Bernanchon, then to Robecq on a little river called the Nave. This minor water course could be widened considerably to help cover the final stretch of works going north and west to the Lys fortress of Saint-Venant.[75]

For all his plan's merits, Villars knew it had an Achilles heel. In order to stand and await the Allied attack in the lines of La Bassée, he explained in a second letter to Louis dated May 4, the Army of Flanders needed plentiful and reliably replenished supplies. Both requirements appeared beyond the powers of the fast-failing French logistical apparatus. The marshal calculated that his army would be able to hold its position for three weeks at most. After that, it would have to seek battle with the Allies or disperse so that its troops could be fed. "I wish for peace because of the extreme difficulty of everything," Villars confessed. "But if we cannot have it, then Your Majesty will find in me all the firmness and confidence fit for the good of his service and the glory of the nation."[76]

The king answered the next day. He too regarded France's predicament as almost irredeemable and wished for an end to the war. For this purpose, he had sent the Marquis de Torcy, his minister for foreign affairs, to The Hague to negotiate personally with the leaders of the Grand Alliance.[77]

The dispatch of a royal minister to sue for peace with France's enemies was unprecedented as well as a humiliation. It was the result of the tortuous talks held between the French envoy Pierre Rouillé and Dutch diplomats for almost two months. When he had set out on his secret mission on March 5, Rouillé had been armed with extensive and detailed instructions drawn up by Torcy. "The most onerous conditions of peace," they declared, "seem less painful to His Majesty than the long suffering of his people." Chief among these onerous conditions was the ceding of Spain, the bulk of its European possessions, and the entirety of its American empire by Philip V to Archduke Charles, the Habsburg claimant. The Dutch would also receive significant concessions. Commercial relations with France would return to the favorable terms and tariffs set in 1664. To assuage its security concerns, the Republic would see its Barrier fortresses in the southern Netherlands restored and enlarged with Ypres and Menin. But the negotiations were not to be completely one-sided. To compensate his grandson for giving up his birthright, Louis demanded that he receive a new realm carved out of Spain's Italian territories: Sicily and Naples at least and preferably also Sardinia and the presidios of Tuscany. France would also keep its most important acquisitions on the Flanders frontier, namely Tournai, Condé, and Maubeuge. Above all, the Allies must return Lille.[78]

Rouillé reached Antwerp on March 9. There, he waited to be informed of the time and location of the talks. On March 17, he made his way to the village of Streydensas near Moerdijk. In a room in a waterside inn, he met the Dutch negotiators, Willem Buys, pensionary of Amsterdam, and Bruno van der Dussen, burgomaster of Gouda. Rouillé opened the discussions by stating that he possessed full powers to negotiate on behalf of his government. Moreover, the king of France's intentions were not just to come to terms with the Dutch Republic but to establish the basis for a general and lasting peace. Buys and van der Dussen responded with calculated coolness. They did not have the authority to conclude anything definitive. They were merely to report the results of their talks to the States General, then follow its instructions on whether and how to proceed.

They received the French proposals equally coolly. On Italy, they indicated that the Republic was open to Louis XIV's grandson receiving Naples and Sicily. However, the British and Habsburgs wanted all of Spain's Italian territories to go to the archduke. Then, raising his voice almost to a shout, Buys declared that if the French insisted on Sardinia and the Tuscan presidios, "it would be useless to continue the conference." As for the Barrier, the Republic wanted a line of strongholds in the southern Netherlands running from the Meuse to the sea. The original Barrier created in 1697 would no longer suffice; it had to include many more fortresses and fortified towns. The French would have to surrender Furnes, Tournai, Condé, and Maubeuge to the Dutch.

The Dutchmen next laid out the key demands of the other Allies. The British sought French recognition of the Protestant Succession to Queen Anne. In addition, Louis must expel the Stuart pretender James from France. For the safety of their seaborne trade, the British wanted possession of Dunkirk, the principal base for French privateers and commerce raiders. The emperor and the German princes were demanding their own barrier against future French aggression. The Rhine frontier therefore had to be restored to what it had been following the 1648 Treaty of Münster, which had ended the Thirty Years' War. As a result, Strasbourg, one of Louis' proudest conquests, would have to be ceded back to the Empire.

After thirteen hours of discussions over two days, Rouillé concluded he had exhausted his instructions and needed new directions from Versailles. Bidding farewell to Buys and van der Dussen, he returned to Antwerp and wrote a full report to the king on March 21.[79] Unfortunately, French hopes that the talks would be secret were almost immediately dashed. Allied spies had identified Rouillé and tracked his movements from Antwerp. Moreover, the Dutch proved remarkably indiscreet: Rouillé's mission was publicized in newspapers and gazettes all over the Republic. In London, the Duke of Marlborough learned of it on March

19. He instantly wrote Count Johann Wratislaw, one of the emperor's chief ministers, and stressed that the Allies needed to rebuff any French attempts to divide them.[80] The meetings between the French and Dutch envoys now became the main focus of all the belligerents.

The French court had been waiting anxiously for word from its envoy. After reading Rouille's report, Louis and Torcy were cautiously optimistic. Although the Dutch responses to their proposals had not been quite what they had hoped, they nevertheless thought they saw room for maneuver. They ordered Rouillé to arrange for another conference as soon as possible. For Philip V, his claims to Sardinia and the Tuscan fortresses were to be abandoned, and those to Naples and Sicily redoubled. For the Dutch, Furnes could be added to their Barrier as long as its fortifications were dismantled. The Republic would then have a solid position from the North Sea coast to the Meuse consisting of Furnes, Oudenarde, Ath, Mons, Charleroi, and Namur. For the British, the Protestant Succession would be recognized. But because of the close ties of family and friendship between the Bourbons and the Stuarts, Louis refused to chase James Stuart from France. For the Germans, the Rhine frontier would be returned to what it had been following the Treaty of Ryswick—in other words, the status quo ante bellum. Torcy did his best to reassure Rouillé that he would eventually prevail in these negotiations: "I believe it is impossible they will not yield to your sound reasoning, for their arguments resemble more those of a Tamerlane than of a well-governed Republic like Holland."[81]

On April 2, Rouillé traveled deep into Dutch territory to the town of Woerden. On a yacht moored in the Utrecht-Leiden canal, he met Buys and van der Dussen for the second time.[82] The French diplomat first tabled Philip V's claims to Naples and Sicily. Buys' evasive reply was that the States General had not yet decided on the matter. Moreover, the Dutch would need to consider the interests of the British, who would likely demand that only Naples go to the French king's grandson. Then, when he turned to the question of the Barrier, Buys' words and tone became ominous. With a feigned bonhomie, he first chided Rouillé that his royal master's demands to retain the Flanders fortresses were excessive and did not reflect France's true circumstances. What he said next revealed how the Allies were viewing and approaching the peace talks:

> Given the unfortunate situation in which France already found itself, and on the eve of falling into an even worse plight during the next campaign, he dared to say that His Majesty ought to think less about losing the places demanded of him and more about keeping any of his conquests at all.

Although the discussions continued for two more days, no progress was made on the substantive issues. The Dutch diplomats then took Rouillé to the village of Bodegraven, where he agreed to remain until the next conference.

In his second report to Versailles, Rouillé made no attempt to conceal the growing difficulties he was facing with Buys and van der Dussen.[83] A further hint of trouble came from the French agent at The Hague, Hermann Petkum, who conversed regularly with Anthonie Heinsius, grand pensionary of Holland and the de facto leader of the Republic. He informed Torcy that Heinsius was displeased with the French proposals, especially the offer of Furnes without its fortifications, and was beginning to believe that the king of France did not actually want to make peace but was merely using the talks to gain more time for his armies to recover their strength.[84]

These warnings made little impression on Louis and Torcy. They were convinced the Dutch were as war-weary as the French. In particular, they believed that a States party—a faction in the Republic that championed the authority of the States General over the monarchical pretensions of the House of Orange—was clamoring for peace. They thus concluded they could still achieve their original aim of drawing the Dutch into a treaty that would break up the Grand Alliance. All they had to do was find the right concessions that would satisfy the Dutch peace party's interests. On April 15, the king sent fresh instructions to Rouillé in Bodegraven. He was willing to grant the Republic all the favorable economic terms with France it desired. He would also add to the Barrier Furnes with its fortifications intact as well as Ypres and Menin. Rouillé could also cede Condé and Maubeuge if necessary to clinch final Dutch agreement on a peace treaty. Louis was offering the other Allies much less. He would give the British all the assurances they required for the Protestant Succession save for the exile of the Stuarts from France and he would treat with the emperor and the Imperial princes on the basis of the Treaty of Ryswick. As for his own demands, they remained Naples and Sicily for his grandson and Lille for himself.[85]

On April 21, Rouillé met the Dutch diplomats at van der Dussen's country villa. When he presented the latest French concessions, he was taken aback by the vehemence and hostility of his counterparts' reaction. The Allies' demands were the minimum they were willing to accept, they thundered, and were the necessary preconditions for a peace treaty. Rouillé tried to coax Buys and van der Dussen back to discussing the French proposals. They spurned his efforts, declaring that "the greatest pleasure His Majesty could give to his enemies was to refuse these preconditions." Then, following a tense dinner, the Dutchmen suddenly announced that they regarded the terms they had laid out during the first conference at Streydensas to be an ultimatum. Louis XIV must accept them all, without negotiation, or the war would continue. All of Rouillé's protests were in vain. He hurriedly left the villa to inform his masters of this disastrous turn of events.[86]

Rouillé's latest account plunged the French court into turmoil. Torcy raged that the Dutch had indeed acted with the utter ruthlessness and perfidiousness of an Asiatic warlord. In fact, the conduct of the Allies during the talks had been driven by their conviction that France was already beaten by battlefield defeats, financial exhaustion, and mass starvation. Another campaign would merely snuff out its last powers of resistance. There was therefore no need to negotiate; they only had to dictate terms to a prostrate foe. As Marlborough told Heinsius on March 22: "We have certain intelligence from France that the King is advised by his ministers to give any conditions rather than venture the next campaign: so that you may insist boldly on such conditions as you think are good for the common cause."[87] And having suffered from the Sun King's ambitions for forty years, the Allies were determined to humiliate him and permanently restrain his kingdom's capacity for aggression. In particular, the Dutch sought revenge for the *Rampjaar* of 1672, when Louis had almost destroyed their Republic.

On April 28, at the palace of Versailles, Louis convened the *Conseil d'en haut*, the state council of ministers, to decide what to do next. Present were the Grand Dauphin, the Duc de Bourgogne, Chancellor Pontchartrain, the Duc de Beauvilliers, Torcy, Chamillart, and Desmaretz. Following the reading of Rouillé's report, Beauvilliers spoke first. "In touching and emotive terms," he dwelt at length on the catastrophic consequences of continuing a war that France could no longer win. Peace had to be made at any price. Chancellor Pontchartrain strongly supported him. The two ministers then turned to Chamillart and Desmaretz to ask if the troops and the treasury could even fight the next campaign.

Before they could answer, Louis himself spoke. The Allied ultimatum was an insult to his honor and an affront to his *gloire*. Yet no one knew better the sad plight of his state, the feebleness of his armies, and the misery of his people. For once, his extraordinary self-control deserted him, and he was overcome by emotion. Tears streamed down his face. God wished to punish him, he declared. Bowing to His will, he would make even more sacrifices for peace. He would order Rouillé to return to the negotiating table.

Now the Marquis de Torcy intervened. After the other ministers departed, he spoke privately with the king. The window for diplomacy was closing fast, he explained. The fighting season was imminent, and once it began, the Allies would become immovable. A new negotiator was urgently needed, one who knew Louis' mind and who could speak with his voice. The minister for foreign affairs volunteered to go and replace

Rouillé. The king accepted gratefully. On April 29, the council met again and approved Torcy's mission. Two days later, he set off for The Hague.[88]

NOTES

1. Rule and Trotter, *A World of Paper*, 421–422; Bély, *Espions et ambassadeurs*, 58.
2. Jean-Christian Petitifils, *Le Régent* (Paris: Fayard, 1986), 148.
3. On Philip V, see Henry Kamen, *Philip V of Spain, the King Who Reigned Twice* (New Haven: Yale University Press, 2001).
4. Jean-Baptiste Colbert, Marquis de Torcy, *Mémoires du marquis de Torcy pour server à l'histoire des négociations depuis le traité de Riswick jusqu'à la paix d'Utrecht*, vol. 62 (vol. 1), in *Collection des mémoires relatifs à l'histoire de France*, eds. A. Petitot et L. Monmerque (Paris: Foucault, 1828), 113.
5. Sourches, *Mémoires*, vol. 11, 206; Dangeau, *Journal*, vol. 12, 321.
6. Archives des Affaires Étrangeres (AAE) Hollande 217, Torcy to van der Dussen, 3 February 1709, ff. 60–60v.
7. Torcy, *Mémoires*, vol. 1, 114–115.
8. Ibid., 115–117.
9. 386, Maintenon to Princess des Ursins, 18 March 1709, *Lettres de Madame de Maintenon*, vol. 4, 521.
10. SHD AG A^1 2150/33, Villars to Chamillart, 18 March 1709.
11. Villars, *Mémoires*, book 3, 35; SHD AG A^1 2150/57, 26 March 1709, Villars to Louis XIV.
12. SHD AG A^1 2150/31, Chanillart to Villars, 18 March 1709.
13. SHD AG A^1 2150/41, Villars to Louis XIV, 20 March 1709; SHD AG A^1 2150/57, Villars to Louis XIV, 26 March 1709.
14. Villars, *Mémoires*, book 3, 34; SHD AG A^1 2150/89, Villars to Louis XIV, 4 April 1709.
15. Archives Nationales (hereafter AN) G^7 290/103, Bernage to Desmaretz, 9 March 1709.
16. AN G^7 263/389, Bernières to Desmaretz, 2 March 1709; Rowlands, *Financial Decline*, 212–213.
17. SHD AG A^1 2150/76, Villars to Chamillart, 30 March 1709.
18. AN G^7 290/124, Bernage to Desmaretz, 10 April 1709.
19. SHD AG A^1 2156/41, Doujat to Chamillart, 12 April 1709.
20. SHD AG A^1 2150/93, Villars to Chamillart, 7 April 1709; SHD AG A^1 2150/113, Villars to Chamillart, 15 April 1709.
21. Vogüé, *Madame de Maintenon et le Marechal de Villars*, 36–37.
22. On Watteau as an artist of war, see Aaron Wile, *Watteau's Soldiers: Scenes of Military Life in Eighteenth-Century France* (New York: The Frick Collection, 2016).
23. The original painting *Recruë allant joindre le Regiment* has been lost. However, Watteau produced several prints of it. The Art Institute of Chicago has one example: https://www.artic.edu/artworks/193123/recruits-going-to-join-the-regiment. On the painting and its possible meanings, see Julie-Anne Plax, "The

Meaning of War in Watteau's *Recruë Allant Joindre Le Régiment*," *Source: Notes in the History of Art* 16/3 (Spring 1997), 17–23.

24. The classic, indispensable work on the social composition of the eighteenth-century French army is André Corvisier, *L'armee francaise de la fin du XVIIe siècle au ministère de Choiseul. Le Soldat*, 2 vols. (Paris: Presses Universitaires de France, 1964). This paragraph is based on Part Two and Part Three of this work.

25. Victor Belhomme, *Histoire de l'infanterie en France*, vol. 2 (Paris: H. Charles-Lavauzelle, 1893–1902), 443, 456.

26. Lynn, *Giant of the Grand Siècle*, 48, 468–469; Oury, *La Guerre de Succession d'Espagne*, 53–54.

27. *Ordonnances militaires du roi de France, reduites en pratique, et appliquées au detail du service. Ouvrage trés utile à tous les Gens de Guerre. Il contient l'explication des fonctions mlitaires, et un abregé des XV tomes d'ordonnances du roi, disposées, selon l'ordre des matières* (Paris: André Chevalier, 1728), 215–229.

28. The best contemporary description of French infantry drill is found in Pierre-Claude de Guignard, *L'école de Mars, ou Mémoires instructifs sur toutes les parties qui composent le corps militaire en France*, book 1 (Paris: Simart, 1725), 616–653.

29. The concept of muscular bonding was coined and developed by William H. MacNeil in his *The Pursuit of Power: Technology, Armed Force, and Society since AD 1000* (Chicago: University of Chicago Press, 1982), 131, and *Keeping Together in Time: Dance and Drill in Human History* (Cambridge, MA: Harvard University Press, 1995), 131–132.

30. *Mémoires de Louis XIV pour l'instruction du Dauphin*, ed. Charles Dreyss, vol. 2 (Paris: Didier et Compagnie, 1860), 112–113.

31. Lynn, *Giant of the Grand Siècle*, 519–524.

32. Oury, *La Guerre de Succession d'Espagne*, 57.

33. Boris Bouget, "'De peu d'effet.' Le fusil et le combat d'infanterie au XVIII siècle (1692–1791). Modèles, tactique et efficacité" (PhD diss., Université Paris-Sorbonne, 2013), 211.

34. *Ordonnances militaires du roi*, 207–215;

35. Lynn, *Giant of the Grand Siècle*, 485–486; Oury, *La Guerre de Succession d'Espagne*, 308.

36. J. A. Houlding, *Fit for Service: The Training of the British Army, 1715–1795* (Oxford: Clarendon Press, 1981), 174–178; Stapleton, "Forging a Coalition Army," 334–336.

37. David Chandler, *The Art of Warfare in the Age of Marlborough* (New York: Hippocrene Books, 1976), 117–121; Brent Nosworthy, *The Anatomy of Victory: Battle Tactics, 1689–1763* (New York: Hippocrene Books, 1990), 55–61.

38. Chandler, *Marlborough as Military Commander*, 232.

39. SHD AG A^1 2080/186, Louis XIV to Vendôme, 20 May 1708.

40. Clement Oury, "L'efficacité du fer et du feu dans les batailles de la guerre de Succession d'Espagne," in *Combattre et gouverner*, 45–47. The quote is found on 47.

41. Boris Bouget, "D'une guerre à l'autre, le double retard de l'infanterie française: un handicap limité (1688–1715)," in *Les dernières guerres de Louis XIV, 1688–1715*, 149–151; Oury "L'efficacité du fer et du feu," 50.

42. Bibliothèque Nationale de France (BnF), Manuscrits françaises 6257 *Traité de la guerre de campagne*, 83.

43. Bouget, "D'une guerre à l'autre," 154–156; Lynn, *Giant of the Grand Siècle*, 487–489; Nosworthy, *The Anatomy of Victory*, 101–106; Oury, *La Guerre de Succession d'Espagne*, 312–314.

44. Oury, "L'efficacité du fer et du feu," 39–40.

45. Chaline, *Les armées du Roi*, 23–27; Lynn, *Giant of the Grand Siècle*, 492–495.

46. Oury, *La Guerre de Succession d'Espagne*, 48–49.

47. Chandler, *Marlborough as Military Commander*, 91.

48. Lynn, *Giant of the Grand Siècle*, 497–500; Oury, *La guerre de Succession d'Espagne*, 314–317.

49. Lynn, *Giant of the Grand Siècle*, 492–495; Oury, *La guerre de Succession d'Espagne*, 50–53.

50. Oury, *La guerre de Succession d'Espagne*, 314–316; Nosworthy, *The Anatomy of Victory*, 127–131; Saint-Simon, *Mémoires*, vol. 12, 182.

51. Chandler, *The Art of Warfare*, 176–183.

52. Lynn, *Giant of the Grand Siècle*, 509–511.

53. Chandler, *The Art of Warfare*, 204–212; Oury, *La guerre de Succession d'Espagne*, 318–319.

54. Monahan, *Year of Sorrows*, 87–89; Rowlands, *Dangerous and Dishonest Men*, 158–162.

55. AN G^7 16/110, letter from Desmaretz to Bernage, 5 May 1709.

56. Stéphane Guerre, *Nicolas Desmaretz. Le Colbert oublié du Roi-Soleil* (Paris: Champ Vallon, 2019), 331; Rowlands, *Dangerous and Dishonest Men*, 164.

57. Erik W. Dahlgren, *Les relations commerciales et maritimes entre la France et les côtes de l'Océan Pacifique (commencement du XVIIIe siècle)* (Paris: Honoré Champion, 1909), 418–419.

58. Vogüé, *Madame de Maintenon et le Marechal de Villars*, 37.

59. Guerre, *Nicolas Desmaretz*, 348; Rowlands, *Financial Decline*, 124–125.

60. Lachiver, *Les années de Misère*, 306–308. The quote is on 307.

61. Jean Nicolas, *La Rébellion française. Mouvements populaires et conscience sociale (1661–1789)* (Paris: Seuil, 2002), 236–237.

62. SHD AG A^1 2157/116, Bernage to Chamillart, 3 April 1709; Boislisle, *Correspondance*, vol. 3, 115–116.

63. 398, Maintenon to des Ursins, 8 April 1709, in *Lettres de Maintenon*, 533.

64. Guerre, *Nicolas Desmaretz*, 292–293; Boislisle, *Correspondance*, vol. 3, 113–114.

65. Lachiver, *Les années de misère*, 310–315.

66. Guerre, *Nicolas Desmaretz*, 296–305.

67. Lachiver, *Les années de misère*, 338.

68. SHD AG A^1 2150/104, Chamillart to Desmaretz, 10 April 1709.

69. SHD AG A^1 2159/168, Fénelon to Chamillart, 24 April 1709; Maurice Sautai, *La Bataille de Malplaquet d'après les correspondants du duc du Maine à l'armée de Flandre* (Paris: R. Chapelot, 1904), 11–12; Fénelon to Chamillart, 6 December 1708, in *Correspondance de Fénelon*, ed. Jean Orcibal, book 14, *Guerre, négociations, théologie 1708–1711* (Geneva: Droz, 1992), 104; Fénelon to Chamillart, 24 April 1709, in ibid., 140; Chamillart to Fénelon, 27 April 1709, in ibid., 141.

70. SHD AG A¹ 2150/100, Chamillart to Villars, 3 April 1709; SHD AG A¹ 2150/127, Villars to Chamillart, 18 April 1709; SHD AG A¹ 2157/169, Chamillart to Bernage, 3 May 1709; SHD AG A¹ 2157/183, Bernage to Chamillart, 13 May 1709; SHD AG A¹ 2157/255, Bernage to Voysin, 18 June 1709.

71. SHD AG A¹ 2150/113, Villars to Chamillart, 15 April 1709; SHD AG A¹ 2150/148, Chamillart to Villars, 25 April 1709.

72. SHD AG A¹ 2150/104, Chamillart to Villars, 10 April 1709; SHD AG A¹ 2150/106, Villars to Chamillart, 12 April 1709; SHD AG A¹ 2150/208, Villars to Chamillart, 15 May 1709.

73. André Corvisier, *La bataille de Malplaquet. L'effondrement de la France évité* (Paris: Economica, 2013), 18.

74. SHD AG A¹ 2157/173, copy of a placard posted in Abbeville.

75. SHD AG A¹ 2150/171, Villars to Louis XIV, 1 May 1709.

76. SHD AG A¹ 2150/183, Villars to Louis XIV, 4 May 1709.

77. SHD AG A¹ 2150/187, Louis XIV to Villars, 5 May 1709.

78. Rouillé's instructions are AAE Hollande 217, ff. 109–159v.

79. AAE Hollande 217, Rouillé to Louis XIV, 21 March 1709, ff. 190–222v.

80. 724, Marlborough to Heinsius, 8/19 March 1709, in *The Correspondence, 1701–1711, of John Churchill, First Duke of Marlborough, and Anthonie Heinsius, Grand Pensionary of Holland*, ed. Bert van 't Hoff (The Hague: M. Nijhoff, 1951), 429; Marlborough to the Comte de Wratislaw, 11 March 1709 (Old Style), in *Letters and Dispatches of John Churchill, First Duke of Marlborough, from 1702 to 1712*, ed. George Murray, vol. 4 (London: John Murray, 1845), 471.

81. AAE Hollande 217, Louis XIV to Rouillé, 26 March 1709, ff. 225–335; AAE Hollande 217, Torcy to Rouillé, 26 March 1709, ff. 236–236v.

82. AAE Hollande 218, Rouillé to Torcy, 2 April 1709, ff. 3–3v.

83. AAE Hollande 218, Rouillé to Louis XIV, 6 April 1709, ff. 13–44v.

84. AAE Hollande 218, Pettkum to Torcy, 5 April 1709, ff. 11–12.

85. AAE Hollande 218, Louis XIV to Rouillé, 15 April 1709, ff. 48–64.

86. AAE Hollande 218, Rouillé to Louis XIV, 22 April 1709, ff. 113–121v.

87. 728, Marlborough to Heinsius, 12/23 March 1709, in *Marlborough-Heinsius Correspondence*, 431.

88. Torcy, *Mémoires*, vol. 1, 190–208.

4

✛

The Negotiations
May–June, 1709

As the Marquis de Torcy's carriage labored northward, it was engulfed by thick fogs and ceaseless rains that blotted out the passing countryside. The absence of a view was hardly marked by Torcy; his attention was entirely given over to the work that lay ahead. Treating for peace with the chiefs of the Grand Alliance was the most daunting challenge he could imagine. Yet he had also spent his entire life learning, practicing, and mastering the subtle, sophisticated arts of diplomacy.

Jean-Baptiste Colbert de Torcy was born in 1665 into a powerful clan of royal servants. His father, Charles Colbert, Marquis de Croissy, was a fast-rising provincial intendant and diplomat. His uncle, godfather, and namesake was the Great Colbert. In his youth, he received an excellent education that included unfettered access to his uncle's library, one of the finest in France. In 1679, Croissy became secretary of state for foreign affairs and a royal minister. The next year, he presented his son to the king, who expressed his approval by observing "he has a pleasing face." Croissy then began grooming Torcy to follow in his footsteps. A crucial part of his apprenticeship was travel throughout Europe. Beginning when he was eighteen, he toured the courts of Iberia, Italy, Scandinavia, and Germany. He became thoroughly familiar with their politics and met many of their key personalities; for instance, in Madrid, he had an audience with Charles the Bewitched, who surprised him with his vigor and intelligence. In 1686, Torcy returned to Versailles to be trained in his father's work. In particular, he learned the intricacies of diplomatic correspondence, including writing letters in the king's name to French envoys abroad and to foreign potentates. So impressed was Louis with the young Torcy's performance that he officially appointed him as his father's successor in 1689.

Croissy died seven years later. But Torcy did not immediately become foreign minister. The post was instead filled by Simon Arnauld de Pomponne, who had held it during the Dutch War and whose dismissal by the king had opened the way for Croissy's ascension. The old minister's return was not meant to thwart Torcy—indeed, he was soon married to Pomponne's daughter—rather, it was to help complete his apprenticeship. For the next three years, the two worked closely and amicably together. They negotiated the Treaty of Ryswick, ending the Nine Years' War. Then, to preserve that hard-won peace, they embarked on talks with William III to divide up the Spanish Monarchy following the extinction of its Habsburg dynasty. The successful conclusion of two partition agreements amply demonstrated Torcy's talent for supple, patient diplomacy.[1]

After Pomponne's death in 1699, Torcy duly became foreign secretary and a minister with a seat on the *Conseil d'en haut*. After 1704, he oversaw the efforts to make peace with the Dutch. Along the way, he had to fend off a number of attempts by War Minister Michel Chamillart to launch his own clumsy démarches. By 1709, he enjoyed the king's full confidence. He was also at the height of his powers: erudite, exceptionally well informed, and blessed with a preternatural calm and patience. Above all, he was convinced that with enough determination and psychological insight into his interlocutors, he could bring any negotiation to a successful conclusion.[2]

Torcy would need all of these gifts. He was going to The Hague not as Louis XIV's plenipotentiary to a public peace conference. Instead, he would be dealing privately with the Allied leaders behind closed doors. He was traveling anonymously—the name on the passport authorizing him to enter and traverse Allied territory had been left blank—and in secret. Approaching Brussels, the military and administrative center of the Allied-occupied Spanish Netherlands, Torcy came close to discovery. By coincidence, Prince Eugene announced an inspection of the garrison and ordered all the gates closed. Thanks to this stroke of good fortune, Torcy's carriage bypassed the city undetected. Then, at Antwerp, Dutch guards demanded to see the passengers' passports. A quick-thinking member of the minister's entourage produced one in his own name permitting him to enter Holland on postal business. The sentries let the French pass. Reaching Rotterdam, Torcy contacted the Dutch merchant banker Sincerf, who had dealings with the Parisian financier Jean-Claude Tourton. Sincerf agreed to conduct Torcy personally to The Hague. On the evening of May 6, the two arrived at Anthonie Heinsius' house on the Denneweg. Sincerf saw the grand pensionary first, leaving Torcy in an adjoining room. He did not have to wait long before Heinsius' entered and expressed his surprise at seeing before him a minister of Louis XIV.[3]

Two days later, Heinsius dashed off a letter to the Duke of Marlborough in England describing his first meeting with Torcy. The French foreign minister had declared that his royal master was still seeking a general peace that would embrace all of the belligerents. Furthermore, he desired a truce before the campaigning season began. Torcy was offering the Dutch a Barrier comprising Furnes, Menin, Ypres, Maubeuge, and Tournai. In return, he insisted that Philip V must have Naples and Sicily. Heinsius retorted that the Allies were unwilling to concede a treaty or even a truce unless the French put forward a much better offer. To this, Torcy did not respond. "Voila, all that happened at this most unexpected conference, one which I cannot foresee the outcome."[4]

Torcy had arrived at The Hague at a triumphant yet also delicate moment for the Allies. Great Britain, the Dutch Republic, and the Austrian Habsburg Holy Roman Emperor had created their Grand Alliance by a treaty signed at The Hague on September 14, 1701. The Allies' principal objective, it declared, was to prevent Louis XIV from uniting Spain and its global empire with France. But the treaty went on to specify other war aims. The emperor was to receive "an equitable and reasonable satisfaction" for his house's claim to the Spanish Monarchy. In effect, this meant partition, with the Bourbons keeping Spain and its overseas empire, while the Habsburgs received Italy and—at the insistence of the Maritime Powers—the Spanish Netherlands. The Dutch were to have their Barrier against France re-established. The Maritime Powers were to obtain extensive trading rights in the Spanish empire; they could also keep whatever Spanish colonies they were able to capture. Six months after the treaty's conclusion, following Louis XIV's recognition of the Stuart pretender and the death of William III, Great Britain appended further goals: French recognition of Queen Anne as rightful sovereign and the succession after her of the Protestant electors of Hanover.[5]

As the Allies' victories over the Sun King mounted, so their war aims increased in number and scope. In 1703, Portugal joined the Grand Alliance, turning Iberia into a theater of war. The next year, Archduke Charles landed in Lisbon and put himself at the head of an army to challenge Philip V. From then on, he and his brother, Holy Roman Emperor Joseph, rejected partition and relentlessly demanded the whole of the Spanish Monarchy for their dynasty. Habsburg pretensions received powerful support in Great Britain from the Whigs, the party in Parliament that championed an all-out continental war against France and Louis XIV. In 1707, the Whigs passed a motion of "no peace without Spain." The next year, after winning a decisive majority in parliamentary elections, they made this formula the basis of British grand strategy and foreign policy. For their part, after the victories of 1706, the Dutch came to think of their Barrier in far more expansive terms. It could, they realized, be more than just a redoubt against France; it would allow the Republic to dominate the southern Netherlands politically and economically. Therefore, in addition to a line of fortresses on the frontier, they began to press for the possession of important towns in the interior and along the coasts.[6]

But tensions among the Allies were escalating as fast as their ambitions. The Dutch revealed that their commitment to no peace without Spain was half-hearted at best by dispatching a bare minimum of troops to the Iberian theater.[7] In the southern Netherlands, Emperor Joseph and Archduke Charles were hostile to an extensive Dutch Barrier, having rightly concluded that it would reduce the Habsburgs to being sovereigns of the country in name only. The British were also opposed, fearing that Dutch control of the Flanders ports would shut London's merchants out of a lucrative market and gateway to the continent. By contrast, the British and Dutch were united against Austrian designs on Italy. Given its immense strategic and commercial importance, they had no desire to see the peninsula dominated by a single power. Finally, Great Britain and the Dutch Republic were vying for the trade of the Spanish Indies. In January 1708, the British convinced Archduke Charles to secretly award them the *Asiento*, the lucrative contract to supply slaves to Spain's American colonies. By 1709, these tensions were threating to become open divisions that could rupture the Grand Alliance.[8]

The increasingly fractious Allies were held together by the will and genius of three men: Marlborough, Heinsius, and Eugene. Torcy described this triumvirate as the animating "soul" of the enemy coalition. Officially, the three were just the servants of their sovereigns, linking their respective capitals to the battlefields and negotiating tables of the contest against France. In reality, they did not just implement the Allies' military and foreign policies; they made them. As the French foreign minister noted, "they drew up the plans, then decided on the moment, means, and manner of their execution."[9] For most of the War of the Spanish Succession, Heinsius' modest office on the ground floor of the Binnenhof in The Hague, where the triumvirs met between campaigns, was the true headquarters of the Grand Alliance.

Marlborough was the triumvirate's fulcrum. He had forged close friendships with both Heinsius and Eugene. Another indispensable friend was Sidney Godolphin, the brilliant administrator who, as lord high treasurer and Queen Anne's most important minister, directed Great Britain's war effort.[10] More than anyone else, Marlborough was committed to the total victory of the Grand Alliance. He did not just want to contain French power; he wished to see it permanently diminished.

French armies were to be broken on the battlefield. Then France was to be prevented from ever again threatening universal monarchy by a ring of powers that included a Habsburg-ruled Spain.[11] The former goal had been largely achieved by the crashing triumphs of Blenheim, Ramillies, Turin, and Oudenarde. The latter would soon be accomplished by dictating peace terms to a humbled Louis XIV and his bankrupt, starving kingdom.

Yet, even as Marlborough stood on the brink of success, the ground was shifting treacherously beneath his feet. He owed his preponderant place in British political, military, and diplomatic affairs to the faithful support of Queen Anne. That faith in turn depended on Anne's friendship with Marlborough's wife, Sarah. Beginning in 1683, the two had been inseparable. Their interactions were marked by an unusual intimacy and informality, with the queen famously insisting they call each other by nicknames: she was Mrs. Morley, Sarah Mrs. Freeman. However, by 1708, their relationship was dissolving. One cause was Anne wearying of Sarah's overbearing, waspish temperament and her constant lobbying for rewards for herself and her family. Another was politics. The queen was a moderate who was determined to rule above the rage of party. The Duchess of Marlborough was, in the words of her husband, a "true-born Whig" who unhesitatingly berated, belittled, and bullied Anne whenever she seemed inclined toward the Tories.[12]

The final dissolution began in August 1708. While on their way in the royal carriage to St. Paul's Cathedral to attend the celebrations for the victory of Oudenarde, the two women had a furious argument. It ended with Sarah peremptorily ordering Anne to be quiet. Then, in October, the queen's beloved consort Prince George of Denmark died. Far from offering comfort and sympathy, Sarah was cold and distant. Anne concluded their friendship was beyond repair. She had already found another companion and confidant in Abigail Masham. The new favorite was cousin to Robert Harley, Marlborough and Godolphin's great enemy and champion of peace with France. Masham became her relative's conduit to the queen.

Marlborough was well aware that his wife's fall from favor posed a mortal danger to his position and policies. In an attempt to shore up both, he made a rash and desperate move. In March 1709, he met with Anne and asked her to appoint him captain general of her armies for life. He then repeated his request in a letter after he returned to the continent later in the spring. On both occasions, Anne was politely evasive. In fact, she was alarmed by his overweening ambition: he was aiming, she feared, to become a new Cromwell. Marlborough would continue to pursue the issue, oblivious to the fact that he was further alienating the queen.[13]

Like Marlborough, Anthonie Heinsius was determined to humble France. Born in 1641, the son of a prosperous sugar refiner and municipal politician, he had been educated in law and philosophy at the universities of Leiden and Angers, then joined the government of his hometown of Delft. At the age of thirty-eight, he became Delft's pensionary. He soon attracted the attention of William III, who came to admire his integrity and considerable political gifts. In 1683, the Stadholder sent him to the French court to try to secure the return of the Principality of Orange. There, he was treated with exemplary harshness by the Marquis de Louvois—at one point, the French war minister threatened to have him thrown in the Bastille.[14] After this experience, he was completely won over to William's view that France and its pretensions to universal monarchy represented the greatest threat to the tranquility and stability of Europe. In 1689, Heinsius was appointed grand pensionary of Holland, becoming William's chief lieutenant in the Republic. After his master's untimely death in 1702, he inherited the struggle against the Sun King.[15]

Thanks to his political moderation, modest demeanor, and masterful handling of his country's byzantine ruling institutions, Heinsius dominated Dutch policymaking. Contrary to both British fears and French hopes, there was never a peace party in the Republic. Heinsius knew his people were growing increasingly war-weary. However, he sought a final peace—"such a one that will prevent us finding France on our necks every seven or eight years." It would require the Republic having a formidable Barrier as well as an extensive system of allies. It could only be achieved, Heinsius calculated, by the continued unity of the Maritime Powers. He therefore refused to contemplate abandoning the Grand Alliance and making a separate treaty with Louis XIV. He was even willing to see Great Britain take the lead in key areas of grand strategy and diplomacy, most notably the fate of Spain.[16]

Of the triumvirs, Eugene had the most reason to hate France and its ruler. He had been born a great aristocrat at the court of the Sun King. But his life there had been deeply unhappy. His mother, the intelligent and strong-willed Olympia Mancini, had been exiled by royal order after being implicated in the infamous scandal called the Affair of the Poisons. Then, when the nineteen-year-old Eugene had asked for the command of a regiment, Louis, out of loathing for his debauchery and rumored homosexuality, had coldly turned him down. These and other humiliations had driven him to take service with France's oldest and most inveterate enemy, the House of Habsburg. He had long since repudiated his origins, instead considering himself a Savoyard prince. He also nurtured a powerful desire for revenge. France, he declared, was "a monster" that must be slain.[17]

At the beginning of 1709, the monster's death appeared to be at hand. Emperor Joseph, his ministers, and Eugene realized they needed to define their goals for a peace treaty. In February and March, they met in Vienna to draw them up. Swept up by a sense of triumph over their ancient adversary, they decided to push for maximum demands. The Spanish Monarchy must go in its entirety to Archduke Charles. For Philip, there could be no compensation in Italy whatsoever. Domination of the entire Italian peninsula had emerged as a Habsburg sine qua non because of an incipient succession crisis in Vienna. Empress Amalia had failed to produce a male child, and the possibility of one was growing more remote with each passing day. Joseph's heir was therefore likely to be his brother Charles. The Habsburgs had to control Italy in order to connect his two great inheritances.

After deciding on the goals of their dynasty, the emperor and his advisors turned to those of the Holy Roman Empire. Having suffered from Louis' ambitions for forty years, the German princes wanted security from French aggression in the form of a *Reichsbarriere*, a buffer zone on the west bank of the Rhine. It would be created by forcing Louis to surrender Alsace, especially Strasbourg, and Franche-Comté. To wring further territorial concessions from him, the Habsburgs would refuse to restore the Wittelsbach electors to Bavaria and Cologne. If the French king insisted on some compensation for his allies, he would then have to cede a series of fortresses on the border with Lorraine.[18]

The snows of the Great Winter had besieged Vienna more closely than the Turks. When they finally retreated and the roads west became passable again, Prince Eugene set out for the Low Countries. He arrived in Brussels on March 27. As soon as he learned of Torcy's meeting with Heinsius, he hurried to The Hague. From England, Marlborough took the first ship for the continent. Together, the triumvirs would give the law to the Sun King.

On May 1, Louis, Madame de Maintenon, and a carefully chosen group of courtiers arrived at the château of Marly. Even in that dreary spring, it was breathtakingly beautiful.[19] It was located five miles north of Versailles in a secluded valley surrounded by forests teeming with game. When Marly's construction began in 1678, the king's architect Jules Hardouin-Mansart eschewed the imposing grandeur of the classic French royal palace, instead taking as his model the graceful Palladian villas of Italy. The chateau's heart was the Royal Pavilion, which had the appearance and dimensions of a stately country house. Its ground floor featured a spacious octagonal salon and just four apartments: one for the king, another for his consort, and two for members of the royal family. Flanking it and arranged around a long water mirror were two rows each of six smaller guest pavilions. The buildings' façades were covered by colorful trompe l'oeil frescoes designed by Charles Le Brun and depicting scenes from Greek mythology—those of the Royal Pavilion of course featured Apollo. The château was set amid gardens and groves of unrivaled sumptuousness. It was also located close to the Seine, and the Machine of Marly—the largest engine of its time, consisting of fourteen gigantic wheels and 259 pumps—brought the river's water to fill vast reservoirs and basins. Unlike at Versailles, Louis could always delight in the play of waterfalls and fountains.

Marly was unlike Versailles in another, even more important respect. It was not accessible to the public. It was the king's private retreat, open only to those who received an invitation from Louis himself. Whenever he announced he was going there, he would be importuned by his courtiers with the famous formula "Sire, Marley?" From among them, he would choose at most a hundred gentlemen and ladies. The resulting guest list was sacrosanct: the uninvited, including the most exalted aristocrats, were barred from going.

At Marly, in the intimate company of his family, friends, and guests, Louis found relief from the turbulent crowds and interminable ceremonies of Versailles. The etiquette of the court, if not abandoned entirely, was considerably relaxed. Men could wear their hats in the king's presence. Women could don more comfortable informal attire instead of their cumbersome, constricting court habits. The chateau and its surrounding domain offered many entertainments. The salon of the Royal Pavilion hosted dinners, balls, masquerades, concerts, and games of all kinds. The gardens and groves contained courses for *jeu de mail* (an early version of golf), a large swing, and a *ramasse* (a kind of primitive roller coaster). Marly's chief diversion, though, was hunting. Louis was addicted to it his entire life. From a young age he had been a crack shot, able to bring down scores of rabbits and birds at each outing. His greatest pleasure was the chase for boar, wolves, and, especially, deer. When old age forced him from horseback, he transferred to a light, two-wheeled carriage called a *soufflet*. According to Saint-Simon, he drove it at breakneck speed with superlative skill on even the narrowest forest paths. Given Marly's many attractions, it is hardly surprising that Louis spent more and more time there: after 1707, a third of the year.

In these Arcadian surroundings, the king might have hoped for a respite from the cares and demands of the war. Any such hopes were soon dashed, for the war found him. On May 9, Marshal Villars arrived at Marly. He had rushed down from Arras for emergency conferences with Louis and the court high command. Although Torcy had begun peace talks with the Allies, it was more important than ever that the Army of Flanders be able to leave its winter quarters, take the field, and occupy the position Villars had chosen for it at La Bassée. Doing so would strengthen Torcy in the negotiations at The Hague. And if the talks failed, the Army of Flanders had to be ready to face the Allied invasion. But the Army's supply situation was desperate. The breakdown of the *munitionnaire* company of François Mauricet de La Cour had left Flanders' magazines empty. Weeks of frantic searching had resulted in promises from various aristocrats, provisioners, and intendants to furnish perhaps 50,000 sacks of grain.[20] These promises fell far short of the army's needs for the campaigning season. In January, Marshal Boufflers had estimated these requirements at 210,000 sacks. Villars had come looking for help.

At five in the evening, he walked into the gardens of Marly. Believing the king was still out hunting, he first went to pay his respects to the vivacious and charming Duchesse de Bourgogne and her companions. He had just begun conversing with these ladies when he was summoned to see Louis, who was changing out of his hunting clothes. The king spoke briefly to the marshal but promised him a longer interview later. It took place that night in the apartment of Madame de Maintenon. Also present was War Minister Chamillart. The next day, another meeting was held, this time including Marshal Boufflers, who, after recovering from his illness, had been serving as the king's personal military adviser. On both occasions, Villars described in detail the plight of his troops and the scarcity of supplies of all sorts on the Flanders frontier.[21] Immediately after this second conference, Villars rushed off to Paris. On May 11, in his wife's house, he conferred with La Cour, who admitted his company had nothing to give the army. He was back at Marly on May 12. After his supper, to the surprise and dismay of his guests, the king retreated to his apartment. There he convened a special war council. In attendance were the Dauphin, the Duc de Bourgogne, Ministers Chamillart and Desmaretz, and Marshals Boufflers, Harcourt, and Villars. For nearly three hours, they discussed and debated France's prospects for the coming campaign. Once again, Villars described the precarious state of his army and stressed his need for more support. But it was clear that little more would be forthcoming. At the war council's end, the king embraced him and said, "I put my trust in God and in you, and I cannot order you to do anything since I cannot give you any help."[22]

Even for a soldier as self-confident and optimistic as Villars, the results of these meetings were sobering. Nevertheless, he remained determined to put his army into the field as soon as possible. His first thought upon returning to Arras on May 15 was for the peace talks at The Hague. The Allies, he feared, were so convinced the French would be unable to resist Marlborough's and Eugene's armies because of lack of supplies that they would dictate the harshest possible terms. He therefore wrote to Torcy, assuring him "that the months of June and July for the army are very secure, the initial fear of running out of grain has ebbed away, and we have found enough in the provinces." The marshal went on to encourage the foreign minister to remain firm in the negotiations, even to be ready to break off the talks if the enemy's demands proved too onerous:

> These are truths I am telling you, monsieur, but solely with the view that you do not believe it would be such a great misfortune if peace is not achieved. I will tell you with all sincerity that every time I look at our troops, I ardently desire that they face the enemy. When I think of our people, I understand they wish for peace, but glory and the true interest of the nation might be to have it later, so long as it is better.[23]

But when Villars tried to give substance to these words, he found himself in serious trouble. On May 18, he met with the intendants of the frontier provinces and the *munitionnaire* François Raffy to ascertain what supplies were actually available in Flanders. To his surprise and dismay, he learned that the bulk of the promised wheat and flour, particularly 18,000 sacks from Lorraine, had failed to arrive. Moreover, the troops of the frontier garrisons were steadily eating up whatever provisions were on hand. According to an inventory drawn up by Raffy, there were just 5,700 sacks of flour left for the field army: 2,000 at Arras, 700 at Douai, and 3,000 on the way from Verdun. This amount was ludicrously paltry—Villars estimated that, once mobilized, the Army of Flanders would consume more than 1,200 sacks per day.[24]

He now resorted to drastic measures. He issued an order to the intendants of Flanders, Artois, and Hainault. The supplies being accumulated for the field army were not to be touched. To feed the troops quartered in their provinces, the intendants were to requisition grain and flour from the king's subjects on the promise of future repayment from the *munitionnaire* companies. But almost immediately, Villars expanded the scope of this order. The frontier towns, in addition to providing for their garrisons, were to furnish extra supplies for the army. The marshal acknowledged to the king that this command was harsh—it effectively imposed a grain tax at a time of burgeoning hunger. Nevertheless, imposing it was the only way that enough provisions could be stockpiled for him to enter the campaign. The king and his ministers agreed. On May 25, Controller General Desmaretz declared that Picardy must also provide grain to the tune of an additional 15,000 sacks.[25]

Villars' measures proved deeply unpopular with the intendants, particularly Louis de Bernage of Artois. His province was the frontline against the Allies. It hosted large garrisons and most of the units of the Army of Flanders. And by late May, it was firmly in the grip of famine. The people of Artois would be infuriated by the sight of grain being taken from their communities to stock the royal magazines. Bernage was a capable administrator with considerable experience in military logistics: he had previously served in Franche-Comté, another frontier province and a key base for French armies operating on the Rhine and in Germany. He was so certain that Villars' orders would provoke a wave of uprisings that he first asked War Minister Chamillart to confirm they had the full support of the king.[26]

As he had feared, when the intendant began requisitioning provisions in Artois and Picardy, he encountered widespread and escalating opposition. It could not be mollified by promises that the royal government would either promptly pay for the seized grain or replace it with fresh supplies brought in from other provinces or from overseas. Bernage dashed off a letter to Villars declaring he required military support if he were to continue making requisitions. Without troops to intimidate the populace, Bernage warned, he would be "lighting a fire of sedition more difficult to extinguish than can be imagined." The marshal sent no support, for he was then assembling the field army. On May 30, Bernage was attempting to levy 1,500 sacks of wheat from the inhabitants of Arras. A crowd of women gathered and besieged the house of the official charged with the task, crying furiously that they would not see their bread taken away from them. The town watch and the town magistrates were at first able to quell the riot. But the next morning the women surged back onto the streets in even greater numbers. They blocked the grain wagons from leaving the town and defied all efforts to disperse them. Order was only restored after Villars finally dispatched troops, including elite companies of the Gendarmes and the Maison du Roi. But resistance to requisitioning did not cease. Just three days after the rebellion at Arras, Bernage was warning Desmaretz that only strong bodies of troops could extract more grain from Artois and Picardy because of the chronic outbreak of revolts.[27]

In spite of this popular hostility, grain at last began to flow into the magazines of the Army of Flanders. The Marquise de Sailly's 3,500 sacks of wheat arrived. More trickled in from Lorraine, the Soissonnais, and Champagne as well as the frontier provinces. Then a new problem arose: turning the wheat into flour. This work was done by mills. Dotting the countryside and found in all cities and towns, these were some of the most important and advanced industrial enterprises of the day. Yet, even when all the mills in the campaigning area were pressed into service, their output was not at all commensurate with the army's urgent needs. A handful of the largest could grind 50–60 pounds of grain per day; most could manage just 8–10 pounds. Such limitations meant that one of the essential duties of a *munitionnaire* was to create a large stockpile of flour well before the beginning of the campaigning season: best practice was to have a two-month supply on hand. Empty magazines during the 1708–1709 winter quarters meant this reserve could not be created. The Flanders provisioners and royal officials now had no choice except to process grain as soon as they could get their hands on some. Swamped, the mills could not keep up with demand. As a result, there was never enough flour. So dire did the situation become that François-Marie

Fargès, the army's fodder supplier who had also become one of its chief *munitionnaires*, begged to be relieved of his post. Villars had to employ all his powers to persuade him to stay on.[28]

And lack of food was just the most serious and urgent challenge the marshal faced as he strove to put his army into the field. Shortage of funds was another. Because of the failures of the treasury of the *Extraordinaire des Guerres*, the principal military paymaster, very little money had reached the forces on the Flanders front over the winter. The April default of Samuel Bernard and Controller General Desmaretz's hugely expensive bailout of the too-big-to-fail banker had then made matters much worse. The wages of the rank and file were weeks or months in arrears. The officers were in even poorer shape. They were missing not just their salaries but also the allowances to refurbish their units with new recruits, uniforms, and equipment. If they had received any money at all, it was in the form of a glut of discredited paper credit instruments which they could only spend at huge discounts. As a result, they were facing enormous difficulties restoring themselves and the troops under their command to fighting trim.

The great dangers posed by unpaid, neglected troops were mutiny, marauding, and desertion. If these had occurred with enough frequency and on a large enough scale, they might have rendered the Army of Flanders hors de combat before it had a chance to enter the campaign. That they did not was due to the efforts of royal intendants, provincial authorities, municipal officials, and army officers, all of whom fed their own funds into the army. Louis de Bernage sent letter after letter to the royal ministers complaining that he was exhausting his personal credit to provide at least some pay to the regiments quartered in Artois and Picardy. His colleagues, Claude Le Blanc of Dunkirk, Charles-Étienne de Bernières of Flanders, and Jean-Charles Doujat of Hainault, were doing the same. In May, Madame Doujat borrowed 28,000 livres in her own name, then handed the money over to her husband for distribution to the troops. Town after town on the frontier raised loans for the wages of their garrisons. The magistrates of Tournai distinguished themselves by their prodigious efforts for the numerous regiments in their city.[29]

Then, there were the colonels and captains of the army itself. They have been aptly described as holders of royal military franchises. The king commissioned them and provided significant financial support in the form not just of pay but allowances for a range of military expenses. It was then understood that these officers would devote their personal fortunes to help sustain their units—regiments for colonels and companies for captains. They used their coin and credit to pay for recruits, uniforms, weapons, horses, rations, even wages. In 1706, Marshal Boufflers had invested 38,000 livres in a new infantry regiment; its colonel was his twelve-year-old son. A captain of infantry spent about 500 livres annually on his company, one of cavalry 1,000–1,500 livres. All in all, officer contributions represented one-fifth of all spending on the royal army. The king knew this was an onerous burden and so he maintained a mechanism that gave his colonels and captains a chance to recoup their investments: they could sell their units. Dangeau's and Sourches' diaries show that Versailles was the site of a lively market in regiments and companies. During the War of the Spanish Succession, the average price of an infantry regiment was 43,500 livres, a dragoon regiment 89,909 livres, and a cavalry regiment 81,292 livres. Prestigious units could be worth much more: in 1704, the Gardes francaises changed hands for 500,000 livres.[30]

But during 1709, the orderly financial arrangements between the king and his officer franchise-holders broke down. As the flow of funds from the royal war treasuries to the army sputtered to a trickle then often dried up completely, colonels and captains found they had to pour more and more of their own resources into their units to keep them viable. Some officers were wealthy enough to cope. Joseph Sevin, Chevalier de Quincy and captain in the régiment de Bourgogne-infanterie, complained bitterly about receiving his pay in almost worthless subsistence bills. Nevertheless, he never seemed short of money. He was able to pass the winter quarters in Paris, where he occupied himself with reading for pleasure, playing music, going to balls, and indulging in gallantries with ladies of quality. He also bought two splendid new uniforms. More importantly, during his sojourn in the capital, he was able to recruit his company up to strength. He claimed to have used a favorite trick to great effect: he put up posters advertising that he was recruiting for the cavalry, which brought in more prospects. Only once they were before him did he announce they would, in fact, be joining the infantry. A more likely explanation for his success was his ability to use his own funds to offer attractive enlistment bounties. He even agreed to supplement the wages of one recruit, a down-on-his-luck English lord.[31]

Few officers were as lucky as the Chevalier de Quincy. Most had to turn to their families for help, go into debt, or both. A typical example was Pierre de Saint-Mayme, a minor noble of Périgord and a veteran captain in the Beaufermé infantry regiment. In March, while in winter quarters at Mons, he asked his older brother, the Chevalier de Cablan, for money "in good coin and not in mint bills (*billets de monnaie*)." "We have not touched even a single sou for a long time," he warned, "and I would be embarrassed if you do not do this for me." Three months later, after his battalion had joined the field army, his predicament had only grown worse, and he pleaded:

> I absolutely need one hundred *écus* for my company. We are in a time when no one has even a single *pistole*; no friend or comrade has any resources. Please try to do me this favor, otherwise I will have to abandon everything.

Money from the Chevalier de Cablan was slow to reach Captain de Saint-Mayme. In the meantime, he was forced to borrow four *louis d'or* for his most pressing necessities. At last, on September 3, he wrote a letter thanking his brother for 250 *livres* that had just arrived. Eight days later, Captain de Saint-Mayme was killed at the Battle of Malplaquet.[32]

Contributions such as these from a wide variety of royal officials, local notables, and army officers were enough to keep the troops obedient and in good order. There were no repetitions in May of the widespread mutinies that had earlier wracked the Flanders frontier. However, Villars knew that he required a substantial delivery of funds from the royal treasury if the Army of Flanders was to enter the campaign. For weeks, he badgered the king, Marshal Boufflers, and the royal ministers. At last, on May 22, Desmaretz was able to respond. The arrival of American silver and the reminting of the currency had brought an influx of specie into the royal mints. The controller general was able to rush carts loaded with 70,000 livres in gold to Arras and 270,000 livres in silver to Douai. Villars immediately employed most of this windfall on the long-suffering subaltern officers, most of whom had gone unpaid since January: infantry lieutenants received 100 livres, cavalry lieutenants 150 livres. Desmaretz promised him more shipments. But five days later, Chamillart cautioned the marshal that he should not expect these anytime soon: coin was pouring into the mints, which were now hopelessly overwhelmed and struggling to produce new money.[33]

Even while he was grappling with shortages of food and funds, Villars also had to deal with the supply of fodder. The Army of Flanders would be bringing into the field an enormous number of horses: at least 60,000. They included not just the cavalry's animals but also those belonging to officers, the artillery, and the supply trains. Feeding them was an immense and complex logistical burden. Each horse's daily ration was either twenty-two pounds of dry fodder (hay, straw, and oats) or fifty pounds of grass and some oats. In January, Marshal Boufflers had calculated the Flanders army's fodder requirements for the entire campaign at four million rations.[34]

Unfortunately, Flanders' magazines were just as empty of fodder as they were of grain. The war ministry had contracted Fargès to be the army's fodder supplier, but the treasury of the *Extraordinaire des Guerres* had failed to pay him: at the beginning of May, he was owed 5 million livres. As with food and funds, French officials and officers were forced to resort to a variety of stopgaps. Louis de Bernage found a merchant of

Béthune named Joffre who was willing to supply fodder. He also prevailed on the Estates of Artois, the province's main administrative body, to provide some. Intendants Le Blanc, Bernières, and Doujat made similar efforts in their provinces. Enough fodder was scraped together in April and May to put the army's horses on short rations: ten pounds of hay or eight pounds of hay and five of straw. The crack cavalry companies of the Maison du Roi and the Gendarmes were kept back at the Somme so that their mounts could be better fed.[35]

The shortages of food, funds, and fodder were serious obstacles to the Army of Flanders being able to take the field. Would the myriad improvisations and makeshift measures be enough to overcome them? On May 22, Villars wrote to the king with an answer:

> By milling everywhere day and night and by exhausting all of the resources on this frontier which can be imagined, I hope to be able to count on eight to nine thousand sacks of flour by the end of the month.
>
> With this very feeble resource, I plan to march the day after tomorrow with fifty battalions and eighty squadrons to La Bassée to begin the building of the lines. Before yesterday, I did not believe that it would be possible to bring the troops out of their garrisons. If I had given any credence to the widespread opinion concerning the impossibility of concentrating the army, I would have kept my forces dispersed, which would have been the most dangerous of all dispositions.

Five days later, Villars led forty battalions onto the Plain of Lens behind La Bassée. They included some of the army's best units: the Gardes françaises, the Gardes suisses, the *vieux* regiments of Picardie, Piémont, and Champagne, and the *petits vieux* Bourbonnais, and du Roi. To make up for the shortage of fodder, the marshal spread his squadrons over a wide area so their horses could fatten themselves on the spring grass. To eke out his scarce rations for as long as possible, he kept the rest of the army a day's march from the front. Despite the precarious state of his logistics, leading out his troops had revived Villars' fighting spirit. "Voila, the king's army on campaign," he gasconaded to Controller General Desmaretz, "despite the opinion of our enemies which was confirmed to them by all their friends."

> I do not know what this cursed opinion will cost us, but I very much desire for the glory of the king and of the nation and the good of the State, that there should be a battle before the fifteenth of June. I see an ardor in our troops, a shame of the last campaign, and a desire to erase it by some great action that gives me great hopes.[36]

Whether Villars' optimism and the ardor of his troops were to be tested depended on the outcome of the peace negotiations at The Hague. On May 30, the Marquis de Torcy called on him at Douai. The foreign minister was hurrying back to court. The Allies' terms, he informed the marshal, were humiliating, and he could not advise the king to accept them.[37]

Before Torcy had left Versailles on May 1, Louis made it clear to him that he was willing to make extraordinary concessions to the Allies in return for peace. For the Dutch, he would include Maubeuge in their Barrier. It would be in addition to the other places already yielded up by Rouillé in April: Furnes, Ypres, and Menin. The Republic would then have a formidable line of fortresses on the Netherlands' frontier with France stretching from the North Sea to the Sambre and Meuse. If the Dutch still demanded more, Torcy was authorized to give them Tournai. As for Lille, the foreign minister was to do his utmost to obtain its return. But if he concluded it was absolutely necessary to secure a peace treaty, he could surrender the capital of Flanders, the first and proudest of the Sun King's conquests. For the Habsburgs and the princes of the Empire, Torcy was to argue strenuously for the Rhine frontier established by the 1697 Treaty of Ryswick. But if the Germans insisted on the boundaries of the 1648 Peace of Westphalia, which would result in much of Alsace as well as Strasbourg restored to the Empire, he was to consent. For the British, the foreign minister was to present an elegant answer to their demand that Louis cease harboring and supporting the Stuart pretender: after peace was made, James Stuart himself would ask to leave France.

Only on one point was Torcy to act forcefully: he was to obtain a crown and realm for Philip. He was to stress to the Allied leaders that Louis' many and far-reaching sacrifices should make them look with favor on his grandson's claims to Naples and Sicily. He was to remind the Dutch that Bruno van der Dussen and Willem Buys, their representatives in the talks with Rouillé, had already signaled the Republic's support for this démarche. Yet, even here, Louis was prepared to compromise if it meant clinching a war-ending agreement. If Habsburg and British opposition to Philip's possession of both Italian territories proved too strong to overcome, the foreign minister could cede Sicily.[38]

When he reached The Hague on May 6, Torcy knew he had been dealt a weak hand. Nevertheless, he was determined to play it skillfully and well. He planned to force the Allies to reveal their true intentions and goals, then exploit divisions among them. He no longer hoped to break up the enemy coalition. He was now aiming to extract the most favorable possible terms for France. The weakest link remained the Dutch, and he intended to entice them from their allegiance to the British and the Habsburgs. Until the arrival of Eugene and Marlborough, he would be dealing only with Heinsius. Over eight days of meetings, the French foreign minister offered every concession on the Barrier. He ceded both Maubeuge and Tournai, then even agreed to surrender Lille. To his dismay, Heinsius did not become any more sympathetic to the French. Instead, he declared that the Republic was tied by treaties as well as goodwill to its Allies and would only make peace if their demands were met. These demands went even further than what the French king was willing to concede. In addition to the recognition of the Protestant Succession and the removal of the Stuarts from France, the British sought the dismantling of the fortifications of Dunkirk and the demolition of its port. The Imperial princes wanted their own barrier carved out of France's eastern frontier territories, including Strasbourg. Most importantly, the British and the Habsburgs would be satisfied only with the entire Spanish Monarchy going to the Archduke Charles. There could therefore be no Italian kingdom for Philip. When the grand pensionary was pressed for what he thought would be a suitable compensation for the Bourbon prince, he responded that it was up to Louis to give him part of France: he suggested Franche-Comté. Torcy summed up the results of this round of negotiations by observing to Louis that "all the nations are conspiring against Your Majesty, using their fear of his power to enrich themselves at his expense in a situation they believe is favorable to their claims."[39]

At Marly, Torcy's dispatches deepened Louis' sense that he was beleaguered on all sides by disaster and danger. Famine was spreading inexorably across his kingdom, and his starving subjects were growing ever more restive. The uprisings that had swept across the provinces were reaching the capital. On April 28, a serious riot took place outside the church of Saint-Roch. It was only quelled by the intervention of the Swiss Guard. Since then, tensions remained high. The Duc de la Rochefoucauld and the Duc de Bouillon reported that extremely insolent posters had been found on walls all over the city.[40] As for the French treasury, what little money and credit it had left had gone to rescue the insolvent Samuel Bernard. No help appeared to be quickly forthcoming from the recently arrived American treasure nor from the imminent reminting of the coinage. Lastly, Louis had just met with Marshal Villars, who had told him about the desperate plight of the Flanders army. It is hardly surprising that Louis' mood became dark and despairing. "What is most unfortunate is the inner pain of the king," Madame de Maintenon confided to the Duc de Noailles. "It makes me fear for everything despite his wonderful temperament." The only remedy his doctors could prescribe was their favorite cure-all, an emetic. Amazingly, this bit of quackery briefly raised the royal spirits.[41]

On May 14, Louis informed Torcy that he was willing to take a hitherto unthinkable step if it meant that peace could be made:

> Although it seems that there is nothing more I can sacrifice in order to procure for my people the peace they so desperately need, nevertheless I want to add a new one. If it is absolutely impossible to induce the English to consent to leave the kingdoms of Naples and Sicily, or just the first, to the king my grandson, and if the latest resolutions of the Dutch are that peace depends on the will of this nation, I finally wish, at the last extremity, to reserve no state for the king my grandson, and to promise also to give him no assistance for his own defense.

This was a momentous decision. Louis had gone to war to make Philip ruler of the entire Spanish Monarchy. When he dispatched his foreign minister to The Hague, he was still resolved to gain him an impressive kingdom in Italy as a consolation for giving up his Spanish throne. Now he was forsaking even this demand, so that nothing remained of his original war aims. Moreover, all that he was seeking in return was to keep Dunkirk and Strasbourg.[42]

Louis did hold out one slim hope that he could still achieve peace on more favorable terms for both him and Philip. It involved the Duke of Marlborough. The king and the Marquis de Torcy had long viewed the captain general as overweeningly avaricious—so much so that they could bribe him into championing their diplomatic efforts. When they had made their first attempt at peace negotiations in 1705, they had instructed their envoy, the Marquis d'Alègre, to secretly offer Marlborough 2 million livres in exchange for his support for French demands.[43] This view of Marlborough as biddable then seemed to be confirmed three years later. Immediately after the fall of Lille to the Allies on October 30, 1708, the captain general contacted Marshal Berwick, his nephew by his sister Arabella. He advised Berwick to urge Louis to seek peace openly and publicly. He then declared he would aid this initiative for a price: "You may be assured that I shall be wholeheartedly for peace, not doubting that I will find the goodwill that was promised me two years ago by the Marquis d'Alègre."[44] Torcy and the other royal ministers considered this proposal seriously enough to conclude that paying Marlborough 2 or even 3 million livres for his services was an excellent value. In the end, though, nothing came of it, for Louis and Chamillart calculated that they could recapture Lille in the next campaign, which would give them the upper hand in peace negotiations. Chamillart wrote a letter in Berwick's name brusquely rebuffing his uncle.[45]

Now Louis ordered Torcy to approach Marlborough as soon as he arrived at The Hague and make him a new offer. Not only was the bid for his services significantly increased, but the exact amount he would receive would also depend on what he was able to achieve. If Marlborough could obtain Naples and Sicily for Philip as well as preserve Dunkirk and Strasbourg for France, his douceur would be 4 million livres. It would be

3 million livres for the Italian lands and one of the two frontier fortresses, and 2 million livres for either the Italian lands or the frontier fortresses. Of these outcomes, Louis emphasized that he preferred a kingdom for his grandson.[46]

Torcy was forced to wait before he could play this gambit: Marlborough's ship was delayed by contrary winds. After a very rough Channel crossing, he finally arrived at The Hague on May 18.[47] The French foreign minister immediately demanded a private meeting. It took place after dinner in Marlborough's quarters in the house of the Earl of Albemarle. The captain general began by expressing his deep respect for the king of France, declaring that he hoped one day to be worthy of his protection. Then, with artful delicacy, he brought up his dealings with the Marquis d'Alègre and Marshal Berwick. Torcy seized this opening. He informed Marlborough that he and Louis were aware of every detail of these interactions and their feelings on them had not changed. The duke blushed deeply. Then he went on to describe Great Britain's peace terms. The message was clear: this time, Marlborough would not be bribed.[48]

His approaches to Heinsius and Marlborough having failed, all that was left for Torcy was to face the triumvirs together. Their first meeting took place on May 20 in Heinsius' house. In a desperate attempt to coax the Allied leaders into a more conciliatory posture, Torcy had informed each of them of Louis' willingness to give up any compensation for Philip vacating the Spanish throne. But the triumvirs were implacable. They instead sought even more territorial concessions in Italy, Germany, and the New World. Most galling for Torcy was Eugene's demand that France return all of Alsace, including Strasbourg, to the Empire. Accepting it would push the French frontier back to what it had been before the Thirty Years' War. Moreover, when added to the other territories France was ceding in Flanders and Italy, it would mean surrendering all of the gains of Louis' reign. During a second conference the next day, the French foreign minister offered to restore Strasbourg as an Imperial Free City. Eugene angrily rejected this compromise, announcing that he was determined to rip up the Peace of Westphalia. Torcy then asked for the return of his passports, intending to leave The Hague and the talks. Before he could go, Heinsius intervened. The grand pensionary beseeched Torcy to reconsider, arguing that they had made too much progress in the negotiations to give up. More importantly, he offered to intercede with Eugene and persuade him to accept the Rhine frontier established by Westphalia. Torcy was mollified enough to return to the negotiating table.[49]

The third meeting between the French foreign minister and the Allied triumvirs took place on May 23. True to his word, Heinsius had persuaded Eugene to accept a compromise on Alsace. Yet no sooner was this issue settled than a new and, as it turned out, far more intractable one appeared. Torcy declared that once his royal master had accepted the terms they had negotiated, an armistice between France and the Grand Alliance would immediately come into effect. The triumvirs strongly objected. They pointed out that the results of The Hague talks only applied to Louis himself; what guarantees did they have that Philip would accept them and agree to meekly leave Spain? Torcy pointed out that his king had promised to withdraw all help from his grandson; the minister was not authorized to offer anything more. Heinsius then proposed that the French surrender three fortified towns in France and three in Spain as pledges for their good behavior; these would be in addition to everything they had already agreed to cede permanently. Torcy angrily rejected this proposal. Fourteen hours of often heated discussion failed to resolve the impasse.[50]

Once again, the talks teetered on the brink of collapse. This time, it was Torcy who ended the deadlock. On the evening of May 24, he went to Heinsius and invited him to set down the Allies' terms in writing as formal articles. Throughout the talks, the Allies had constantly changed and escalated their demands. Torcy wished to put an end to this. He also had a more devious motive. By having the Allies define exactly what they wanted, he was making a final attempt to encourage divisions among them.[51]

Torcy's stroke was well timed. Since his arrival at The Hague, the Allies had maintained an impressive unity. It was based on the triumvirs' conviction that France was close to collapse. Their frontier outposts and patrols had fed them a steady stream of information about the ramshackle state of the French forces in Flanders. The Dutch and the British had excellent intelligence networks in France itself, which kept them apprised of widespread hardships and escalating turmoil. Perhaps most importantly, Marlborough had a well-placed spy at the French court whose regular reports told of deepening despair among Louis and his chief servants.[52] As Torcy had feared, the Allied leaders were determined to make use of France's desperate condition to push for maximum gains.

But the cracks in the Grand Alliance were also threatening to emerge. On May 23, Count Philippe von Sinzendorf, one of Emperor Joseph's most trusted ministers and an experienced diplomat, arrived at The Hague to assist Eugene. He quickly became embroiled in a bitter dispute with the Dutch over their schemes for an expansive Barrier. The arguments became so heated that Marlborough at first feared the Allies would be compelled to break off discussions with the French. Fortunately, Eugene and Heinsius were able to finesse the issue. The articles presented to Torcy would name only the French fortresses that were to be included in the Barrier. Strongholds from the Spanish Netherlands would be designated only after further negotiations between the Dutch Republic and the Habsburgs.[53]

The most contentious and difficult issue remained Spain. The British and Habsburgs had made no peace without Spain their fundamental war aim. The Dutch were committed to this policy out of a desire to preserve their alliance with Great Britain at all costs. Yet the Allied position in Iberia was weak. In April 1707, Marshal Berwick had crushed the main Allied army in Spain at the Battle of Almanza. Philip V had gone on to consolidate his grip on Castile, the largest, most populous, and most powerful of the Spanish kingdoms. In April 1709, the Castilians had made a spectacular show of their loyalty to their Bourbon ruler when the Cortes, their national assembly, did homage to Philip's heir, the one-year-old Louis, Prince of Asturias. By contrast, the Allies were largely confined to Portugal and Catalonia, where the Archduke Charles had his court at Barcelona. Then, on May 7, the Allies suffered a fresh setback when the Earl of Galway's army was beaten by a Spanish force under the Marquis de Bay at Campo Maior in Portugal.[54]

Since the Allies lacked a guarantee that Philip would obey The Hague conditions, they faced the very real possibility of having to fight a new, costly, possibly prolonged war to drive him out of Spain. Marlborough had already considered this eventuality and come up with a plan. As soon as the king of France had agreed to an armistice, the Allies would transport their main armies to Iberia. Marlborough would invade Castile with one army from Portugal, Eugene with another from Catalonia. They would effect a junction at Madrid. The captain general did not anticipate the Spanish offering much serious resistance. One campaigning season would likely be enough to secure Spain for its new Habsburg king.[55]

Despite Marlborough's confidence, this option was completely unacceptable to the Dutch. Removing the Allied armies from Flanders would leave their Republic exposed and defenseless. Meanwhile, a respite from war would allow France to rapidly recover its strength. Heinsius and the other Dutch statesmen did not trust Louis XIV at all. In their eyes, throughout his long reign, he had shown a dangerous combination of boundless ambition and lack of respect for international agreements. He would have no scruples about abrogating the armistice with the Grand Alliance and invading the Low Countries to recover everything he had lost. He might even overrun the Dutch provinces as he had during the disaster year of 1672. For the Dutch, then, the only acceptable outcome of The Hague negotiations was a general peace that embraced both France and Spain. As for the problem of evicting Philip from his kingdom, it was likely the grand pensionary who came up with an altogether different solution: have Louis accomplish it for the Allies.[56] This would not mean he would have to resort to arms. Although Torcy had told Heinsius during their first conference that Louis "could not, even if he were willing, oblige the king of Spain to resign all his dominions," his warning was ignored.[57] For the Allies remained convinced that Versailles completely controlled and dominated Madrid. Surely it would be enough for the French king to command his grandson to depart. The trick would be to compel Louis to do so.

Heinsius needed two days to transform the Allies' demands into forty articles. He first showed them to Marlborough and Eugene, who approved them. On the morning of May 27, he summoned Torcy to his house on the Denneweg. There, the grand pensionary presented the articles to the French foreign minister as the Preliminaries of The Hague. Most constituted a long list of surrenders that Louis would have to make on every one of his kingdom's frontiers; he would be giving up all the gains of his earlier wars. But two articles would subsequently become notorious as the rocks on which peace would founder. Article Four required Philip to leave Spain within two months of the Preliminaries' ratification. If he did not, then his grandfather "and the stipulating princes and states will take appropriate measures in concert to ensure its entire effect, so that all Europe, by the accomplishment of the said treaties of peace, may without delay enjoy perfect tranquillity." The meaning of this diplomatic formula was clear to all: if his grandson defied the peace terms, Louis would be required to join the Allies in making war on him. Article 37 established a truce of two months. At the end of that time, if Louis had failed to execute all of the articles, the Allies would be free to resume the war. However, by then, Louis would have already evacuated the fortresses of Flanders and Alsace. France would thus be at the Allies' mercy.[58]

As soon as Heinsius had finished reading out the Preliminaries, Torcy's reaction was immediate and unequivocal: the articles were repugnant. If it had been within his power, he would have repudiated them on the spot and broken off negotiations. However, since it was not, he would present them to Louis for his decision. Torcy promised the grand pensionary that he would have his answer by no later than June 4. He forwarded the Preliminaries to Versailles accompanied with the advice that "Your Majesty is entirely free to reject absolutely these conditions, as I trust the state of your affairs will permit, or to accept them if unhappily you conceive it your duty to end the war at any price." He then prepared to follow. By May 28, his carriage was on the road to Rotterdam and Mons.[59]

At The Hague, the triumvirs were exultant. The Preliminaries satisfied all the war aims of Great Britain, the Dutch Republic, and the Habsburgs. They also offered a seemingly elegant solution to the fiendish problem of Spain. As for Torcy's repugnance toward them, the Allied leaders were convinced it amounted to mere posturing. Given the disastrous state of his kingdom, the suffering of his subjects, and the weakness of his armies,

Louis would have no choice but to sign. On the last day of May, Marlborough wrote to his duchess:

> Since the going away of Monsieur de Torcy, I have some time to myself, so that I begine to write this letter though the post does not go til tomorrow. I have the satisfaction to tel my dear soull that I have now a prospect of living quietly some time with you, for I do veryly beleive the condition of France is such, that thay must submitt to the conditions we have given them, and thay are such that I hope everybody will be pleased with them.[60]

At half past seven in the evening on June 1, Torcy arrived at Versailles. Louis took him to Madame de Maintenon's apartments. The pair passed through the King's Guard Room and two antechambers before coming to the consort's bedroom. There, Louis settled himself on an armchair with a small round table placed in front of it. Torcy sat opposite him on a little folding chair. On the other side of a guttering fireplace, in another armchair set in an alcove decorated in red damask wallpaper, was Madame de Maintenon, the king's beloved Votre Solidité. She busied herself with her needlework but listened intently as the two men talked for hours about the Preliminaries.[61] Outside Maintenon's apartments, the adjoining corridors and chambers filled with courtiers impatiently waiting to learn about the peace terms. When Torcy at last emerged at half past one in the morning, they discovered that the enemies' proposals were "impossible to execute and too shameful even to wish to undertake." All believed that the peace talks should be broken off and the war resumed in earnest.[62]

All except for Louis. As the triumvirs had expected, the desperate situation of his kingdom meant that he could not dismiss the Grand Alliance's terms out of hand. Instead, he pondered them with great care through a sleepless night, Madame de Maintenon remaining at his side, his indispensable partner and bulwark of his spirits. At eleven in the morning, in the cabinet room adjacent to his bed chamber, he convened his *Conseil d'en haut* of royal ministers to advise him and help him reach a decision. Torcy first read out the Preliminaries. In the debate that ensued, the council split. The Duc de Beauvilliers had long been the principal proponent of peace in French ruling circles. He acknowledged the exceptional harshness of the Allies' demands; nevertheless, he begged the king to accept them. He received strong support from the Duc de Bourgogne, Louis' eldest grandson. The debacle of the 1708 campaign had confirmed his abhorrence of war. Torcy was the loudest voice calling for the rejection of the Preliminaries and the rupturing of negotiations. For over two hours, the arguments raged. Throughout, the king said nothing. His demeanor, though, suggested he was inclining to the position of the peace party.

At last, Louis the Grand Dauphin spoke. Aged forty-seven, he was known to everyone as a lover of pleasure, an indefatigable hunter—especially of wolves—and a great patron of music and the arts. By contrast, he had little reputation as a statesman. Yet, in 1700, his forceful intervention on behalf of Philip had convinced the king to accept the will of Charles the Bewitched. Now he again came to the defense of his second son. Usually tranquil and exquisitely courteous, he angrily condemned the abandonment of a king of Spain who had won the love of his people and had courageously defended his throne against long odds. Then he addressed his father and, with a lack of respect that made the other councilors blanch, reproached him for even considering such a dishonorable act. The Dauphin next turned on the ministers and announced that he would soon be their master and they would have to render a long account to him of their deeds this day. Then he stood up from the table and stormed out of the king's cabinet.

The furious prince swept through the royal apartments and into the Hall of Mirrors, where a throng of courtiers and dignitaries was waiting to learn the fate of the peace terms. A short while later, Torcy rushed up to him. After his departure, the Duc de Bourgogne had forsaken the Duc de Beauvilliers and declared himself in favor of his father. The king had then bowed to the opinions of his heir, his heir presumptive, and his foreign minister. He was rejecting the Preliminaries of The Hague.[63]

Having decided to continue the war, Louis at once turned his attention to the Flanders front. In his hands was a new strategic appreciation drawn up by Villars. It began with all of the marshal's inimitable optimism. The Army of Flanders, he assured the king, had enough bread until the end of June. However, the rest of his letter made for more sobering reading. The army's scarce supplies were stockpiled only between Béthune and Douai. If the Allies opted for a war of movement and marched westward for the sea or eastward for the Sambre and Meuse, Villars would be able to follow only with the greatest difficulty. He would thus do his utmost to entice Marlborough and Eugene to fight. Either they would attack him in his fortified lines, or he would lead the army out of his emplacements to seek battle. Louis replied, "I have great confidence in your good will, your energy, and your good conduct." He assured the marshal that he and his ministers were doing everything in their power to find enough food and funds for the army. He then set out what he hoped Villars would accomplish:

> If you can sustain this campaign without ill events, the conditions of peace will be very different and the Dutch, oppressed by the will of their allies and by the great forces that they must sustain in the midst of their country, shall then feel that it is in their true interest to come to terms with France in order to obtain a reasonable barrier.

This exchange between the king and the marshal began a debate within the French high command that would continue until the end of 1709. On the one hand, Villars was always aware that shortages of supplies and money might result in the disbanding of his army. He believed he had to do something significant before that happened. Moreover, his generalship had always been characterized by boldness and aggression. For these reasons, he would be the advocate of a battle-seeking strategy. On the other hand, Louis regarded the campaign as an extension of the diplomacy begun at The Hague. Its purpose was to demonstrate to the Allies that France could not be beaten militarily, and they should offer better terms for peace. This could only be achieved if the French limited their losses and, above all, preserved their last major field army. The king would champion passive defense and the avoidance of battle.[64]

Louis knew his decision to break off negotiations was a perilous gamble: France, bankrupt and prostrated by hunger, was about to be invaded by powerful armies led by great captains with an unbroken record of victories. He had originally intended to send the Bourbon princes to the front—the Grand Dauphin to Flanders and the Duc de Bourgogne to the Rhine. He now ordered them to remain at court. The field armies would be left entirely in the hands of the professionals Villars and Harcourt. More importantly, the king's heirs would be safeguarded from the humiliation of defeat.[65] Louis then made another, even more consequential change in the composition of the court high command. For months, War Minister Michel Chamillart had been depressed and defeatist, hardly concealing his longing for peace. The marshals, including Boufflers and Villars, were growing more and more critical of his management of the war effort. Louis regretfully concluded that his long friendship with Chamillart and his reluctance to dismiss his chief servants were no longer enough to keep him in office. On June 9, the king asked for and received the war minister's resignation. His replacement was Daniel Voysin, an experienced jurist and administrator and a protégé of Madame de Maintenon, who had appointed him the intendant of her school at Saint-Cyr. All of his contemporaries regarded him as capable, conscientious, and exceptionally hard working. However, he at first lacked experience in military affairs, so the king appointed Marshal Boufflers to serve as his mentor.[66]

When the news of the French rejection of the Preliminaries reached The Hague, the triumvirs were shocked. They were particularly dumbstruck that Louis and Torcy were rupturing the negotiations without offering any counterproposals. Their dismay quickly gave way to disgust and a determination to finish not just the war but perhaps the Sun King's regime itself. On June 7, Marlborough wrote to Sidney Godolphin that once the French had been beaten in the coming campaign,

> I think the Queen should then have the honour of insisting upon putting the French government upon their being againe governed by the three Estates, which I think is more likly to give quiet to Christdome, then the tearing of provences from them for the inriching of others.

This proposal was breathtakingly far-reaching. In demanding the reestablishment of the Estates General—the French national assembly that had last been summoned in 1614 and would not be again until 1789—Marlborough was calling for nothing less than a revolution in France: the dismantling of the absolute monarchy and its replacement by a government more resembling Great Britain's. Two days later, in a letter written to Sarah, the captain general was in a quieter, more reflective mood as he left The Hague to join his army mustering around Ghent:

> I confess I thought it sure, beleiving it very much for the interest of France to have agreed with us; but since thay seeme to think otherways, I hope God has a farther blessing in store. I was in hopes to have had the happiness of being with you before the winter; I wish I could still flatter myself with those thoughts.[67]

In France, a surge of martial enthusiasm followed in the wake of the Preliminaries' repudiation. "We are no longer talking about anything other than the war," Madame de Maintenon assured Villars,

> and it seems to me that everyone is zealous to find money, everyone is offering their silver plate, we will see who will give it first; you can well believe, Monsieur, that our Marshal de Boufflers will not be the last.

In Bordeaux, the judge Joseph de Labat de Savignac was kept abreast of the latest developments by his father-in-law, the city's agent at Versailles. In his diary, he vented his indignation at the "insolent propositions of our enemies" and applauded their rejection. And from Flanders, Villars informed the king how his troops responded to the news:

> I was at the head of your infantry when the courier gave me the dispatch of Your Majesty and on the first lines which made known his resolution, I marked my satisfaction with it to your troops, who all returned a great cry of joy and ardor to come to blows with the enemy.[68]

Yet Louis believed that he needed to do more to spur his people to make still greater sacrifices for the war effort. It was Torcy who proposed that he directly appeal to them. The king ordered his foreign minister to draw up something suitable. The result had never been seen before in French history, nor would it be repeated after: an absolute monarch answerable only to God addressing his subjects to explain and justify his actions. It took the form of a letter, dated June 12, to the governors of the provinces, who were commanded to disseminate it as widely as possible. "The expectation of a speedy peace was so generally diffused throughout my kingdom," it began,

> That I think it my duty, in return for the fidelity which my people have shown me during the course of my reign, to give them the satisfaction of being acquainted with the reasons which still hinder them from enjoying that repose which I intended to procure for them.

The bulk of the letter detailed the harshness and injustice of the Allied peace terms, particularly Article Thirty-Seven. It climaxed with a ringing call to rally around the king:

> But though my affection for my people is as sensible as that which I have for my own children; though I share with them all the calamities which war draws on such faithful subjects; and though I have shown to all Europe that I was sincerely desirous of procuring a peace for them, yet I am persuaded that they themselves would be against receiving it, upon conditions equally opposite to justice and the honor of the FRENCH NAME.
> It is therefore my intention, that all those who for such a series of years have given me proofs of their zeal, in contributing by their labor, their property, and their blood, to support so burdensome a war, should be informed, that the only return the enemy pretended to make to my offers, was a suspension of arms; which being limited to the space of two months, would have procured them much greater advantages, than they can expect from the confidence they put in their troops. As I put mine in the protection of the Almighty, and as I hope that the purity of my intentions will draw down the Divine Blessing upon my arms, I am willing that my people within your jurisdiction should know from you, that they should already enjoy peace, had it depended merely on my will to procure them a blessing which they wish for with reason; but which must be obtained by new efforts, since the immense concessions I was ready to make are of no effect for restoring the public tranquility.[69]

Louis' subjects enthusiastically greeted what has come to be called the appeal of June 12. The provincial governors made and distributed thousands of copies, which were read aloud in public and posted up on walls in prominent places. In Paris, the first printing sold out in a day, and new editions had to be made that night, with crowds waiting impatiently outside the printers' workshops. Madame de Maintenon declared to the princesse des Ursins that anyone "with even a drop of French blood" was aroused to fury by the unjust peace. At court, more aristocrats and dignitaries followed the example of Marshal Boufflers by donating their silver and gold vessels to the mint to be turned into new coin for the armies.[70]

But this burst of national zeal did not last. No amount of royal eloquence could for long conceal the breadth and depth of the crisis engulfing France. The donations of precious plate quickly stopped. In August, Controller General Desmaretz's clerks drew up a detailed inventory of what the mint had received. It totaled 1,489,343 livres from seventy-six individuals, including the king. While a tidy sum, it represented only an insignificant proportion of the needs of the field forces.[71] As for the king's ordinary subjects, their enthusiasm for his appeal to arms was even more short-lived than his courtiers'. In the provinces of the Flanders frontier, they continued to resist the royal government's efforts to requisition supplies for the army. At the beginning of June, Controller General Desmaretz contemplated another grain tax in Artois and Picardy. Intendant Bernage dissuaded him by warning that unless the measure was backed by the full weight of Villars' army, the people would rise up in a "terrible revolt." At Tournai, the Marquis de Surville, commander of the fortress-city, reported that when his troops tried to expropriate 300 sacks of wheat, they found themselves blocked by a crowd of angry women. Later, attempts to acquire grain in Valenciennes and Cambrai provoked rioting.[72]

There was one group for whom Louis' appeal of June 12 had profound and lasting results: the officers and soldiers of his army. They heard the king's call to defend the honor of the French name and they answered with pride and fierce enthusiasm. For they lived and died for honor. More than four-fifths of French officers were noblemen; their ethos pervaded the entire corps. Like their king—whom they regarded as the first gentleman of France—they pursued reputation in life and renown in posterity. Acquiring these required adherence to a code of honor which, though unwritten, was as unbending as iron. Its demands could be satisfied by punctilious devotion to professional duties: the mustering of a well-manned and -equipped company or regiment; the rigorous application of discipline and drill; and, especially as the monarchy slipped ever closer to financial collapse, the sacrifice of private fortunes to keep units viable and combat ready. But the consummation of an officer's honor was the performance of conspicuous courage on the battlefield. Once, this would have involved prowess at arms, preferably in single combat against a worthy foe. The evolution of warfare had led to courage's transformation. On battlefields now dominated by musket volleys and cannon shot, bravery no longer meant inflicting wounds but risking or even suffering them. An officer was most worthy of honor by standing unflinchingly with his men under the fiercest fire; by refusing to leave his post after being wounded; by insisting on returning to the fighting as soon as his injuries were dressed; and by obeying an order willingly, even cheerfully, whatever the danger to himself.[73]

The monarch was a key arbiter of honor. He could recognize it and reward it by bestowing numerous favors: promotions to higher rank, appointments to lucrative or prestigious postings, cash gratifications, and annual pensions. In 1694, he founded the chivalric Order of Saint Louis for officers, noble or commoner, who had at least ten years of service, performed distinguished deeds, and received wounds in the line of duty. By 1715, it consisted of 2,450 knights, each of whom had been inducted by Louis personally in a special ceremony.[74] But even the Sun King could not completely control honor. For an officer, the most important judges of his honorableness were his fellow nobles, particularly his brothers in arms. It was his standing in their eyes that mattered most and that had to be defended at all costs and by all means, including recourse to armed violence. If an officer publicly challenged another's character or conduct—particularly by casting doubt on his courage—it was an injury that could only be redressed by a duel. Louis loathed dueling, considering it a form of rebellion, even *lèse majesté*. Throughout his reign, he made great efforts to stamp it out everywhere in his kingdom. Yet it flourished clandestinely in his army with the silent complicity of his generals and officers. According to one estimate, during the last thirty years of his reign, 10,000 officers fought duels. Nor were these trivial affrays: 400 duelists died on the field of honor and countless more succumbed to their wounds afterward.[75]

Honor was not supposed to be a quality possessed by common soldiers. The French upper classes, including officers, regarded them as vile persons drawn from the margins of society who could only be controlled by incessant drill and harsh, unrelenting discipline. The reality belied such prejudiced aristocratic stereotypes. The rank and file were, in fact, poor but solidly respectable men who had enlisted largely to escape economic hardship. Moreover, they came from a world suffused with powerful ideals of popular honor. Far from being merely passive subjects, French commoners demanded respect for their dignity in exchange for deference. They were intensely sensitive to their reputations and went to great lengths, including violence, to defend them. This acute attention to public esteem extended to innumerable social groups and associations: craft guilds, confraternities, lay charities, militia companies, city neighborhoods, and country villages. The army's recruits would have been familiar with—and likely have themselves participated in—the "youth abbeys," the gangs of unmarried men who policed the moral behavior of their neighbors. And the artisans among them would have known of the *compagnonnages*, the clandestine brotherhoods of journeymen who had embarked on the *tour de France*, the peripatetic search for work.[76]

Joining the army entailed not just beginning a new life; it meant forging a new identity. One key rite of passage for the recruit was his acceptance of the king's silver, the enlistment bounty. Another was the donning of his uniform. Consisting of tricorn hat, cravat, justaucorps coat, waistcoat, shirt, breeches, and shoes, it was not merely functional but modeled on a gentleman's suit. The infantryman's small sword, a weapon of almost no lethal value, was indispensable as the symbol of his soldierly status. Together, uniform and sword served as the most visible signs separating the recruit from civilian society; at the same time, they united him with his comrades, his officers, and, ultimately, the king himself. Sealing the soldier's new identity was his assumption of a name by which he would be known throughout his time in the ranks—the *nom de guerre*. A distinctive feature of the French royal army, these names exhibited a dizzyingly colorful variety: they could denote geographical origins ("Parisien"), civilian profession ("Boulanger," Baker, "La Lime," a small file used by a locksmith), favorite plants and flowers ("La Rose," "La Tulipe"), or personal characteristics ("Blondin," Blondy, "Sans Souci," Carefree, "Sans Quartier," Merciless).[77]

With a new identity came a new community: the regiment. It was profoundly masculine in composition and character. One of Louis XIV's main military reforms was to drastically reduce the number of women who were permitted to accompany his troops. Whereas at the beginning of his reign each regiment had been followed by a long train of women, at its end only about fifteen remained. They did such essential jobs as needlework and laundry. As *vivandières*, they were peddlers of small, essential comforts such as liquor and tobacco. A few undoubtedly provided more intimate services, although Louis made strenuous efforts to stamp out prostitution in his army.[78]

The new soldier's integration into the life and culture of his regiment would have begun at once and been carried out by a number of mechanisms. One was the efforts of his closest comrades, the members of his fifteen-strong squad. In garrison, they lived together in houses close to each other; on campaign, they shared the same tents. They mounted guard together, cooked and ate their food together. The squad's older hands played an invaluable role in introducing recruits to the ways and customs of the army. Another crucial mechanism of social integration was drill. By training all of the men in a unit to move and act together, it not only imparted military skills; it also fostered deep feelings of belonging and solidarity.[79]

More than anything else, the regiment was a community of honor. It imposed a strict code on all who belonged to it. The code's tenets included esprit de corps—a fierce pride in the unit's reputation along with a responsibility to uphold it—and loyalty to one's comrades. The most important of all was bravery in battle. It won esteem for the soldier and glory for his regiment. Conversely, cowardice brought shame and opprobrium to both. The main enforcers of the code were the soldiers of the regiment themselves. It was not unknown for them to petition their officers to drum out a man for behavior they considered dishonorable, such as harming a comrade or cowardice in combat.[80]

The conviction that courage was the ultimate expression of masculine honor was the most powerful bond tying soldiers to their officers. The rank and file judged an officer's worth based not on administrative acumen, technical ability, or tactical skill but on bravery under fire. For their part, officers knew that successful command depended on providing a good example to their men. An incident from the Battle of Ramillies illuminates these relationships between leadership and emulation, courage and shame. Jean-François Martin de La Colonie was a veteran French engineer and officer who had entered the service of the elector of Bavaria at the beginning of the War of the Spanish Succession. By 1706, he had risen to the rank of lieutenant colonel and command of a regiment of grenadiers recruited from French deserters. At a critical moment in the battle, de La Colonie deployed his unit to block the advance of a much larger enemy force. Suddenly, from somewhere behind him, he heard one of his soldiers cry out "with an oath that it would all end in a butchery." He immediately turned and faced them:

> I myself, swearing like a grenadier, demanded in stentorian tones where the scoundrel was who confessed to such a fear, declaring that I was the only proper person to act as his butcher, and finally did all I knew to find him. But not being successful in this search, I continued my impassioned address, crying out that he and his like ought to know that at any time an occasion might arise when it would be our duty to sacrifice ourselves, such things were in the nature of our business and that at any rate the example set by the gallant men who led them ought to be quite sufficient for the miserable cowards who showed such a fear for their skins. At last, the temper into which I had worked myself had the effect I desired, and my troops appeared to be much more reassured.[81]

In the summer of 1709, de La Colonie and his grenadiers joined the forces facing the Allied invasion of France. They and the rest of the Army of Flanders, from Marshal Villars to the lowest common soldier, were about to subject their honor to a trial by fire.

NOTES

1. John C. Rule, "King and Minister: Louis XIV and Colbert de Torcy," in *William III and Louis XIV: Essays 1680–1720 by and for Mark A. Thompson*, eds. Ragnhild Hatton and J. S. Bromley (Liverpool: Liverpool University Press, 1968), 216–217; Rule and Trotter, *A World of Paper*, 44–137.

2. Olivier Chaline, *L'année de quatre dauphins* (Paris: Flammarion, 2009), 110; Rule, "King and Minister," 223–224.

3. Torcy, *Mémoires*, vol. 1, 209–210.

4. 733, Heinsius to Marlborough, 8 May 1709 in *Marlborough-Heinsius Correspondence*, 433.

5. An English text of the treaty can be found in *A Collection of all the Treaties of Peace, Alliance, and Commerce, between Great Britain and Other Powers, From the Treaty signed at Munster in 1648, to the Treaties signed at Paris in 1783*, volume 1 (London: J. Debrett, 1785), 226–231.

6. Olaf van Nimwegen, "The Dutch Barrier: Its Origins, Creation and Importance for the Dutch Republic as a Great Power, 1697–1718," in *Anthonie Heinsius and the Dutch Republic 1688 1720: Politics, War, and Finance*, eds. Jan A.F. de Jongste and Augustus J. Veenendaal Jr. (The Hague: Institute of Netherlands History, 2002), 152–153.

7. On the War of the Spanish Succession in Iberia, see Henry Kamen, *The War of Succession in Spain, 1700–1715* (Bloomington: Indiana University Press, 1969) and David Francis, *The First Peninsular War, 1702–1713* (New York: St. Martin's Press, 1975).

8. On the development of the Allies' various war aims and the growing tensions in the Alliance, see Roderick Geikie and Isabel A. Montgomery, *The Dutch Barrier, 1705–1719* (New York: Greenwood, 1968); John Hattendorf, *England in the War of the Spanish Succession: A Study of the English View and Conduct of Grand Strategy, 1702–1712* (New York: Garland, 1987); Charles Ingrao, *In Quest and Crisis: Emperor Joseph I and the Habsburg Monarchy* (West Lafayette, IN: Purdue University Press, 1979); H. G. Pitt, "The Pacification of Utrecht," in *The New Cambridge Modern History*, vol. 6, *The Rise of Great Britain and Russia, 1688–1715*, ed. J. S. Bromley (Cambridge: Cambridge University Press, 1970), 446–479; J. G. Stork-Penning, "The Ordeal of the States: Some Remarks on Dutch Politics during the War of the Spanish Succession," in *Acta HistoriaeNeerlandica*, volume 2 (Leiden: Brill, 1967), 107–141.

9. Torcy, *Mémoires*, vol. 1, 211.

10. The only scholarly biography of Godolphin is Roy A. Sundstrom, *Sidney Godolphin, Servant of the State* (Newark: University of Delaware Press, 1992). On his partnership with Marlborough, see Frances Harris, *The General in Winter: the Marlborough-Godolphin Friendship and the Reign of Queen Anne* (Oxford: Oxford University Press, 2017).

11. Hattendorf, *England in the War of the Spanish Succession*, 193–201.

12. On Sarah Churchill, see Frances Harris, *A Passion for Government: the Life of Sarah, Duchess of Marlborough* (Oxford: Clarendon Press, 1991). On Queen Anne, see Edward Gregg, *Queen Anne* (London: Routledge and Kegan Paul, 1980).

13. Henry L. Snyder, "The Duke of Marlborough's Request of His Captain-Generalcy for Life: A Re-examination," *Journal of the Society for Army Historical Research* 45/182 (1967), 70–72.

14. Torcy, *Mémoires*, vol. 1, 210

15. Augustus J. Veenendal, Jr., "Marlborough and Heinsius: Friends, Colleagues or Just Working Together for the Common Cause?" in *Marlborough: Soldier*

and Diplomat, eds. John Hattendorf, Augustus J. Veenendal, Jr., and Rolof van Hövell tot Westerflier (Amsterdam: Karawansaray Publishers, 2012), 173–175.

16. Stork-Penning, "The Ordeal of the States," 110–120.
17. Mckay, *Prince Eugene of Savoy*, 119–120.
18. Ingrao, *In Quest and Crisis*, 172–176.
19. The following description of Marly is based on Stephane Castelluccio, *Marly. Art de vivre et pouvoir de Louis XIV à Louis XVI* (Montreuil: Gourcuff Gradenigo, 2014).
20. 30,000 from Lorraine, 4,000 from Archbishop Fenelon of Cambrai, 12,000 from the Marquise de Mailly, 7,000 from the Marquise de Sailly.
21. Sourches, *Mémoires*, vol. 11, 331–332; Dangeau, *Journal*, vol. 12, 411–412.
22. Sourches, *Mémoires*, vol. 11, 333; Dangeau, *Journal*, vol. 12, 413; Villars, *Mémoires*, vol. 3, 41.
23. SHD GR A^1 2150/208, Villars to Chamillart, 15 May 1709; Villars, *Mémoires*, book 3, 247–248.
24. SHD GR A^1 2150/228, Villars to Chamillart, 19 May 1709; SHD GR A^1 2150/229, Report on flour available for the Army of Flanders, 19 May 1709; Villars, *Mémoires*, book 3, 42.
25. SHD GR A^1 2150/229, Villars to the frontier intendants, 19 May 1709; SHD GR A^1 2150/237, Villars to Louis XIV, 22 May 1709; SHD GR A^1 2157/220, Bernage to Chamillart, 26 May 1709.
26. On Louis de Bernage, see Darryl Dee, *Expansion and Crisis in Louis XIV's France*, chapters 6 and 7; SHD AG A^1 2157/202, Bernage to Chamillart, 19 May 1709.
27. SHD AG A^1 2157/
28. On mills, see Perjes, "Army Provisioning," 8–9. On the need for *munitionnaires* to mill grain into flour before the campaigning season, see Nodot, *Le munitionnaire*, 130–133. SHD AG A^1 2150/238, Villars to Chamillart, 22 May 1709.
29. AN G^7 263/389, Bernières to Desmaretz, 2 March 1709; AN G^7 290/99, Bernage to Desmaretz, 4 March 1709;AN G^7 290/103, Bernage to Desmaretz, 9 March 1709; SHD AG A^1 2156, Doujat to Chamillart, 2 April 1709; AN G^7 290/124, Bernage to Desmaretz, 10 April 1709; G7 290/132, Bernage to Desmaretz, 26 April 1709; SHD A^1 2150/233, Chevalier de Luxembourg to Chamillart, 21 May 1709; SHD A^1 2156/71, Voysin to Doujat, 16 June 1709.
30. On the French version of military enterprise, see Chaline, *Les armées du Roi*, 41–57; Hervé Drévillon, *L'impot du sang. Le métier des arms sous Louis XIV* (Paris: Tallandier, 2005), 179–211; Lynn, *Giant of the Grand Siécle*, 221–247; David Parrott, *The Business of War: Military Enterprise and Military Revolution in Early Modern Europe* (Cambridge: Cambridge University Press, 2012), 266–279; Guy Rowlands, *The Dynastic State and the Army under Louis XIV: Royal Service and Private Interest, 1661 1701* (Cambridge: Cambridge University Press, 2002), 166–171, 200–231.
31. Quincy, *Mémoires*, vol. 2, 318–319 and 322–325.
32. Georges Girard, ed., "Un soldat de Malplaquet: lettres du capitain de Saint-Mayme," *Carnets de la Sabretache. Revue militaire retrospective*, troisième série (Paris: La Sabretache, 1922), 534–541.
33. SHD A^1 2150/239, Chamillart to Villars, 22 May 1709; SHD A^1 2150/267, Chamillart to Villars, 27 May 1709.

34. On fodder, Lynn, *Giant of the Grand Siècle*, and Perjes, "Army Provisioning," 14–16. Boufflers' estimate of the Army of Flanders' fodder requirement is SHD AG A^1 2149/97, Rations for the 1709 campaign.

35. SHD AG A^1 2157/86, Bernage to Chamillart, 22 February 1709; SHD AG A^1 2157/100, Bernage to Chamillart, 9 March 1709; AN G^7 290/116, Bernage to Desmaretz, 4 April 1709; SHD AG A^1 2157/161, Bernage to Chamillart, 30 April 1709; SHD AG A^1 2157/169, Bernage to Chamillart, 1 May 1709; SHD AG A^1 2150/183, Villars to Louis XIV, 4 May 170; SHD AG A^1 2156/55, Doujat to Chamillart, 15 May 1709; SHD AG A^1 2150/237, Villars to Chamillart, 22 May 1709.

36. SHD AG A^1 2150/245, Villars to Louis XIV, 24 May 1709; SHD AG A^1 2150/261, Villars to Louis XIV, 26 May 1709; André Corvisier, *La bataille de Malplaquet*, 42.

37. SHD AG A^1 2151/1, Villars to Louis XIV, 1 June 1709.

38. AAE Hollande 218, Louis XIV to Rouillé, 29 April 1709, ff. 129–136. At the bottom of the last page of this letter, Louis personally wrote, "I approve what is contained in this dispatch and my intention is that Torcy executes it."

39. AAE Hollande 218, Torcy to Louis XIV, 7 May 1709, ff. 166–177v.; AAE Hollande 218, Torcy to Louis XIV, 9 May 1709, ff. 178–178v; Torcy, *Mémoires*, vol. 1, 212–240.

40. Dangeau, *Journal*, vol. 12, 409.

41. 414, Maintenon to the Duc de Noailles, 14 May 1709, *Lettres de Maintenon*, vol. 4, 548–549.

42. AAE Hollande 218, Louis XIV to Torcy, 14 May 1709, ff. 179–188.

43. Legrelle, *La diplomatie française et la succession d'Espagne*, vol. 4, 368.

44. AAE Angleterre 226, Marlborough to Berwick, 30 October 1708, f. 157.

45. Arsène Legrelle, *Une negotiation inconnue entre Berwick et Marlborough, 1708–1709* (Paris: Cotillon, 1893), 25–36.

46. AAE Hollande 218, Louis XIV to Torcy, 14 May 1709, ff. 179–188; Torcy, *Mémoires*, volume 1, 334–342.

47. 1270, Marlborough to Godolphin, 8/19 May 1709, *Marlborough-Godolphin Correspondence*, volume 3, 1251.

48. AAE Hollande 218, Torcy to Louis XIV, 22 May 1709, ff. 212–225v.; Torcy, *Mémoires*, volume 1, 262–263.

49. AAE Hollande 218, Torcy to Louis XIV, 22 May 1709, ff. 212–225v.

50. Torcy, *Mémoires*, vol. 1, 282–289.

51. AAE Hollande 218, Torcy to Louis XIV, 28 May 1709, ff. 241–246; Torcy, *Mémoires*, volume 1,

52. Churchill, *Marlborough*, book 2, 549.

53. 1276, Marlborough to Godolphin, 14/25 May 1709, *Marlborough-Godolphin Correspondence*, volume 3, 1253–1254; 1278, Marlborough to Sarah, 14/25 May 1709, *Marlborough-Godolphin Correspondence*, volume 3, 1255; Ingrao, *Quest and Crisis*, 181–182.

54. Churchill, *Marlborough*, book 2, 541; Francis, *First Peninsular War*, 336.

55. Churchill, *Marlborough*, book 2, 545.

56. Stork-Penning, "The Ordeal of the States," 122–124.

57. Torcy, *Mémoires*, vol. 1, 222.

58. The text of the Preliminaries of The Hague is found in Torcy, *Mémoires*, volume 1, 304–326.
59. AAE Hollande 218, Torcy to Louis XIV, 28 May 1709, ff. 241–246.
60. 1285, Marlborough to Sarah, 20/31 May 1709, *Marlborough-Godolphin Correspondence*, volume 3, 1260.
61. Sourches, *Mémoires*, vol. 11, 346–347. The description of Madame de Maintenon's apartments is from Saint-Simon, *Mémoires*, vol. 7, 13–14.
62. Dangeau, *Journal*, vol. 12, 427.
63. Churchill, *Marlborough*, book 2, 548–550; Rule, "King and Minister," 226–227.
64. SHD AG A^1 2151/1, Villars to Louis XIV, 1 June 1709; SHD AG A^1 2151/7, Louis XIV to Villars, 3 June 1709.
65. Oury, *Guerre de Succession*, 296.
66. Penicault, *Michel Chamillart*, 151–159; Thiérry Sarmant, ed., *Les Ministres de la guerre, 1570 1792* (Paris: Belin, 2007), 308–315.
67. 1291, Marlborough to Godolphin, 27 May/7 June 1709, *Marlborough-Godolphin Correspondence*, vol. 3, 1266; 1294, Marlborough to Sarah, 29 May/9 June 1709, *Marlborough-Godolphin Correspondence*, vol. 3, 1268–1269.
68. 425, Maintenon to Villars, 6 June 1709, *Lettres de Maintenon*, vol. 4, 561; *Le Mémorial de Savignac*, 112; SHD AG A^1 2151/15, Villars to Louis XIV, 6 June 1709.
69. This text is from a 1757 English translation of Torcy's *Mémoires* quoted in Joseph Klaits, *Printed Propaganda under Louis XIV* (Princeton: Princeton University Press, 1976), 214–216. "Nom Francois" is capitalized in most printed editions of the letter.
70. Klaits, *Printed Propaganda*, 219; 433, Maintenon to des Ursins, 17 June 1709, *Lettres de Maintenon*, vol. 4, 571; Villars, *Mémoires*, book 1, 49.
71. Lynn, *Giant of the Grand Siècle*, 448–449.
72. AN G^7 290/155, Bernage to Desmaretz, 3 June 1709; SHD AG A^1 2151/31, Surville to Chamillart, 8 June 1709; SHD AG A^1 2151/63, Chevalier de Luxembourg to Voysin, 18 June 1709.
73. Drévillon, *L'Impot du sang*, 321–351, 398–407; Lynn, *Giant of the Grand Siècle*, 248–252; Guy Rowlands, "Keep Right on to the End of the Road: the Stamina of the French Army during the War of the Spanish Succession," in *The War of the Spanish Succession: New Perspectives*, eds. Matthias Polig and Michael Schaich (Oxford: Oxford University Press, 2018), 324–328.
74. Lynn, *Giant of the Grand Siècle*, 252–254; Rowlands, *The Dynastic State and the Army*, 218–225.
75. Drévillon, *L'Impot du sang*, 393–398; Lynn, *Giant of the Grand Siècle*, 255–259.
76. William Beik, *A Social and Cultural History of Early Modern France* (Cambridge: Cambridge University Press, 2009), 224–237; idem., *Urban Protest in Seventeenth-Century France: the Culture of Retribution* (Cambridge: Cambridge University Press, 1997), 28–40.
77. Ilya Berkovich, *Motivation in War: the Experience of Common Soldiers in Old-Regime Europe* (Cambridge: Cambridge University Press, 2017), 163–170; Corvisier, *L'Armée francsaise*, book two, 851–861.
78. Lynn, *Giant of the Grand Siècle*, 337–343.

79. Berkovich, *Motivation in War*, 215–225; Lynn, *Giant of the Grand Siècle*, 439–443.

80. Berkovich, *Motivation in War*, 181–194; André Corvisier, *Armies and Societies in Europe, 1494 1789*, trans. Abigail T. Siddall (Bloomington: University of Indiana Press, 1979), 182.

81. Jean-Baptiste de La Colonie, *The Chronicles of an Old Campaigner: M. de La Colonie, 1692–1717*, trans. Walter C. Horsley (London: John Murray, 1904), 310–311.

5

The Campaign
June–August, 1709

On June 9, 1709, Captain Joseph Sevin, Chevalier de Quincy, left Paris to join his regiment at La Bassée. He spent most of the four-day carriage journey pleasurably in the amorous company of two fair ladies. Soon after his arrival at the army, Marshal Villars held a grand review of his troops. It took place on a day that alternated between bright sunshine and sudden downpours. During the fair interludes, Villars sported a magnificent hat bedecked with medallions, cockades, and plumes. Whenever the rain began falling, he quickly doffed it and put on an old, battered cap. Quincy mocked the marshal's crass, indecent vanity.[1]

Meanwhile, John Marshall Deane, a gentleman volunteer serving as a sentinel or private soldier in the British First Regiment of Foot Guards, was marching on the road west out of Brussels. He and his comrades had spent the winter in the city, "living as we oughtt to doe, like men who carry our lives in our hands; not knowing how soone it may be our turns to be cutt off, as we have been eyewittneses that many brave fellows have been before us." On June 18, at Courtrai, his regiment met the rest of the Allied army, which had come down from Ghent. The whole force then made ready to go into action on the plains south of Lille.[2]

The most powerful armies Europe had ever seen were assembling in Flanders. The French Army of Flanders mustered 136 battalions and 255 squadrons, about 80,000 troops in all.[3] Louis XIV had mobilized other forces to defend his kingdom's frontiers on the Rhine and in the Alps and to help his grandson in Spain. But Marshal Villars commanded the Sun King's only major field army. It was also his last. So enervated was France that if the Army of Flanders ever suffered a crushing defeat like Blenheim, Ramillies, or Oudenarde, it could never be rebuilt.

Villars led a largely national army: more than four-fifths of his soldiers were French. The native regiments included most of the elite corps—Maison du Roi, *vieux*, *petits vieux*, Gendarmes, carabineers—as well as the pick of the regulars. Of the foreigners, the Swiss represented the most substantial contingent, providing the Gardes suisses and numerous line battalions. The Swiss had fought for French kings for over two centuries. The Irish were, by comparison, newcomers. They were Wild Geese, Catholic Jacobites who had rejected the Glorious Revolution and then chosen to follow the Stuart pretenders into exile. Many were veterans of the brutal Williamite War in Ireland and they fought with particular ferocity whenever they faced British troops. Five regiments—Lee, Dorrington, O'Donnell, O'Brien, and Galmoy—were with Villars.[4] Germans were found in their own mercenary regiments as well as the refugee armies of the Duke of Bavaria and the prince-archbishop of Cologne, Louis' Wittlesbach allies. Lastly, there were the troops in Spanish service, mostly Walloons recruited locally in the Low Countries.

Save for the king's household troops, the units of the Flanders army were understrength. The defeats of the previous year had thinned their ranks, and the disastrous conditions of the winter months, particularly the chronic shortages of provisions and pay, had provoked waves of desertions. Replacements had been almost impossible to find. Having received almost no money from the royal war treasuries, most officers could not offer enlistment bounties to entice new men to join the regiments. Ironically, it was the famine that improved this dire situation. Hunger proved to be a highly effective recruiting sergeant. Throughout the spring, especially in the frontier provinces, poor men flocked to the colors in hopes of getting something to eat; many even agreed to waive payment of the king's silver. "The misery of the people," Villars observed, "was the salvation of the state."[5]

The French were even more fortunate that the Army of Flanders did not have to depend solely on raw recruits. Each regiment contained an irreducible core of hard-bitten veterans. These were the most committed and professional soldiers France possessed. Whether originally volunteers or impressed militiamen, they had been at war for many years and had come to regard arms as their métier. For them, enduring hardships had become badges of soldierly honor and masculine pride. They had learned to make do with few comforts, eking out a living on a couple of sous, a crust of bread, a skin of piquette, and a shred of tobacco. Above all, despite the many defeats they had suffered, they still regarded themselves as the equals of their foes. It was the least of Villars' gasconades when he boasted that his troops wished to wipe away the stain of the last campaigns through some glorious action.[6]

Their commanders were also hardened veterans who had seen considerable combat. Villars' chief subordinate was Pierre de Montesquiou, Comte d'Artagnan, lieutenant general and director general of infantry. Cousin of the musketeer who would be immortalized by Dumas, he had fought in Flanders for many years, earning a reputation for courage and tenacity. In 1706, he had stoutly defended the village of Ramillies against waves of enemy assaults, only withdrawing after the rest of the French army had been overwhelmed. The Flanders army's leading cavalry commander was Chrétien-Louis, Chevalier de Luxembourg. He was the youngest son of the hunchbacked marshal of the Nine Years' War but had won fame in his own right for a spectacular feat of arms. During the siege of Lille, he had led a force of French cavalry in a daring dash through the Allied siege lines to resupply the beleaguered garrison with gunpowder. The artillery was under Armand de Mormès de Saint-Hilaire. A seasoned gunner, an old comrade of Vauban, and an innovative tactician, he had turned his batteries into a fearsome battlefield instrument. Other notable general officers were Antoine de Gramont, Duc de Guiche, one of France's most exalted aristocrats and commander of the French and Swiss Guards; Louis-Vincent, Marquis de Goësbriand, a tenacious fighter who had played an important part in the repulse of Prince Eugene from Toulon; Jacques-François de Chastenet, Marquis de Puységur, who would later become an influential military theorist; François-Frézeau, Marquis de La Frézelière, a celebrated artillerist; and François Zénobie Philippe, Comte d'Albergotti, a Florentine in French service well known for his bravery.

Against the enemy they were about to face, the French would need all their veteran pluck and determination. The Allied host assembling around Ghent and Courtrai was of unprecedented size and strength: 170 battalions and 263 squadrons, more than 130,000 men. The Duke of Marlborough commanded the Confederate Army, the combined British and Dutch forces. His troops testified to the diversity and breadth of the European coalition arrayed against the Sun King.[7] The British element consisted of twenty battalions and thirty-five squadrons, or about twenty thousand men. They included some of the British army's most historic regiments: the First Foot Guards, the Coldstream Guards, the Royal Scots (the senior regiment of the line, which gloried in the nickname "Pontius Pilate's bodyguard"), the Buffs, the Green Howards, and the Scots Greys.[8] The British had an importance out of all proportion to their relatively small numbers, for Marlborough frequently entrusted them with particularly difficult and crucial missions. This was recognized by the French.

Already in 1706, Louis himself warned Marshal Villeroy to "pay particular attention to what will be the first shock of the English troops."[9]

The core of Marlborough's command was the Dutch States Army, *Het Staatsche Leger*. After the Dutch War, it had become one of the most advanced, most professional, and best-trained forces in Europe. The infantry, sixty-two battalions strong, was widely considered the finest of its kind and counted such crack formations as the Holland or Blue Guards, the Frisian Guards, the Scottish Brigade, and the Prince of Orange's regiment.[10] The sixty cavalry squadrons, both horse and dragoons, also had a very high reputation.[11]

Most of Marlborough's soldiers were neither British nor Dutch but foreigners in the pay of London and The Hague. The Maritime Powers purchased the services of nine battalions and twenty-one squadrons of the Danish army. The Danes, particularly the cavalry, were highly regarded as shock troops. There were also the ubiquitous Swiss. Nine battalions formed part of the States Army's order of battle. The bulk of the Confederate Army was made up of Germans. The Dutch Republic had long supplemented its own slender manpower with mercenaries from Europe's most fertile recruiting grounds: the small states and Free Cities of the Holy Roman Empire. They represented a significant share of the rank and file of the "national" regiments of the States Army. Furthermore, for the 1709 campaign, the Dutch augmented their forces with 4,743 soldiers from Saxony, Brunswick-Wolfenbüttel, and Holstein-Gottorp. The British also hired numerous units of German infantry and cavalry.[12]

Distinct from and more numerous than the mercenaries were the auxiliaries contributed by the *Armierten*, the armed princes of the Empire. They received large subsidies from Parliament and the States General to send their armies to fight under Marlborough in Flanders. Of these auxiliaries, the Prussians were the most important. For 1709, Frederick I, Elector of Brandenburg and King in Prussia, agreed to supply nineteen battalions and twenty-one squadrons. Georg Ludwig of Hanover—the future King George I of England—also sent a sizable contingent: fifteen battalions and twenty-nine squadrons. Augustus the Strong of Saxony, despite being simultaneously embroiled in the Great Northern War, still managed to dispatch eight battalions and twelve squadrons. Other auxiliaries were provided by Hesse-Kassel (nine battalions and sixteen squadrons), the Palatinate (eight battalions and eighteen squadrons), and Württemberg (six battalions and four squadrons).[13]

Alongside Marlborough's Confederate Army was Prince Eugene's Imperial corps. During the War of the Spanish Succession, the Habsburg emperors raised an impressive army—by 1705, 113,000 troops—from their dynastic lands in Central Europe. However, most of it had been committed to the conquest of Italy and the defeat of Ferenc Rakoczi's rebellion in Hungary.¹⁴ Eugene had eight battalions and thirty squadrons of Habsburg troops together with seven battalions of auxiliaries from the minor German states of Ansbach, Mecklenburg, and Würzburg. To flesh out the prince's corps, Marlborough assigned him the Danes and most of the German contingents in the pay of the Maritime Powers, so that Eugene came to lead 66 battalions and 108 squadrons. The captain general retained command of the British and Dutch national troops as well as the Prussians and Hanoverians, a total of 104 battalions and 163 squadrons.¹⁵

The generals of the Allied armies were as diverse and colorful as the soldiers they led. Marlborough's indispensable lieutenant was the Irishman William Cadogan. Their professional association and close friendship had begun during the Nine Years' War when they served together in Flanders in the army of William III. Cadogan's intelligence, resourcefulness, and calm, efficient conduct of his duties won Marlborough's complete trust. In 1701, after taking charge of the Confederate Army, he appointed Cadogan Quartermaster-General. In this post, he was responsible for the critical matters of supply and logistics. But much else fell within his remit. He was the army's chief scout and gatherer of intelligence. On campaign, he chose its campsites, routed its marches, found forage for its horses, searched for the enemy, and reconnoitered their positions. Not least, he often led troops in critical actions.¹⁶ At Oudenarde, commanding the Allied vanguard, he surprised the French, seized vital crossings over the Scheldt, and tenaciously held his ground against repeated attacks. His activities frequently exposed him to great peril. In 1706, while riding ahead of the army, he was captured by French cavalry. A frightened Marlborough wrote to Sarah that "poor Cadogan is taken prisoner or killed, which gives me a great deal of uneasiness, for he loved me, and I could rely on him." Fortunately, the Duc de Vendôme chivalrously agreed to release the quartermaster-general in exchange for a French officer taken at Ramillies.¹⁷

In addition to Cadogan, Marlborough could call upon other talented British officers. One of his best combat commanders was George Hamilton, Earl of Orkney. Immensely pugnacious, courageous, and indomitable, this taciturn, humorless Scot led British infantry with distinction in all of the captain general's battles and sieges. At Blenheim, Orkney assaulted the village's walled church and forced a much larger enemy force to surrender. At Ramillies, he conducted a diversionary attack so successfully that when ordered by Marlborough to withdraw, he did so only with the greatest reluctance. Far less happy was the captain general's relationship with another Scottish officer, John Campbell, Duke of Argyll. A rising star in both the British army and politics, he distinguished himself at Ramillies, the siege of Ostend, and Oudenarde. Yet his fiery personality, arrogance, and ambition would eventually lead him to clash bitterly and openly with Marlborough.[18]

In skill, experience, and dedication, the Dutch generals were the equals of their British comrades in arms. The most prominent among them was Johan Willem Friso, William III's cousin and successor as Prince of Orange. Just twenty-two years old, he had fought bravely and well at his baptism of fire at Oudenarde, where he delivered the climactic attack that nearly encircled Vendôme's army. The other leading Dutch generals were capable and doughty veterans who had been schooled in war by the Stadholder-King: Claude Frederic T'Serclaes, Count Tilly; Arnold Joost van Keppel, Earl of Albemarle; and François Nicolas, Baron Fagel. In addition, the Republic had always made good use of talented foreigners. Two highly regarded infantry officers, Bengt van Oxenstiern and Karel Willem van Sparre, were Swedes. One of the States Army's most important cavalry commanders was Frederick, Hereditary prince of Hesse-Kassel. Not just a high lord of the Holy Roman Empire, he was also heir by marriage to the greatest warrior of the age, Charles XII, King of Sweden. Another cavalry general was a French aristocrat, François Egon de La Tour d'Auvergne, styled the prince d'Auvergne, who was a great nephew of Turenne. With characteristic viciousness, Saint-Simon describes him as a "fat, very obtuse and very disagreeable youth, extremely full of his birth and the chimeric pretentions of his family." In 1702, feeling that his ambitions were being thwarted by War Minister Chamillart and his other enemies at court, d'Auvergne deserted to the Allies. The Parlement of Paris promptly sentenced him to death for high treason and hanged his effigy in the place de Grève.[19]

Distinguished captains were also found among the Germans. The Prussians were led by Carl Philipp, Graf von Wylich und Lottum. Nearly sixty years old yet still vigorous, Lottum had first faced the French as an officer of the States Army during the Dutch War. He had been made Prussia's chief general at the beginning of the War of the Spanish Succession and had then fought in its greatest battles. Prince Eugene's most important subordinate was Johann Matthias, Graf von der Schulenburg. In command of the Saxon auxiliaries, he was a grizzled mercenary of vast and varied experience, having fought against the Turks, the Swedes, and the French. He would end his long life as a field marshal of Venice, having amassed one of the finest art collections in eighteenth-century Europe.[20]

The Allied generals were a solid, competent lot; some even rose to the level of greatness. But the Dutch Republic regarded war as too important to be left solely up to military men. The Council of State, the governing body of the Republic that administered its armed forces, dispatched representatives, the *gedeputeerden te velde* or field deputies, to accompany the army on campaign. They attended councils of war, participated in making command decisions, and, most importantly, could exercise a veto on the use of Dutch troops. Marlborough and his historians, including his great descendant and biographer Winston Churchill, cast the field deputies as militarily amateurish politicians and bureaucrats and blamed them for unnecessarily restraining his genius. Time and again, their excessive caution quashed the captain general's boldest schemes.[21] The wariness was mutual. Sicco van Goslinga of Friesland was the most important field deputy of the War of the Spanish Succession and knew Marlborough exceedingly well. He praised his impeccable manners, courage, judgment, penetrating intelligence, and ability to plan and fight victorious campaigns. Alongside these perfections, though, were a host of less admirable qualities:

> The Duke is a profound dissimulator, all the more dangerous because he covers it with mannerisms and expressions which seem to convey frankness itself: he has an excessive ambition, is sordidly avaricious, which influences all his conduct; if he has courage, as he undoubtedly does despite what his envious enemies say, he certainly does not have that firmness of soul which makes the true Hero; he is sometimes irresolute, and, especially on the eve of some great action, is discouraged by difficulties and sometimes allows himself to be beaten down by disasters.[22]

The field deputies in fact made essential contributions to Allied success. They were indispensable for the organization and smooth running of the army's logistics. Far from being ignorant of war, most were long-serving members of the Council of State who possessed expertise and experience that rivaled those of the professional soldiers. In particular, their knowledge of finances and supplies often made them better placed to realistically reconcile the Allies' strategic and operational ends with their material means. Marlborough and Eugene had to cooperate with them. For the 1709 campaign, four field deputies were with the army: Goslinga, Jacob van Randwyck, Willem Hooft, and Philip Frederik Vegelin van Claerbergen.[23]

The Allied army poised to invade France was polyglot, multi-confessional, and drawn from all the nations of Western and Northern Europe. Ironically, if the army had a common tongue, it was French. Yet, this disparate force had deep wellsprings of cohesion. Its veteran soldiers had campaigned together for many years. They had developed a common approach to fighting—what modern military theorists call a doctrine. They also took enormous confidence from their unblemished record of success. Not least, they had an unshakable faith in Marlborough and Eugene, the two great captains who had brought them victory after victory. France could not have faced a more formidable foe.

How to stop this foe consumed Marshal Villars. As more and more reports reached him about the Allied army, he became increasingly worried about its considerable superiority in numbers, and he began lobbying the court for reinforcements. He now argued that Ypres and Tournai were adequately garrisoned. A few battalions could be safely taken from each for the campaign army. After receiving authorization from the king, Villars extracted four battalions from Ypres and three from Tournai. For more cavalry, he had to go further afield. On June 14, Daniel Voysin, the new minister of war, ordered Marshal Harcourt, commander of the Army of Germany, to detach twenty-two squadrons, a third of his mounted arm, and send them to Flanders.[24]

Villars' chief worry remained bread. Just enough had been scraped together for his troops to take up position south of La Bassée. But feeding the Army of Flanders remained a hand-to-mouth and day-by-day affair. The French authorities had to continue searching everywhere for grain. Voysin turned to Normandy and Brittany, which appeared to have suffered less from the Great Winter than the rest of the kingdom. Supplies from these provinces could be shipped through the English Channel to the port of Saint-Valéry at the mouth of the Somme, barged upriver to Amiens, then carted to Arras.[25] However, the British government, after learning of the destruction of the harvest in France, immediately imposed a naval blockade to prevent the movement of food into French ports. To reach Flanders, the grain ships would have to run a gauntlet of Royal Navy men of war.[26]

Even if the ships could get through, Norman and Breton grain would take many weeks to arrive. Villars' hungry army could not wait. None other than the king himself proposed a stopgap: eke out the available wheat by combining it with oats. With the horses now able to forage on grass, most of their feed could be redirected to meet the needs of the men. Louis told Villars that bakers at the Invalides, the great veterans hospital in Paris, had successfully made loaves from a mixture of wheat and oat flours. On June 11, Intendant Bernage was ordered to make this new *pain de munition* with the oats he had stockpiled for the cavalry. Although production would be plagued by technical difficulties—expert bakers from the Invalides had to be dispatched to Arras—this bread was helping to feed the Army of Flanders by the end of June.[27]

Yet, as Villars wrestled with the difficulties of grain supplies and flour milling, a new logistical problem arose. When the army went into the field, it left behind in the rear its magazines and bread ovens. Its troops then depended on the convoys of the supply train to bring them their rations. The creation, maintenance, and running of this train, the *équipages des vivres*, were among the most important duties of the army's bread contractors, the *munitionnaires*. It had to be of high quality, replete with sturdy wagons driven by skilled teamsters and pulled by robust draft horses. The munition bread itself had to be packed and transported in special waterproof chests called caissons. The *équipages* shuttled constantly between the ovens and the camps, bringing four days of food at a time to the troops.[28] But, as with almost everything else under their purview, the *munitionnaires* of the Army of Flanders had completely failed to marshal an adequate supply train. French officers and officials had been left to improvise one by pressing into service carts owned and driven by local peasants. These soon proved to be hopelessly inadequate: country horses, for instance, were too feeble and lacking in endurance to pull heavy loads of bread. "The supply train is very weak," Villars complained to Voysin on June 17, "bread was delivered today for only one day and it arrived in the evening so that the troops worked all day without eating." The marshal would make many more such complaints as the fighting season unfolded.[29]

Villars needed his starving soldiers to work long and hard. His hopes of stopping the enemy rested on the completion of the fortified lines running from the Scarpe near Douai to the Lys at Saint-Venant, barring the most direct invasion route into France. During the first weeks of June, he constantly visited his troops, encouraging and exhorting them to bend to their shovels with a will. He also promised they would soon receive more bread and back pay. "I stand with the men as they labor," he explained to Voysin, "talking to them in such a way as to encourage their patience. Then many even cry out, 'The Marshal is right: you sometimes have to suffer.'"[30]

Thanks to the stoic toil of Villars' troops, the lines took shape. By the middle of June, they had become strong in the crucial La Bassée sector. There they consisted of two broad, deep ditches fronting a continuous earthen parapet studded with bastions and ravelins for cannon. More artillery batteries were massed in redoubts on the heights of Cambrin, from where they could bring down a storm of shot on advancing enemy troops. The La Bassêe defenses were anchored by impassable marshes at either end—Cuinchy to the west and Hulluch to the east. On the western stretch running to the Lys, the lines consisted of fortified outposts. Many of these were buttressed by forbidding terrain, especially water obstacles swollen by the relentless spring rains.[31] On the eastern flank near Douai, the French planned further inundations by opening the sluices that channeled the Scarpe. This would only be done once the Allied advance was imminent because the river's water was needed to power the mills supplying the army with flour.[32]

Villars encamped most of his infantry and cavalry near Lens and at the villages of Benifontaine and Annequin, all located within easy reach of the La Bassée front. He scattered the rest across Flanders from Aire in the west to Valenciennes and the Abbey of Crespin near Mons in the east to Arras and Cambrai in the south. This dispersal was necessary both for reasons of supply and to guard against an Allied descent on an unexpected quarter. The marshal intended to quickly concentrate all his troops as soon as he learned when and where the Allies were approaching.[33] The large number of battalions and squadrons in his army posed a challenge to efficient command and control: he would have had to send individual orders to each one. Following long-standing French practice, he and his subordinates grouped these smaller units into brigades, temporary larger formations created for the campaign. Each had four to ten battalions or eight to sixteen squadrons. The Irish brigade consisted of the five single-battalion Jacobite regiments, while the Le Roi brigade comprised the four battalions of the elite régiment du Roi and the two of the Saintonge regiment.[34]

Building the lines was Villars' main countermeasure against the Allied invasion. But he also took another. Beginning in early June, he sent out his cavalry to forage. One body from the stronghold of Saint-Omer ate up all the grass along the roads leading to the Lys. Another thirty squadrons descended on the countryside between Lille and the Deûle and stripped it bare of clover and sainfoin. The marshal's aim was to hinder enemy operations in large stretches of the Flanders theater. Without food for their horses, the Allies would find it difficult, if not impossible, to move their armies west of Lille or toward Douai.[35]

Meanwhile, the Allies were completing their own preparations. They too were struggling with feeding their armies. This huge task was undertaken by specialist provisioners who, like the French *munitionnaires*, were civilian contractors. For the 1709 campaign in Flanders, the Republic was furnishing rations to 62,500 troops and Great Britain to 37,500. The Dutch also assumed responsibility for the subsistence of the Imperial and Prussian contingents. This meant that the key figure in Allied logistics was the supplier of bread and forage to the States Army, the *provediteur-generaal van den staat*. From 1673 until 1706, this post had always been held by Moses (alias Antonio Alvarez) Machado. A Sephardic Jew of Amsterdam, he had been a close and invaluable associate of William III. No one could match his financial resources nor his expertise and experience in finding, gathering, and distributing food to tens of thousands of men and horses. After his death, the Republic's Council of State awarded his contracts to his son, Jacob Hiskia Machado. The younger Machado worked in partnership with one of his father's old associates, Solomon de Medina. Also a Sephardic Jew, Medina had become the provisioner of the British forces in Flanders after 1688. For his services, he had been knighted, the first person of his faith to be so honored.[36]

Unfortunately, Machado and Medina proved inadequate to the challenges they faced. They were first tormented by the fast-rising cost of grain. The ravages of the Great Winter had caused prices to shoot up in Great Britain, the Dutch Republic, the Spanish Netherlands, and Germany. Matters were little better when they turned to their other main source of supplies. Thanks to the Maritime Powers' control of the sea, they had long been able to avail themselves of the rich grainlands of Eastern Europe. But in 1708, the Swedish King Charles XII had launched an invasion of Russia. His army had consumed much of the harvests in Prussia and Poland. Then the fighting and Russia's scorched-earth strategy had caused widespread destruction in Ukraine, Lithuania, and the Baltic lands. As a result, imports from the east were exorbitantly dear. On May 24, Machado and Medina complained to the Dutch Council of State that they had already exhausted the funds it had advanced to them to buy grain. They would need much more if they were to provision the armies for the entire campaigning season. The hard-headed leaders of the burgher Republic rejected their demand, pointing out that the provisioners' contract stipulated that they were solely responsible for any increases in costs. Forced to resort to their own funds and credit, Machado and Medina dragged their feet on stockpiling grain.[37]

As the opening of the campaign neared, the provisioners revealed other shortcomings. The supply train they assembled had an insufficient number of wagons drawn by poor-quality horses. The field deputies had to supplement them at great expense with two hundred vehicles with better draft animals. Worse yet, Jacob Hiskia Machado showed that he lacked his father's administrative talents. At a meeting between the army's commanders and the provisioners on June 13, it was discovered that he had failed to transport enough grain to the Allied armies' forward base at Lille and had fallen seriously behind schedule in milling flour and baking bread. The field deputies now forcefully intervened. Machado was placed under the close supervision of Vegelin van Claerbergen. Then, at the end of June, he was forced to hand over most of his duties to Joshua Castano, another Sephardic Jewish provisioner, who managed to put the bread supply on a much sounder footing. Following the dismal experience of the 1709 campaign, Machado would give up the post of *provideteur-generaal* and abandon the business of army provisioning altogether. As for Sir Solomon de Medina, he would rack up such enormous debts that his fortune would be ruined.[38]

Problems with provisioning slowed the entry of the Allies into the campaign. The atrocious weather imposed further delays. The heavy spring rains continued until well into June. The Confederate and Imperial armies marked time on the heights of Courtrai, while their commanders cooled their heels at Lille. "We have rain every day," complained Marlborough to Godolphin, "which gives us the spleen, and is of great advantage to the Marishal de Villars, since it gives him the time to finish his lins, which he is working at the head of his army."[39] At last, on June 21, a brilliant sun broke through the banks of clouds. The Allies shipped the heavy guns of their siege train down the Lys from Ghent to Menin and their armies began assembling on the waterlogged plains south of Lille. Villars immediately called in his troops and sent them into the La Bassée lines. Crucially, he drew more battalions out of Tournai, leaving the fortress with just thirteen, the minimum required for its defense. A shipment of coin from Paris enabled him to distribute some morale-boosting pay. But a shortage of bread forced him to leave the large corps of the Chevalier de Luxembourg below Douai.[40]

On June 23, the Allied armies advanced down both sides of the Deule toward La Bassée. Villars dashed off dispatches to the court warning that an attack on his lines was imminent.[41] Eugene and Marlborough, however, stopped short and sent out scouts to examine the French works. One reconnaissance was carried out by Daniel Wolf von Dopff, who had been William III's Quartermaster-General during the Nine Years' War and was reputed to have an unequaled knowledge of the geography of Flanders. Another was conducted by William Cadogan. To get a closer look at the fortifications, he disguised himself as a laborer and mingled among the French troops.[42]

Dopff and Cadogan returned to the Allied camp on June 24. A council of war convened that night. In attendance were Marlborough, Eugene, Count Tilly (the senior Dutch general), the two quartermaster-generals, and the field deputies. On the goal of the campaign, there was no debate. All were certain that France was at its last gasp and Louis' defiance mere bravado. One more dose of pressure and the French king would be forced to admit the futility of resistance and accept whatever terms the Grand Alliance cared to impose. But by entrenching his army, Villars had robbed the Allies of the most straightforward means of achieving this end—a pitched battle in the open field. Instead, the council of war had to consider four alternative courses of action: assault the Army of Flanders in its lines; attack the Lys strongholds of Béthune and Saint-Venant; beleaguer Ypres; or besiege Tournai.

On the first option, Dopff and Cadogan spoke at length. They had carefully studied Marshal Villars' position and determined it was too strong to successfully storm. Without demur, Marlborough and Eugene agreed with this opinion. The second option was also quickly dismissed. If the Allies marched for Béthune and Saint-Venant, they would expose their lines of communication to constant enemy attacks from both Ypres and La Bassée. Under such conditions, they would be unable to sustain sieges of these fortresses.

The Duke of Marlborough then spoke forcefully in favor of making an attempt on Ypres. He was hoping to resurrect the boldest of all his strategic designs. During the summer of 1708, in the heady aftermath of the victory at Oudenarde, he had proposed that the Allied armies should sweep west to the Channel coast, then south to the mouth of the Somme. There, they would rendezvous with the Royal Navy and seize the port of Abbeville. Such a move would completely outflank Vauban's *pre carré*. A march up the river would then bring the armies into the defenseless heart of France. Marlborough acknowledged that the Allies would be cutting themselves off from their bases in the Netherlands. However, the Anglo-Dutch fleets would be able to land everything they needed at Abbeville. In the end, Eugene had concluded that the scheme was too risky and had opted instead for besieging Lille.[43]

It had been Sidney Godolphin who brought up the plan again. Following the collapse of The Hague talks, he enthusiastically endorsed it in letter after letter to the captain general:

> This therfore I should think were the proper time to attempt it. Wee can certainly bee masters of the sea in the channell, and carry bread for your whole army to the bay of Bolloin or St. Valery, whenever you give us notice. And I should think this must force the enemys to a battell, or to abandon all Picardie and Normandy to the very gates of Paris.[44]

Marlborough needed little convincing. Lille gave the Allies a firm lodgement in the *pré carré* but little more. If they wished to break into the interior of France, they would have to batter their way through a barrier of strong fortresses as well as Villars' field army, now entrenched in fortifications that were becoming more forbidding by the hour. Taking Ypres would be the necessary first step to opening the road to the sea. Unknown to Marlborough and the other Allied commanders, one of Marshal Villars' chief fears was, as he had confessed to Louis, a wide turning movement against his left flank. His grain stores were so meager and his supply trains so weak that he would be hard-pressed to pursue the Allies westward.

Prince Eugene remained unconvinced. Above all, he was deeply skeptical that the Allied navies could keep the armies supplied. Unlike Marlborough, he had recent experience of an amphibious operation, and it had been an unhappy one. During his descent on Toulon in 1707, the Royal Navy had promised to provision and support his army as it marched across southern France and attacked the port. But the fleet of Admiral Cloudesley Shovell had failed to keep this promise, an important reason for the campaign's failure.[45] Consequently, Eugene rejected Ypres and opted for Tournai. Count Tilly and the field deputies immediately ranged themselves alongside him. The Dutch raised several reasons in favor of

Tournai. While it was a powerful fortress—Goslinga dubbed it "perhaps one of the strongest in the Universe"—its garrison had been gravely weakened by Villars. Taking it would widen the breach in the *pré carré*. The siege could be easily sustained from nearby friendly strongholds. At the same time, the Allied armies would be covering Brabant from French attack. Finally, Marshal Villars would discover that it was almost impossible to relieve Tournai without giving battle on disadvantageous terms. The captain general realized he was alone in favoring an attack on Ypres. He at once abandoned it and fell into line with Eugene and the Dutch.[46]

Having chosen a course of action, Eugene and Marlborough concocted a brilliant plan to invest Tournai before Villars could stop them. The marshal had been keeping a close eye on the Allies and was trying to anticipate what they would do next. He fixed on the positioning of their siege artillery at Menin and interpreted it as a sign they would move against his left. On June 26, he warned the court that:

> We have learned that the enemy no longer intends to attack us since they carried out a reconnaissance of our camp by Monsieur de Catogan, who it is said walked in disguise along the whole length of our works. He and some other enemy officers who entered the ramparts estimated they could not be taken. We are also told that their intention now is to try to shift us out of our lines by marching towards Saint-Venant.[47]

That very day, at twilight, the Allies struck camp. Thanks to the efforts of Vegelin van Claerbergen and the provisioner Joshua Castano, the troops' haversacks and the bread wagons were stuffed with six days of rations, giving the Allied armies great freedom of action. Eugene and Marlborough first moved threateningly toward the French position south of La Bassée. Villars saw this as a feint and acted to strengthen his left flank but without moving his main army. He immediately rushed reinforcements to Aire, Béthune, and Saint-Venant. Meanwhile, he himself hurried with three hundred cavalry to La Gorgue, to the west of La Bassée. Along the way, his troopers lit fires to simulate an advancing French vanguard. However, during the night, Eugene and Marlborough turned east, marched directly for Tournai, and arrived there at daybreak. By nightfall on June 27, the Allies had completely surrounded the great fortress. When he learned of it, the marshal claimed to the king that his precautions had forced the Allies to alter their original plans of marching to the Lys and instead settle for besieging Tournai. It was a ludicrous boast. In reality, in Goslinga's memorable words, "Monsieur de Villars had been caught with his head in the basket."[48]

Nevertheless, Villars and the king quickly regained their equilibrium. As Goslinga had observed, Tournai was one of the strongest of all French fortresses. Its centerpiece was its state-of-the-art pentagonal citadel. Designed by Vauban's colleague Deshoulières and built by the engineer and long-serving governor Jean de Mesgrigny, it featured a particularly intricate system of underground defenses called countermines.[49] Tournai's garrison had been weakened by Villars' frequent withdrawals. When the Allies surrounded the city, it consisted of just thirteen battalions and a motley collection of independent companies, in all about seven thousand troops, barely enough to man the fortifications. But there were no doubts about its commander, Louis-Charles de Hautefort, Marquis de Surville. A lieutenant general of infantry, he had been Marshal Boufflers' second-in-command during the legendary defense of Lille.[50] He could be counted on to offer a skillful, obstinate resistance. Tournai also seemed to be well provisioned: according to Charles-Étienne de Bernières, intendant of Flanders, its magazines stored four months of food for both the garrison and the townsfolk. The French high command hoped that it could hold out for most, if not all, of the campaigning season.[51]

Villars also realized that by tying down their armies in a siege, Eugene and Marlborough were handing him the initiative. At the beginning of July, he sent the king his assessment of the transformed strategic situation. The Army of Flanders could now maneuver freely. It could attempt to lift the siege of Tournai, which would almost certainly bring on a battle with the enemy, or march west and invest Menin, the capture of which would yield a valuable fortress on the vulnerable seaward flank, or strike east toward Brussels with the goal of subjecting virgin enemy territory to contributions—Villars was the undisputed master of this system of formalized extortion and plunder. Although each of these operations had its challenges, particularly in terms of securing adequate supplies for the army, given his predilection for bold, offensive action, the marshal pressed the king to choose one of them. If Louis judged all three options too risky, the army could remain in place and complete the westward extension of the La Bassée lines by finishing the fortifications out to Saint-Venant. This would seal off Artois and Picardy from enemy raids.[52] Villars entrusted his letter to a mounted courier, who immediately set off for the court. The journey from the marshal's headquarters at the camp of Annay near Lens to Versailles took most of a day. On the evening of July 2, the courier galloped through the palace's gilded gates.[53]

Louis accepted the letter, read it, and considered his response. For more than two decades, his most trusted military adviser had been the Marquis de Chamlay. However, the influence of the king's favorite officer was waning. Much of his attention this year was given over to the famine and to the financial crisis. The king also customarily turned for advice to his war minister. But Daniel Voysin had been in office for less than a month and, despite previously serving as intendant of the frontier province of Hainault, he was quite inexperienced in military affairs. He had therefore been placed under the tutelage of Marshal Boufflers. During the first months of his tenure, Voysin hesitated to opine on strategic and operational questions, confining himself to administrative matters.[54] Perhaps like no other time during his long reign, in the summer of 1709, Louis made decisions about his armies by himself.

In his answer, the king first lavished praise on Villars' conduct of the campaign so far:

> I count for much that by your wise dispositions and the precautions you have taken, all of their vast projects have been reduced to this single enterprise; and you cannot have rendered me a more important service, for this fortress is so well fortified I have cause to hope this siege will occupy the enemy army for the best part of the campaign.

But he then urged caution on his general. A relief of Tournai must only be tried late in the siege, and only if the Allies had been considerably weakened by combat, fatigue, and disease. No attempts on Menin or Brussels should be made because the Army of Flanders would be exposed to battle for too little gain. Louis concluded by reminding Villars:

> That my principal objective has always been to prevent the enemy penetrating my kingdom and this view must not be abandoned. And it is to this that you must principally attach yourself, never leaving the camp and the posts which you occupy, unless you consider it possible to do so in complete safety, always remaining in such a position that you cannot be forced to leave. Fight only as much as you think you can do so with advantage and that you do not also give opportunity to my enemies to make detachments which can penetrate into my kingdom.[55]

Villars reluctantly followed his master's wishes. He set his army to work completing and strengthening the lines from La Bassée to Saint-Venant. Yet even explicit orders from the king could not entirely curb his aggressive instincts. Instead, he looked for opportunities to harass the Allies. The marshal led a strong corps of cavalry to reconnoiter and forage the countryside around Lille. By feeding his horses on the fresh grass, he denied it to the enemy armies at Tournai. While on this expedition, Villars also learned that the Allies had established an outpost at Warneton near Menin. He decided to attack it. On July 3, the Comte d'Artagnan sallied out of the La Bassée lines with fifteen battalions and twenty squadrons. The next day, he was joined by a brigade of infantry and six cannons dispatched by Claude Le Blanc, the bellicose and enterprising intendant of Ypres. The combined force surprised and stormed Warneton. Eight hundred Allied soldiers were killed: most drowned while attempting to flee across the Lys. A further eight hundred were taken prisoner. D'Artagnan pillaged the outpost, razed it, then got clean away before a strong relief force led by Prince Eugene arrived on the scene.[56]

Louis effusively praised Villars and d'Artagnan for this tidy success. It raised French spirits, as even the Allies acknowledged.[57] But the campaign's focus was now besieged Tournai. After effecting its encirclement, the Allies divided their forces into two. Eugene took charge of the army of observation that covered the siege and guarded against French interference. Marlborough commanded the sixty battalions and seventy-six squadrons that went against Tournai itself. For all his reputation as a fearsome battle captain, Marlborough had surprisingly little experience against first-rate French fortresses. To this point, he had only faced antiquated German strongholds or dilapidated Low Countries fortlets. Additionally, the British army had had almost no exposure to modern, scientific siege warfare as it was practiced on the continent. For the entire duration of operations at Tournai, the captain general would exercise a mainly hands-off, supervisory role.[58]

The real work was done by the Dutch. The States Army had a long tradition of excellence in assailing strong places. It employed an approach that had been developed by the great military engineer Menno van Coehoorn. Eschewing the efficient, yet time-consuming methods of his archrival Vauban, Coehoorn had emphasized massive artillery bombardments and vigorous infantry assaults to overwhelm even the strongest enemy defenses. Expensive in terms of both money and materiel, these methods were taxing even for the wealthy Dutch Republic. But they had produced results time and again during the Nine Years' War and the War of the Spanish Succession.[59]

The Allies first surrounded Tournai with a long perimeter of entrenchments and earthworks.[60] These lines of circumvallation cut off the fortress from resupply and relief. Then, on the night of July 7, the trenches were opened. Under the direction of the experienced Huguenot siege engineers Guillaume Des Rocques and Lucas Du Mée, thousands of Allied soldiers took up their tools and began to dig. Their trenches crept toward the beleaguered stronghold, zigzagging for increased protection from incoming fire. The Allies were making three different attacks on widely separated sectors of the defenses. The first and largest was led by the Prussian Lottum and was aimed at the eastern front of the citadel and the gate of Valenciennes. The second was launched by the Dutch Fagel on the north bank of the Scheldt against the gate of Marvis and two adjoining bastions. The third was commanded by the Saxon Schulenberg and threatened the western walls of the city, especially the hornwork protecting the gate of the Seven Fountains.

From Tournai's ramparts, the Marquis de Surville was closely watching all of these enemy moves. He was ably assisted by the seven-seventy-year-old governor Mesgrigny, who knew every inch of the defenses. The three attacks, they realized, were designed to overstretch the garrison. Their paucity of troops forced them to be extremely sparing with sorties and raids against the Allied trenches. What they could do was lay down a continuous curtain of fire. Musketry and cannon shot were soon inflicting serious losses on the besiegers.

The French had the advantage in firepower until the arrival of the Allied siege train on July 11. The great guns and all their impedimenta had been floated down the Scheldt from Ghent on 160 boats and barges. The Dutch engineers had already selected and prepared positions for the batteries. On the night of July 12, 104 cannons and 78 mortars opened fire on Tournai. Their crescendos were heard by French outposts near Condé, fifteen miles to the southeast.[61]

Under their cover, the Allied troops drove their trenches steadily forward. Schulenburg's attack made particularly dangerous progress. By July 16, his troops had reached the Seven Fountains hornwork and the nearby Blandinoise bastion. Surville did not have enough soldiers to adequately defend both, and he was forced to evacuate this sector's covered way—the infantry fighting position directly in front of the curtain wall and bastions. When he learned of this setback, Villars told the king it gave him "an extreme pain." But the besieged were mounting a stout resistance; in addition, they still had deadly tricks to play. On July 18, they detonated one of the underground countermines, destroying a battery firing on the citadel. Two nights later, a well-judged sortie overran a long stretch of the besiegers' works. Proof of the ferocity of the fighting and the dismal conditions in the Allied trenches came in the steady stream of enemy soldiers deserting to the French.[62]

While the siege of Tournai raged, Villars was struggling with the seemingly endless problem of subsistence for his army. Ministers, intendants, and other royal officials continued to scour provinces on the frontier and as far away as Normandy and Brittany for grain. The *munitionnaires* François-Marie Fargès and the Paris brothers—who had taken over the Army of Flanders' bread contract from the defunct La Cour company—imported more from the Bishopric of Liège and the Duchy of Jülich.[63] Yet there was never enough. When supplies were found, it was often difficult getting them to the magazines. At the beginning of July, Intendant Bernage had too few carts to move a desperately needed shipment of wheat from Peronne on the Somme to Arras and Douai. He had to seize munitions wagons, empty them of their cargoes of gunpowder and ammunition, and load them up with sacks of grain instead. When even this measure failed to produce a large enough convoy, he ordered the *maréchaussée*, the rural constabulary, to round up local peasants with their wagons.[64] There were chronic challenges with milling enough flour and with transporting bread to the troops. As Villars complained to War Minister Voysin

> I confess to you, Monsieur, that worries about our provisions are killing me. How can I be expected to make the least march if I do not have two days' worth of bread? We consume more flour than the mills can make. In truth, Monsieur, one must have a little courage to always appear cheerful and calm when one endures such bad nights.[65]

Now when the marshal inspected his troops, he heard them muttering, "Panem nostrum quotidianum da nobis hodie." The plight of the French soldiers was truly desperate. They were surviving on poor-quality munition bread that they received neither daily nor in adequate quantity. They had not received their pay in weeks or even months. Most were clad in ragged uniforms and worn-out shoes. Unsurprisingly, their behavior soon became much more dangerous than mere grumbling in the ranks. Many deserted, particularly from the foreign regiments and the Wittelsbach contingents. Many others took to marauding. They despoiled French villages and hamlets, taking whatever they needed or fancied. On July 6, the deputies of the Estates of Artois complained to War Minister Voysin that the soldiers' depredations were causing peasants to abandon their communities all over the province. Villars understood that he had to act. On July 11, he issued an order to all the troops on the Flanders frontier prohibiting marauding on pain of death. Strictly enforced, it succeeded in restoring discipline and order to the army. Yet, it could do nothing for subsistence.[66]

Faced with this avalanche of logistical troubles, Villars feared that his field army would not be able to see the fighting season through to its end. He concluded he had no choice except to reject the defensive strategy favored by the king. The crisis of subsistence was becoming worse by the day, he warned Louis. "If we cannot hope for peace," he argued, "and if supplies are not entirely assured,"

> Then it is necessary to seek battle because it could be successful, whereupon all would be restored and because it would be better that the army were dissolved by arms then by hunger.[67]

When this first appeal received no reply, the marshal pressed his case. On July 18, he sent Louis his latest assessment of the strategic situation. Although the defenders of Tournai were still holding out, the Allies were making uncomfortably rapid progress. It was now likely that they would have enough time to continue the campaign after taking the fortress.

Their probable targets would then be Condé and Valenciennes, strongholds on the upper reaches of the Scheldt barring one of the main avenues into the interior of France. The Army of Flanders could take up a strong defensive position covering both, but Villars declared he would prefer to seek battle, particularly because the terrain around Valenciennes was well-suited to cavalry action. Louis still possessed a powerful mounted arm, but he might not be able to preserve it over the winter because of the parlous state of France's finances. The marshal then concluded:

> A victory, for which I hope by the grace of God, the justice of your arms and the courage of your troops, will reestablish everything and a defeat will be no more dangerous than the misfortune of seeing the troops waste away from lack of funds and food.[68]

Villars' pleas for permission to seek battle at last drew a comprehensive response from the king in the form of a long letter written on July 20. Louis agreed that Marlborough and Eugene would likely next set their sights on Condé and Valenciennes. But he disagreed about both the necessity of a battle and the benefits one would bring. As he explained

> I risk more than my enemies because if they lose, the result will not place me in a position to make great gains against them and if on the contrary they have the advantage, they will be able to profit from it by penetrating into my kingdom and making themselves masters of places in Artois that are less well defended than those on my frontier.

The king's counsel against battle was not just based on the current strategic situation; it also drew on hard-won experience. Each great battlefield defeat of the War of the Spanish Succession had produced far-reaching consequences. Blenheim had led to the eviction of the French and their Wittelsbach allies from Germany, Ramillies to the Allied conquest of the Spanish Netherlands, Turin to the loss of northern Italy, and Oudenarde to the fall of Lille and the breaching of the *pré carré*. There were good reasons to fear even worse if the last French field army was defeated on the kingdom's most important frontier.

Louis was also unconvinced by Villars' argument that he had to use his field army or lose it to starvation and dissolution. The shortages of money and supplies would not last, he explained:

> I know that what is alarming you is the lack of subsistence and the uncertainty about whether I will have the necessary funds to maintain my troops during the winter and to put a similar army in the field next spring. Although having sufficient funds is presently extremely difficult, I have reason to believe that when the reformation of the currency is more advanced, money will be more plentiful. The fear of running out of funds for the next year will

not induce me to order you to risk a general action. By winning through to the end of the campaign, the peace negotiations can resume their course.

But then he made a significant concession to his marshal:

> I repeat to you nevertheless that I leave you the liberty to profit from the advantages that you are able to take over the enemy in the event that, after the siege of Tournai, they formulate new enterprises. I give myself over entirely to your prudence and your good conduct, without seeking an extreme position, to seize the opportunities that the movements of the armies will bring and which you alone can judge perfectly.[69]

Ever since the death of the Marquis de Louvois in 1691, Louis had been the sole commander-in-chief of his armies. While he always sought counsel from a circle of trusted military advisers and often followed their counsel, he made all major and many minor decisions himself. Now, during the crucial phase of the most important campaign of his greatest war, while strenuously arguing against seeking battle, he was nevertheless granting his field commander wide discretion about where, when, and how to fight.

In time, Marshal Villars would make full use of the freedom he had been afforded. For the moment, he understood that the royal wishes were that he remain on the defensive and only fight a battle if it was unavoidable. He assigned the Comte d'Artagnan to hold the lines of La Bassée with 36 battalions and 73 squadrons. He then shifted the bulk of the Army of Flanders—in all 92 battalions and 195 squadrons—eastward to a new line extending from Hélesmes on the Scarpe to Denain on the Scheldt. This position, which was rapidly and formidably fortified, protected Condé, Valenciennes, and Bouchain. To further bolster their defenses, extensive flooding was undertaken around the first two fortresses. Specially built gunboats patrolled the waters.[70]

Villars continued to seek out fresh opportunities to harass the enemy. He followed his usual practice of sending out his cavalry to forage. The horses ate up the countryside between the two rivers, which denied fodder to the enemy in this crucial part of the Flanders front. On July 24, Villars learned that enemy troops had occupied the Abbey of Hasnon near Valenciennes. A picked force of 600 grenadiers attacked it, killing or taking prisoner the entire Allied garrison of 200 men. By energetically prosecuting the little war of ambushes, raids and skirmishes, the marshal kept his troops active and boosted their morale with small victories. But the Army of Flanders mostly settled into its new fortifications to wait upon events.[71]

Louis was pleased that he had been able to persuade his marshal to pursue a passive, defensive strategy. For, as he had made clear to Villars, he was placing his hopes on diplomacy to bring a satisfactory end to the war. The goal of the Flanders campaign was not to win victories; it was to avoid defeat. Then the Allies would realize that France could not be beaten on the battlefield, and they would have no choice except to offer more reasonable terms at the negotiating table.

Yet Louis also knew that the Allies distrusted him. In particular, they did not believe he wished to see Philip V lose the Spanish Monarchy. In reality, Louis' position was a nuanced one. He would always steadfastly refuse to go to war to drive his grandson from his throne. However, he was willing to withdraw his support from Philip, leaving him to face the Allies alone. During The Hague talks, he had made an offer to the Allies to remove all French troops from Spain. After the conference broke down, he decided to go through with it as a demonstration of his good faith. On June 3, he wrote to Amelot, his ambassador in Madrid, informing him of it. A fortnight later, he broke the news to Philip. The king of Spain had been expecting this turn of events. He implored his grandfather to temporarily retain a few French battalions in Iberia in order to give the Spanish time to raise more troops of their own. The queen of Spain personally pleaded with him not to leave her and her children defenseless. With both his honor as paterfamilias and his chivalry piqued, Louis hesitated. The Grand Dauphin, who had come into his own as the conscience of the Bourbon dynasty and the champion of its interests, then intervened, arguing forcefully in favor of Philip. In the end, it was decided that twenty-five French battalions would remain in Spain for up to six weeks. They would leave as soon as the new Spanish regiments were ready. This cumbersome compromise would do little to enhance the king of France's trustworthiness in the eyes of his enemies.[72]

Nevertheless, Louis sought to reopen negotiations with the Allies. Even after breaking off formal talks, he and the Marquis de Torcy had preserved a channel of communication to the Allies through Herman Petkum, envoy of Holstein-Gottorp to the Dutch Republic and long-time French agent. Barely a week after the rejection of The Hague Preliminaries, Petkum began sounding out Grand Pensionary Anthonie Heinsius about renewed discussions. He declared that, from the French perspective, the main stumbling block to a peace treaty was Article 37 of the Preliminaries. Torcy was sanguine about these approaches. "I hope that with affairs becoming more equal," he wrote to Petkum, "we can renew talks by August, at which time you will again employ your services." But Louis chose not to wait and instead promptly extended an olive branch to the Allies. On June 27, the French foreign minister contacted Heinsius directly. If he wished to restart discussions, Petkum was ready to carry his proposals to the French court.[73]

Heinsius reacted to this approach with caution. Faithful to his principle that he must always act in concert with his British allies, he forwarded Torcy's missive to the Duke of Marlborough. From his army's camp before Tournai, Marlborough responded that "my opinion is that if there can be an expedient agreed upon as to the 37 article, I should think it a great happiness." The Allied leaders interpreted Louis' initiative as a sign of weakness. According to the intelligence they were receiving from France, famine and financial collapse were biting hard, causing deepening misery and instability. The French king was under intense pressure to end the war. Given these circumstances, there was no reason for the Allies to compromise on their terms. It would be up to the French to arrive at new ones.[74]

On July 18, Heinsius presented Torcy's letter to the States General. It duly authorized him to resume discussions. The next day, the grand pensionary wrote to the French minister, telling him that "because you find difficulties with Article Thirty Seven of the Preliminaries, we believe that progress will only be made if you proposed such expedients as would satisfy your objections." These words left Torcy puzzled, and he was forced to turn to Petkum for clarification. His agent answered that the Dutch were demanding the French hand over three towns in Spain and three in Flanders as "hostages" to be returned only when Philip V had abandoned the whole Spanish Monarchy. The six would be chosen by the Allies and would be in addition to all the other surrenders that France would be making.[75]

Louis and Torcy were taken aback by these demands. They appeared excessive, especially because the Allied armies were pinned down before Tournai and the Flanders campaign appeared likely to end with few losses for the French. In their reply to the grand pensionary, written on August 1, they pushed back strongly. Louis would not cede any Spanish towns because:

> As you saw, the king has withdrawn from Spain the greater part of his troops, His Majesty wishing to make known, even before this time, that he would no longer assist the king his grandson either directly or indirectly. As a result, he would be less able than ever to hand over places where the commandants are Spanish and where the Spanish troops outnumber the French troops in the garrisons.

In Flanders, Louis was willing to surrender three towns, but only if he could choose them and only if the Allies promised to return them without difficulty. And in exchange for these hostages, he demanded a significant concession: instead of the two-month ceasefire of the original Article 37, a general peace treaty would be concluded.[76]

It was now the Allies' turn to be confounded. They were entirely unconvinced by Louis' claim that he had few troops and thus little power left in Spain. His clumsy compromise with Philip was now redounding back on him. "If the French would have us believe them sincere in their promises of giving up Spain," Sidney Godolphin asked Marlborough, "why won't they imediatly putt into the hands of the Allys such towns (I mean) belonging to Spain as are unquestionably in their power, such as Pampelona, Lerida, Badajou, and Cadiz?" The most frustrated of the Allies were the Dutch. Heinsius reminded Marlborough of the Republic's fundamental concern: "We here are extremely opposed to continuing the war in Spain after peace has been made with France." Any treaty had to embrace both Bourbon powers at once. Beginning with The Hague Preliminaries, Heinsius' stratagem had been to force the king of France to put pressure on his grandson to abandon his throne. By refusing to concede the Spanish towns, Louis was failing to play the part expected of him.[77]

The grand pensionary prepared his reply with the help of Lord Charles Townshend and Count Philippe von Sinzendorf, respectively the British and Habsburg plenipotentiaries to The Hague. It was written in the coldly formal language of European diplomacy. But its tone betrayed irritation and impatience. Heinsius declared that the hostage towns and the two-month suspension of arms were intended to guarantee that France would fulfill all The Hague Preliminaries, particularly Philip V's evacuation of Spain. The Allies refused to accede to any agreement that lacked these sureties. If Louis persisted in refusing to cede places in Spain, then he should propose other expedients that offered just as much security.[78]

The Dutch note reached the French court on August 22. The king called together an emergency session of his *Conseil d'en haut* of ministers. With Chancellor Pontchartrain and Controller General Desmaretz away, it consisted of Torcy, Voysin, the Duc de Beauvilliers, and the Duc de Bourgogne. The council debated Heinsius' missive for hours. The next day, Louis considered the Dutch terms again with Torcy and the Dauphin.[79] They concluded that they would have to make significant concessions. The foreign minister's answering letter began by stating that his master "is willing that the Preliminaries remain as they have been drawn up, with regard both to the suspension of arms as well as to the other terms." For Spain, Torcy reiterated that the French did not possess the power to hand over any towns to the Allies. Instead, he was offering two expedients. First, the king of France would prohibit his subjects from aiding or even entering Spain after the signing of the Preliminaries. He would then publicly inform his grandson that he would consider any violation of this ban an act of war and he would join his forces to those of the Allies to expel him from his kingdoms. Second, the French would surrender Bergues, Douai, and Charlemont as hostages to the Allies. Possession of these strongholds would immeasurably strengthen the Allies' grip on France's northern frontier. Louis and Torcy calculated that these concessions would be enough to satisfy the Allies. They called for the immediate convening of a new peace conference at The Hague.[80]

The king and his foreign minister were wrong. The Allies regarded the French proposal on Spain as completely inadequate. No one trusted Louis to keep his word that he would not help his grandson, much less declare war on him. The surrender of the Spanish towns was regarded as the minimally acceptable show of faith. On August 25, Petkum warned Torcy that Heinsius was considering breaking off all contact with the French court.[81] Yet, soon after, diplomacy was overtaken by events on the battlefield.

Negotiations between the French and the Allies had taken place at the speed of the written letter, the mounted courier, and the postal diligence. Meanwhile, the siege of Tournai and the campaign of Flanders were grinding on at their own paces. Against the beleaguered city, the Allies were advancing bloodily. On Fagel's front on the northern bank of the Scheldt, the siege guns had battered down a long stretch of the city wall. But the Dutch general's men were badly hampered by a deep ditch filled with fast-flowing water. Attempts to cross it suffered severely from the fire of the besieged. Lottum was making only fitful progress toward the citadel. Here, the Prussian's every move was threatened by exploding French mines. Against the Valenciennes gate, his battalions were doing much better, pushing steadily forward despite numerous sorties by the garrison. Schulenburg's attack on the western sector remained the most dangerous of all. The Saxon's troops had established firm lodgements at the Seven Fountains hornwork and the Blandinoise bastion. Three large breaches had been opened in the defenses.

The Allied and French commanders realized that the fight for Tournai was approaching its climax. On July 24, Eugene and Johan Willem Friso rode over from the army of observation to confer with Marlborough. Together, the three generals and their lieutenants toured the siege trenches and closely gauged the intensity and effectiveness of the resistance. They concluded that the time had come to storm the weakest points of the fortifications. Inside Tournai, Surville knew that he would be unable to repel these assaults. Although his men had mounted a tenacious defense and inflicted very heavy losses on the besiegers, they were just too badly outnumbered and overstretched.

On July 26, Lottum launched his troops against the Valenciennes gate. Thrown back twice, they finally managed to capture the covered way and a small outwork that served as the bridgehead for the gate. The next night, Schulenburg attacked. His troops quickly seized the Seven Fountains hornwork and the Blandinoise bastion. At daybreak, the French tried to retake these positions but were repulsed and driven back into the city in great disorder.

Following these events, Surville convened a council of war. He and his officers decided that they could no longer hold on to the ramparts at any of the three locations under attack. The moment had come for talks with the enemy. At eight in the evening on July 28, a lone French drummer appeared at the Valenciennes gate and beat out the chamade. Surville then met with the Allied generals. They agreed that the Allies would occupy the city of Tournai, while the French would retreat to the citadel to continue its defense.

On July 30, the gate of Lille was opened, and the Allies marched into Tournai. Their success had been dearly bought. Three weeks of fighting had cost them 3,310 dead and wounded. Surville retreated into the citadel with the survivors of the garrison. They amounted to over 4,000 infantry and dragoons. In addition, 800 wounded and invalids were in the fortress' infirmary. All in all, the French had lost about 1,500 casualties.[82]

Surville intended to defy the Allies for a long time yet. The fortifications of the citadel were formidable and had suffered little damage from the enemy's artillery. Its perimeter was much more compact than the city's enceinte. Furthermore, the opposing commanders had agreed that the city itself would be demilitarized: the Allies would not attack out of it and the French would not fire their cannons into it. So, unlike during the first part of the siege, there were now ample troops to fully man the walls and works. An even more important advantage was the citadel's extensive and state-of-the-art system of countermines. Surville's second-in-command Mesgrigny had already employed mines to devastating effect against Lottum's attack. But all these strengths were outweighed by a grave weakness: a lack of provisions. In the months and weeks leading up to the siege and even during it, Surville had done his best to requisition food for his troops from Tournai's inhabitants. They had vigorously resisted his efforts. A final attempt on July 20 almost provoked a riot. As a result, the citadel's magazines and storerooms remained largely empty.

The Allies were sufficiently worried about the strength of the citadel that, to avoid besieging it, they approached Louis with an unusual offer. There would be a local ceasefire in Tournai. The French garrison would stay inside the fortress unmolested, while the Allied siege army of thirty battalions and ten squadrons would remain around the city. If the Army of Flanders failed to relieve Tournai by September 5, the garrison would surrender the citadel and withdraw under safe conduct to French lines. Louis was unimpressed by this arrangement. The Allies, after waiting for just a month, would receive his strongest fortress intact and at no cost. Meanwhile, their main army would be entirely free to operate as it pleased. He countered by trying to convert the Allies' offer into another opportunity for diplomacy. The ceasefire would extend until September 10. More importantly, it would cover the entire Flanders theater, including the field armies. Allied and French diplomats would then try to hammer out an agreement over Article 37 of the Preliminaries. Marlborough and Eugene rejected this proposal out of hand.[83]

At Tournai, the pause in the fighting was brief. No sooner were Surville and his troops ensconced in the citadel than Lottum resumed his assault. He was joined by a second attack under Schulenburg aimed at the Orléans bastion located on the western face of the citadel. The Allies also unleashed an intense bombardment. In particular, they fired heavy barrages of mortar bombs in an attempt to raze the stronghold's interior. For his part, Surville conducted a very active defense. Strong sorties were continually sent out against the Allied trenches to kill their occupants and fill them in. But by far his most effective weapons were mines. From their network of permanent countermine galleries, the French dug tunnels reaching out beneath the Allied siegeworks. The ends of the tunnels were then packed with gunpowder. The resulting explosions killed and maimed everyone above them. Even worse, they often caused the works to collapse, burying alive even more victims.

These deadly invisible menaces slowed the besiegers' attacks to a crawl. As Marlborough complained to Godolphin:

> By the enemys dayly springing of new mynes our ingeniers advance so very slowly that the Prince of Savoye and myself thought it for the Service to come hether in order to push on the attacks. But as this is the first siege where we have meet with myns, we find our soldiers apprehend them more then thay aught, so that we must have patience for some litle time, that thay may be used to them.[84]

The Allies had no choice except to dig mines of their own: over thirty during this phase of the siege. Their purpose was defensive: to find and break into the French mines before they could be detonated. When the two sides encountered each other in the tunnels, there were gruesome close-quarter combats with spades, picks, daggers, hand grenades, and pistols. In this underground contest, the Allies found themselves at a decided disadvantage. They had no professional miners in their siege army. Their tunnels had to be worked by soldiers detached from the trenches and paid a special premium for these novel and very dangerous duties. The Allies' Huguenot siege engineers were also inexperienced in mining. Then, on August 27, one of them, Lucas Du Mée, was fatally wounded by a splinter from a stone mortar shot. By contrast, Surville's garrison included fifty-two expert miners, and old Mesgrigny was a master of subterranean warfare. After four weeks of costly and creeping progress, Marlborough and Eugene began to despair of taking Tournai's citadel before the end of the campaigning season.[85]

The Allies were not alone in feeling a sense of desperation as the summer wore on. At the end of July, the Army of Flanders' subsistence crisis reached its nadir. Intendant Bernières of Flanders warned War Minister Daniel Voysin that "our misery knows no bounds and I tremble every day that the army will finally disband." The troops had not been paid at all during the winter months and had only received a modicum of wages since the campaign began. They were subsisting on very poor munition bread that often arrived late or not at all. "I dare to say to you, Monsieur," he concluded, "the monarchy has not been in greater danger since its establishment." Marshal Villars wrote to Madame de Maintenon in a similar vein:

> What is happening here with the subsistence of the army is in truth, Madame, dismaying. The army very often lacks bread for a day or two days, and it is a miracle that the service is sustained. When I arrived at the camp where I am presently, the army was thirty hours without bread, and if I were ordered to relieve Tournai on the day after, it would have been impossible to attempt it because people who go for thirty hours without eating cannot for sixty.[86]

The frightful state of his army's supplies provoked Villars to raise with the king once again the prospect of seeking battle. The marshal's constant fear was for his left flank. He had no choice but to keep his field army at Denain because it could now only draw supplies from the magazines of Maubeuge. Those of Arras and Douai were empty. Should the enemy move against his left, he would not be able to reach his old lines near La Bassée in time. The Allied armies would then overwhelm d'Artagnan's corps defending the entrenched camp of Cambrin and break into the Plain of Lens. They would then be free to besiege the Lys fortresses of Béthune, Aire, and Saint-Venant, all of which were weakly defended and badly provisioned. Their capture would open an avenue into the interior of the kingdom. The only way that Villars could prevent this outcome was to force a battle somewhere on the plains between Lens and Mont-Saint-Éloi.[87]

The king found this argument unconvincing. Negotiations with Heinsius had been underway for some time, he informed Villars, and discussions about a truce at Tournai had just begun. Both approaches were showing promise, and an agreement over Article 37 was altogether possible. Therefore, he wanted the marshal to avoid the risks of a battle and continue pursuing a defensive strategy. He explained at length why it should be done and how:

Although I have told you that in the event of new enterprises by our enemies, you have the discretion to attack and fight them when you believe you could do so with some advantage, I consider that it is always better not to be forced to seek the occasion of combat. For this reason, I believe that you must, by preference, hold your first camp and your entrenchments between Hulluch and Cambrin. This position, as when you first took it up, covers Douai, Béthune, and Aire, which I prefer to protect rather than Condé or Valenciennes, because these latter places, being well equipped, can easily stop the enemy for the remainder of the campaign.

Louis ordered Villars to move the Army of Flanders from Denain back to La Bassée. He was to leave garrisons of eighteen battalions in Valenciennes and ten in Condé. As for his supplies, the stockpiles at Maubeuge could be carted to Douai. At the same time, the *munitionnaires* and royal officials would make renewed efforts to refill the magazines of Arras.[88]

Before Villars could carry out Louis' orders, the Allies acted first. After Surville retreated into the citadel of Tournai, Marlborough rejoined Eugene with most of his force. On August 6, the two Allied commanders marched to Orchies, halfway between Tournai and Lille. From there, their army could threaten both the La Bassée lines and the fortresses on the upper Scheldt. Marlborough preferred to see Villars return to his old position. The Allies could then besiege Valenciennes and subject the country around it to contributions (map 5.1).[89]

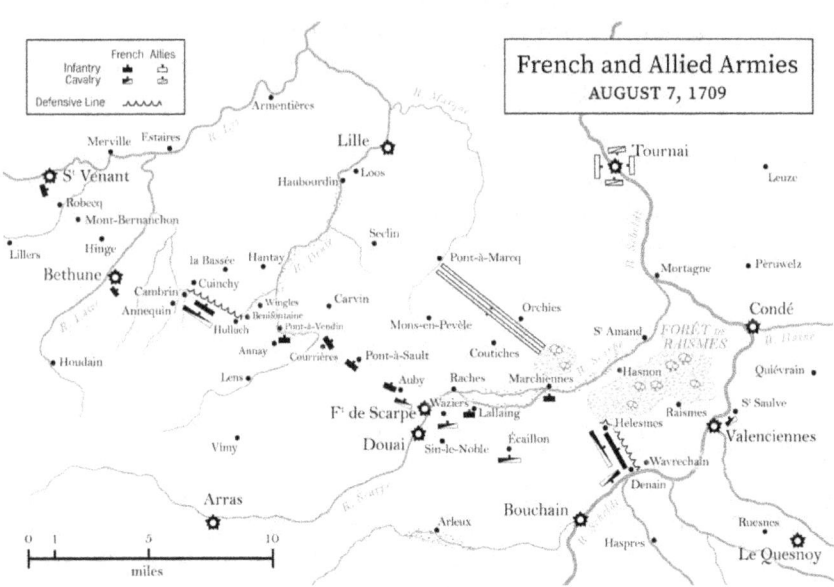

Map 5.1   French and Allied Armies, August 7, 1709.

The marshal did not take the bait. He concentrated most of his infantry in his lines at Denain while sending strong cavalry forces to guard both his flanks. Then, on August 8, the Allies attacked Marchiennes, a town with an important crossing of the Scarpe. Leading a detachment of grenadiers, Count Tilly attempted to take it by surprise. But the garrison detected his approach, and its lively fire held him up. Villars then arrived, leading the Bretagne and La Marine infantry brigades and some dragoons. Realizing that the town was now too strongly held, the Dutch general withdrew.[90]

This minor action convinced the marshal that he was right and the king wrong about where the Army of Flanders should be deployed. Marchiennes showed that Marlborough and Eugene might force their way over the Scarpe, bypass Condé and Valenciennes, and fall upon Bouchain. This fortress was in poor repair and without provisions; it would be able to hold out for just six days at most. Its loss would open an invasion route into the heart of France as dangerous as the Lys corridor. Additionally, the Army of Flanders was still drawing all of its supplies from Maubeuge. If it marched to La Bassée and then the enemy broke through to Bouchain, it would be cut off from its sole source of food. Hunger, Villars estimated, would cause it to dissolve in no more than twelve days. For these reasons, the army had to remain in the lines and entrenched camp of Denain. But this left the old problem of an Allied sweep westward that would result in sieges of the Lys strongholds. To save them, the marshal could still see no alternative except to fight a battle.[91]

Villars' arguments succeeded in persuading the king to keep the Army of Flanders at Denain. Yet he still remained firmly opposed to fighting a battle. As Voysin explained:

> Seeking out the enemy to fight a battle near the Lys is always regarded here as an extreme position in which the king would risk much more than he could gain. His Majesty is convinced that you should not determine on it unless you are somehow stronger and able to fight with advantage.

The solution proposed by the court was to restock the magazines of Douai and Arras, which would allow Villars to reinforce d'Artagnan's corps as well as march his army to the La Bassée lines should the enemy attack them.[92]

As the marshal and the king were debating strategy, the supply situation of the Army of Flanders began to improve. As Louis had hoped, the American silver and the reminting of the French currency brought a transfusion of money into his treasury. Controller General Nicolas Desmaretz was able to send large shipments of coin to Flanders. At the beginning of August, Intendant Bernières took in 400,000 livres from the mints of Rheims and Paris; he would receive even more as the month passed. He handed a good portion of these funds over to the *munitionnaire* François-Marie Fargès to buy grain and flour in Liège. On August 6, the intendant was able to write to Voysin,

> After insurmountable difficulties, I managed to furnish bread to the army for three days, which will begin today. We only have to wish that it continues. I am to meet this evening at Valenciennes with the Sieur Fargès, who is the real restorer of our affairs.

On August 11, Voysin assured Villars that the money flowing to the intendant of Flanders should enable him to reliably arrange three- or even four-day bread runs for his troops. Bernières' colleague in Artois, Louis de Bernage, dipped again and again into the coffers of the Amiens mint: from late July to the end of August, he took 77,000 livres for food supplies and 116,725 livres for the soldiers' wages. In the process, he learned that while the people of Artois and Picardy were ready to riot whenever he attempted to expropriate their grain, they were more than happy to sell it to him for 40 livres a sack. At Maubeuge, Charles Doujat turned foodstuffs bought in Champagne and the Soissonais into bread, then convoyed it to Villars' army at Denain. Desmaretz came up with still more expedients. By August, the barley that had been sown by France's peasants in the spring was ripening. The controller general imposed a tax of 20,000 sacks of barley on Picardy, Champagne, and the Soissonais; the proceeds were intended to feed the frontier garrisons and restock the magazines of Arras and Douai.[93]

The easing of his army's subsistence troubles led to Villars changing his plans a final time. On August 25, he informed the king that his position at Denain was now so strong he could afford to reinforce that of La Bassée. He stated that "I am beginning to believe that I can make an attack on my first camp very dangerous without weakening my center." Five days later, he drew up a "Memoir for the Defense of the Line." It described the Army of Flanders holding a continuous barrier of field works and entrenchments running from the Lys to the Scheldt. Outposts and fortresses extended west to the sea and east to the Sambre. The most crucial and heavily defended points were the entrenched camps at Cambrin and Denain. The enemy would have to deal with the former if they chose to move against the strongholds of the Lys; they had to attack the latter if they decided to besiege Condé, Valenciennes, or Bouchain. The troops in the camps were to hold off the enemy until the rest of the army arrived. The marshal gave detailed instructions to each of his generals about when and where to move. The whole scheme depended on swiftly detecting Marlborough and Eugene's movements, then rushing forces to the threatened points. Villars added a further refinement on September 1. He identified another possible Allied objective: Mons. Located thirty miles southeast of Tournai, Mons was not covered by the lines. Therefore, "if the enemy wishes to march there, we hope to arrive there before him." In earlier campaigns, the French had built fieldworks along the banks of the River Haine and the La Trouille stream. By reoccupying them, Villars might prevent a siege of this fortress. This latest plan confirmed that he had once again come to embrace the battle-averse, defensive strategy urged on him by the king.[94]

For Louis, the Flanders campaign was only one aspect of the general crisis that continued to remorselessly unfold during the late summer of 1709. All over France, the famine was now at its height. The king and his chief servants had to devote much attention and energy to trying to combat its worst effects. Their greatest fear was popular unrest. As Madame de Maintenon described to the Duc de Noailles:

> Our court is very distressed. We only talk about wheat, oats, barley, and corn. We are very preoccupied with the relief of the people, but so far what has been done for them only irritates them. There are people with bad intentions who excite them.[95]

Paris was never far from Versailles' thoughts. The capital was a teeming, turbulent anthill of 600,000 people, and the Parisians never hesitated to take to their streets to decry their misery as well as to punish those whom they believed were responsible for it. Maintaining order in the city was a perennial preoccupation of French kings. It was the charge of Marc-René de Voyer, Marquis d'Argenson, lieutenant general of police of Paris since 1697. D'Argenson was intelligent, tireless, and ruthless—according to Saint-Simon, during interrogations, he made even the innocent tremble. He closely monitored grain prices, sending a daily digest to the king, and strove to ensure that the markets were well-stocked with provisions; among other methods, he hunted down hoarders and forced them to disgorge their caches on pain of severe punishment. As a last resort, he also disposed of a considerable armed force. Companies of the Gardes francaises, Gardes suisses, and Musketeers had been held back from the front.[96]

Yet even d'Argenson's energy and methods were overborne by the crisis. In August, food prices began an ominous rise. There was so little wheat that bakers were mixing it with oats to make crude, barely edible loaves. To make matters still worse, many workers and craftsmen had not received their wages for many weeks. In the markets, women—who, as elsewhere in France, played the leading role in popular protest against food shortages—began crying out that they and their families were being starved. On the twentieth, a large group of poor Parisians was working on a rampart beside the Porte Saint-Denis. When they did not receive the bread and wages they were promised, they rose up in rebellion. They first pillaged the house of their overseer, then marched through the city. As they went, their ranks were swelled by more malcontents; soon the rebels numbered over 15,000. They decided to attack the Mint and the Arsenal in order to seize weapons. Marshal Boufflers, who happened to be in Paris, rushed to the scene in his carriage, dismounted, and remonstrated with them, promising to tell the king of their plight and their need for bread and money. He managed to persuade many to go home, yet not all. The Guards and mounted Musketeers then arrived. They first fired three volleys into the air. These were answered by showers of stones. The troops shot into the crowds, killing two men and one woman. Only then did the rebels disperse, pursued by the guardsmen who arrested many of them. The next day, d'Argenson had extra quantities of bread brought to the markets and there was no resurgence of rioting. But the capital would remain restive for weeks after.[97]

At the same time as tumult was engulfing Paris, another element of the crisis was coming to a head. Nicolas Desmaretz had managed to prop up the monarchy's failing fisc with the windfall of silver from Spanish America and a massive devaluation of the French currency. These measures had allowed the controller general to send the Army of Flanders the money it desperately needed for its troops' pay and provisions. But they could not be repeated. Desmaretz could hardly count on the arrival of more specie from the Indies. Another devaluation of the currency would wreck whatever residual confidence French subjects had in the economy.[98]

On August 26, the controller general drew up a long report to Louis comprehensively detailing the disastrous state of the royal finances. "The present situation of business is so bad," Desmaretz began, "it causes those who are acquainted with it just anxieties about the unforgettable events that might be feared." Since the default of Samuel Bernard in April and the massive bailout mounted to rescue him, all money had ceased to circulate. Because of the Great Winter and the famine, the common people were no longer paying their taxes. The nobles and clergy were still contributing to theirs, but their complaints were growing louder and more frequent. The manifold financial expedients called extraordinary affairs had been exploited to exhaustion. Finally, there was no credit available from the king's usual lenders, as

> the fall of the Sieurs Hogguer, Bernard, and Nicolas, those of the Sieurs Tourton and Guiges and all the others who practice banking have thrown the

money markets in Lyon, Paris, and Geneva and other places into disorder. No resource can be expected from the bankers.

Desmaretz had managed to scratch together just enough money for the rest of the campaigning season. However, the winter quarters would bring colossal new expenses. Rebuilding the armies would cost at least 19,000,000 livres. Yet "the bad disposition of the spirits of all the people is well known. For four months, a week has not passed without some sedition." Therefore, the money could only be collected by force of arms. The controller general concluded: "for all these evils, it is not possible to find remedies except for a speedy peace."[99]

Beset by many misfortunes, Louis' spirits plunged further still. "You would be touched," said Madame de Maintenon to the Duc de Noailles, "by the sadness of the king and by his courage." Then, on September 5, a dust-covered horseman arrived at Versailles. He was a courier from Marshal Villars, and he was the bearer of more bad news: the citadel of Tournai had capitulated, and the enemy armies were on the move.[100]

NOTES

1. Quincy, *Mémoires*, vol. 2, 326–333.
2. John Marshall Deane, *A Journal of Marlborough's Campaigns during the War of the Spanish Succession, 1704–1711*, ed. David Chandler (London: Society for Army Historical Research, 1984), 79–80. In his journal, Deane employs Old Style dating. I have converted all his dates to New Style.
3. SHD AG A¹2151/49, "État des endroits où sont les Trouppes destinés pour la campagne, 13 juin 1709."
4. On the Irish regiments in French service during the War of the Spanish Succession, see Nathalie Genet-Rouffiac, *Le Grand Exil: Les Jacobites en France, 1688–1715* (Paris: Service historique de la Défense, 2007), 203–206.
5. Georges Girard, *Le service militaire en France à la fin du règne de Louis XIV: racolage et milice (1701–1715)* (Paris: Plon, 1921), 72.
6. Andre Corvisier, "La morale des combattants, panique et enthousiasme: Malplaquet, 11 septembre 1709," in *Les hommes, la guerre et la mort* (Paris: Economica, 1985), 293–294; Berkovich, *Motivation in War*, 182–183.
7. The total strength of the Allied forces is given in François-Eugene Vault and Jean-Jacques-Germain Pelet, eds., *Mémoires militaires relatifs à la Succession d'Espagne: extraits de la correspondance de la cour et des généraux*, vol. 9 (Paris: Imprimerie Impériale, 1855), 33, and Jan Willem Wijn, *Het Staatsche Leger*, part VIII, *Het Tijdperk van de Spaanse Successieoorlog, 1702–1715*, book II, *De Veldtochten Van 1706–1710* (The Hague: Martinus Nijhoff, 1959), 476. The breakdown of the various national contingents is found in *Feldzüge des Prinzen Eugen von Savoyen*, book 11, *Spanischer Successions-Krieg. Feldzug 1709* (Vienna: Verlag des K.K.

Generalstabes, 1886), 69 and 72–74. The description of the Allied army in 1709 is based on these sources.

8. On the regiments of the British Army during the War of the Spanish Succession, see Scouller, *Armies of Queen Anne*, 93–97.

9. SHD AG A¹ 1933/36, Louis XIV to Villeroy, 6 May 1706.

10. On the Scottish Brigade, John Childs, "The Scottish Brigade in the Service of the Dutch Republic, 1688–1782," *Documentatieblad werkgroep Achttiende eeuw*. Jaargang 1984 (1984), 59–74.

11. On the evolution of the States Army up to and during the Nine Years' War, Stapleton, "Forging a Coalition Army," 102–122 and 240–337, and van Nimwegen, *The Dutch Army and the Military Revolutions*, 325–360.

12. On the large number of foreign, especially German recruits, in "national regiments" of the States Army, see Stapleton, "Forging a Coalition Army," 248–251. On the German troops added to the States Army in 1709, see Douglas S. Coombs, "The Augmentation of 1709: A Study in the Workings of the Anglo-Dutch Alliance," *The English Historical Review* 72/285 (1957), 657–658.

13. Frederick's unique royal title was awarded to him by Emperor Leopold in 1701. On the auxiliary forces contributed by the *Armierten*, see Peter Wilson, *German Armies: War and German Society, 1648–1806* (London: Routledge, 1998), 105–106, 108–111, and 120.

14. Hochdilinger, *Austria's Wars of National Emergence*, 102–104.

15. Wijn, *Het Staatsche Leger*, part VIII, book 2, 476–477.

16. On the importance and range of Cadogan's duties as Quartermaster-General, see Stewart Stansfield, *Early Modern Systems of Command: Queen Anne's Generals, Staff Officers, and the Direction of Allied Warfare in the Low Countries and Germany* (Solihull: Helion and Company, 2015), 34 and 194–225; see also Stapleton, "Forging a Coalition Army," 314.

17. 652, Marlborough to Sarah, 16 August 1706, *Marlborough-Godolphin Correspondence*, vol. 2, 645.

18. H. H. E. Cra'ster, ed., "Letters of the First Lord Orkney During Marlborough's Campaigns," *The English Historical Review* 19 (1904), 307–311 and 315; Lawrence B. Smith, "Hamilton, George, First Earl of Orkney (bap. 1666, d. 1737), Army Officer," *Oxford Dictionary of National Biography*, 23 September 2004. Accessed 28 July 2023, https://www.oxforddnb.com/view/10.1093/ref:odnb/9780198614128.001.0001/odnb-9780198614128-e-12069; Alexander Murdoch, "Campbell, John, Second Duke of Argyll and Duke of Greenwich (1680–1743), Army Officer and Politician," *Oxford Dictionary of National Biography*, 23 September 2004. Accessed 28 July 2023, https://www.oxforddnb.com/view/10.1093/ref:odnb/9780198614128.001.0001/odnb-9780198614128-e-4513; Stansfield, *Early Modern Systems of Command*, 56–57.

19. Saint-Simon, *Mémoires*, vol. 4, 3–5.

20. On Lottum, Ernst Friedländer, "Lottum, Philipp Karl Reichsgraf von Wylich und Lottum," in *Allgemeine Deutsche Biographie*, vol. 19 (Leipzig: Duncker & Humblot, 1884), 284–285; On Schulenburg, see Paul Zimmerman, "Schulenburg, Matthias Graf von der," in *Allgemeine Deutsche Biographie*, vol. 32, 667–674 and his memoirs, *Leben und Denkwürdigkeiten Johann Mathias Reichsgrafen von der*

Schulenburg. Erbherrn auf Emden und Delitz, Feldmarschalls in Diensten der Republik Venedig, 2 vols. (Leipzig: Weidmann, 1834).

21. David Chandler, for example, describes them as "veritable political commissars" in *Marlborough as Military Commander*, 99.

22. Sicco van Goslinga, *Mémoires relatifs à la Guerre de Succession d'Espagne de 1706–1709 et 1711*, ed. U. A. Evertsz and G. H. M. Delprat (Leeuwarden: G.T.N. Suringar, 1857), 43.

23. On the Dutch Republic's Council of State and the field deputies, see Stapleton, "Forging a Coalition Army," 340–361; The field deputies of 1709 are discussed by Wijn, *Het Staatsche Leger*, part VIII, book 2, 475.

24. SHD AG A^1 2151/7, Louis XIV to Villars, 3 June 1709; SHD AG A^1 2151/15, Villars to Louis XIV, June 6, 1709; SHD AG A^1 2151/54, Voysin to Villars, 14 June 1709. Harcourt's army initially consisted of 38 battalions and 68 squadrons or about 25,000 troops.

25. Boislisle, *Correspondence*, vol. 3, 151.

26. Hattendorf, *England in the War of the Spanish Succession*, 200–201.

27. SHD AG A^1 2151/32, Louis XIV to Villars, 9 June 1709; SHD AG A^1 2157/241, Voysin to Bernage, 11 June 1709; SHD AG A^1 2157/254, Voysin to Bernage, 17 June 1709.

28. In *Le Munitonnaire des armées de France*, his 1697 handbook for fellow *munitionnaires*, François Nodot devotes one of nine chapters and 105 out of 615 pages to detailed information about how to create, organize, and operate the *équipages des vivres*. See also Perjes, "Army Provisioning," 26–29.

29. SHD AG A^1 2151/60, Villars to Voysin, 17 June 1709; SHD AG A^1 2157/274, Bernage to Desmaretz, 24 June 1709.

30. SHD AG A^1 2151/60, Villars to Voysin, 17 June 1709.

31. Vault and Pelet, *Mémoires militaires*, vol. 9, 33–34.

32. SHD AG A^1 2151/87, Villars to Voysin, 22 June 1709.

33. SHD AG A^1 2151/49, "État des endroits où sont les Trouppes destinés pour la campagne, 13 juin 1709."

34. On the French use of brigades, see Lynn, *Giant of the Grand Siècle*, 534.

35. SHD AG A^1 2151/15, Villars to Louis XIV, 6 June 1709.

36. Stapleton, "Forging a Coalition Army," 361–365; Olaf van Nimwegen, *De subsistentie van het leger: logistiek en strategie van het Geallieerde en met name het Staatse leger tijdens de Spaanse Successieoorlog in de Nederlanden en het Heilige Roomse Rijk (1701–1712)* (Amsterdam: De Bataafsche Leeuw, 1995), 26–27.

37. Van Nimwegen, *De subsistentie van het leger*, 246–247, 257–258.

38. Ibid., 259–268.

39. 1307, Marlborough to Godolphin, 9/20 June 1709, *Marlborough-Godolphin Correspondence*, vol. 3, 1280.

40. SHD AG A^1 2151/85, Contades to Villars, 21 June 1709; SHD AG A^1 2151/87, Villars to Voysin, 22 June 1709.

41. SHD AG A^1 2151/98, Villars to Voysin, 23 June 1709; SHD AG A^1 2151/99, Villars to Voysin, 24 June 1709.

42. On Dopff, Stapleton, "Forging a Coalition Army," 314. Churchill, *Marlborough*, book 2, 569–570; SHD AG A^1 2151/101, Villars to Voysin, 25 June 1709 and SHD AG A^{1}2151/103, Villars to Voysin, 26 June 1709.

43. Churchill, *Marlborough*, book 2, 398; Chandler, *Marlborough as Military Commander*, 224–225.

44. 1304, Godolphin to Marlborough, 6 June 1709 (OS), *Marlborough-Godolphin Correspondence*, vol. 3, 1277.

45. Paoletti, "The Toulon Expedition of 1707," 954–957.

46. Goslinga, *Mémoires*, 104.

47. SHD AG A¹ 2151/103, Villars to Voysin, 26 June 1709.

48. SHD AG A¹ 2151/119, Villars to Louis XIV, 28 June 1709; SHD AG A¹ 2151/122, Villars to Louis XIV, 29 June 1709; 1314, Marlborough to Godolphin, 16/27 June 1709, *Marlborough-Godolphin Correspondence*, vol. 3, 1285–1286. Goslinga, *Mémoires*, 105.

49. On countermines, see Christopher Duffy, *Fire and Stone: The Science of Fortress Warfare, 1660–1860* (London: Greenhill Books, 1996), 48–49 and 82–84.

50. On Surville, see Beckman, "Sword of the Sun," 238–239.

51. SHD AG A¹ 2151/122, Villars to Louis XIV, 29 June 1709.

52. SHD AG A¹ 2151/130, Villars to Louis XIV, 1 July 1709.

53. Dangeau, *Journal*, vol. 12, 459–460; Sourches, *Mémoires*, vol. 12, 1–2.

54. Cénat, *Le roi stratège*, 217–220; Cénat, *Chamlay*, 161–166; Sarmant, ed., *Les Ministres de la guerre*, 308–315.

55. SHD AG A¹ 2151/134, Louis XIV to Villars, 2 July 1709.

56. SHD AG A¹ 2151/152, Villars to Louis XIV, 5 July 1709; SHD AG A¹ 2151/153, Villars to Voysin, 5 July 1709.

57. SHD AG A¹ 2151/157, Louis XIV to Villars, 6 July 1709; 755, Heinsius to Marlborough, 13 July 1709, *Marlborough-Heinsius Correspondence*, 445.

58. Jamel Ostwald, "Marlborough and Siege Warfare," in *Marlborough: Soldier and Diplomat*, 130–143.

59. Jamel Ostwald, *Vauban under Siege: Engineering Efficiency and Martial Vigor in the War of the Spanish Succession* (Leiden: Brill, 2002), 253–308.

60. Good accounts of the opening events of the siege of Tournai are found in Vault and Pelet, *Mémoires Militaires*, vol. 9, 53–54; Wijn, *Het Staatsche Leger*, part VIII, book 2, 490–493.

61. SHD AG A¹ 2151/214, Frézelière to Villars, 15 July 1709.

62. SHD AG A¹ 2151/221, Villars to Louis XIV, 18 July 1709; SHD AG A¹ 2151/218, Broglie to Villars, 17 July 1709.

63. On the four Paris brothers—Antoine, Claude (nicknamed La Montagne), Jean, and Joseph—see Daniel Dessert, *Argent, pouvoir et société au Grand Siècle* (Paris: Fayard, 1984), 663–665.

64. SHD AG A¹ 2157/285, Bernage to Voysin, 2 July 1709; SHD AG A¹ 2157/289, Bernage to Voysin, 4 July 1709.

65. SHD AG A¹ 2151/101, Villars to Voysin, 25 June 1709.

66. Corvisier, *Malplaquet*, 43–45; SHD AG A¹ 2151/150, Voysin to Villars, 6 July 1709; SHD AG A¹ 2151/189, Order against Marauding, 11 July 1709.

67. SHD AG A¹ 2151/183, Villars to Louis XIV, 10 July 1709.

68. SHD AG A¹ 2151/221, Villars to Louis XIV, 18 July 1709.

69. SHD AG A¹ 2151/232, Louis XIV to Villars, 20 July 1709.

70. SHD AG A¹ 2151/254, Villars to Louis XIV, 25 July 1709; SHD AG A¹ 2151/263, Villars to Voysin, 26 July 1709; SHD AG A¹ 2151/265, Broglie to Voysin, 25 July 1709. SHD AG A¹ 2151/267, Louis XIV to Villars, 27 July 1709.

71. SHD AG A¹ 2151/254, Villars to Louis XIV, 25 July 1709.

72. CLXXIII, Louis XIV to Amelot, 3 June 1709, in *Correspondence de Louis XIV à M. Amelot, son ambassadeur en Espagne, 1705–1709*, ed. Auguste Théodore, Baron de Girardot, vol. 2 (Nantes: Merson, 1864), 142–146; Chaline, *Le règne de Louis XIV*, vol. 1, 679–680; Alfred Baudrillart, *Philippe V et la cour de France, 1700 1715* (Paris: Bureau de la Revue, 1889), 348–360.

73. AAE Hollande 219, Torcy to Petkum, 20 June 1709, ff. 62–65; AAE Hollande 219, Torcy to Heinsius, 27 June 1709, ff. 89–89v.

74. 752, Heinsius to Marlborough, 6 July 1709, *Marlborough-Heinsius Correspondence*, 443–444; 753, Heinsius to Marlborough, 7 July 1709, *Marlborough-Heinsius Correspondence*, 444; 754, Marlborough to Heinsius, 10 July 1709, *Marlborough-Heinsius Correspondence*, 444–445; 755, Heinsius to Marlborough, 13 July 1709, *Marlborough-Heinsius Correspondence*, 445; 1340, Godolphin to Marlborough, 10 July 1709 (OS), *Marlborough-Godolphin Correspondence*, vol. 3, 1307–1308.

75. AAE Hollande 219, Heinsius to Torcy, 19 July 1709, ff. 156–156v; AAE Hollande 219, Petkum to Torcy, 25 July 1709, ff. 141–142v.

76. AAE Hollande 219, Torcy to Heinsius, 1 August 1709, ff. 158–160.

77. 1346, Godolphin to Marlborough, 15 July 1709 (OS), *Marlborough-Godolphin Correspondence*, vol. 3, 1313; 777, Heinsius to Marlborough, 17 August 1709, *Marlborough-Heinsius Correspondence*, 455–456.

78. AAE Hollande 219, Heinsius to Torcy, August 16, 1709, ff. 215–216.

79. Dangeau, *Journal*, vol. 13, 18; Sourches, *Mémoires*, vol. 12, 41.

80. AAE Hollande 219, Torcy to Heinsius, August 23, 1709, ff. 217–220v.

81. 785, Marlborough to Heinsius, 2 September 1709, *Marlborough-Heinsius Correspondence*, 462; AAE Hollande 219, Petkum to Torcy, August 30, 1709, ff. 245–246v.

82. Vault and Pelet, *Mémoires militaires*, vol. 9, 68–69; Wijn, *Het Staatsche Leger*, part VIII, book 2, 494–498 The original copy of the capitulation is SHD AG A¹ 2151/292.

83. 770, Marlborough to Heinsius, 8 August 1709, *Marlborough-Heinsius Correspondence*, 453.

84. 1366, Marlborough to Godolphin, 4/15 August 1709, *Marlborough-Godolphin Correspondence*, vol. 3, 1332.

85. Wijn, *Het Staatsche Leger*, part VIII, book 2, 502–507.

86. SHD AG A¹ 2154/110, Bernières to Voysin, 27 July 1709; Vogüé, *Madame de Maintenon et le Maréchal de Villars*, 50.

87. SHD AG A¹ 2152/12, Villars to Louis XIV, 4 August 1709.

88. SHD AG A¹ 2152/24, Louis XIV to Villars, 5 August 1709.

89. 770, Marlborough to Heinsius, 8 August 1709, *Marlborough-Heinsius Correspondence*, 452–453.

90. SHD AG A¹ 2152/36, Villars to Louis XIV, 9 August 1709.

91. SHD AG A¹ 2152/36, Villars to Louis XIV, 9 August 1709; SHD AG A¹ 2152/56, Villars to Voysin, 14 August 1709; SHD AG A¹ 2152/69, Villars to Louis XIV, 17 August 1709.

92. SHD AG A¹ 2152/68, Voysin to Villars, 17 August 1709; SHD AG A¹ 2152/77, Louis XIV to Villars, 19 August 1709.

93. SHD AG A¹2158/6, Voysin to Bernage, 2 August 1709; SHD AG A¹ 2154/131, Bernières to Voysin, 6 August 1709; SHD AG A¹ 2152/44, Voysin to Villars, 11 August 1709; AN G7 90/252, "État des fonds qui ont esté tires de la monnoye d'Amiens suivant les orders de M. de Bernage pour le service des vivres"; AN G7 90/253, "État des fonds qui ont esté tires de la monnoye d'Amiens suivant les orders de M. de Bernage pour le payement de la subsistence des troupes"; SHD AG A¹2158/13, Bernage to Voysin, 8 August 1709; SHD AG A¹ 2156/174, Doujat to Voysin, 5 September 1709; SHD AG A¹ 2158/35, Voysin to Bernage, 19 August 1709.

94. SHD AG A¹ 2152/97, Villars to Louis XIV, 25 August 1709; SHD AG A¹ 2152/127, "Mémoire pour la deffense [sic] de ligne," 30 August 1709; SHD AG A¹ 2152/131, Villars to Voysin, 1 September 1709.

95. 465, Maintenon to the Duc de Noailles, 30 July 1709, in *Lettres de Madame de Maintenon*, 610.

96. Pierre Clément, *La Police sous Louis XIV* (Paris: Didier, 1866), 330–372.

97. Dangeau, *Journal*, vol. 13, 16–17; Sourches, *Mémoires*, vol. 12, 34–35.

98. Rowlands, *Financial Decline*, 46–47.

99. "Mémoire de M. Desmaretz au Roi," 26 August 1709, in Boislisle, *Correspondance*, vol. 3, 603–604.

100. 485, Maintenon to the Duc de Noailles, 2–3 September 1709, in *Lettres de Madame de Maintenon*, 633; SHD AG A¹ 2152/146, Villars to Louis XIV, 4 September 1709; Dangeau, *Mémoires*, vol. 13, 28.

6

✣

The Battle
September–December, 1709

One night in the middle of August, a French soldier stealthily slipped out of the citadel of Tournai. He picked his way through the siege works and the lines of circumvallation, carefully avoiding watchful sentries. Once in open country, he made his way south, eluding enemy patrols and raiding parties until he reached the nearest French outpost. He was then taken to the Army of Flanders' headquarters, where he handed Marshal Villars a letter from the Marquis de Surville.

In this way, Villars learned on August 16 that the citadel's garrison was running out of food. He hastily drew up a message to be smuggled back into the besieged fortress. In tones brimming with surprise and indignation, he reminded Surville that he had been expected to hold out for most of the campaigning season or at least until the end of September. He must put his troops on half-rations or even less to eke out what supplies he had available. "Your glory and that of the nation, your fortune and that of your officers," Villars warned, depended on prolonging the defense for as long as possible. But neither encouragement nor threats had any effect. Eleven days later, Surville declared he had just four days of provisions left. He planned to beat the chamade on the last day of August and negotiate surrender terms with the enemy. The marshal lost his temper completely. He condemned this action as "the most disgraceful thing in all the world." Nevertheless, on September 6, Surville and his men marched out of the citadel. Only about half of the original 7000-strong garrison had survived unscathed. Among them was the septuagenarian governor Mesgrigny, who had done more than anyone else to turn the siege into a costly slog. The Allies had lost a further 1,900 dead and wounded in addition to the 3,300 casualties they had already suffered capturing the town.¹

The realization that the citadel of Tournai was about to fall alarmed the court high command. The king approved of Villars' plan to stand on the defensive in his fortified lines, which were now formidably strong and stretched from the North Sea to the Sambre. But he feared that the Allies' next move would be to attack the Army of Flanders in its entrenchments. In the ensuing pitched battle, Villars, a captain of undoubted courage who led from the front, faced more than a passing chance of being wounded or even killed. If this happened, another general would be needed to take over the leadership of the army. None of Villars' lieutenants possessed the requisite experience, skill, and force of personality. There was only one suitable candidate: Marshal Boufflers. During the winter, illness had forced him to abandon the army and return to court. Since then, he had served as the king's military adviser and War Minister Voysin's mentor. Now fully recovered, he longed to return to action.

Sending him to Flanders, however, raised a delicate, potentially dangerous complication. In the order of precedence of France's marshals, Boufflers was senior to Villars. This meant that he could claim command of the army. The notoriously proud and arrogant Villars could hardly be expected to accept his presence willingly or with equanimity. Divided command and disputes among generals were scourges of the French throughout the War of the Spanish Succession. They had been fundamental causes of the defeats of Blenheim, Turin, and, above all, Oudenarde.²

It was Boufflers himself who offered a solution. He declared that he would serve as a simple volunteer under his junior. As soon as he reached Arras on September 3, he sent Villars a message of singular grace and generosity: "I can assure you that none of your aides-de-camp will carry out your orders with more eagerness or more pleasure than me. Do not regard this, I beseech you, as a compliment or a manner of speaking, but as an unshakeable truth." Villars could only respond by embracing him and agreeing to share command.³

Bouffler's arrival was initially greeted with great joy by the officers and rank and file of the Flanders army—they thought he had come to negotiate an armistice with the Allies.⁴ They were soon to be badly disabused. For even before the surrender of Tournai's citadel, Marlborough and Eugene were already planning the next stage of the campaign. Despite Villars' harsh criticisms of Surville, his obstinate defense had consumed the best months of the fighting season. All that the Allies could do now was to keep up the pressure on Louis XIV in hopes of forcing him to finally submit to their peace terms. The Allied generals carefully considered their options. One was a wide swing west against Ypres. But many reasons argued against it. Ypres was a strongly garrisoned, powerful fortress. A long march westward would take time and could not be concealed, giving the French ample opportunity to take effective countermeasures. The autumn rains were about to fall in coastal Flanders, which would turn the region's clay soil into a morass. Not least, Villars' foraging expeditions had stripped the countryside of the Lys bare of fodder. The Allies would face considerable difficulties keeping their horses fed. Another option was to attack either Douai or Condé and Valenciennes. This would bring the Allied armies directly against Villars' lines. Contrary to Louis' fears, Marlborough and Eugene had no intention of throwing their troops at field fortifications the French had spent the entire summer perfecting.

Only one option remained: Mons. Located thirty miles southeast of Tournai, it was an important town, the seat of the government of the Spanish Netherlands and the refuge of Bavarian Elector Max Emmanuel. Though it did not stand on any of the major river highways leading into France, its capture would give the Allies possession of another first-class fortress, widen the breach in the French frontier defenses, threaten the Sambre stronghold of Maubeuge, and provide a good starting position for the next campaign. Finally, the Dutch coveted Mons for their Barrier.

As they had with Tournai, Marlborough and Eugene hoped to invest Mons before Villars could stop them. They did not expect the marshal to

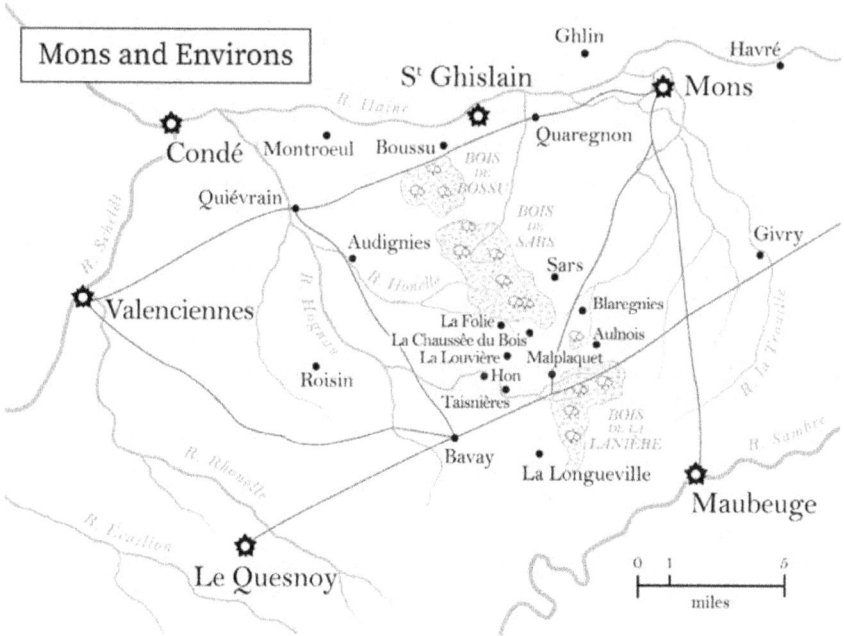

Map 6.1 Mons and Environs.

fight a battle for it. Instead, they guessed, correctly, that he intended to entrench his army in the old French lines along the River Haine and the stream of La Trouille. They aimed to reach and occupy these lines before he did (map 6.1).

A race to Mons now began. The Allies had further to go. The combined armies of Marlborough and Eugene were encamped at Orchies between Lille and Tournai, some forty miles west of Mons. Villars' right wing at Denain was ten miles closer. A further obstacle was the French-held fort at Saint-Ghislain, which controlled a key crossing over the Haine. The Allied generals did enjoy the priceless advantage of the initiative. They could decide when to move and, more importantly, Villars had no idea about their choice of target. The marshal had to assume that his foes could strike almost anywhere between the coast of Flanders and the foothills of the Ardennes. Until he knew where they were going, he had to remain rooted to his lines.

The Allies were in motion as soon as they were confident that Surville would surrender. On September 1, 1,400 cavalry and grenadiers commanded by the Earl of Orkney and General Johann Werner van Pallandt set out to capture Saint-Ghislain. Then, late on the night of September 3, Frederick, Hereditary prince of Hesse-Kassel, left Orchies leading sixty cavalry squadrons. At the same time, General Coenraad Willem van Dedem marched from Tournai with 4,000 infantry drawn from the regiments of the siege force. The two detachments were to rendezvous on the road, then together dash for Mons. The next day, the main army followed.[5]

As he had explained to the king, Villars' plans depended on the early detection of the Allies' movements. The first inklings came from Saint-Ghislain. The fort's alert commander discovered the approach of Orkney and Pallandt's force during the early hours of September 3. Soon, more reports from patrols and outposts were pouring into French headquarters at the village of Sin-le-Noble near Douai. On September 4, Villars learned that Marlborough's and Eugene's armies had crossed the Scheldt at Tournai, Antoing, and Mortagne. He was now sure they were marching for Mons. His own army was separated into several corps distributed between Cambrin and Denain. He immediately ordered all of them to follow him. Then he hastened eastward with the army's elite cavalry—the Maison du Roi, the Gendarmes, and the carabineers. At the same time, the Comte d'Albergotti, commander of the Army of Flanders' right wing at Denain, sent the Chevalier de Luxembourg with thirty squadrons and the infantry brigade of Picardie rushing for Mons.[6]

After leaving Orchies, Hesse-Kassel drove his horsemen onward relentlessly. Soon after crossing the Scheldt, he was joined by Dedem's infantry. But on the night of September 4, the force was caught in a tremendous downpour that completely blotted out visibility and halted all movement.

At the same time, the prince learned that the Allies had failed to take Saint-Ghislain, which prevented him from crossing the Haine and reaching Mons from the southwest. He was forced to take a more circuitous route, circling round to the north of the fortress-city and approaching it from the east. He renewed his advance on September 5. At two o'clock in the morning of September 6, he passed over the Haine at Obourg and Havré. Noon saw him seizing the old French lines along the La Trouille stream. Then, at dusk, the Chevalier de Luxembourg came hurrying up at the head of his cavalry.[7]

In the fading light, Luxembourg took stock of the situation. Facing him was Hesse-Kassel in line of battle with a force at least twice the size of his own. Behind the Allied squadrons, their main armies would be coming up. The French cavalry commander decided not to challenge the prince, even though this meant abandoning the lines of La Trouille. He threw a regiment of dragoons into Mons as reinforcements for its garrison. Then he fell back to join Villars, who had managed to reach Quiévrain on the little River Hogneau. The French had lost the race.

Hesse-Kassel's dash to Mons was a splendid feat of arms for which he won much praise. It also wrecked Villars' plans. Having failed to get to the Haine and La Trouille lines first, he could no longer stop Marlborough and Eugene from besieging Mons. Yet the marshal did not hesitate about what to do next: "We will assemble Your Majesty's army behind the Hogneau today, tonight, and tomorrow," he informed the king on September 6, "then we will cross this river and attempt to engage the enemy in an action."[8]

Why did Villars seek battle now? There was little reason for one. Mons itself was hardly worth fighting for. It was much less important than Tournai. Its fall would not have opened a way into France. With it in their hands, the Allies would still have had to break through a barrier of powerful *pré carré* fortresses, including Douai, Condé, Valenciennes, Le Quesnoy, and Maubeuge. In addition, the French army itself was safe from attack. Quiévrain was fifteen miles from Mons and the intervening ground was difficult, replete with defiles and woods. Even Marlborough and Eugene would have been able to advance only slowly. Villars would have had ample warning of their approach and could easily have pulled his forces back safely out of range.

Villars was seeking a battle for its own sake. He had been spoiling for one since taking command in Flanders in March. Then, throughout the spring and summer, he had been tortured by his army's chronic shortage of supplies, which had brought it dangerously close to dissolution. Its plight had eased of late, yet, like Controller General Desmaretz, the marshal feared that financial failure would lead over the winter to the withering away of French military power. The Army of Flanders had to fight now or never.

A still more important reason for Villars' decision was his towering self-confidence. Although he had never faced Marlborough and Eugene in battle before, he had no doubt he could beat them. For, as he had once reminded his patron Madame de Maintenon, he was the only French general who remained undefeated in the field. Moreover, he was convinced that a great victory would completely change the course of the war. It would stop the Allied invasion of France. It would allow the Army of Flanders to go on the offensive and regain much of the ground lost in past campaigns. It would break the diplomatic stalemate and give Louis the upper hand at the negotiating table.

The king was much less sanguine than his marshal about the prospects and promise of a battle. From the beginning of the campaign, he had always urged caution, advising Villars never to initiate an action himself and to engage the enemy only if he had a clear advantage in numbers or position. In addition, he was skeptical that a victory would produce significant results. The Army of Flanders was too weak and too badly supplied to make great gains against the Allies. He had, though, given Villars permission in July to fight if he chose. Now, after learning of the marshal's intention to seek battle, Louis made one last appeal for restraint. He suggested that the proximity of the French field forces and the difficult terrain around Mons might suffice to hinder the Allied siege. But suspecting that Villars had already made up his mind to bring on a general engagement, the king stressed that he must first assemble his entire army.[9]

Villars had arrived at Quiévrain on September 6 with the elite cavalry. He was soon joined by the forty infantry battalions of Albergotti. The next day, the rest of the infantry—eighty-one battalions—under his second-in-command, the Comte d'Artagnan, marched in. The Army of Flanders then crossed the Hogneau. Before it could close with the enemy, it needed to be fed. The troops were famished after their long, hard marches. From Maubeuge, Intendant Charles Doujat sent 54,000 rations of bread, about half of what the army would normally have consumed.[10] On September 8, Villars sent another message to the court:

> I have the honor of informing Your Majesty of the resolution that has been taken to assemble the army and seek combat with the enemy. They have surrounded Mons, so we must march this night to reach the Bavay road and then occupy the Aulnois Gap, which is the most open country by which to approach them. I have the honor to once again tell Your Majesty that I am delighted that Marshal Boufflers is with me. If we attack, he will testify that we do so with good reason; if we do nothing, he will confirm that we could not have done better.[11]

From Versailles came no eleventh-hour objections. Louis waited with bated breath.

On the morning of September 9, Marlborough was writing a letter to his wife. Sarah had complained bitterly about the harsh treatment she was suffering at the hands of Queen Anne as well as the conspicuous favor being shown to Abigail Masham. She scolded her husband for not rushing to her defense. He reassured her that he would soon write to the queen to speak up for her interests.[12]

Marlborough had his headquarters in the village of Blaregnies. His Confederate Army was encamped in a line running north to Genly. Less than three miles separated it from the Army of Flanders. But in between was a belt of dense forests running northwest to southeast. It was pierced by only two passages wide enough for the movement and deployment of armies. The first was the Boussu Gap, between the wood of that name and the River Haine. The other was the Aulnois Gap, between the forests of Sars and La Lanière, at the center of which was the little village of Malplaquet. Prince Eugene was covering the former from his camp at Quaregnon. Marlborough was guarding the latter. Neither of the Allied generals was anticipating that Villars would court battle. Instead, they expected him to act as he had during the siege of Tournai: he would shadow the Allied armies from a safe distance, harass them with raids, pick off isolated detachments and convoys, and strip the countryside bare of fodder.

Suddenly, Marlborough received electrifying news: the French were marching for the Aulnois Gap. He immediately set aside his letter and called for his horse. Protected by an escort of thirty squadrons under the prince d'Auvergne, he hurried to the windmill of Sars. Eugene was already there. From the windmill, the two commanders had an excellent view of the gap. Auvergne and a strong body of cavalry then pushed into it. They immediately ran into a party of Gardes du Corps. The blue-uniformed French troopers were commanded by the Chevalier de Luxembourg, and they had been sent by Villars during the night to occupy the vital ground; having accomplished their mission, they withdrew without a fight. Auvergne rode forward only a short distance before he spotted the entire Army of Flanders advancing toward him. It was now his turn to fall back. Upon hearing the prince's report, Marlborough and Eugene dispatched urgent orders for their armies to concentrate against the enemy. Then they watched the French filling up the open ground between the Sars and La Lanière woods.[13]

It was an impressive sight. First, they saw dark, moving masses. Soon these became four huge columns, two each of infantry and cavalry. As the French drew closer, the observers at the windmill would have been able to make out more details. Wan, watery sunlight glinted off muskets and cannons, half-pikes and halberds, cuirasses and breastplates. Above the closely packed ranks waved and fluttered a multitude of flags—each battalion carried three, each squadron two. The infantry's standards were emblazoned with a white cross, the quarters colored in myriad hues. Many of the cavalry's pennons bore a golden, many-rayed sun, others a field of fleurs-de-lys. To the Allied generals' ears would have come the tramp of marching feet, the rattle of drums, and the blare of trumpets.[14]

If Marlborough and Eugene could have peered closer, they would have noticed that the French soldiers cut much less prepossessing figures. Their army's dire poverty had meant that few had received new uniforms during the winter quarters. Almost all were making do with old kit, and, after another grueling fighting season, these were stained, torn, and tattered. Once white coats, waistcoats, and breeches had been so mended and patched with whatever cloth came to hand they now resembled motley. Most were shod in worn-out shoes; more than a few were barefoot. Their faces were gaunt, and their arms, legs, and torsos thin—the result of subsisting for too many months on meager rations of bad bread. Yet, in spite of it all, the French had a lively, spirited air, stepping out with shoulders back and heads high.

This ragged army had stolen a march on its opponents. The Chevalier de Quincy's company of the régiment de Bourgogne was in the van of the leading infantry column. In his memoirs, he describes the scene that unfolded before him in the Gap of Aulnois: "I saw with a single glance the entire enemy army encamped, its tents still pitched. There was not a single sign of movement. A complete tranquility reigned everywhere in their camp."[15] Throughout September 9, Marlborough and Eugene scrambled to assemble their forces. Much of the captain general's troops were widely dispersed, the cavalry out foraging, the infantry marauding. They had to march through sudden downpours that sowed much confusion, with whole contingents losing sight and touch with each other in the gloom. For his part, Prince Eugene needed several hours to bring his corps down from its cantonments around Quaregnon. Only at the end of the day were the Allied armies finally formed in line of battle.[16]

In the discomfiture of the enemy, the Chevalier de Quincy saw a priceless opportunity: "I had every reason to notice at my ease that, if Marshal de Villars wanted to take advantage of the negligence of the enemy generals, he would obtain an assured victory without much difficulty." A number of Quincy's contemporaries—and after them, many historians—shared his view that the marshal should have attacked the Allies while they were struggling to concentrate.[17] But Villars had good reasons not to do so. His army had been on the march since five o'clock in the morning. His troops were in poor physical condition. Many of them would have been tired and in need of a pause to recuperate. The sudden bursts of heavy rain that bedeviled the Allies would have equally played havoc with his attacks. Moreover, Marlborough had no reason to stand and fight. Even at the cost of losing a rearguard or two, he could have retreated northward out of the Army of Flanders' reach, which would have also hastened his junction with Prince Eugene. Most importantly, Villars knew that advancing beyond the shelter of the forests would be playing into his enemies' hands. On the wide-open plain of Mons, Marlborough and Eugene would have been able to bring to bear their overwhelming advantages of greater numbers, superior firepower, and the unmatched prowess in maneuver of their well-founded, veteran regiments. Despite all his bombast, Villars had a realistic appreciation of his troops' more limited capabilities. Their best hope of success against the enemy lay in fighting on the tactical defensive and from the protection of prepared positions. As a result, he never had any intention of leaving the ground around the village of Malplaquet. Instead, he ordered his artillery to open a long-range bombardment of the Allies and his troops to dig in along the whole length of their line.[18]

After they had recovered from their initial alarm, Marlborough and Eugene welcomed Villars' move. They had resigned themselves to another grinding siege of a frontier fortress. Now they were being offered what they had desired from the beginning of the campaign: a pitched battle. They threw themselves into preparations. They first decided to capture Saint-Ghislain in order to secure their line of retreat to Tournai. Two thousand infantry drawn from the force blockading Mons set out under General Dedem. On the night of September 10, they stormed the fort and took it. The Allied commanders also wanted to fight Villars with as much of their strength as possible. Here, though, they faced a quandary. The detachment that had been besieging the citadel of Tournai—nineteen battalions and ten squadrons led by General Henry Withers—was still on the road and would not arrive until late on the tenth. From their vantage point at the windmill of Sars, Marlborough and Eugene could see the French troops toiling like ants on their trenches, redoubts, and barricades. Should the Allies attack immediately, before the enemy defenses became too strong, or should they wait for Withers? The captain general argued strenuously for the former course of action, the prince of Savoy for the latter. Eugene eventually carried the debate. A council of war was then scheduled for the night of September 10 to draw up final plans for a battle the next day.

During these hectic hours, Marlborough still found a moment to pick up his pen and continue his letter to his duchess:

[The French] have last night intrenched their camp, by which thay show plainly that thay have changed their mind and will not attack us, so that we must take our measures in seeing which way we can be most troublesome to them. This afternoon the redgiments which made the siege of Tournay will join us, and then wee shall have all the troupes we can expect for those we have left for the blocking upp of Mons must continu where they are. I do not yet know if I shall have an opportunity of sending this letter tonight. If not I shall add to it what may passe tomorrow.

He then assured her that her problems at court were still close to mind, writing "in the meantime I can't hinder saying to you, that though the fate of Europe if these armys ingage may depend upon the good or bad success, yet your uneasiness gives me much great trouble." (See maps 6.2 and 6.3)[19]

Meanwhile, Villars was meticulously preparing the battlefield. The Army of Flanders had taken up a position measuring about two and a half miles from end to end as the crow flies. On the left flank was the Bois de Sars; thick with trees and undergrowth, it was difficult and slow to traverse. Behind it were the villages of La Folie and La Chausée du Bois.

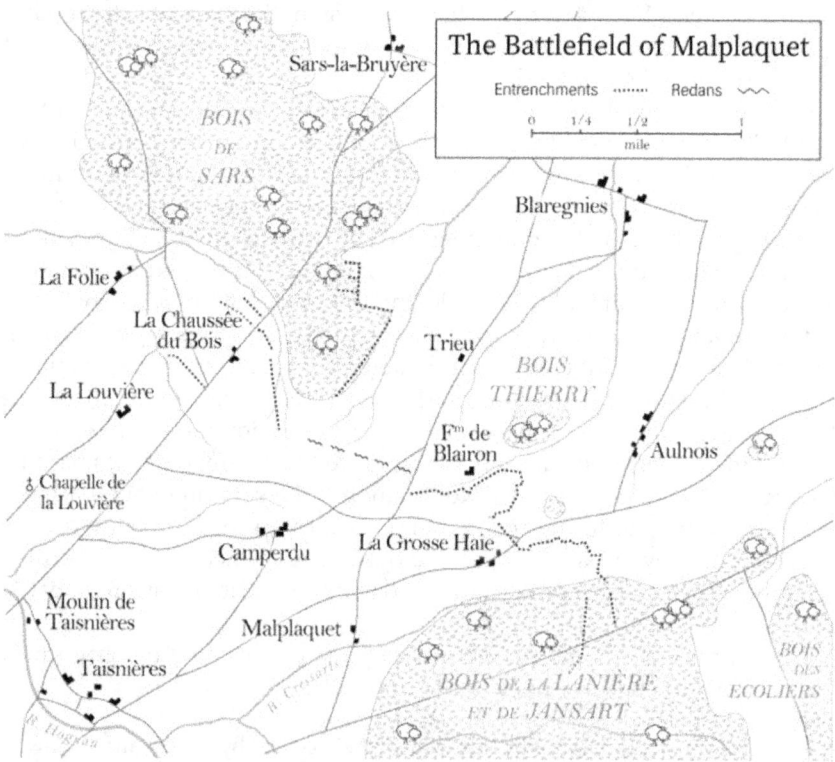

Map 6.2 The Battlefield of Malplaquet.

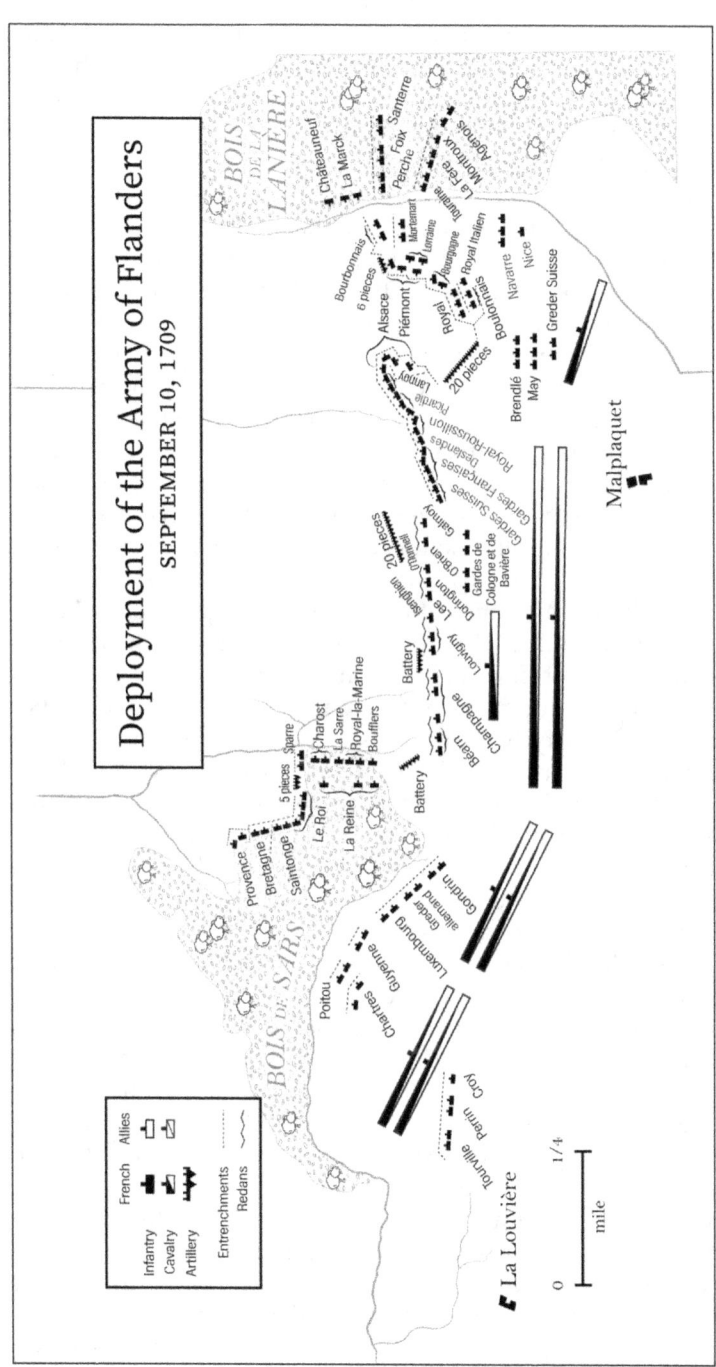

Map 6.3 Deployment of the Army of Flanders, September 10, 1709.

On the right flank was the Bois de La Lanière, so dense its interior was impenetrable to formed bodies of troops. In front of it were the hamlet of La Grosse Haye and the walled farm of Blairon. In between the two forests was a plain just under a mile wide. It was bisected by the little Bois de Thierry. To the south, it gradually rose up to a low plateau on which was the village of Malplaquet.[20]

On this battlefield, Villars deployed 125 battalions and 260 squadrons, some 80,000 troops in all. Following their marshal's orders, they had spent the better part of two days and nights energetically entrenching themselves. The key to the left flank was the southeastern corner of the Bois de Sars, where a triangle-shaped tongue of woodland stuck out toward the Allied lines—in military parlance, a salient. Its entire perimeter was fortified by breastworks, trenches, and abatis—barriers made from felled trees and sharpened stakes. This bastion was garrisoned by the brigades of Le Roi, La Reine, La Sarre, Charost, and Bretagne with a total of twenty-one battalions. More fieldworks had been constructed in and on either side of La Chaussée du Bois. These were occupied by the seventeen battalions of the brigades of Tourville, Gondrin, and Poitou. On the right flank, the edge of the Bois de La Lanière was girded by redoubts and barricades and held by the twenty-four battalions of the brigades of Bourbonnais, Touraine, La Fère, and La Perche. A long stretch of fieldworks ran from the wood to La Grosse Haye and then on to the farm of Blairon. Here from right to left were the brigades of Piémont, Royal, Lannoy, Picardie, and the Guards, in all thirty-two battalions. In support were the six battalions of the brigade of Navarre and the eight Swiss battalions of Brendlé. In the plain at the center of the French line were five arrowhead-shaped redans. They were defended by the thirteen battalions of the Champagne and Irish brigades. The four battalions of the Guards of Bavaria and Cologne were in reserve behind them.

As for his cavalry, Villars massed the bulk of it in four long lines on the plateau of Malplaquet. In front and on the right, the traditional place of honor, were the companies of the Maison du Roi and the Gendarmes. On the left, near La Folie, were the carabineers. The marshal sent a strong detachment of fifty squadrons under the Chevalier de Luxembourg to La Longueville, three miles southeast of Malplaquet. The dependable Luxembourg had orders to guard the Army of Flanders' lines of communication to Maubeuge, its sole source of supplies, and to watch for any outflanking moves by the enemy.

The field artillery had a vital role to play in supporting the foot and horse. Its eighty guns were distributed in batteries of varying sizes along the army's entire front. The veteran gunner Saint-Hilaire chose positions that afforded clear fields of fire on the most likely enemy approaches. One battery would prove particularly deadly. Near the hamlet of La Grosse

Haye, where the French field fortifications bent back to create a so-called re-entrant, Saint-Hilaire tucked twenty cannons hidden from Allied view. They could fire down the length of a shallow natural trough running in front of the French entrenchments from the hamlet to the tip of the wood of La Lanière. They would turn this ground into the site of a veritable massacre.

Villars just as meticulously made command arrangements. He reserved for himself overall direction of the army. In deference to Marshal Boufflers, he assigned him the forces on the right from Blairon to the Bois de La Lanière. Assisting him was a cohort of trusted generals, including the Comte d'Artagnan, the Duc de Guiche, and the Marquis de La Frézelière. In charge of the center and the left were the Marquis de Goësbriand, the Marquis de Puységur, and the Comte d'Albergotti.[21]

The position of the Army of Flanders was exceptionally strong. It resembled a fortress more than a trace of hastily thrown-up entrenchments. Moreover, in deploying his troops, Villars had considered his opponents' preferred tactics. Marlborough had won two great set-piece battles, Blenheim and Ramillies, with massive assaults that had crashed through the French center. By manning the middle of his own line relatively lightly with seventeen battalions, Villars was baiting the captain general to try again. But, in reality, this sector was a deathtrap. An Allied attack would be hit and devastated by crossfire from the Bois de Sars, the redans, and the strongpoint of Blairon. After it had been repulsed, Villars could then launch a counterattack with his cavalry. Led by the glittering squadrons of the Maison du Roi and the Gendarmes, the French horsemen would ride through the gaps deliberately left between the redans and charge onto the open plain beyond to complete the defeat of the enemy.

Villars' plan was excellent. It maximized his army's strengths, minimized its weaknesses, went a long way to countering Allied superiority in numbers, and gave him an opportunity to win a major victory. Yet it suffered from three flaws. First, Villars overestimated the impassability of the flanking forests, particularly the Bois de Sars. Second, by fixing the bulk of his troops in field fortifications, he robbed them of much of their mobility and flexibility. This was especially significant on a battlefield where the wooded, rugged terrain frequently prevented generals and officers from knowing what was happening in different sectors. Third, Villars' deployment of his army was markedly unbalanced: seventy battalions were on the right against just fifty-five in the center and on the left. He thought he had good reasons for doing this. His army's position was more open between Blairon and La Grosse Haye and so needed to be held by considerable bodies of troops. More importantly, the marshal was acutely concerned about protecting his line of retreat to his supply base at Maubeuge. He therefore deliberately weighted his strength toward the east.

If Villars was worried about these flaws, he did not show it. On the morning of September 10, he wrote a final message to the king brimming with all of his old optimism:

> Never have the troops marched so well or with such order. The valor of the soldier and the cavalier inspires everyone. I must especially praise the conduct of Messieurs d'Albergotti, d'Artagnan, Chemerault, La Frézelière, and Puységur. Finally, I must say that all have shown a vivacity and an ardor which has redoubled my desire to come to grips with the enemy on equal ground and has given me complete confidence, with God's help, to defeat them utterly.[22]

Having chosen not to attack on the tenth, the Allied commanders spent the day methodically reconnoitering the enemy's lines. While this was going on, a curious incident took place. During an inspection of his troops in the Bois de Sars, the Comte d'Albergotti noticed that the Allies had pushed their outposts very close to the forest. He sent one of his officers to demand a parley. The Florentine then met the prince of Hesse-Kassel, the electoral prince of Brandenburg, and Quartermaster-General Cadogan in no-man's land. While their superiors conversed amicably, a huge crowd of officers and ordinary soldiers from both sides fraternized. Many joined forces to harvest the peas they found in the fields. But when Villars learned of what was happening, he feared that Cadogan was using the opportunity to study the French forces and fortifications in a crucial sector. He ordered the parley ended at once. With salutes and sincere well wishes, the soldiers of the two armies went back to their lines. This courtesy would contrast starkly with the brutality and savagery that were about to follow.[23]

The Allies held their council of war in the early evening. Given the import of the next day's events and the enormity of the decisions to be taken, it was attended by the generals of all the national contingents that made up the army. Marlborough and Eugene were united in urging an attack on the French. Without demur, the other Allied commanders concurred. The decision then passed to Sico van Goslinga. Of the Dutch field deputies, he was the only one present; the other three had remained behind at Tournai to oversee its occupation. Should he veto the use of the States Army's troops, a battle would be impossible. Yet, for all his often skeptical and suspicious view of Marlborough, he shared the captain general's desire for a decisive engagement. He enthusiastically endorsed the attack. The council was unanimous.

Marlborough and Eugene then made their plan. They recognized the difficult challenges posed by Villars' fortified position. The forests girding the French flanks would slow and break up the attacking Allied infantry's

The Battle 185

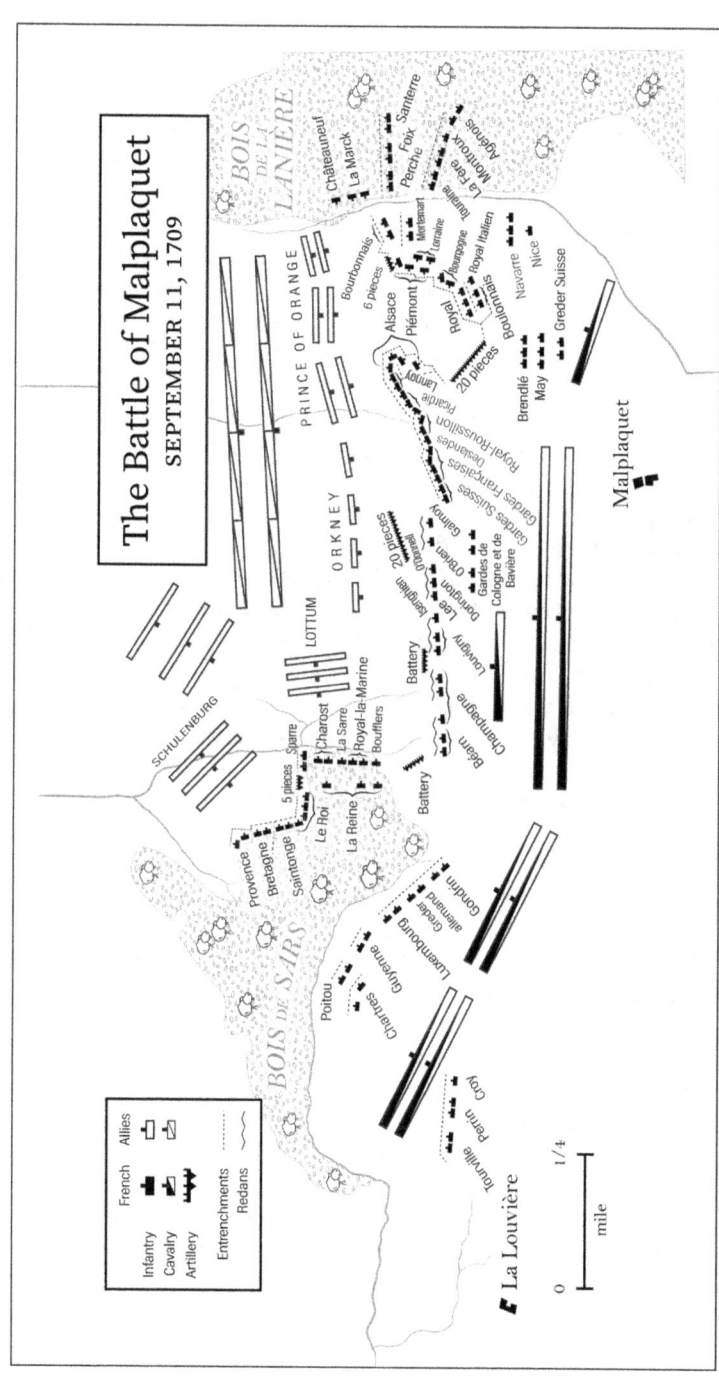

Map 6.4 The Battle of Malplaquet, September 11, 1709.

orderly lines, largely nullifying their advantages in numbers, maneuver, and firepower. Moreover, the captain general and the prince spotted the trap that had been set for them in the French center. Their solution was to retry the scheme that had won their great triumph at Blenheim in 1704. They would first mount heavy attacks on the French flanks. A particularly powerful stroke would be aimed at the Bois de Sars—the fruit, perhaps, of some surreptitious scouting by Cadogan during Albergotti's ill-advised afternoon parlay. These thrusts, however, were feints meant to deceive Villars and force him into making a mistake that would then enable the Allies' real main effort. With his flanks under increasing pressure, the marshal would be compelled to reinforce them with troops pulled from his central redans. The Allied infantry reserve would then advance and capture them. Finally, the massed Allied cavalry would deliver the coup de grace by passing through the occupied fieldworks and sweeping on to the plateau of Malplaquet, cleaving the enemy army in two.

Marlborough's clerks wrote up the orders. Altogether, the Allies had 126 battalions and 253 squadrons, totaling over 100,000 men. The French entrenchments from the Bois de Thierry to the tip of the Bois de La Lanière were to be assailed by the Allied left wing, comprising thirty battalions of the States Army and the nineteen battalions of the Tournai detachment, all commanded by the youthful Prince of Orange and the veteran Count Tilly. In support would be twenty-one squadrons under Hesse-Kassel. After the infantry had taken the earthworks, they and the cavalry were to advance together onto the plain beyond the woods. On the other end of the battlefield, the triangle-shaped French salient in the Bois de Sars was the target of two attacks. General Schulenburg would storm the salient's northern face with the forty battalions of the Allied right wing. At the same time, General Lottum would lead twenty-two battalions from the Allied center against its eastern side. They would be backed by thirty squadrons under Auvergne. The remaining forces in the center, fifteen battalions under the Earl of Orkney and the 182 squadrons of the Allied cavalry reserve, would wait for their moment to move on the redans. Most of the 100 cannons of the Allied artillery were supporting the attacks, except for twelve that Schulenburg's infantry were laboriously dragging with them through the forest of Sars.[24]

The written orders went out from Marlborough's headquarters at Blaregnies sometime on the night of September 10. Soon afterward, a final, crucial change was made to the plan. Despite hours of hard marching, Henry Withers' Tournai detachment had only managed to reach the western edge of the battlefield. The troops were now exhausted, and moving them during the night through the Allied camps to the post originally intended for them on the left wing would cause enormous disruptions.

Marlborough and Eugene decided to keep the whole force of nineteen battalions and ten squadrons on the extreme right of the Allied line. They now ordered Withers to take his corps through the Bois de Sars, emerge near La Folie, and turn the flank of the French army, perhaps even roll it up from west to east. This last-minute modification added a new and unexpected dimension to the battle plan—the prince dubbed it "a special attack." But it also significantly weakened the Allied left wing, which was reduced from forty-nine to thirty battalions. This would have grave consequences the next day.[25]

Over many successful campaigns, Marlborough and Eugene had forged a close, remarkably effective partnership. They trusted each other implicitly and agreed completely on how they would fight the battle. The prince took charge of the Allied right, the captain general the center and left. But they shared overall command. At day's end, Eugene recorded in his diary: "Tomorrow morning, September 11, in the name of God, we attack the enemy." The Allies would begin at first light, the signal a salvo from the massed guns of the British artillery (map 6.4).[26]

The night was restless and full of disturbances. With the armies so close together, both sides feared a raid or a surprise attack. French and Allied cavalry patrols ranged between the lines, alert for any sign of enemy movement. They clashed constantly, skirmishing and exchanging fire. In the camps, the infantry were repeatedly called to arms, only to be stood down again once the false alarms had passed. At last, at three o'clock in the morning, the Allied troops were summoned to prayers. These were led by chaplains of every confession: Church of England, Roman Catholic, Lutheran, and Calvinist. As soon as the rites of salvation were done, the regiments were fed, then marched to their battle stations. The French were also forming up. They had gone to mass and received general absolution from their priests. Those who had any food left had eaten a meager breakfast. Then their marshals rode through the ranks, showing themselves to their men, pausing frequently to speak words of encouragement. Cries of "Vive le roi!" "Vive le maréchal de Villars!" and "Vive le maréchal de Boufflers!" rang up and down the Army of Flanders.

By dawn, 180,000 soldiers were crammed into a battlefield of little more than four square miles. There would be no larger battle in Europe until Wagram almost exactly a century later. Malplaquet's beginning was delayed by an early morning fog that blotted out all visibility. The impenetrable gray gloom greatly benefited the Allies, who were able to deploy unobserved and unmolested. At seven-thirty, the sun broke through the murk. Half an hour later, the last tendrils of mist were gone, replaced by brilliant sunshine. Marlborough gave the order for the signal salvo. The forty British guns thundered together. The Allied batteries massed in the center then opened a bombardment so heavy and rapid that the Chevalier de Folard, a captain on the staff of the Marquis de Goësbriand, likened it to volleys of musketry.[27]

The French guns replied in earnest. They were well commanded by Saint-Hilaire and well served by veteran gunners. But the Allies had much the better of the exchange of fire. The French found they had few targets: the enemy forces in the center, the infantry and cavalry reserves, were mostly drawn up out of range. By contrast, the Allies relentlessly pounded the redans and the fieldworks along the edges of the Bois de Sars. Even worse, the French cavalry lined up in the open behind the central earthworks were within easy reach. Shot after shot slammed into the serried ranks of the Maison du Roi and the Gendarmes, mangling men and mounts. With superb discipline and splendid sangfroid, the elite French horsemen held their ground. Their ordeal would last for almost six hours.[28]

The Allied attack began on their right. Withers led his nineteen battalions into the heart of the Bois de Sars. His ten cavalry squadrons did not follow. Instead, reinforced by ten more squadrons of Imperial dragoons and hussars, they set out under the Saxon Major General Moritz Friedrich von Milkau on a long ride around the western edges of the wood, hoping to find the open end of the French left flank. Schulenburg had arranged his forty battalions—20,000 men—in a compact formation of three successive lines. They marched toward the northern face of the French salient. Eugene himself accompanied them.

The trees and undergrowth slowed Schulenburg's troops and broke up their lines. They had not gone far before they encountered French skirmishers. A flurry of shooting and the French retreated, fading into the forest. The Habsburg, German, Danish, and Walloon infantry marched on until they were brought to a halt by a row of abatis. Beyond them, at close musket range, were the first French fieldworks, packed with the ten battalions of the Bretagne and Le Roi brigades. Schulenburg and his subordinates sent out a few platoons to try to tempt the French to throw away their first volley. They did not react. The Allied soldiers then began clambering over the barricades of sharpened wooden stakes; they lost their last semblance of order and cohesion. The French opened fire. Some battalions loosed a mass volley. Others employed *feu par rang*. Still others resorted to parapet firing, a technique normally used in the defense of besieged fortresses: six ranks each took turns marching up to the breastwork, shot, then moved to the back of the formation to reload. Whatever method they chose, Count August Christoph von Wackerbarth, the Saxon general commanding Schulenburg's first line, thought the French shot like the best infantry in the world. Hundreds of Allied troops fell dead and wounded. Officers and sergeants, shouting, swearing, and swinging their spontoons and halberds, struggled to form the survivors into a coherent front. Lacking time and under unremitting pressure, they had no opportunity to organize platoon volleys. The Allies instead returned fire as best they could. Wackerbarth's battalions were some of the finest in the Allied army, including the Saxon Guards and the Danish Guards. But they began to shrink back from the remorseless French musketry.[29]

Meanwhile, the other prong of the Allied attack on the Bois de Sars was also under way. Lottum had deployed his twenty-two British, Hanoverian, and Prussian battalions in a close column of three successive lines. They first had to march from the Allied center toward the French redans. But in order to strike their real target, the eastern face of the forest salient, they had to execute a turn to the right. The French artillery was at last presented with an inviting target. Standing with his Bavarians behind the redoubts, Jean-François Martin de La Colonie had a clear view of what transpired:

> As soon as this dense column appeared in the avenue, fourteen guns were promptly brought up in front of our brigade almost in line with the regiment of Gardes francaises. The fire of this battery was terrific, and hardly a shot missed its mark. I could not help noticing the officer in command, who although he seemed elderly was nevertheless so active that in giving his orders there was no cessation of action anywhere, the cannon shot continued to pour forth without a break, plunged into the enemy's infantry and carried off whole ranks at a time, but a gap was no sooner created than it was immediately filled again, and they even continued their advance upon us without giving us any idea of the actual point determined on for their attack. At last the column, leaving the great battery on its left, changed its direction a quarter right and threw itself precipitately into the wood on our left.

In the elderly artillery officer, de La Colonie might have glimpsed the fifty-eight-year-old Saint-Hilaire. Racked and raked by the French guns, Lottum's formation, the eight British battalions of the Duke of Argyll's brigade in the lead, nevertheless continued advancing straight at the field fortifications held by the brigades of Charost and La Sarre. The six French battalions unleashed their first volleys at murderously close range. Staggered, the Allies halted and returned fire. Argyll himself was in the thick of the fighting. When he heard some of his men complaining that he must be wearing a bulletproof breastplate hidden under his clothing, he ripped open his shirt. "You see, brothers, said he, I have no concealed armor. I am equally exposed with you and I require none to go where I shall refuse to venture."[30]

Both Allied attacks on the Bois de Sars had been checked by fierce French resistance. Schulenburg and Eugene strove to restore momentum by committing more and more fresh battalions from their unengaged second and third lines. The brigades of Bretagne and Le Roi were soon fighting desperately to hold back an overwhelming number of foes. But it was Lottum who achieved a breakthrough. From the beginning of the battle, the morale of the régiment de La Sarre had been dangerously shaky. During the initial Allied bombardment, it had panicked and abandoned its post, only to be rallied and brought back into line. Under heavy pressure from Argyll's brigade, it suddenly broke and fled. Into the resulting gap surged the Allied infantry. The regiments of La Reine, Royal-la Marine, and Boufflers began to retreat. The commander of the La Sarre brigade, Charles, Comte d'Angennes, already twice wounded, tried to stem the flight of his troops; a shot to the head killed him. Though the two battalions of Charost fought with remarkable tenacity, they were overwhelmed and forced from their positions. Lottum could now attack the French brigades facing Schulenburg in the right flank and rear. Worse still, his troops overran a five-gun French battery sited at the northeastern corner of the salient. The gun crews managed to limber up and evacuate three of their pieces. The Allies captured the remaining two, turned them on the régiment du Roi, and blasted away at point-blank range. Already hard-pressed by the masses of Schulenburg's infantry, this elite formation collapsed and ran.

Realizing the fieldworks were lost, the Marquis de Goësbriand brought off the battered regiments of Bretagne, Provence, and Saintonge. They retired deeper into the forest to continue the fight. In the process, Goësbriand had his horse killed under him, and a spent musket ball struck his right arm. Schulenburg was at last able to occupy the French positions on the northern face of the salient. His corps had paid a very heavy price. All the colonels, lieutenant colonels, and majors of Wackerbarth's battalions were killed or wounded. Some of these units were down to just two or three officers.[31]

By midmorning, on their right, the Allies had succeeded in breaking into the Bois de Sars and were about to advance deeper into it. On their left, they had suffered a bloody disaster.

Between eight-thirty and nine o'clock, the thirty battalions of the States Army began their attack. Their target was a mile-long front from the walled farm of Blairon to the Bois de La Lanière. They were organized into five columns. The Prince of Orange led the three columns on the right (seventeen battalions), General Fagel the two on the left (thirteen battalions). Behind them were the twenty-one squadrons of Hesse-Kassel.

Fagel's columns were aimed at the formidable French defenses on the fringes and in front of the forest of La Lanière. Under the veteran general were some of the States Army's best troops. The first column included two battalions of the Scottish Brigade. Scots had fought for the Dutch since 1572, even before the formal foundation of the Republic. For the clansmen of the impoverished Highlands, enlisting in the best-paid and best-provisioned army in Europe had an irresistible appeal: a constant stream of recruits flowed out of the mountains and across the North Sea to the lowlands of Holland. Many of the officers were scions of families with a tradition of service in the Brigade. Some were as much Dutch as Scottish: they were bilingual and completely at home in the urbane, cosmopolitan society of the Netherlands. The second column was led by two battalions of the Holland or—thanks to the color of their uniforms—Blue Guards. Once the personal bodyguards of William III, they were the finest infantry on the field, renowned for their fortitude and firepower.[32]

The Scots and the Guards came on superbly, drums beating, pipes playing, flags flying. But they were about to run a deadly gauntlet. As soon as they stepped down into the long, shallow trough that ran from La Grosse Haye to the tip of La Lanière, they came into the sights of the twenty guns of the French battery concealed in the re-entrant near the hamlet. Their gunners were presented with an unmissable target: tightly packed masses of men marching slowly across their muzzles at short range. Their first salvos of shot and canister enfiladed the Dutch lines, sweeping through them from end to end. Within minutes, they had inflicted horrific casualties. The Swedish general Oxenstiern was killed, his countryman Sparre mortally wounded. Major General George Hamilton, the Scots' commander, was badly hit and had to be carried from the field. Caught closest to the guns, the Guards' losses were appalling. For dozens of yards, broken blue-clad bodies blanketed the ground.

Somehow, Fagel's columns pressed home their attacks. The four battalions of the first column, the Scots in the lead, engaged the Bourbonnais brigade in its entrenchments on the extreme right of the French line. After a grueling firefight, the German mercenaries of the La Marck regiment suddenly abandoned their posts and retreated into the forest. Their disappearance shook the Chateauneuf and Bourbonnais regiments, and they too fell back. Some Scots pursued the enemy into the trees but were then stopped dead in their tracks by the brigade of La Perche, which was behind an impenetrable barrier of abatis. The other Scots found a seam in the French defenses that brought them behind La Grosse Haye. From there, they threatened to take the hamlet's defenders in the rear. The Marquis de La Frézelière, who was in command of the second line of the French right wing, was alert to the danger and ordered a counterattack. The *vieux* regiment of Navarre charged with the bayonet, overran the Scots, killed many, forced the survivors into flight, captured four flags, and retook the Bourbonnais brigade's fieldworks. The Scottish Brigade's losses were fearsome. The Chevalier de Quincy, whose régiment de Bourgogne had played no small part in its repulse, poignantly described seeing "two-thirds, at least, of these regiments lying face down in the dirt." Among them were the colonels of both battalions, John Murray, Marquess of Tullibardine, and James Hepburn.

Fagel's other column fought with even more valor and met with even less success. Its nine battalions hurled themselves against the fortifications of the Piémont and Royal brigades. Already terribly ravaged by the hidden battery, they were then struck again and again by close-range fire from the French infantry. Amazingly, they stood fast and shot back, platoon volleys rippling up and down their lines. The Comte d'Artagnan, who had stationed himself with the régiment de Piémont, had his horse shot from under him and a ball ricochet off his cuirass. Gallant Dutch guardsmen charged forward, planted their flags on the parapets of the enemy works, and fought it out hand-to-hand with their occupants. It could not last. After half an hour of unequal struggle, Fagel's remnants retreated. The Blue Guards had been practically annihilated. They left behind their flags for the enemy.[33]

Even as Fagel's assault was coming to grief, Orange's was reaching its climax. The young prince, surrounded by a phalanx of Dutch generals and accompanied by Deputy Goslinga, led his three columns against the salient between Blairon and La Grosse Haye held by the Picardie and Lannoy brigades. As the seventeen Dutch and Swiss battalions advanced, they were hit by French artillery and musketry. But they escaped the attentions of the guns that had savaged the Scots and Guards. Nearing the French positions, they entered a patch of broken ground and thick hedges which lent them cover and concealment. As a result, they were able to attack in good order and with the full weight of their numbers and firepower. They prised the Picardie brigade out of its fieldworks, then took the Lannoy regiment in the flank and drove it off in disorder. The next French regiment in line, Alsace, made a determined stand. In vicious close-quarters combat, its four battalions lost half their strength; after the action, the dead and wounded were found piled high in the trenches. Overpowered, Alsace, too, was forced to retreat.

The French were now facing a crisis. The Prince of Orange's columns had torn a gaping hole in their right wing and were about to take the twenty-gun battery and La Grosse Haye. The rout of the régiment de Picardie was especially shocking—it was the oldest of the *vieux* and considered one of the Flanders army's best formations. Marshal Boufflers sent four squadrons of the Maison du Roi to block its flight. Even they could not rally and round up all the fugitives and the Picardie brigade played little further part in the battle.

The French right wing was rescued by another timely counterattack. After seeing to the fleeing troops, Boufflers galloped over to Brigadier Jost Brändle and ordered his Swiss brigade forward. The eight Swiss battalions fixed bayonets and charged. They were joined by the Royal and Navarre regiments, which went into action for the second time after helping beat back the Scots. They piled into the enemy. The French Swiss regiments of May and Brendlé found themselves face to face with the Dutch Swiss regiments of May and Stürler. Ignoring their common origin, both sides gave no quarter. Already bloodied, exhausted, and disorganized by their initial assault, the States Army's troops began giving ground before the onslaught of fresh forces. In a desperate attempt to halt this retrograde movement, the Prince of Orange seized the colors of the May regiment, rushed headlong into enemy fire, and thrust them into an earthen parapet. "Follow me, my friends," he cried, "here is your post!" Somehow, he came away unscathed. His heroics and those of his soldiers were unavailing. They gave up the fieldworks they had fought so hard and paid so much blood to take and retreated back to their own lines. The Royal and Navarre regiments chased after the enemy, seizing nine flags and overrunning a battery. Their officers did not want them to go too far and quickly recalled them.[34]

By half past ten or eleven o'clock, the Dutch attack had been repulsed everywhere. They had fought with all the valor, discipline, and skill of Europe's finest army. Yet their endeavor had been ill-fated from the beginning. The eleventh-hour diversion of Withers' force had fatally weakened it. Thirty Dutch battalions had challenged seventy French ensconced in formidable field fortifications. Why, despite these long odds, had they attacked with such fierce determination and persistence? Some British historians, most notably Winston Churchill, have looked to the Prince of Orange for the answer. After moving Withers, Marlborough had reduced the role of the Dutch to merely staging a demonstration to hold the attention of the powerful French right wing. Excessively proud and hungry for glory, Orange had recklessly converted what should have been a feigned attack into a real one. There is no evidence to support this interpretation. The original orders issued to the Dutch had been to drive the enemy from their works, then advance onto the plateau of Malplaquet. These were never rescinded or modified. In fact, they were entirely in keeping with how Marlborough fought his battles. He always mounted a flurry of attacks to unbalance the enemy and to give himself as many options for success as possible. And as the Earl of Orkney had learned at Ramillies, he did not always tell his commanders they would be leading a secondary effort. The captain general never blamed the prince for the Dutch debacle. In the end, both were guilty of grossly underestimating the tenacity and prowess of the French.[35]

Moreover, the States Army's sanguinary sacrifice would not be in vain. The remnants of the Dutch having retreated in disarray, a priceless opportunity beckoned to the French to launch a counterattack. La Frézelière and Claude, Marquis de Ceberet, commander of the La Perche brigade, rushed to Marshal Boufflers. Their troops had left their entrenchments, they declared, and were clamoring to be led against the enemy. Would the marshal authorize an attack, and would he support it with the cavalry, especially the Maison du Roi? Boufflers demurred. He could not, he said, take such a decision without the consent of Marshal Villars. There were other reasons as well. The squadrons could not easily pass through the fieldworks, and there was too little open ground between the forests of Thierry and La Lanière for them to deploy properly. Boufflers was also hesitant to commit the French right wing without knowing the situations of the center and left. Lastly, the Dutch appeared to be recovering quickly: their battalions were back in line, and their drum calls suggested they were preparing for a fresh effort. Disappointed, La Frézelière and Ceberet returned to their posts.[36]

During his long career in the service of the Sun King, Boufflers had shown himself time and again to be a doughty fighter. Yet, his generalship had seldom been marked by great daring or imagination. At this crucial juncture, his caution and rigid adherence to tactical orthodoxy got the better of him, and he kept the strongest part of the Army of Flanders passive and immobilized. In doing so, he threw away France's best chance for victory.

A prolonged calm now settled over the French right wing. The Chevalier de Quincy posted sentries to watch over his company and prevent any of his soldiers from leaving the ranks to despoil the enemy corpses lying in front of their trenches. Then he and his fellow officers sat down to a lunch of roasted leg of lamb. While they were enjoying their repast, on another part of the field, the battle was being decided.[37]

After the loss of the salient on the edges of the Bois de Sars, the Marquis de Goësbriand redeployed the Bretagne brigade and the La Reine regiment in field fortifications deeper in the forest. There they were attacked by Schulenburg's and Lottum's corps. Because of the density of the trees and undergrowth, the Allied troops lost all semblance of order and cohesion. Battalions and brigades became hopelessly intermingled. The fighting was savage and chaotic, a soldiers' brawl over which the generals and officers could exert almost no control. At terrible cost, the Allies pushed the French out of their works. Realizing that his left wing was in grave danger, Villars raced over to La Chaussée du Bois and ordered Albergotti to take the seventeen battalions of the brigades of Poitou, Tourville, and Gondrin into the Bois de Sars. The battle flared up with redoubled intensity. John Wilson, a self-described "Old Flanderkin Serjeant" of the British Fifteenth Regiment of Foot, has left a vivid portrait of the struggle:

> Wee beat them from that post and they beat us back again with as great courage and resolution as wee had them. Whereupon ensued an obstinate engagem't for the space of two hours in which there was a great effusion of blood on both sides; the Armys fireing at each other bayonett to bayonett. And after came to stab each other with their bayonetts and several came so close that they knocked one another's brains out w'th the butt end of their firelocks.

Prince Eugene was with the Habsburg and German troops. He was exhorting them to greater efforts, rallying shaken battalions, and feeding in fresh ones when a musket ball grazed his neck. With studied nonchalance, he refused to seek medical care. If the Allies won, he declared, there would be plenty of time to dress the wound; if they lost, it would not matter.[38]

Albergotti's intervention failed to tilt the balance in favor of the French. Marlborough and Eugene had committed two-thirds of their infantry—eighty-two battalions—to capturing the Bois de Sars. Allied strength was overwhelming. Slowly but inexorably, the French were forced back. As he watched his beaten battalions retreat, Villars realized he had made a serious error in placing so much of his army's strength on its right wing. He had now run out of fresh formations on its left. Just two regiments of dismounted dragoons remained in the entrenchments running from La Chaussée du Bois to La Folie. The Allies could easily smash through this threadbare line as soon as they emerged from the trees. The entire left wing would then collapse, and with it the Army of Flanders.

The marshal's solution to this dangerous crisis was characteristically bold and aggressive. He would rally and reinforce the battalions of the left wing, then launch an all-out counterattack to recapture the Bois de Sars. To carry out this plan, he needed troops and time. He sent aides galloping to Marshal Boufflers to ask for whatever battalions he could spare. But worried about another Dutch assault, Boufflers and his subordinates turned down this request. It was the old marshal's second crucial blunder of the day. It ensured that several still fresh and relatively unbloodied right-wing infantry brigades would not be usefully employed all day. It also meant that the most powerful Allied attack would be met with inadequate strength. Most importantly, it forced the decision that Marlborough and Eugene hoped Villars would make: the denuding of his center.

For the only infantry now available to Villars was those in the redans. He did not hesitate. He ordered the thirteen battalions of the Champagne and Irish brigades to leave the earthworks and attack into the wood. The Guards of Bavaria and Cologne moved up from their reserve position to take their places.

The Champagne and Irish brigades surged into the Bois de Sars from the southeast. Their onset initially knocked the Allies back on their heels.

The Irish fought with noteworthy fury, overrunning an enemy brigade and, according to one report, mercilessly massacring 1,500 Allied troops who had thrown down their arms and attempted to surrender. Yet they soon became mired in combat with vastly superior numbers of foes in the tangled labyrinth of the forest. And in the confusion, they even had to fear their own side. Mistaking the red-coated Irish for the enemy, the Le Roi regiment blasted them with a volley at close range. This friendly fire killed almost one hundred officers and soldiers, and the generals commanding the Irish brigade, Armand, Comte de Villars (younger brother of the marshal), and Louis-Armand de Brichanteau, Marquis de Nangis, had to exert all their authority to stop their men from falling upon the culprits.[39]

The intervention of the Champagne and Irish brigades bought Villars some valuable time. But he needed more in order to finish rallying the battalions of the left wing and form them up in a new line. He turned to his last available force of infantry: the Guards of Bavaria and Cologne. Yet, when the order arrived for these four battalions to attack into the Bois de Sars, Brigadier de La Colonie realized it would mean abandoning the redans and leaving them completely undefended. "When the first order was brought to the brigade-major, who reported it to me, I refused to obey it," de La Colonie recalled, "and pointed out the absolute necessity that existed for our maintaining the position we were holding; but a lieutenant-general then arrived on the scene and ordered us a second time to march off so sharply that all our remonstrances were useless." The Wittelsbach guardsmen duly plunged into the forest.[40]

In the end, the Allies overpowered the French through superior numbers and forced them from the Bois de Sars. According to John Marshall Deane, sentinel in the British Foot Guards:

> we drove them cleare out of the wood, and there, some of our forces, being drawne up, fell upon them and broke them confusedly. And they runn, all that could runn, behind their horse for shelter; ffor the French doth really think that they have no business to stand against us in the feild except they have eyther a ligne or breastwork, a wood or a wall, before them to cover them.

But Deane's bravado was tempered by his battalion's casualties, which amounted to "240 private centinells, 12 sarjeants and 3 colonells and 2 captains" out of a total strength of little more than five hundred men. Many of the Habsburg, German, Danish, and Walloon units that had been fighting since the early morning were even more grievously hurt.[41]

In addition to the heavy losses they had suffered, the Allied forces were in a state of utter chaos. Brigades, battalions, even individual companies were mixed together pell-mell. Thousands of fugitives from the ranks were wandering about freely. Worse still, Henry Withers' detachment had become completely lost. During its fruitless anabasis, it had somehow gone from the extreme right of the Allied line to the left of Lottum's battalions. General Schulenburg and his lieutenants had to devote themselves to sorting out the mess. It took them more than an hour to reorganize their units and form them into a coherent front along the southern edge of the Sars wood.[42]

The Allies' confusion gave Villars the time he needed to complete his preparations. By noon, he was ready to launch his counterattack. The marshal had managed to stitch together a new line facing the forest from La Folie to La Chausée du Bois, consisting of three regiments of dismounted dragoons and fifty battalions, all the remaining infantry from the Army of Flanders' left wing and center. These formations were battered from earlier fighting. But Villars and his officers had done their utmost to force stragglers back to their units, bolster their soldiers' morale, and prepare them for a renewed onslaught.

Before Villars could give the order to advance, General Saint-Hilaire came rushing up. All morning, he had been directing his batteries at the center of the French line. Now he had an urgent warning for the marshal: the redans were completely abandoned, he declared, and the enemy could capture them at any moment without resistance. Villars responded curtly that it would be up to Marshal Boufflers to find the troops to plug this gap. Yet he knew he was making an enormous gamble: he had to drive the Allies from the Bois de Sars before they could take advantage of his empty center.[43]

Surrounded by his generals, Villars sped to the right of his line and placed himself at the head of the brigades of Le Roi and La Reine. Commanding the soldiers to keep their ranks closed and not to stop to shoot, he led them toward the Bois de Sars. The rest of the French left wing followed. Villars and his entourage had not gone far when Allied skirmishers fired a fusillade. It tore through them, sorely wounding Albergotti and killing another general, Jean-Noël de Barbesières, Comte de Chemerault. Villars' horse was hit and he struggled to control it. Then a second volley struck. A shot smashed into the marshal's knee. He swooned in his saddle. The counterattack stopped in its tracks.[44]

At about the same time as Villars was wounded, the Duke of Marlborough rode from his post just behind the Allied center to the Bois de Sars. He was going to confer with Prince Eugene. The captain general sensed that the climax of the battle was at hand. Although bloodily repulsed, the Dutch attack had at least succeeded in fixing the powerful French right wing in place. The prince and his lieutenants had finally secured the western woods. Had the time come to commit the Allied reserves against the French center?

Under the eaves of the forest, Marlborough met Eugene and Schulenburg. The prince declared that Lottum had struck a decisive blow. The remark annoyed Schulenburg, and he spoke up to claim his fair share of the credit. His troops had brought into action the cannons they had laboriously hauled through the forest. These guns, he observed, were sweeping the redans and had driven back the supporting enemy cavalry. Then he turned to Marlborough and said: "My lord, the French have abandoned their entrenchments. I beg you not to delay in having them occupied by a few battalions."[45]

Marlborough needed no further urging. His aides spurred with his orders to the Earl of Orkney. At once, the pugnacious Scot led out nine British and four German battalions. With drums rattling and colors flying, they rolled across the half-mile of open ground separating them from the redans. The only opposition they faced was from a score of French guns. But they were largely out of ammunition. Saint-Hilaire calculated that his artillery had fired off 8,000 shots during the battle and had less than 400 left by its end. Orkney recalled that "it was about one o'clock that my 13 battalions got up to the retrenchments, which we got very easily." He went on to say, modestly, "not that I pretend to attribute any glory to myself (for it was the nature of our situation), yet I verily believe that these 13 battalions gained us the day, and that without firing a shot almost."[46]

The Earl of Orkney was not alone in mounting an attack. After rallying their troops, the Dutch generals had been carefully following the battle's course. Seeing Orkney preparing to advance, they implored the Prince of Orange that their honor demanded they too go forward. Their allies could not have all the glory of victory. Johann Willem Friso agreed. So, for the second time that day, the States Army launched an assault on the entrenchments of the French right wing. Because of the severe losses they had suffered in the morning, the Dutch no longer had sufficient strength to attempt the entire front from the Bois de Thierry to the Bois de La Lanière. They aimed their depleted battalions at a stretch of the French line east of the redans.

The Dutch were assailing fieldworks defended by the most vaunted troops in the Army of Flanders: the Gardes francaises and the Gardes suisses, Louis XIV's household infantry. Undaunted, the Dutch marched up and began blasting out their platoon volleys. In reply, the guardsmen loosed a single massive salvo. Then, suddenly, they broke and ran. The guards' brigadier, the Duc de Guiche, tried to halt their flight; he fell with a wound in the leg. The collapse of the guards exposed the flanks of the neighboring brigades of Piémont and Lannoy, and they were forced to withdraw from their entrenchments. In an attempt to retrieve the situation, La Frézelière rushed up with the Royal regiment. But these soldiers were exhausted physically and morally from their earlier exertions. They were caught up by the rout and swept away. The triumphant Dutch troops then overran the grand battery that had earlier caused so much devastation to the Blue Guards.

As in the morning, the Dutch had, against all odds, smashed a yawning breach in the French line. And as then, a well-timed, well-handled counterattack saved the French. François-Marie, Marquis de Hautefort, hurried two brigades of infantry from the right wing to strike the Dutch near La Grosse Haye. The men of the Navarre regiment—who, said de La Colonie, were very short and clad in little more than rags—charged with the bayonet for the third time. They threw the Dutch back in disorder, inflicting such a slaughter on them that Field Deputy Vegelin van Claerbergen afterward dubbed it a hecatomb. Fully living up to their regiment's motto "Navarre sans peur," they completed their tour de force by reoccupying the works vacated by the guards and capturing a battery of guns the enemy had brought up. The States Army's gallant last gasp had failed. Yet, once again, the sacrifice of the Dutch had not been in vain. They had distracted the French right wing at a crucial moment and prevented it from interfering with Orkney's occupation of the redans.[47]

Meanwhile, another dramatic event was playing out on the opposite end of the battlefield. General Milkau's twenty cavalry squadrons had finally rounded the Bois de Sars and were nearing the exposed end of the French left wing. It was the only element of Withers' special attack that had gone according to plan. But Francois, Chevalier du Rozel, commander of the carabineers deployed around La Folie, had been warned by Villars to guard against just such an outflanking move. Before the Allied horsemen could properly deploy, he charged them. The crack French cavaliers were in a vengeful mood: a number of their captured comrades had been murdered by enemy hussars a few days before. In a swirling melee, they shattered and chased Milkau's squadrons from the field. The Allied wounded left behind were killed on the spot.[48]

For all the action taking place on the wings, it was in the center where the battle was being decided. After his wounding, Villars had tried to continue giving orders, but the pain from his mangled knee caused him to faint. His aides deposited him in a sedan chair that carried him from the field. Then they sent a message to Boufflers that he must assume command of the army. The old marshal received it shortly before one o'clock in the afternoon. Leaving d'Artagnan in charge of the right wing, he raced to the high ground near Malplaquet, looked out over the battlefield, and saw disaster unfolding.[49]

A vast mounted host was filling the plain between the Bois de Sars and Blairon farm, flowing forward like an irresistible tide. As soon as

Orkney's infantry had secured the French fieldworks, Marlborough had committed the Allied cavalry reserve. Leading it were Auvergne's and Hesse-Kassel's corps. In all, 230 British, Dutch, German, and Danish squadrons—almost 40,000 men and horses—were poised to smash through the middle of the French army and split it asunder.

Boufflers knew what he had to do. He rushed to the waiting French cavalry formed up in four long lines on the Malplaquet plateau. He drew his sword and pointed it at the enemy now beginning to stream through the gaps between the redans. For six hours, the French horsemen had been stoically enduring artillery fire; the order to charge came as a relief. More than a hundred squadrons followed Boufflers into the largest cavalry battle Western Europe would ever see. To the fore were the Maison du Roi and the Gendarmes. In the front rank of the Gardes du Corps was a young officer even more splendidly uniformed and mounted than the rest. Called the Chevalier de Saint-Georges, he was in reality James Francis Edward Stuart, the twenty-one-year-old pretender to the British throne. With the Scottish Company of the Gendarmes was another foreign volunteer of far less illustrious pedigree and even more colorful background. Peter Drake was an Irish soldier of fortune of irresistible charm and malleable loyalties. In his long and eventful career, he had fought in the Jacobite, Spanish, Dutch, and French armies. After a spell in an English prison, he had arrived at Douai in August and talked his way into one of the most elite formations in the Army of Flanders.[50]

The French cavalry swept down the slopes, accelerating from a walk to a fast trot. Meanwhile, the narrow passages between the redans were greatly hampering the Allies' deployment: according to the Earl of Orkney, no more than thirty squadrons had got through before the French were upon them. The captain of Peter Drake's squadron ordered six picked marksmen on each flank to fire their carbines into the enemy while the rest of the troopers rushed in with their sabers. Other squadrons used different combinations of fire and shock, while yet others charged home with cold steel alone. A dusty, smoky, tangled melee of slashing, stabbing, and shooting horsemen spread swiftly across the plain behind the redans and between the Bois de Sars and Blairon. The Scots Greys under Lieutenant Colonel James Campbell, whom Orkney declared "behaved like an angell," broke through two lines of opponents. But the French soon gained the upper hand. Led by the Maison du Roi and the Gendarmes, they overcame their foes and pursued them back to the redans. There, they were confronted by Orkney's infantry. The British and German battalions lined the parapets and poured their platoon volleys at close range into the pursuers, bringing them down in droves. Reeling and disordered, the French retreated back to the plateau, where they rallied.

The great cavalry contest now settled into a grim pattern. The Allies would advance through the redans. Before too many enemy squadrons had reached the plain, the French would set upon them, break them, and chase them back to the fieldworks. The French would then in turn be stopped and forced to retreat by the withering fire of the Allied infantry. During these actions, Marshal Boufflers earned the everlasting admiration of friends and foes alike for his determination and courage. He seemed to shed most of his sixty-five years, becoming again the fire-breathing dragoon of his youth, fighting at the head of the Gardes du Corps, and several times crossing swords with an enemy. The blue and red companies of the Maison du Roi performed prodigies of valor, redeeming the honor and reputation of the Sun King's household troops from the disgraceful flight of the French and Swiss Guards. Their heroics were matched by their close comrades, the Gendarmes. Other regiments that charged repeatedly included the Italians of Royal-Piémont and the Germans of Royal-Allemand.

"I realy believe, had not ye foot been there, they would have driven our horse out of the field," asserted the Earl of Orkney. The French cavalry swept its opponents back each time they dared venture out onto the plain. However, without supporting infantry and artillery of their own, Boufflers' squadrons could not dislodge the Scot's battalions from the redans. Behind their shield, the Allied cavalry could lick its wounds and reform in perfect safety. In addition, their platoon volleys took a steady toll of French men, mounts, and morale. After six consecutive charges, even the Maison du Roi and the Gendarmes were spent. The Allies were finally able to pass the full force of their cavalry through the redans and onto the plain. They then employed a tactic that had been successful at Blenheim. They advanced on the plateau at a walk with ranks strictly ordered and tightly closed. The exhausted and outnumbered French cavalry were unable to make any impression on this moving wall. At three o'clock in the afternoon, Marshal Boufflers realized his squadrons could do no more. He ordered them to retreat.[51]

The French left wing had begun to retreat an hour earlier. After Villars' wounding, command of the left wing had been assumed by the senior lieutenant general on the spot, Jacques-François de Chastenet, Marquis de Puységur. A talented staff officer and military intellectual who would write an important treatise on the art of war, he still enjoyed a high reputation despite committing a series of disastrous blunders at Oudenarde. Now he feared that the cavalry battle in the center was beginning to turn against the French and that it would only be a matter of time before Prince Eugene would burst out of the forest in overwhelming strength. Choosing discretion over valor, he ordered the entire left wing to withdraw to

Valenciennes. Whatever his deficiencies as a tactician, Puységur was a master organizer. He quickly had fifty battalions and one hundred squadrons arranged in four columns. The cavalry rearguard was confided to the carabineers under the redoubtable Chevalier du Rozel. At about two o'clock, the columns began to move off. The French went not as broken, fleeing troops but as formed units which, though battered, were still full of fight.

On the other end of the battlefield, the Comte d'Artagnan proved more reluctant to retire. His right wing had not yielded an inch of ground all day and had bloodily repulsed two attacks by the finest troops in the Allied army. D'Artagnan himself had fought with exemplary courage, having three horses shot out from under him and escaping serious injury only by the luck of having several musket balls bounce off his cuirass. He finally gave the order after seeing Boufflers' squadrons begin to go and Hesse-Kassel's cavalry threaten to outflank and roll up his line from near the farm of Blairon. Even then, many of his subordinates received it with incredulity. As the Chevalier de Quincy relates, he and the other officers of the régiment de Bourgogne protested fiercely to their brigadier, the Marquis de Vieuxpont:

> Surprised by this order, we said to him; "Monsieur, why are we retiring? As you know, we have beaten and driven back all the troops that have attacked us. No one is facing us."
>
> "Messieurs," he replied, "you must obey me: I am your general. Retreat quickly as you are about to be enveloped. There is an enemy column marching behind you for this purpose."
>
> We therefore abandoned a post that we had defended so well. We retired, heartily distressed and aggrieved, by our right.

With more haste and less order than the other parts of the Army of Flanders, the right wing withdrew shortly after three o'clock.[52]

The Battle of Malplaquet ended with the Allied pursuit of the retreating French. It was an anticlimax. Marlborough and Eugene dispatched what squadrons they had to hand that were still comparatively fresh and able to fight. Some tried to press Puységur's columns. But du Rozel kept them at bay in a series of bloody skirmishes until the French left wing crossed over the Hogneau near Audignies. The artillery forded the river further south. Saint-Hilaire managed to bring off sixty-four of his guns. Boufflers' cavalry and d'Artagnan's right wing retreated in a different direction toward Bavay and Le Quesnoy. Their pursuers were repelled by the expertly handled rearguard of the Chevalier de Luxembourg, who had brought in his cavalry corps from La Longueville. By nightfall, the entire Army of Flanders was safely away. Marlborough would claim that the Allies had failed to mount an effective pursuit because their cavalry had lacked adequate infantry support. In reality, the Allied army was simply too exhausted and exsanguinated after its brutal ordeal to achieve anything of consequence.[53]

That evening, Marlborough was at last able to finish his letter to Sarah:

> I am so tiered that I have but strengh enough to tel you that we have had this day a very bloody battaile. The first part of the day we beat their foot, and afterwardes their horse. God almighty be praised, it is now in our powers to have what peace wee please, and I may be pretty well assured of never being in another battel. But that nor nothing in this world can make mee happy if you are not kind.

The Allied army camped on the battlefield. The night offered no rest, for it was filled with the cries, shrieks, and groans of the innumerable wounded and dying lying in woods and fields, hedges and ditches. Daylight revealed the full extent of the horror. The dead of the Dutch Blue Guards presented a particularly shocking sight. Over a thousand had fallen in their ranks in front of the French breastworks. During the hours of darkness, scavengers had stripped them of their uniforms. The naked corpses carpeted the ground so thickly that not an inch of bare earth could be seen. Veterans at once recognized that they had fought in a combat of singular ferocity. The Earl of Orkney, who had served in all of his country's wars for twenty years and had seen many a stricken field, told his younger brother:

> As to ye killed and wounded. I leave you to the publick letters; but depend upon it, no two battles this war could furnish the like number. You will see great lists of generals and officers. I can liken this battle to nothing so much as an attack of a counterscarp from right to left; and I am sure you would have thought so, if you had seen the field as I did ye day after. In many places they lye as thick as ever you saw a flock of sheep; and, where our poor nephew Tully-Bardine was, it was prodigious. I realy think I never saw the like; particularly where the Dutch gaurds attacked, it is a miracle. I hope in God it will be the last battle I may ever see.[54]

Malplaquet was the most sanguinary battle of Louis XIV's reign. Allied casualties totaled 21,000. Of these, the Dutch accounted for 2,400 dead and 6,100 wounded. Only eight out of thirty battalions of the States Army had fewer than 200 casualties. By comparison, the British had got off more lightly with 600 dead and 1,300 wounded. French losses were 11,000, of which 4,400 had been killed and 6,600 wounded. Among individual units, the casualties of the Gardes du Corps amounted to 39 officers and 395 men or one-third of the four companies' total effectives—a testament to the valor of the Sun King's mounted bodyguards. The hardest-fighting line units had suffered even more. The two battalions of the régiment Royal-infanterie, which had charged twice with the bayonet on the right wing, together lost 40 officers and 500 soldiers, more than half their strength. The Brétagne regiment, which had stoutly defended the Bois de Sars against daunting odds, had a similar proportion of losses. Malplaquet's butcher's bill would not be equaled in Europe for fifty years.[55]

Caring for the vast numbers of wounded proved a Herculean task for both armies. For days, they lay out in the open or crammed into every hovel in the vicinity of the battlefield. The Allies were eventually able to gather up theirs and evacuate them to Brussels, Mechelen, and Antwerp. Bundled into goods and bread wagons that then struggled with excruciating, jolting slowness on pitted, muddy roads, many perished before they reached their destinations. The French had managed to bring away most of their wounded when they retreated. Nevertheless, hundreds had to be left behind to fall into Allied hands. The overburdened Allied medical services could not cope with such numbers. Marlborough wrote to Villars and Boufflers, offering to return them all on the stipulation that those who recovered from their injuries could not fight again until they had been exchanged for Allied prisoners of war. On September 15, the Chevalier de Luxembourg and Quartermaster-General Cadogan met at Bavay and effected the transfer.[56]

The French wounded were taken to military hospitals in Le Quesnoy, Valenciennes, Maubeuge, and Cambrai. Each of these establishments should have been staffed by fifty doctors and fifty surgeons. In addition, when the first news of the battle and its losses reached Versailles, the court high command acted with urgency and vigor. War Minister Voysin drafted civilian surgeons from Paris to reinforce the hospitals, while Controller General Desmaretz dispatched a wagon with 10,000 livres in coin for the purchasing of provisions and medical supplies. The king sent his personal surgeon Georges Mareschal to tend to Marshal Villars as well as to inspect the medical facilities in Flanders. A few of those hurt at Malplaquet received excellent, lifesaving care. Peter Drake had been wounded seven times charging with the Gendarmes. One head wound was feared mortal, "my skull being cut open, so that the *dura mater* of the brain was to be seen in dressing me." Captured, then repatriated by the Allies, he had been brought to Le Quesnoy, where he received treatment from the Gendarmes' surgeon. Thanks to this worthy's skillful ministrations as well as a diet of hearty soups, Drake was back on his feet in three weeks. Most of the wounded were far less fortunate. A fortnight after the battle, six thousand were packed into the hospitals. Despite the best efforts of French officers and officials, not all could receive the care they needed. Between one-fifth and one-third would die from their injuries, infections, illnesses, or the insalubrious conditions all too often found in the army's hospitals.[57]

The Allies claimed the laurels of victory. They had forced the French to retreat and were masters of the battlefield. It was a claim that Allied soldiers, statesmen, diplomats, and propagandists would repeat again and again until the end of the war. But they could boast of few other trophies. They had captured just thirteen infantry flags, sixteen cavalry standards, three pairs of kettle drums, and sixteen cannons. The number of unwounded French prisoners taken on the field was a paltry five hundred. These were hardly the marks of an overwhelming triumph (there had been 7,000 prisoners at Ramillies). Moreover, they were overshadowed by the staggering Allied losses. A wave of grief and revulsion swept over the Dutch Republic at the destruction of the flower of the States Army. The Prince of Orange and Sico van Goslinga became scapegoats—the former for attacking too recklessly, the latter for authorizing Dutch participation in the battle in the first place. After Malplaquet, the Council of State and its field deputies would exercise an iron grip on the Dutch forces and would never again agree to commit them to a similar action. In England, the Tories and their pamphleteers excoriated Marlborough for squandering the lives of so many of his troops. In a fiery speech in the House of Lords, the Duke of Argyll, who had fought so courageously in the Bois de Sars, denounced him for mismanaging the campaign. Worse still was the attitude of the queen. She greeted the news of the victory with a distinct lack of enthusiasm, failing even to inquire about her captain general's safety. The Whigs managed to use their control of parliament to secure Marlborough a vote of thanks from both houses. But the shrill chorus of criticism was another unmistakable sign of the erosion of his once-dominant political position.[58]

The French immediately challenged the Allies' claim that they had won a great victory. In his first report to the king written at ten o'clock on the night of September 11, Boufflers declared:

> Marshal Villars was sorely wounded today. The surgeons assure me that he is out of danger. I am very distressed, Sire, that this misfortune compels me to announce to you the loss of a new battle. But I can assure Your Majesty that never has misfortune been accompanied by more glory. All of Your Majesty's troops have acquired the greatest glory by their valor, firmness, and obstinacy. They finally yielded only to the vastly superior numbers of the enemy and after having all done marvels.

"The enemy have lost three times more men than we have," he concluded, "and they cannot draw any other advantage from this unfortunate action than the possession of the battlefield." In the days and weeks that followed, letter after letter arrived at the court from other officers repeating and amplifying the old marshal's contentions: the battle, they said, had been a glorious feat of French arms in which the Army of Flanders had only been forced to abandon the field by the Allies' overwhelming strength and after inflicting grievous losses on them. Then, on September 17, Louis received more tangible proof of what his soldiers had achieved. The Marquis de Nangis, who had bravely commanded the Irish brigade, came to Versailles to give a detailed account of the action. Louis honored him with a lengthy audience immediately after his rising. During it, Nangis presented thirty-two captured Allied flags.[59]

The king realized that Malplaquet ought to be celebrated as something of a success. He told Villars:

> I have such great reasons to be satisfied with everything you have done during the course of this campaign. You stopped, with your wise arrangements, the vast projects that the enemies had formed, and you have given me invaluable signs of your zeal, particularly in the battle of the 11th of this month, in which my troops, encouraged by your good example, gained the main advantage over our enemies.

He ordered the captured colors displayed in the nave of Notre-Dame de Paris. Then he distributed largesse. Marshal Villars was raised to a Peer of France, the highest aristocratic rank, and the Comte d'Artagnan to Marshal of France. Promotions, pensions, and other rewards cascaded down to the lowest-ranking regimental officers.[60]

From his bed of pain at Le Quesnoy, Villars pithily summed up Malplaquet thus: "finally, Sire, if God grants us the grace to lose a similar battle, Your Majesty can count on his enemies being destroyed." The marshal deserved much of the credit for this outcome. His planning and preparations had transformed what should have been an open-field engagement into something resembling an assault on a fortress. On the day itself, his leadership had been inspiring, his energy inexhaustible, and his courage redoubtable. Yet he should never have fought at Malplaquet at all. In choosing to fight, Villars had broken with the strategy championed by the king, which had sought to seal off France with fortified lines and the barrier of the *pré carré* while avoiding a pitched battle. This strategy had succeeded beyond all expectations: after a summer of campaigning, Allied gains had been limited to a single fortress. The marshal should have persisted with it. After losing the race to Mons, he should have entrenched the Army of Flanders to cover the strongholds of the Scheldt and the Sambre. Although Mons would have fallen, he still would have blocked Marlborough and Eugene from invading France for the remainder of the fighting season.[61]

Malplaquet was not just an unnecessary battle; it was also one whose rewards were far outweighed by its risks. Villars had challenged

Marlborough and Eugene because he hoped to win a sweeping victory that would transform France's military and diplomatic situation. However, such hopes were misplaced, even foolhardy: the Allied armies were too strong, too skilled, and too well led to be so easily vanquished. The most the Army of Flanders could have accomplished was to repel the enemy's attacks and retain control of the battlefield. Moreover, Villars would not have been able to follow up this result: the continuing paucity of provisions would have prevented him from attempting any ambitious operations. Not least, the French were incapable of causing enough damage to permanently weaken their opponents. They inflicted unprecedented losses on the Confederate Army at Malplaquet. Marlborough was able to quickly make them good by replacing the worst-hit battalions with thirty drawn from garrison duty.[62]

Against the modest advantages that would have been gained from a victory must be set the dire consequences that would have attended a defeat. By deciding to fight at Malplaquet, Villars had handed Marlborough and Eugene the chance to end the war by a decisive battle. Another Blenheim, Ramillies, Turin, or Oudenarde would have left Louis XIV's last major field army shattered beyond repair. French morale would have plunged to its nadir. Equally importantly, despite the lateness of the season, Marlborough and Eugene could have exploited their victory by penetrating into the weakly defended interior of Hainault, Artois, and the Cambresis. They would then have been lodged deeply inside France and perfectly placed to make further advances in the next campaign. Faced with such a catastrophe, it is hard to see how Louis could have avoided making peace on the Grand Alliance's terms. Villars was exceedingly fortunate that his tactical skills and the stubborn valor of his troops had confined the Allies to a pyrrhic victory.

That valor left a deep and lasting impression on the Duke of Marlborough. Never before, he declared, had the enemy resisted so obstinately or so ferociously, neither asking for nor giving quarter. Why had the French fought so hard and so well? The answer is found in the honor of the officers and soldiers of the Army of Flanders. In his appeal of June 12, their king had called on them to defend the honor of the French name. At Malplaquet, they had answered in full measure. The consummation of the French officer's code of honor was the performance on the battlefield of stoic courage even in the face of certain injury or death. The code's burden is revealed by an anecdote told by the Chevalier de Quincy. Just before the Allies attacked, a friend and fellow officer was so ill with fever he was shaking uncontrollably. He asked Quincy if he should leave the ranks and go to the rear. The chevalier told him no, "for it was in these moments of greatest danger that one must stay with the colors, even if afflicted by the most unbearable suffering." If his friend departed, he would be disgraced forever. He stayed and behaved with steadfast gallantry. Innumerable other French officers succeeded in living up to this iron standard. From Marshal Villars to the lowest subaltern, they led from the front, exposed themselves heedlessly to enemy fire, crossed spontoons and swords with the foe, refused to abandon their posts after being wounded, and again and again rallied their men and led them back into the fray. They paid a terrible price: 240 of them were killed, 593 wounded, and 17 taken prisoner. But they had met, or even surpassed, the demands of honor.[63]

It was through their conspicuous courage and self-mastery that French officers exercised leadership and command over their men. They served as examples to follow into the fiercest fire. Quincy noted with pride that just one man of the régiment de Bourgogne broke ranks during the most desperate close combat. The common soldiers, though, more than just emulated their officers. They also fought for their own honor as embodied in the glory and reputation of their regiments. On the day after the battle, one hundred and fifty soldiers of Navarre, wearing bearskins seized from enemy grenadiers and brandishing twenty captured flags, marched proudly from their camp to Marshal Boufflers' headquarters at Ruesnes. At about the same time, the French Guards were shamed for their panicked flight. When they paraded before the army, they were subjected to vicious mockery by the assembled troops. Later, guardsmen were insulted, even assaulted by furious comrades. The disgrace of the king's household infantry was the exception; so many other units of the Army of Flanders had more than done their duty. Letters and dispatches to the court picked out for particular praise the Irish brigade and the regiments of Champagne, Royal-Infanterie, Piémont, Bourbonnais, Charost, Bretagne, Provence, Saintonge, May, Royal-Piémont, and Royal-Allemand. The Allies and the French would long dispute the result of Malplaquet. But the battle had one clear and unambiguous outcome: it was the triumph of honor.[64]

After Malplaquet, the last act of the campaign unfolded. On September 12, Marshal Boufflers reunited the two wings of the Army of Flanders, then took up a position along the Rhonelle stream from Valenciennes to Le Quesnoy. To help make up the army's losses, War Minister Voysin was sending it fifty men from each of the 43 battalions in garrison between the Flanders coast and the Meuse. On September 16, Boufflers reviewed his troops. He pronounced them to be in higher spirits than before the battle and eager to take on the enemy again.[65]

Meanwhile, the Allies were embarking on the siege of Mons. This time, the arrangements of Tournai were reversed, with Eugene taking charge of the besieging force and Marlborough commanding the covering army. The need to wait for the siege train, which had to move overland from

Brussels, imposed a considerable delay. Only on September 25 was the prince of Savoy able to open the trenches.[66]

Mons was strongly fortified, and its walls were in good repair. Its governor, the Marquis de Ceva Grimaldi, an Italian in Spanish service, was a tough, dependable veteran. In addition, the Comte de Bergeyck chose to remain in the city, and it was hoped that the presence of Spain's chief minister in the Netherlands would stiffen the resolve of the civilian population. But the garrison of 3,000 mainly Spanish troops was both inadequate in size and doubtful in quality. To bolster it, the Chevalier de Luxembourg managed to slip three French battalions into the fortress-city before the Allied ring closed.

Boufflers had at first hoped to play an active role in the defense of Mons. He had planned to advance the Army of Flanders to the River Hogneau from where it could regularly raid the enemy siege lines. His hopes, however, were dashed by the long-standing nemesis of the French in Flanders: lack of supplies. With the magazines of Maubeuge now exhausted, bread was only coming fitfully from Valenciennes and Le Quesnoy. Moreover, the pitiable state of the supply trains meant that the field army could not venture far from these fortresses. Boufflers conducted a series of large-scale foraging expeditions to the Hogneau to strip the countryside bare of fodder. He also dispatched a strong detachment under Luxembourg to Charleroi with orders to harass Allied convoys and raiding parties. But he otherwise abandoned a forward posture. Instead, he decided to extend the French fortified lines from the Scheldt to the Sambre. The new works ran from Valenciennes along the Rhonelle to Le Quesnoy then through the forest of Mormal to just above Maubeuge. The intendants of the frontier provinces conscripted thousands of peasants to labor on them. When they were finished, they were very strong and closed off the interior of France to Allied incursions.[67]

Unexpectedly, Grimaldi and his garrison resisted tenaciously. On October 3, Boufflers told the court the siege of Mons would drag on until the end of the campaigning season. The Army of Flanders' next move would be into winter quarters, and he had drawn up plans for them. In doing so, he was dismissing rumors that the Allies would attack Le Quesnoy or Maubeuge after Mons. Having already undertaken two major sieges and fought a battle of unparalleled ferocity, the Allies would be in no condition to attempt anything else. But Louis and his military counselors were haunted by the memory of the 1708 campaign when the Allies had remained in the field long after the French and had scored significant successes as a result. Voysin sternly instructed Boufflers to treat seriously the enemy threat against Maubeuge. The king considered this Sambre stronghold of such importance that he was authorizing Boufflers to risk a second battle to prevent its fall. This did not mean that Louis was forsaking his cautious defensive strategy. For, as the minister explained,

His Majesty believes nevertheless that it would be easy for you, when the siege of Mons reaches its end, to place yourself in such a way that it would be impossible for our enemies to fall on Maubeuge and at the same time safeguard Le Quesnoy.

The Army of Flanders, Voysin went on to advise, should be posted on the Sambre from Barlaimont to Maubeuge. This exchange touched off a new debate between the high command at court and the general at the front. Boufflers argued that he could not protect both Le Quesnoy and Maubeuge. He preferred to guard the former because it was both less well fortified and barred a more direct route into France. The king continued to stress the value of the latter.[68]

To break the impasse, Boufflers proposed an operation to relieve Mons: a surprise attack by a picked force on the Ghlin quarter, a weakly held section of the Allied lines. Louis approved this scheme on the condition that it did not provoke a general engagement. He also sent Boufflers help in the person of Marshal Berwick. Marlborough's nephew was fresh from a successful campaign in Dauphiné, where he had stopped an attempted invasion of southeastern France by the Duke of Savoy.[69]

Before Boufflers could carry it out, the Ghlin project was wrecked by the Army of Flanders' chronic problem of paucity of provisions. Its magazines were largely empty. The long-awaited grain from Brittany had failed to appear: the transports had been unable to sail from Saint-Malo for lack of adequate naval escorts. The supply trains were in terrible condition, with scores of peasant horses dying daily from overwork. They had begun the campaign with 3,200 horses and 800 caissons; they were now down to 1,280 horses and 320 caissons. The troops were only receiving bread rations from day to day. However, Boufflers calculated that the army would need to stockpile four days of provisions to carry out the Ghlin operation. On October 17, the *munitionnaire* Pâris reported he had gathered 2,300 sacks of flour at Cambrai, Le Quesnoy, and Valenciennes. Four days of rations for the army required 2,800 sacks. Intendant Bernage was rushing the remaining supplies from Artois and Picardy; they would arrive on October 26 at the earliest. Mons surrendered on October 20.[70]

With the Allied armies once again free to maneuver, Boufflers kept most of his army near the Scheldt to protect Condé, Valenciennes, and Le Quesnoy. Marshal Berwick began construction of an entrenched camp at Maubeuge for twenty-five battalions and seventy squadrons. If the enemy attacked him, Berwick was to hold out until Boufflers arrived. This scheme resembled Villars' August plan for the defense of the lines. Perhaps fortunately, it was never put to the test. Marlborough and Eugene noted the worsening weather and the weariness of their troops. Above all, they observed that the countryside between the Sambre and Meuse had been completely stripped of fodder. For these reasons, they ruled out further operations. As Boufflers had anticipated, as soon as Mons was in their hands, they began to disperse their armies to winter quarters. On October 28, the court high command authorized Boufflers to follow suit. The Flanders campaign of 1709 was over.[71]

Yet further memorable events were still in store before the year was out. In the aftermath of Malplaquet, Anthonie Heinsius launched another attempt to end the war by diplomacy. The grand pensionary of Holland believed it was an especially propitious moment for the Republic. For several years, the British had feared that the Dutch would make a separate peace with the French. Although he never had any intention of doing so, Heinsius had nevertheless skillfully played on these fears in order to extract maximum advantage from his allies. At the beginning of 1709, the Whig ministry approached him with an offer of highly favorable terms of trade and a formidable Barrier in the Low Countries. The failure of The Hague Conference gave powerful momentum to these negotiations, and by the fall they were bearing fruit. On October 27, the Dutch and the British concluded a Treaty of Succession and the Barrier. By it, the British gave full support to Dutch possession of Neuport, Furnes, Ghent, Dendermonde, Ypres, Menin, Lier, Lille, Tournai, Halle, Condé, Valenciennes, Maubeuge, Charleroi, Namur, and numerous forts. Taken together, these acquisitions would give them military and economic domination of the southern Netherlands. In return, the Republic confirmed its commitment to the Grand Alliance. It also recognized the Protestant Succession to the British throne, pledged to defend it militarily, and promised to make no peace unless Louis XIV expelled the Stuart pretender from his domains.[72]

The Dutch thus had much to gain if a general peace treaty could now be secured between the Allies and France. Heinsius' last contact with the French court had been Torcy's letter of August 23, in which Louis' foreign minister had made a handful of concessions on Spain but had not surrendered the three surety towns demanded by the Allies. On September 28, Heinsius told Marlborough that he was at last replying: "with this letter, we will see their sentiments after the victory [of Malplaquet]." Although the captain general was skeptical that anything meaningful would come of it, he approved this resumption of discussions.[73]

Heinsius' reply reached Torcy in Paris on October 2. It expressed grave disappointment that the French were unwilling to meet the Allies' full demands. However, it ended on a conciliatory note: "I assure you I am extremely displeased at this turn of events and wish for nothing more ardently than to have a favorable occasion to advance a work so much desired by all Christendom." Torcy showed the letter to the king. Together, they decided it afforded an opening for serious, face-to-face negotiations.

The foreign minister invited his agent at The Hague, the Holstein-Gottorp envoy Hermann Petkum, to come to the French court with the Allies' proposals for a peace agreement. The grand pensionary initially hesitated: he regarded the French refusal of the Spanish surety towns as a serious stumbling block. In the end, after long discussions with Eugene and Marlborough, he accepted the invitation.[74]

On the afternoon of November 19, Petkum arrived at Versailles. That evening, he dined in public with Torcy and several other ministers; rumors swept the court and the capital that serious peace negotiations were now afoot. The next day, Torcy took Petkum into the gardens of the great palace. As they wandered along secluded pathways, past idle fountains, and through quiet groves, the German diplomat laid out the latest Allied terms. They were, Torcy learned to his dismay, far from favorable. In fact, the Allies had not budged at all from the harsh demands they had first laid down in the spring at The Hague. They wanted the entire Spanish Monarchy for the Habsburgs and regarded Article 37 of the Preliminaries as indispensable for the achievement of this end. They were willing to offer just a single minor concession: an extension of the article's truce from two to three months.[75]

The royal council convened on November 24 to decide how to respond to the enemy's propositions. The king and his ministers carefully reviewed the military situation. At the beginning of the campaigning season, the Allies had threatened to invade on almost every frontier. Famine and financial collapse had cast doubt on whether the French armies could fight at all. A range of desperate expedients found enough food and funds to put them into the field. They then repelled the enemy in every theater. In Dauphiné, Marshal Berwick successfully held the crests of the Alps. On the Rhine, Marshal Harcourt turned back an Imperial incursion into Alsace thanks to a tidy victory in the action of Rumersheim. In Spain, King Philip's forces retook Alicante in Valencia and beat the British and Portuguese at Campo Maior. Louis' grandson remained secure in Madrid and in full control of Castile and Aragon.[76] Most importantly, in Flanders, Marshal Villars stopped Marlborough and Eugene from penetrating into the heart of France. He had fought them at Malplaquet, which, far from being a clear-cut victory as the grand pensionary claimed, had been a bloodbath for the Allies.

The king, his commanders, and soldiers had amply demonstrated their mettle. But could they repeat their performance in the coming year? In August, Controller General Nicolas Desmaretz had despaired of the royal treasury's ability to continue the war. The transfusion of funds from the windfall of Spanish silver and the reformation of the French currency had been exhausted. He now spoke. He informed the council that he had bent all his energy and considerable ingenuity to finding the means to support the king's forces. He had come up with a scheme to bring together twelve leading receivers-general—the wealthy financiers who collected the state's direct taxes—into a single consortium called the Caisse Legendre. It would pay for military expenses by issuing new credit instruments backed by the most reliable remaining revenue sources and would go into operation on the first of January. The controller general assured his colleagues and his royal master that he could sustain the armies through the winter quarters as well as the next fighting season.[77]

The spirits of the king and his servants soared. "At a stroke, courage appeared reborn," Torcy declared triumphantly. The royal council unanimously decided to reject The Hague Preliminaries. Instead, Louis would make peace based on the offers he had previously made to the Dutch, the British, and the Habsburgs. He was ready to name his plenipotentiaries to a new conference embracing all of the belligerents. But if the Allies refused this proposal, they would then force France to wage war to the last extremity.[78]

Petkum sent a letter to the grand pensionary communicating the French decision. When it reached The Hague, it provoked outrage. Marlborough wrote to Heinsius:

> As Petkoms letter of the 29th in my opinion is a demonstration that the intentions of France were never sincere as to peace, I hope and beg the States will be on this occasion make such a publick declaration, that not only France, but all the world may see that wee will not any longer be imposed upon, but immediately take such measures as may be the most proper for the carrying on of the war with vigor.

The States General duly announced the Republic's intention to fight until France submitted to the Grand Alliance. Louis was ready to take up the gauntlet.[79]

NOTES

1. SHD AG A¹ 2152/71, Villars to Surville, 17 August 1709; SHD AG A¹ 2152/125, Surville to Villars, 27 August 1709; SHD AG A¹ 2152/126, Villars to Surville, 30 August 1709. Wijn, *Het Staatsche Leger*, part VIII, book 2, 506–510.

2. Clement Oury, "Les défaites françaises de la guerre de Succession d'Espagne, 1704–1708" (PhD diss., Université de Paris IV-Sorbonne, 2011), 505.

3. SHD AG A¹ 2152/132, Voysin to Villars, 1 September 1709; SHD AG A¹ 2152/141, Boufflers to Villars, 3 September 1709.

4. Dauger to the duc du Maine, 5 September 1709, in Sautai, *La bataille de Malplaquet*, 39.

5. Churchill, *Marlborough*, book 2, 588–591; *Feldzüge des Prinzen Eugen*, vol. 11, 93–94; Wijn, *Het Staatsche Leger*, part VIII, book 2, 511–513.

6. SHD AG A¹ 2152/146, Villars to Louis XIV, 4 September 1709; SHD AG A¹ 2152/155, Villars to Louis XIV, 6 September 1709.
7. Churchill, *Marlborough*, book 2, 591–592; *Feldzüge des Prinzen Eugen*, vol. 11, 94–95; Wijn, *Het Staatsche Leger*, part VIII, book 2, 513.
8. SHD AG A¹ 2152/155, Villars to Louis XIV, 6 September 1709.
9. SHD AG A¹ 2152/163, Voysin to Villars, 8 September 1709.
10. SHD AG A¹ 2156/180, Doujat to Voysin, 7 September 1709.
11. SHD AG A¹ 2152/165, Villars to Louis XIV, 8 September 1709.
12. 1391, Marlborough to Sarah, 29 August/9 September 1709, *Marlborough-Godolphin Correspondence*, vol. 3, 1358–1359.
13. Churchill, *Marlborough*, book 2, 596–597; *Feldzüge des Prinzen Eugen*, vol. 11, 97–98; Wijn, *Het Staatsche Leger*, part VIII, book 2, 516–518.
14. Pierre Charrié, *Drapeaux et étendards du roi* (Paris: Le Léopard d'or, 1989).
15. Quincy, *Mémoires*, vol. 2, 352.
16. Cra'ster, "Letters of the First Lord Orkney," 817; Churchill, *Marlborough*, book 2, 598; *Feldzüge des Prinzen Eugen*, vol. 11, 98–100; Wijn, *Het Staatsche Leger*, part VIII, book 2, 519–520.
17. Quincy, *Mémoires*, vol. 2, 352. Other veterans of Malplaquet also thought Villars should have attacked, most notably the Chevalier de Folard: see Chevalier de Folard, "Relation de la bataille de Malplaquet, donnée le 11 septembre 1709, par un officier particulier qui était à la gauche," in Sautai, *La bataille de Malplaquet* 160–161; Modern historians tend to agree: Corvisier, *Malplaquet*, 68–71; Oury, *La Guerre de Succession d'Espagne*, 301; and the Austro-Hungarian General Staff, *Feldzüge des Prinzen Eugen*, vol. 11, 98.
18. Jean-Francois Frézeau de La Frézelière, "Relation de la bataille de Taynières et des événements qui l'ont précédée, donnée le 11 septembre 1709," in Sautai, *La bataille de Malplaquet*, 186–187.
19. 1391, Marlborough to Sarah, 29 August/9 September 1709, *Marlborough-Godolphin Correspondence*, vol. 3, 1359.
20. Folard, "Relation," 158–159. Corvisier, *Malplaquet*, 76–80.
21. Corvisier, *Malplaquet*, 80–82.
22. SHD AG A¹ 2152/167, Villars to Louis XIV, 10 September 1709.
23. Folard, "Relation," 161–162; Churchill, *Marlborough*, book 2, 599.
24. Stansfield, *Early Modern Systems of Command*, 238–240.
25. Chandler, *Marlborough as Military Commander*, 257; Jan Willem Wijn, "Les troupes hollandaises à la bataille de Malplaquet," *Revue Internationale d'Histoire Militaire* 19 (1957), 352.
26. *Feldzüge des Prinzen Eugen*, vol. 11, 101.
27. Folard, "Relation," 165.
28. Corvisier, *Malplaquet*, 84.
29. Folard, "Relation," 165–166; Johann Matthias von der Schulenburg, "Relation de la bataille de Malplaquet, donnée le 11. Septbr. 1709, par le Général d'infanterie de Schulenburg," in Johann Matthias von der Schulenburg, *Leben und Denkwürdigkeiten Johann Mathias Reichsgrafen von der Schulenburg, Erbherren auf Emden und Delitz, Feldmarschalls in Diensten der Republik Venedig: Aus Original-Quellen bearbeitet*, vol. 1 (Leipzig: Weidmann, 1834), 426–427; August Christoph von

Wackerbarth, "Extrait d'une relation de la bataille de Malplaquet addressee au Roi par le Comte de Wackerbarth, d. d. 27 Septbre. 1709," in ibid., vol. 1, 435–436.

30. De La Colonie, *Chronicles*, 338; *The Life and Adventures of Christian Davies, Commonly called Mother Ross* (London, 1741), 145.

31. Folard, "Relation," 167–169; Schulenburg, "Relation," 427.

32. Childs, "The Scottish Brigade," 66–68.

33. La Frézelière, "Relation," 191–192; SHD AG A^1 2152/188, d'Artagnan to Voysin, 13 September 1709; Wijn, "Les troupes hollandaises à la bataille de Malplaquet," 356–359; Wijn, *Het Staatsche Leger*, book 2, 529–531.

34. La Frézelière, "Relation," 193–195; Wijn, *Het Staatsche Leger*, book 2, 531; James Ferguson, ed., *Papers Illustrating the History of the Scots Brigade in the Service of the United Netherlands, 1572–1782*, vol. 2, *1698–1782* (Edinburgh: University of Edinburgh Press, 1899), 15; Corvisier, *Malplaquet*, 88–89.

35. Churchill, *Marlborough*, book 2, 607–608. A similar interpretation is made by C. T. Atkinson, *Marlborough and the Rise of the British Army* (London: Putnam, 1921), 399–402 and Frank Taylor, *The Wars of Marlborough 1702–1709*, book 2 (Oxford: Blackwell, 1921), 370–372. Its echoes can still be found in the popular history of Malplaquet by Osprey, Simon McDowell, *Malplaquet 1709: Marlborough's Bloodiest Battle* (Oxford: Osprey, 2020), 66–74. Even André Corvisier suggests that Orange exceeded or perhaps even overrode Marlborough's orders. ("Outrepassant peut-être les orders de Marlborough"). See *Malplaquet*, 88.

36. Des Bournays, "Relation de la bataille de Malplaquet, par M. des Bournays," in Sautai, *La bataille de Malplaquet*, 211–212; La Frézelière, "Relation," 193–194; Corvisier, *Malplaquet*, 90.

37. Quincy, *Mémoires*, vol. 2, 367.

38. Folard, "Relation," 174–175; John Wilson, "The Journal of John Wilson, an 'Old Flanderkin Serjeant' of the 15th Regiment and Later of the 2nd Troop of Life Guards, who served 1694–1727," in *Military Miscellany II: Manuscripts from Marlborough's Wars, the American War of Independence, and the Boer War*, ed. David G. Chandler, Christopher L. Scott, Marianne M. Gilchrist, and Robin Jenkins (Gloucestershire: Society for Army Historical Research, 2005), 78.

39. Fadi El Hage, "À propos d'une relation de la bataille de Malplaquet (1709) comme source de *L'histoire militaire du règne de Louis le grand* du Marquis de Quincy (1726)," *Revue du Nord* 395/2 (2012): 10–11.

40. De La Colonie, *Chronicles*, 340.

41. Deane, *Journal*, 91–94.

42. Schulenburg, "Relation," 427–428; Wackerbarth, "Relation," 436; *Feldzüge des Prinzen Eugen*, vol. 11, 106–107.

43. Saint-Hilaire to the duc du Maine, 12 September 1709, in Sautai, *La bataille de Malplaquet*, 129.

44. SHD AG A^1 2152/177, Villars to Louis XIV, 12 September 1709; Folard, "Relation," 175; Corvisier, *Malplaquet*, 92.

45. Excerpt from a letter from Schulenburg to Adolph Friedrich von der Schulenburg in Schulenburg, *Leben und Denkwürdigkeiten*, 417.

46. Saint-Hilaire to the duc du Maine, 12 September 1709, 131; Cra'ester, "Letters of the First Lord Ordkney," 319.

47. Wijn, "Les troupes hollandaises à la bataille de Malplaquet," 360–364; Wijn, *Het Staatse Leger*, part VIII, book 2, 535 and 537; des Bournays, "Relation," 212–213; La Frézelière. "Relation," 106–197 and 203–204.

48. Chevalier du Rozel to the duc du Maine, 12 September 1709, in Sautai, *La bataille de Malplaquet*, 135.

49. Villars, *Mémoires*, book 3, 72; SHD AG A^1 2152/171, Boufflers to Louis XIV, 11 September 1709.

50. Corvisier, *Malplaquet*, 97; Peter Drake, *Amiable Renegade: The Memoirs of Capt. Peter Drake, 1671–1753* (Stanford: Stanford University Press, 1960), 148–163.

51. Cra'ster, "Letters of the First Lord Orkney," 319–320; La Frézelière, "Relation," 197–201; des Bournays, "Relation," 213–214.

52. SHD AG A^1 2152/188, d'Artagnan to Voysin, 13 September 1709; Quincy, *Mémoires*, vol. 2, 371–372.

53. Saint-Hilaire to the duc du Maine, 12 September 1709, 131; SHD AG A^1 2152/185, Contades to Voysin, 13 September 1709.

54. Cra'ster, "Letters of the First Lord Orkney," 320.

55. Corvisier, *Malplaquet*, 125–132; Wijn, *Het Staatsche Leger*, part VIII, book 2, 540–543; Lynn, *Wars of Louis XIV*, 334–335.

56. Wijn, *Het Staatsche Leger*, part VIII, book 2, 544–545; SHD AG A^1 2152/194, Marlboroough to Boufflers, 14 September 1709; SHD AG A^1 2152/197, Luxembourg to Voysin, 15 September 1709.

57. Lynn, *Giant of the Grand Siècle*, 420–426; Oury, "Défaites françaises," 813–818; Corvisier, *Malplaquet*, 126; Drake, *Amiable Renegade*, 167–171; SHD AG A^1 2152/180, Voysin to Boufflers, 13 September 1709; SHD AG A^1 2152/192, letter from Broglie to Voysin, 19 September 1709.

58. SHD AG A^1 2152/259, "État des Régiments qui ont perdus des drapeaux à la bataille donnée le onze septembre 1709"; SHD AG A^1 2152/313, "État des timbales et entendards qui ont esté perdus le jour de la bataille données le onze septembre 1709"; James Q. Whitman, *The Verdict of Battle: the Law of Victory and the Making of Modern War* (Cambridge, MA: Harvard University Press, 2012), 172–179; Wijn, *Het Staatsche Leger*, part VIII, book 2, 543; Churchill, *Marlborough*, book 2, 630–633.

59. SHD AG A^1 2152/171, Boufflers to Louis XIV, 11 September 1709; SHD AG A^1 2152/185, Contades to Voysin, 13 September 1709; Goësbriand to duc du Maine, 17 September 1709, in Sautai, *La bataille de Malplaquet*, 154–157; SHD AG A^1 2152/192, Broglie to Voysin, 19 September 1709; Sourches, *Mémoires*, vol. 12, 73–74.

60. SHD AG A^1 2152/211, Voysin to Villars, 18 September 1709; SHD AG A^1 2152/222, Louis XIV to Villars, 20 September 1709.

61. SHD AG A^1 2152/190, Villars to Louis XIV, 14 September 1709.

62. Chandler, *Marlborough as Military Commander*, 267.

63. 1395, Marlborough to Godolphin, 2/13 September 1709, *Marlborough-Godolphin Correspondence*, vol. 3, 1363; 1396, Marlborough to Sarah, 2/13 September 1709, *Marlborough-Godolphin Correspondence*, vol. 3, 1364; Quincy, *Mémoires*, vol. 2, 382; SHD AG A^1 2152/225, "État des officiers tués, blessés et prisonniers à la bataille de Malplaquet, donné le 11 septembre 1709."

64. Quincy, *Mémoires*, vol. 2, 366–367 and 384–385; Anonymous cavalry officer to the duc du Maine, 14 September 1709, in Sautai, *La bataille de Malplaquet*, 209; Corvisier, *Malplaquet*.

65. SHD AG A¹ 2152/181, Boufflers to Louis XIV, 13 September 1709; SHD AG A¹ 2152/189, Voysin to Boufflers, 14 September 1709; SHD AG A¹ 2152/202, Boufflers to Voysin, 16 September 1709; SHD AG A¹ 2152/207, Contades to Voysin, 17 September 1709.

66. 1396, Marlborough to Sarah, 2 September/13 September, *Marlborough-Godolphin Correspondence*, vol. 3, 1364; 1409, Marlborough to Godolphin, 15 September/26 September 1709, *Marlborough-Godolphin Correspondence*, vol. 3, 1376.

67. SHD AG A¹ 2152/242, Boufflers to Louis XIV, 22 September 1709; SHD AG A¹ 2152/243, Boufflers to Voysin, 22 September 1709.

68. SHD AG A¹ 2153/13, Boufflers to Voysin, 3 October 1709; SHD AG A¹ 2153/14, Project for the winter quarters; SHD AG A¹ 2153/38, Voysin to Boufflers, 6 October 1709; SHD AG A¹ 2153/60 Boufflers to Louis XIV, 9 October 1709; and SHD AG A¹ 2153/101, Boufflers to Louis XIV, 14 October 1709.

69. SHD AG A¹ 2153/89, Boufflers to Louis XIV, 13 October 1709; SHD AG A¹ 2153/104, Boufflers to Louis XIV, 15 October 1709; SHD AG A¹ 2153/114, Louis XIV to Boufflers, 16 October 1709; and SHD AG A¹ 2153/122, Louis XIV to Boufflers, 17 October 1709.

70. SHD AG A¹ 2153/42, Boufflers to Voysin, 7 October 1709; SHD AG A¹ 2153/44, "Equipages des vivres à l'armée de Flandres, campagne 1709," 7 October 1709; SHD AG A¹ 2153/70, Boufflers to Voysin, 10 October 1709; SHD AG A¹ 2153/124, Boufflers to Louis XIV, 17 October 1709; SHD AG A¹ 2153/156, Report of Pâris la Montagne.

71. SHD AG A¹ 2153/148, Berwick to Louis XIV, 21 October 1709; SHD AG A¹ 2153/150, Boufflers to Louis XIV, 22 October 1709; SHD AG A¹ 2153/207, Voysin to Boufflers, 28 October 1709; Marlborough to the Council of State, 22 October 1709, in *Letters and Dispatches of John Churchill, First Duke of Marlborough*, vol. 4, 634.

72. Geikie and Montgomery, *The Dutch Barrier, 1709–1719*, 99–164. The text of the treaty is found in Appendix E, 377–386.

73. 799, Heinsius to Marlborough, 28 September 1709, and 800, Marlborough to Heinsius, 30 September 1709, *Marlborough-Heinsius Correspondence*, 467–468.

74. Legrelle, *La diplomatie française*, vol. 4, 505.

75. Sourches, *Mémoires*, vol. 12, 120–121; Jean-Baptiste Colbert de Torcy, *Journal inédit de Jan-Baptiste Colbert, Marquis de Torcy, ministre et secretaire d'état des affaires étrangéres, pendant les anées 1709, 1710, et 1711*, ed. Frédéric Masson (Paris: Librairie Plon, 1881), 25–26, 30.

76. Lynn, *Wars of Louis XIV*, 335–336; Oury, *La Guerre de Succession d'Espagne*, 331–332.

77. Guerre, *Nicolas Desmaretz*, 353–355; McCollim, *Louis XIV's Assault on Privilege*, 168–169; Rowlands, *Financial Decline*, 74–75.

78. Torcy, *Journal*, 38–39; Sourches, *Mémoires*, vol. 12, 123.

79. 812, Marlborough to Heinsius, 29 November/9 December, 1709, *Marlborough-Heinsius Correspondence*, 473; John Rule, "France and the Preliminaries of the Gertruydenberg Conference," in *Studies in Diplomatic History: Essays in Memory of David Bayne Horn*, eds. Ragnhild Hatton and M. S. Anderson (London: Longman, 1970), 107.

7

✢

A New Year

On January 1, 1710, in his bedchamber in the château of Versailles, the old king rose at his usual hour.

Louis XIV's day then unfolded with all the splendor and exactitude for which he and his court were renowned. His rising, the semi-sacred ritual of the *lever du roi*, was crowded with courtiers eager to see their monarch and be seen by him. After it, he led the procession of the chivalric Order of the Holy Spirit from the Bullseye Antechamber through the Hall of Mirrors and the State Apartments to the Royal Chapel. There, he and the knights worshiped at a high mass performed by over a hundred singers and instrumentalists of the King's Music. Other ceremonies, major and minor, followed. At last, in the evening, Louis returned to the Chapel and sat in the royal tribune surrounded by his family to hear Vespers.

But the war was never far from his thoughts that day. As he had strode through the Hall of Mirrors, he had bowed to the throng of onlookers and declared that he was going to pray to God that this year's campaign would have a better outcome than the last. Later, he had announced that he would be foregoing his custom of distributing New Year's gifts to the members of the royal house. Instead, he would be sending the money to the troops in Flanders.[1]

The war had also consumed him during the preceding weeks. He had discussed it regularly with his ministers, either in council or in more intimate *liasses* in the apartment of Madame de Maintenon. He had also been consulting his generals. Marshal Boufflers had returned to court on November 12. At the château of Marly, he was greeted affectionately by Louis, who had brought him into his cabinet and conversed with him at great length. The old dragoon was, however, a spent force. His heroism at Malplaquet and his exertions during the siege of Mons had ruined his health. He never held a field command again. During the spring and summer of 1711, he precipitously declined, and he died on August 22. The king mourned him, and Madame de Maintenon grieved the loss of one of the best of her friends.[2]

More than ever, Louis needed Marshal Villars. By slow stages to spare his mangled knee, he was brought down from Le Quesnoy to Paris, arriving on November 15. The king summoned him to Versailles and installed him in the apartments of the late prince de Conti. Then, on December 22, Louis paid him a personal visit—itself an exceptional mark of honor. For two hours, they spoke privately together.[3]

As a new year began, Louis had few illusions about what lay ahead. The euphoria that had closed the old year had given way to a more sober outlook. Though he and his subjects had survived an unprecedented concatenation of catastrophes, their plight remained bleak. In Flanders, Marlborough and Eugene were poised to break through the *pré carré* and drive on to Paris and Versailles. Only the king's last field army stood in their way. Moreover, the royal state could not long afford even a straitened war effort. For all of his ingenuity and resourcefulness, Nicolas Desmaretz could only hope to temporarily prop up the collapsing edifice of French finances. France badly needed an end to the war. Yet Louis wanted a peace with honor, one that would preserve something of the pre-eminence of his monarchy, the prestige of his dynasty, and, above all, his hard-won *gloire*. Too enervated to win it by military means, his only hope was to obtain it by exploiting the fissures among his enemies and causing the breakup of the Grand Alliance. He would finally succeed after a long and dramatic struggle.

Until the armies could once again take the field in the spring, the main theater of this struggle would be diplomacy. The Marquis de Torcy's fundamental principle was always to keep channels of communication open with the Allies. As they had been since 1704, his chief interlocutors were the Dutch. Torcy employed Petkum to sound out Heinsius' willingness to reengage in peace talks. In early January, he believed he had an opportunity to present a fresh proposal to the grand pensionary. He declared that while the French rejected the specifics of The Hague Preliminaries, they were willing to negotiate on their substance. In addition, they would cease all support for Philip of Spain and surrender to the Allies four surety towns in Flanders—essentially the same concessions Torcy had offered to Heinsius in August. The royal council approved this démarche, and it was sent to Petkum.[4]

Torcy received the Dutch reply on January 27. It completely ignored the French terms. Instead, it demanded negotiation solely of Article 37 of the Preliminaries, which gave France two months to convince Philip to abandon the entire Spanish Monarchy. The foreign minister was taken aback by this ultimatum. The staunch French stands in the last campaign and at Malplaquet had seemingly made no impression on the enemy, who remained determined to impose a harsh and humiliating peace. Nevertheless, Torcy believed there was no choice except to treat with the Allies without delay; France's condition was simply too dire. But when he laid out this argument to Louis that evening in the apartment of Madame de Maintenon, he provoked a furious response:

> The king regarded as a delusion or even a sort of foolishness the notion that one day more or less would have any effect on the negotiations. He lashed out against those who were only making matters worse by showing the enemy too much eagerness and desire to conclude peace at any price.

Although Torcy protested that he was only doing his best to serve his royal master, Louis would not be mollified. Lying in her bed knitting, Madame de Maintenon had been closely following the exchange. Now she intervened, urging her husband to make peace with his foes. At last, following more heated debate, Louis reluctantly agreed to allow Torcy to present the Dutch terms to the *Conseil d'en haut*.[5]

Over the course of three meetings, Louis learned that he was alone in his defiance and all his other ministers were in full agreement with Torcy. They unanimously decided to renegotiate Article 37, then chose two plenipotentiaries: Nicolas du Blé, Maréchal d'Huxelles, a bluff, plain-speaking soldier, and Melchior, Abbé de Polignac, a distinguished diplomat and trusted confidant of the foreign minister. The two departed for the Republic on March 5.[6]

On March 9, the French emissaries arrived at the border village of Moerdijk, located on a little island in the middle of the Hollands Diep. They boarded a yacht and met their counterparts, Willem Buys and Bruno van der Dussen, the veteran negotiators who had played a prominent role in the peace talks the previous year. The four then proceeded to Gertruydenberg. The Dutch had deliberately chosen this nondescript garrison town as the site of the conference in order to isolate and control Huxelles and Polignac. There they were cut off from their contacts at The Hague and had their letters regularly opened. They complained bitterly about their boredom, their ignorance of the latest news, and their monotonous diet of fish. In these difficult circumstances, they would try for five months to come to terms with the enemy.[7]

As the Gertruydenberg conference got underway, so did the Flanders campaign. Eugene and Marlborough were determined not to repeat their mistake of waiting for the conclusion of peace talks before bringing their armies into action. Over the winter, they meticulously made their preparations. They convinced the German princes to send strong contingents once again to the Low Countries. They ordered the Dutch and British provisioners to stockpile ample rations in their magazines. Most importantly, they prevailed upon the States General to create, at immense cost, depots of dry fodder at Tournai and Lille. The two captains intended to borrow an old French trick and begin campaigning as soon as the spring weather arrived. Battlefield success, they hoped, would place intolerable pressures on the French diplomats at the negotiating table.[8]

The French were also laying their plans. At the beginning of November, Villars had urged that the Army of Flanders should take the offensive in the next campaign. What drove him was a lingering fear of logistical weakness. Defending against the enemy, he argued, would require filling and maintaining food stores along the entire front from the sea to the Meuse, something that might be beyond the capacities of the French provisioners. An attack, by contrast, would require far fewer supplies. He and War Minister Daniel Voysin debated this as well as other possibilities during several lengthy meetings in the marshal's apartments at Versailles.[9]

In the end, the king rejected an aggressive posture in Flanders. The great lesson of 1709 was that the French did not have to win a victory; all they had to do was avoid defeat. Louis chose to implement an improved version of the defensive strategy he had always favored in Flanders. The French adopted what could be called "an army in being." Much like a "fleet in being" (a term coined in 1710), such an army avoided large-scale combat yet still exerted an inordinate strategic and operational influence by its very existence. By keeping close to its enemies, the Army of Flanders could constrain their movements, canalize their offensives, and limit their advances. Yet it would not be risked in battle. Its overriding goal was survival.[10]

The strategy of an army in being featured two further refinements. First was the resort to greatly improved and strengthened fortified lines. In Marlborough and Eugene, the Army of Flanders faced notably aggressive opponents keen to force it to fight. Another lesson the French had learned in 1709 was that they could more than hold their own against the Allies by going to ground in field fortifications. Henceforth, the Army of Flanders always sought to dig in. Moreover, its entrenchments and redoubts became so formidable and intricate they compared favorably to the trench systems of the Western Front that would crisscross the same countryside two centuries later. Second was the reliance on the defense in depth of the *pré carré*. Even after taking Lille, Tournai, and Mons, the Allies remained deeply enmeshed in Vauban's web of mutually supporting strongholds. Breaking through it would require numerous sieges. Each would exact a toll in blood, treasure, and, not least, time.[11]

Keeping an army in being required substantial and, above all, reliable logistical and financial support. Contrary to Villars' fears, the Army of Flanders' supply situation eased as harvests improved and the Pâris brothers came into their own as *munitionnaires*. Finding money for the troops proved much more difficult. The Caisse Legendre went a little way to repairing the monarchy's battered credit. As a result, Nicolas Desmaretz was able to recruit a new coterie of bankers willing to advance hard currency to the king's forces. Among them was the irrepressible Samuel Bernard, who became closely connected to the Pâris provisioning company. But the most important new banker was Antoine Hogguer. A Swiss Protestant of Saint Gallen, he channeled 600,000 *livres* in coin each month to the Army of Flanders between 1709 and 1713.[12]

In addition to credit, the controller general realized he had to find new sources of revenue. Captain Chabert's ships were not the last to bring New World silver to Bourbon-held shores. More continued to arrive from time to time for the remainder of the war. Although they represented invaluable injections of specie, Desmaretz could hardly depend on these windfalls. In October 1710, he carried out the most significant and far-reaching reform of his career: he introduced a new direct tax. Called the *dixième*, it was levied on an individual's private income. What made it even more revolutionary was that it was imposed on all of Louis XIV's subjects, including even privileged nobles. Hugely unpopular, it provoked shirking and tax avoidance on a massive scale. Nevertheless, the *dixième* brought in 22 million *livres* annually. The French war effort could not have gone on without it.[13]

Thanks to these efforts, Desmaretz was able to provide a modicum of money regularly to the field forces. Yet it was never enough: according to Voysin, the troops were only receiving at most a quarter of what they were owed. The army in being also had to be sustained by more nefarious means. It became accepted practice for officers to exaggerate the strength of their units; when money finally arrived for uniforms, equipment, or pay, they pocketed the difference. As for ordinary soldiers, they took part in a whole host of illicit activities. Entire companies organized and led by their sergeants and corporals counterfeited coins or smuggled salt. Louis' ministers had no choice except to tolerate this rampant peculation and criminality. They were the price to pay for upholding morale as well as keeping officers and men in the ranks.[14]

The Allied captains immediately put the new French strategy to the test. Marlborough's design for the 1710 Flanders campaign was to take Douai, then Arras. The capture of the latter would enable an advance on Calais and Boulogne. Capturing the Channel coast and eliminating the privateers' nest of Dunkirk were fundamental British goals.[15]

Marlborough and Eugene made an excellent start. Drawing on their depots of dry fodder, they gathered their armies and marched on Douai on April 21. With Villars and Boufflers both confined to Versailles, the Flanders frontier was in the hands of Marshal Montesquiou—the newly promoted Comte d'Artagnan. The French had been unable to afford laying up stocks of fodder themselves, which meant they could not feed their horses until the grass returned to the meadows in May. As a result, Montesquiou could not muster the field army. The best he could do was throw a strong garrison into Douai under the command of the Comte d'Albergotti, now recovered from the wounds he had suffered at Malplaquet.

Facing little opposition, the Allies overran the lines of La Bassée and invested Douai on April 25. The fortress was one of the most powerful and important of the second line of the *pré carré*. Louis wished to save it. He summoned Villars from his sick bed and ordered him to take command of the Army of Flanders. To be able to mount his horse, the marshal had to make use of a contraption that kept his injured knee rigidly straight. Accompanying and assisting him was Marshal Berwick.

On May 30, Villars, leading 153 battalions and 262 squadrons, neared Douai. He had permission from the king to fight a battle if he believed he could win it. He discovered that Marlborough was covering the siege and that his Confederate Army was strongly entrenched. At a council of war the next evening, Berwick, the most cautious of all the French marshals, and Montesquiou opined that the enemy position was too daunting to attack. Uncharacteristically, Villars agreed with them. The knowledge that he commanded France's last army curbed his natural boldness and aggression. He was also depressed and pessimistic because of the chronic pain from his unhealed wound. The French withdrew. Marlborough let them go. The captain general's own desire for a battle was tempered by the fragility of his political position back home. He knew that his Tory enemies would not allow him to survive another Malplaquet.[16]

Louis had to accept the decision of his field commanders. Douai was resolutely sacrificed. Nevertheless, Albergotti defended it with vigor and skill. Thanks to the tenacity of the Florentine and his garrison, it only fell on June 25, a month later than the Allies had intended. Villars had correctly guessed that Arras would be the next Allied target. He entrenched the Army of Flanders just south of the Scarpe along a ten-mile line that protected this fortress-city as well as Cambrai, Bouchain, and

Valenciennes. It was now Marlborough and Eugene's turn to judge the enemy's works impregnable. Although they would have liked nothing better than to fight a war-winning battle, they deemed the risks of severe casualties and a repulse too great. With the approaches to Arras blocked, the captain general decided to try to open another way to the sea by turning west.

On July 20, the Allies surrounded Béthune, a minor stronghold that controlled vital waterways, and opened their trenches four days later. The court high command now gave Villars orders to risk a battle only as a last resort; the fortresses were to be left to their fates. Instead, he did his utmost to hinder and delay the besiegers: he raided enemy outposts, harassed convoys and foraging parties, and denuded the countryside of fodder. Béthune yielded on August 28. The next Allied objectives, Saint-Venant and Aire, were only seven miles apart; they were besieged together on September 6. Saint-Venant was an earthen-walled fortlet, and it fell quickly within the month. By contrast, Aire was a first-class *pré carré* strongpoint stoutly defended by a numerous garrison ably led by the Marquis de Göesbriand, another notable veteran of Malplaquet. It held out far longer than the Allies expected. By the time Göesbriand beat the chamade on November 28, the weather had already turned wet and wintry, bringing the fighting season to a close. Villars had left the front long before. While Saint-Venant was besieged, he had asked the king to be relieved of command, claiming exhaustion and lingering agony from his wounded knee. On September 25, he had departed to take the healing waters of Bourbonne-les-Bains. His replacement, Marshal Harcourt, maintained his watching brief of the enemy.

Marlborough and Eugene had badly battered the *pré carré*, capturing four strongholds against determined French resistance. But these gains were more apparent than real. Vauban's great barrier remained unbroken. Ypres continued to close the route to the sea. Arras and Cambrai still barred the road into France. The four sieges had devoured an unusually lengthy campaign of eight months. They had been exorbitantly expensive. The Dutch, who had borne most of the financial burden, were brought close to bankruptcy. The cost in lives had been hideously high. The Allies had suffered 9,000 casualties at Douai, 3,300 at Béthune, 900 at Saint-Venant, and 6,500 at Aire: in all, 19,700 dead, wounded, missing, and captured, almost another Malplaquet.[17] As for the Army of Flanders, it remained intact and ready to fight. The Flanders campaign of 1710 was a vindication of the strategy of the army in being.

The goal of this strategy was to buy time for French diplomats to secure an honorable peace. Huxelles and Polignac had been armed with detailed instructions about how they were to proceed. As he had ever since

President Rouillé's mission the previous year, Louis insisted on a kingdom for Philip as compensation for abandoning Spain—preferably Naples and Sicily, although the negotiators could, *in extremis*, settle for the little Pyrenean territory of Navarre. In exchange, he would hand over to the Dutch four Flanders towns—Bergues, Douai, Charlemont, and Aire—as sureties as well as agree to Article 37 of The Hague Preliminaries.[18]

During their first meetings at Gertruydenberg, the French plenipotentiaries were horrified as Buys and van der Dussen flicked away their terms one by one. The Flanders towns were insufficient. An Italian kingdom for the Bourbon prince was "a chimera." The Dutch emissaries even refused to discuss Article Thirty-Seven. Instead, they presented an entirely new demand: Louis must use his own armies to drive Philip from his throne. It was the logical end of Anthonie Heinsius' policies. The Dutch had tied themselves to their Habsburg and British allies' war aim of no peace without the undivided Spanish Monarchy going to the Archduke Charles. But they were unwilling to wage a new, certainly costly, possibly prolonged war in Iberia to achieve it. To cut this Gordian knot, the grand pensionary had, at The Hague Conference, hit upon the seemingly elegant solution of having Louis do the Allies' work for them. However, all his efforts in this regard had met with delay, evasion, and obfuscation. Heinsius now believed he had no choice except to issue an ultimatum.[19]

Louis received it as an insult. Although he had shown himself willing to make far-reaching, even humiliating concessions, he always steadfastly refused to make war on his own grandson. He at first considered recalling his envoys from Gertruydenberg. In the end, he decided France needed peace too much. Instead, he and Torcy ordered Huxelles and Polignac to strive to soften the enemies' terms. Through the spring and summer, the talks twisted and turned. But the Allies were implacable. Moreover, they announced that their armies would stand idly by while France fought to conquer Spain for the Habsburgs. As paltry compensation, they were willing to offer Philip Sardinia or Sicily.

On June 21, Louis and Torcy met to formulate an answer. The foreign minister argued that the military situation was exceptionally grave. Douai was about to fall. The Army of Flanders was suffering from a spate of desertions. Peace must be made in order to pull France back from the precipice. However, Torcy compared Louis' acceptance of the Allied terms to the "promise a man makes to highwaymen who wish to murder him in a clearing in some wood"—he had no obligation to keep it. A respite from war would restore French power. At the same time, internecine quarrels would break up the Grand Alliance. In a few years, Louis could seek a new and far better settlement.

The king rejected this argument. With words full of emotion that almost brought the minister to tears, he explained that his advanced age meant he could not place his hopes in the future. Torcy then advised offering the enemy a subsidy of up to a million livres per month for their armies to campaign in Spain. When Huxelles and Polignac presented this proposal to Buys and van der Dussen, they dismissed it outright. On July 20, Louis recalled his plenipotentiaries, officially breaking off the negotiations.[20]

At Gertruydenberg, the Allies had fallen victim to hubris. Spurning the evidence of Malplaquet, they had convinced themselves that the collapse of France was imminent and that they could have their way with the Sun King. It was a grave mistake. Louis would never again be forced to offer such humiliating concessions to his enemies. Events in Spain and Great Britain were about to transform his fortunes.

Such a transformation was hardly evident at first. In fact, the opening months of the 1710 campaign in Spain encouraged the Allies to believe they would not need Louis to drive out Philip after all. The Allied commanders in Iberia, the Habsburg Guido von Starhemberg and the British Alexander Stanhope, had received considerable reinforcements in men and money. They launched a powerful invasion of Aragon and Castile, defeating Philip's armies at Almenar, then at Saragossa. Philip evacuated Madrid. On August 28, Archduke Charles entered the city.[21]

The Bourbon cause was saved by two developments. The first was the resistance of Philip's Castilian subjects against the invaders. The nobles demonstrated their loyalty by rushing to join Philip at Valladolid. The peasants rose up in arms. In a way that would become all too familiar to Napoleon's troops a century later, they waged a merciless *guerilla* against Allied outposts, foraging parties, detachments, and convoys. Charles and his generals' grip on the capital and Castile quickly became tenuous.[22]

The second development was a sea change in France's policy toward Spain. Beginning at The Hague Conference, Louis had convinced himself that by withdrawing his assistance from his grandson—particularly the majority of his troops—he could entice favorable terms from his enemies. When the Allies remained intransigent, he became disillusioned with this approach. In January, he decided that if the latest peace negotiations failed, he would revert to giving Philip his full support.[23] Perhaps Bourbon successes in Spain would compel the Allies to moderation. After the breakdown of the Gertruydenberg talks, he sent his troops back over the Pyrenees. More importantly, he placed them under the command of the Duc de Vendôme. Since the debacle of Oudenarde, he had been sulking in disgrace at his château of Anet. But he was a battle captain at least the equal of Villars, and the king could now not do without him.

In late November, the Allies abandoned Madrid and withdrew toward Catalonia, despoiling the countryside as they went. Vendôme pursued them, driving his 25,000-strong army onward by forced marches. On

December 8, at Brihuega, he caught and surrounded the Allied rearguard under Stanhope. The British general and his 4,000 troops surrendered. Worse was to come. Starhemberg had been hurrying back with the main body of the Allied army to try to rescue his colleague. On December 10, Vendôme fell upon him at Villa Viciosa. The action was bloody and inconclusive. The next day, the Habsburg commander chose to continue his retreat. It turned into a fiasco, the Allies shedding guns, horses, pack animals, stores, and thousands of men as they went. Only 7,000 of his original 18,000 troops remained to Starhemberg by the time he reached safety in Barcelona. In Spain, the Allies were now reduced to the triangle of territory enclosed by the Catalan capital and the towns of Igualada and Tarragona.[24]

Philip V returned to Madrid in triumph on December 3. Though scarcely comparable in scale and carnage to the titanic clash of Malplaquet, Brihuega and Villa Viciosa were the decisive battles of the War of the Spanish Succession. For with them, the Bourbons won Spain for good.

Nowhere were their reverberations felt more keenly than in Great Britain. They arrived in the midst of momentous political changes. Since 1708, the Whigs, the party of all-out continental war against France and no peace without Spain, had dominated both parliament and the ministry of Queen Anne. Their popularity had been sliding as the conflict dragged on, the burden of taxes mounted, and the national debt soared. A domestic cause célèbre then precipitated their downfall. The botched impeachment and trial of the Tory zealot Dr. Henry Sacheverell in early 1710 turned public opinion completely against them.

The queen had become disenchanted with the Whigs and their policies. She now decided to refashion her government under the leadership of Robert Harley, the bitter opponent of the Whigs, sworn enemy of Marlborough, and champion of peace with France. Together, they moved to create a new ministry and secure a Tory parliament. In April, Anne dismissed Sarah Churchill, so ending the remarkable thirty-year friendship of Mrs. Morley and Mrs. Freeman. Then, over the following months, she replaced her ministers one by one with Harley's supporters. Her stealthy coup culminated in August when she forced out Sidney Godolphin, the chief architect of Great Britain's war effort and Marlborough's great friend and closest ally. The captain general was completely isolated, and he feared his own dismissal was imminent. But Harley chose to retain him in command of the Allied armies while he searched for a way out of the war.[25]

In September, Anne engineered the resignations of her last Whig ministers and dissolved parliament. The ensuing elections produced a thumping Tory majority. In the meantime, Harley had discovered a conduit to the French court. Abbé François Gaultier had been the chaplain of the last pre-war French ambassador to Britain. Amiable, speaking excellent English, and as a result well-liked by his hosts, he had managed to remain behind and become a secret agent of the Marquis de Torcy.[26] The French foreign minister had been closely following events in London and, in July, he instructed Gaultier to contact the queen's new favorites and sound them out about the possibility of peace talks. The abbé began a clandestine dialogue with Edward Villiers, Earl of Jersey, a Jacobite Tory and close associate of Harley. It had few results at first. Then, in December, a breakthrough. Vendôme's victories had rendered no peace without Spain a dead letter. Harley had long opposed this Whig policy, and he now decided on a decisive shift in British war aims: Philip V could keep his throne in exchange for favorable trading relations for the British in Spanish America. He dispatched Gaultier to the French court with this offer. He landed at Neuport on January 15, safely crossed the frontlines, and arrived at Versailles four days later.

For Louis and Torcy, the unforeseen outbreak of negotiations with the British was a godsend. They had always regarded the Dutch as the weakest link in the Grand Alliance and thus their most likely peace partners. By contrast, the British under Godolphin and Marlborough had seemed the most obstinate of enemies. But now the positions were completely reversed. When Gaultier asked Torcy on behalf of the British ministers if the French wanted peace, he replied that it was like asking a sick man if he wanted to be healed. During the spring of 1711, the diplomatic pace quickened. In April, Harley produced a fresh set of peace preliminaries for the French court. They included trading concessions for Great Britain throughout Spain's empire, a barrier of fortresses in the southern Netherlands for the Dutch Republic, and concessions for the remaining Allies. The final disposition of Spain was left deliberately vague, opening the way for Philip to retain it. Harley then demanded that Louis and Torcy publicly send these so-called Seven Articles to London as if they were French terms. This subterfuge was necessary, he explained, in order to preserve the British ministry's credibility with parliament and with the Grand Alliance. Entrusted with this new proposal, Gaultier went back to France.[27]

When the abbé returned to Versailles on April 16, he found it plunged into mourning. Two days before, Louis the Grand Dauphin had died of smallpox.[28] Since 1709, he had shaken off any lingering doubts about his statesmanship to become one of the chief voices in his father's councils as well as the principal defender of the interests of the Bourbon dynasty. The king now displayed immense tenacity and resolve. Even as he grieved his son, he was determined to grasp the opportunity afforded to him by the British. He summoned his ministers and sought their advice on Harley's proposals: all were in favor. He then commanded Torcy to draw them up virtually unchanged and give them to Gaultier to take back to London.

No sooner had he left that news of a second, even more consequential death reached the French court: Holy Roman Emperor Joseph had also contracted smallpox and died on April 17. Because he had no sons, his heir was his brother Charles. The very real possibility now existed of the joining of his two inheritances, the Spanish and Austrian monarchies, into an empire even greater than that of Charles V. Louis and Torcy realized at once that this event dangerously destabilized the Grand Alliance. The Imperial princes feared that the emperor would become too powerful in Germany. The Savoyards felt threatened by Austrian domination of Italy. And Great Britain regarded a Habsburg super-state to be as dangerous to the balance of power in Europe as a Bourbon one. Negotiations with France were thus given irresistible impetus. On May 5, the British cabinet approved the Seven Articles and immediately sent them to Anthonie Heinsius.[29]

The ripening of French–British relations shaped the Flanders campaign of 1711. Harley needed Marlborough to maintain pressure on the French so that Louis and Torcy would continue bargaining in good faith. He also wanted vigorous action in this crucial theater in order to convince the Dutch and the Habsburgs that Britain remained fully committed to the original war aims of the Grand Alliance. As for the captain general, he understood that battlefield success was the only way he could shore up his position with his new political masters in London.[30]

Marlborough was once again opposed by Villars. His health was now restored, and with it his inimitable pugnacity; he incessantly lobbied the court high command for permission to fight a great action. Yet Louis had a far better appreciation of France's strategic and political situation than the marshal. He refused to allow military events to interfere with the promising diplomatic developments then unfolding. The 1711 campaign was the apogee of the strategy of the army in being. Villars received strict instructions not to run even the least risk with the Army of Flanders. "His Majesty prohibited me to give battle," the marshal recalled, "trusting that divisions among the enemy powers would reduce their forces. His orders were that I should confine myself to defending the lines that I occupied."[31]

These lines were the most formidable example of French field fortifications of the entire war. They ran for two hundred miles from the Channel coast at Montreuil to the confluence of the Sambre and Meuse at Namur, covering Arras, Cambrai, Valenciennes, Le Quesnoy, Landrecies, and Maubeuge along the way. They consisted of layers of abatis, infantry entrenchments, and artillery emplacements. They incorporated the obstacles afforded by hills, ridges, marshes, watercourses, inundations (both natural and manmade), and the Rivers Scarpe, Sensée, and Scheldt. In a fit of bravado, Villars dubbed these lines "Ne Plus Ultra" because they would stop the enemy from going any further.

They more than lived up to their name during the opening months of the campaign. In May, Marlborough and Eugene marched from Douai with 120,000 troops with the aim of taking Arras. Villars confronted them with the 80,000-strong Army of Flanders along the River Sensée. The obvious strength of the French defenses stopped the Allies short. A month-long stalemate ensued. In June, the leaders of the Grand Alliance became worried about the security of the upcoming election to Holy Roman Emperor of Archduke Charles. Louis cannily played on their fears by having Villars send reinforcements to Marshal Harcourt's Army of Germany. In response, Eugene was then ordered to the Rhine. He left on June 14 with his corps of 20,000 Imperial and Palatine troops. The two great Allied captains would never fight together again.

Marlborough was facing another frustrating campaign. He responded with one of his greatest feats of generalship. At the beginning of August, he feinted west toward Arras. Suddenly, on the night of the fourth, he launched his army eastward for the Sensée crossing at Arleux. His march was concealed behind Vimy Ridge and went undetected by Villars. On the fifth, the Allies surged over the river unopposed and overran the unmanned French fieldworks. The captain general had breached the lines of Ne Plus Ultra without losing a single soldier.

Villars, having arrived too late to stop the captain general, deployed the Army of Flanders near the forest of Bourlon with his right protecting Cambrai. As was now his custom, he ordered his troops to dig in. Marlborough had the choice to attack. Many of his generals, including not a few of the Dutch, were in favor. He declined; the precarity of his political position prevented him from running any risks. Instead, he invested Bouchain, a key fortress of the second line of the *pré carré*. The siege was grueling, with Villars doing everything he could to hinder and harass the besiegers. Bouchain fell on September 12. Now only a final line of fortresses—Arras, Cambrai, Le Quesnoy, Landrecies—stood between the Allies and a march on Paris. Just one more campaign would be required to break through it. But Marlborough had run out of time.[32]

For negotiations between London and Versailles were rushing to their end. By sending the Seven Articles to Heinsius in May, Harley had been initially willing to include the Dutch in the discussions. The grand pensionary and the Republic's other leaders reacted cautiously to what they believed was the latest French démarche. Privately, they worried that the Tory ministry was intending to bargain away the 1709 Barrier Treaty in exchange for commercial advantages for Britain in France and Spain.

Publicly, Heinsius complained that the proposed preliminaries were extremely vague and insisted on more details. In doing so, he was hoping to coax both the British and the French to reveal their true intentions.

The British, however, deliberately and deceitfully treated their ally's reply as a refusal to participate. Harley had concluded that the British could win better terms for themselves without Dutch meddling. Moreover, he had been joined in the negotiations by Secretary of State Henry St. John. A prominent Tory, St. John loathed the Allies in general and the Republic in particular. Together, he and Harley ditched the Dutch.[33]

The decisive phase of the talks took place between July and October. The British ministry sent an envoy, the poet-diplomat Matthew Prior, to Versailles to treat with Louis and Torcy. When he came back to London in August, he brought a French emissary, the Rouen merchant and seasoned negotiator Nicolas Mesnager. By the beginning of October, Versailles and London had finalized two documents. The first was kept secret and detailed the advantages that Britain was receiving from France and Spain: the recognition of the Protestant Succession; the demolition of the port of Dunkirk; the cession of Gibraltar, Port Mahon, and various territories in the New World; and the award of the *Asiento* for thirty years. The second, public document described in very general terms the French concessions that would constitute the preliminaries for a final peace treaty and called for the convening of a general congress embracing all the belligerents.

The British ministry revealed the London Preliminaries to the Allies on October 24. Their outrage was immediate. The Imperial ambassador Gallas leaked the text to the Whig press, which then waged a pamphlet war to try to turn British public opinion against the dealings of the Tories. It was defeated, however, by the government's propagandists, prominent among them Jonathan Swift. The Dutch were just as furious. But fearing the British would go ahead and sign a separate treaty with France, they agreed to host a peace conference. The promulgation of the London Preliminaries also spelled the end for Marlborough. Harley no longer needed him. On January 11, 1712, Queen Anne dismissed him as captain general of her armies.[34]

At the beginning of 1712, diplomats from all over Europe gathered in the city hall of Utrecht. As they talked, soldiers mustered in Flanders one last time.[35] For the Habsburgs and the Dutch, a successful campaign would be the means to impose their terms on the peace conference. The British did not join them. The Harley ministry had received everything it wanted from Louis. In May, it issued secret "restraining orders" to Marlborough's replacement, James Butler, Duke of Ormond. He was to avoid all contact with French forces. Then, in July, he took his 12,000 British troops to occupy Dunkirk. Even without them, the remaining Allies fielded an imposing army. The States General agreed to take into its service the 35,000 German auxiliaries who had been in British pay. As for the Habsburgs, having conquered Italy and put down the Hungarian revolt, they were able to send substantial strength to Western Europe.

The Allies still had a great captain in command in Prince Eugene of Savoy. For five years, he and Marlborough had been battering away at the *pré carré*. Now he was ready to finish the job. He set his sights on the fortresses of Le Quesnoy and Landrecies. Taking them would complete the dismantling of the French frontier defenses and open up tantalizing prospects. To the southeast of Landrecies was the rich, largely untouched countryside of Champagne and the French coronation city of Reims. To the southwest was Saint-Quentin on the Somme. Beyond it were the valley of the Seine and Paris. As Eugene explained to Count Sinzendorf, the Habsburg foreign minister, he intended to ravage the heart of France up to the gates of the capital, then winter his army on the Sambre.[36]

Louis knew he and his kingdom were in grave danger. Then, just as the fighting season was about to open, he suffered a new and staggering personal and dynastic tragedy. An epidemic of measles carried away first the Duchesse de Bourgogne, whose charm and vivacity had so enchanted the king in his old age, on February 12, followed by her husband the Duc de Bourgogne, who had been heir to the throne for less than a year, on February 18, and, finally, their eldest son on March 8. Louis' successor was now his great-grandson, a two-year-old boy. This hecatomb of his heirs prostrated him with grief and the conviction that God was punishing him for his transgressions.[37] Yet, with a resolution and courage that cannot fail to astonish and impress, Louis rose from these sorrows to face the war. On April 12, he summoned Villars to Marly. In the seclusion of his cabinet, he let slip his public mask to reveal his private pain, saying "God punishes me, and I well deserve it. I will suffer less in the next world. But let us set aside our own personal misfortunes and see what can be done to avert those of the state." After confirming the marshal as commander of the Army of Flanders, he asked what he intended to do. When Villars equivocated, Louis declared:

> Very well, this is what I think, and afterward you will tell me your own sentiments. All my courtiers are advising me to retire to Blois before the enemy army marches on Paris, which is certainly possible if mine is defeated. Yet great armies are never completely defeated and mine should be able to rally behind the Somme. I know this river. It is very difficult to cross and there are fortresses on it. I intend to go to Peronne or Saint-Quentin and gather there all my remaining troops to make a last effort with you. We will either perish together or save the state. I will never allow my enemies to approach my capital.

Fortified with these words, Villars departed for the front.[38]

Eugene struck on June 5 by investing Le Quesnoy. Villars brought the Army of Flanders, 70,000 strong, up to the Scheldt below Allied-held Bouchain, but he could do nothing more until the British troops had left for Dunkirk. Le Quesnoy capitulated on July 4. Louis had expected it to hold out much longer; he had its commander thrown in the Bastille. Two weeks later, even as Ormond was marching away, the prince of Savoy turned his army of 130,000 men against Landrecies. This fortress was strongly garrisoned and had been expertly fortified by Vauban. The siege was made even more difficult for the Allies by daunting logistical challenges. Because Condé and Valenciennes were still held by the French, the lower reaches of the Scheldt were closed to them. They had to draw their supplies from a depot established at Marchiennes on the Scarpe. Huge convoys lumbered overland thirty miles to Landrecies. To protect them, the Allies built a double line of entrenchments and redoubts along the whole route. They christened these works—in what would soon be revealed as a sign of fatal overconfidence—"the Grand Highway to Paris." The key node of the supply system was the entrenched camp of Denain.[39]

For two years, Louis had determinedly pursued the strategy of the army in being. Now he realized he had to set it aside and seek a great action that would utterly transform the strategic situation. On July 6, War Minister Voysin ordered Villars to fight a battle to save Landrecies. A brilliant plan then came from an unexpected source. Jean-Robert Le Fèvre d'Orval was a lawyer in the Parlement of Flanders and an intelligence agent in the service of the war minister. Fancying himself a military strategist, he proposed an attack on Denain, which would cut the enemy's supply lines and force them to abandon the siege of Landrecies. Voysin passed the scheme on to Villars. On July 18, the marshal set in motion what would come to be celebrated as the "maneuver of Denain." Letters detailing that the French intended to cross the Sambre to attack the Allies were allowed to fall into enemy hands. The ruse worked—Eugene kept the bulk of his forces firmly fixed in his siege lines.[40]

Unopposed, Villars swept up the corridor between the Rivers Selle and Scheldt to Denain, reaching it on July 23. Suddenly, his nerves failed him, and he ordered Marshal Montesquiou, who was leading the strike force of the Army of Flanders, to halt the attack. Why did Villars, normally so combative, shy away from battle at this crucial moment? He was likely daunted by Eugene's fearsome reputation: he simply could not believe that he could take the prince so completely by surprise. He was also keen to preserve his reputation as an undefeated general, especially with the end of the war so near. Montesquiou ignored the order. On July 24, he stormed the fortified camp and overran it in an hour of furious fighting. He was ably supported by another general, Charles de

Montmorency-Luxembourg, Prince de Tingry, governor of Valenciennes, who sallied out his garrison to block a key bridge over the Scheldt, stopping a relief force hastily sent by Eugene. The entire 8,000-man Dutch garrison of Denain was killed or captured. More importantly, the Grand Highway to Paris had been severed.

Denain, the only major French battlefield success in Flanders during the entire war, had swift and far-reaching results. The Army of Flanders beleaguered Marchiennes and took it on August 2. His depot and supply lines both lost, Eugene retreated in disarray from Landrecies. Villars then mounted an energetic counteroffensive, retaking lost strongholds one by one: Douai on September 8, Le Quesnoy on October 3, and, finally, Bouchain on October 20. By the campaign's end, the breach in the *pré carré* had been sealed.[41]

Villars had brilliantly exploited the aftermath of Denain. But the victory itself had been won by Le Fèvre d'Orval, Montesquiou, and Tingry. Therefore, even as he was beleaguering the Flanders fortresses, Villars was waging another campaign to take credit for Denain. He was ably assisted by his allies and protectors at court, especially his patron Madame de Maintenon. By the time his friend Voltaire dubbed him, in his *Age of Louis XIV*, the "restorer of France," he had won the war for posterity. For the remainder of his life, he was laden with rewards commensurate with his reputation as France's greatest soldier. This culminated in 1733, a year before his death, when he was promoted to *Maréchal général des camps et armées du roi*, one of only seven men to ever hold this dignity.[42]

The denouement of the War of the Spanish Succession followed the end of the fighting in Flanders. The Dutch Republic realized it could gain nothing further from continued hostilities. It was also in no shape to go on. It had been the financial Atlas of the Grand Alliance, shouldering a disproportionate share of the immense costs of the contest. It had finally buckled under the strain: in 1715, the States General would be forced to declare bankruptcy. Bargaining at the peace conference yielded the Dutch their coveted Barrier in the southern Netherlands, one more extensive than they had possessed after the Peace of Ryswick but much less than what they had been promised in 1709. In the early morning of April 13, 1713, the Republic signed the Treaty of Utrecht. The British and the minor Allies had already done so hours earlier.

Only one major belligerent against France remained in the field: the Habsburgs and the Holy Roman Empire. During the fighting season of 1713, Villars and Eugene squared off along the Rhine. Yet even a terminally war-weary France outmatched a Habsburg Monarchy bereft of allies. With his army heavily outnumbered, Eugene could not stop Villars from capturing Landau, then Freiburg. In the fall, the two generals met in the city of Rastatt to negotiate a peace. The old comrades in arms and friends from the Turkish Wars quickly reached an agreement. France and the Habsburg Monarchy concluded the Treaty of Rastatt on March 7, 1714. Only the cumbersome machinery of the Imperial government delayed the Holy Roman Empire's signing of the Treaty of Baden until September 7, 1714.

In the three war-ending treaties, France was forced to make concessions and to suffer territorial losses. The French Guinea Company surrendered to the British South Seas Company the *Asiento*, the lucrative slave trade to Spanish America. In Flanders, Furnes, Ypres, and Tournai were handed over to the Dutch Republic for its Barrier. In Germany, French forces evacuated the right bank of the Rhine, leaving it to the Empire. In America, Hudson's Bay, Acadia, and Newfoundland were ceded to Great Britain. Louis found personally painful Utrecht's requirement that he expel the Stuarts from his kingdom: he and his family had grown very close to the exiles of Saint-Germain. But compared to what his enemies had sought at The Hague and Gertruydenberg—essentially the reduction of France to what it had been at the beginning of his father's reign—Louis could bear all these reverses. And he could take real satisfaction in the accomplishment of the goal for which he had taken up arms in the first place: his grandson was king of Spain. The outcome of the War of the Spanish Succession was far more favorable to him and to France than he could ever have hoped for during the dark days of 1709.[43]

In hindsight, 1709 was the pivotal year of the War of the Spanish Succession. When it began, France was already reeling from military defeat and financial decline. The Great Winter and its consequences then struck like hammer blows. The harvest failed all over the kingdom, and hunger reached the very gates of Versailles. Six hundred thousand French perished from starvation. Riots and revolts broke out everywhere. In April, Samuel Bernard, the king's principal banker, defaulted on his debts. The royal finances came close to complete collapse. Coin and credit both vanished. Starving and unpaid royal troops mutinied. On every frontier, the Allies' armies were set to invade. With his kingdom on its knees, the king had sought peace from his enemies. Their response had been the onerous, humiliating Preliminaries of The Hague. Louis might still have accepted them if not for the impassioned intervention of his son and heir. During the whole war, France never stood closer to defeat. The crisis of 1709 was the greatest France faced between 1649, when the ten-year-old Louis XIV was forced to flee Paris by the rebels of the Fronde, and 1789, when his descendant confronted the first stirrings of the Revolution.

But France then experienced a remarkable recovery. The rallying of the kingdom was due largely to the strength and capabilities of a seasoned absolute monarchy. For the first and only time, a French king directly addressed his people, summoning them to defend their collective honor. Orders and commands issued from the royal councils, leaving no one in doubt that Louis and his chosen servants kept an unwavering grip on the state. From the capital to the smallest villages, the authorities succeeded in preserving order, so that the many popular tumults never coalesced into larger, more dangerous uprisings. At first on their own, then with the approval of the royal ministers, the peasants plowed under their fields and planted new crops in the spring; in the fall, the "miracle of the barley" put an end to the last famine of the eighteenth century. By resorting to a windfall of American silver and the desperate expedient of reminting France's entire stock of currency, Controller General Nicolas Desmaretz managed to prop up the royal finances and to find the means to keep the French war effort going.

The resilience of the royal regime was matched by the tenacity of the army. The king, his ministers, and marshals constantly feared that it might disband from lack of provisions and pay. They exploited every possible makeshift to channel resources to the troops. In addition, officers, officials, and local notables dipped again and again into their own fortunes to keep regiments and companies in the field. Though half-starved and barely paid, an irreducible core of veterans remained steadfastly with the colors. At Malplaquet, the threadbare Army of Flanders fought the Allies to a sanguinary standstill. Moreover, the Flanders campaign of 1709 gave Louis a successful strategy that he would pursue until the end of the war. It was based on avoiding defeat rather than winning victories. After Malplaquet, the field army did not fight another pitched battle for three years. Instead, it sought the protection of field fortifications of increasingly forbidding strength. As an army in being, it kept close to the enemy's forces, harried them, and limited their advances. The king and Marshal Villars successfully preserved it until negotiations had transformed France's fortunes. When the strategic and diplomatic circumstances were right, they boldly risked it to win a great action.

The Grand Alliance's triumvirate of Marlborough, Heinsius, and Eugene underestimated the strength and stability of France and its absolute monarchy. Ignoring the evidence of the 1709 Flanders campaign and Malplaquet, they were convinced its collapse was imminent. It was a fatal error that snatched defeat from the jaws of victory. After 1709, a race began pitting the breakdown of French finances against the breakup of the Grand Alliance. Desmaretz resourcefully and ruthlessly found the funds to maintain the French armies. Meanwhile, Torcy worked patiently and cunningly to exploit the tensions among the Allies. France would at last crumple into financial exhaustion in 1714. But Great Britain had already abandoned its Allies and so forced the end of the war.

No one was more responsible for France's resilience and resurgence than Louis XIV. If Marshal Villars skillfully commanded his principal army, talented ministers advised him and administered his state, his heir reminded him of his duty to his family, and Madame de Maintenon buttressed his emotions, he was nevertheless the animating spirit in all affairs and the maker of all decisions, great or small. If he at times wavered and suffered from self-doubt, his determination to win a peace that would protect France's power, uphold the prestige of his dynasty, and preserve his *gloire* always returned. In 1709 and the handful of years left to him, he achieved a stoic grandeur and endurance that outshone even the brilliant vigor and daring of his youth and the first half of his reign. The twilight of the Sun King was his finest hour.

NOTES

1. Dangeau, *Journal*, vol. 13, 85–86; Sourches, *Mémoires*, vol. 12, 133–134.
2. Sourches, *Mémoires*, vol. 12, 115; Beckman, "Sword of the Sun," 323–326.
3. Sourches, *Mémoires*, vol. 12, 129–130; Villars, *Mémoires*, book 3, 76–78; El Hage, *Le maréchal de Villars*, 97; Ziegler, *Villars*, 210–211.
4. Torcy, *Journal*, 90–91.
5. Ibid., 122–126.
6. Ibid., 148.
7. Lucien Bély, *L'art de la paix en Europe. Naissance de la diplomatie modern, XVIIe-XVIIIe siècle* (Paris: PUF, 2007), 446–447.
8. Van Nimwegen, *De subsistentie van het leger*, 269–279.
9. SHD AG A^1 2153/230, Villars to Voysin, 1 November 1709; Dangeau, *Journal*, vol. 13, 81.
10. Olivier Chaline developed the concept of the "army in being" in "Le sursaut Francais, 1710–1712," *Revue historique des armées* 281 (4e trimestre 2015), 18.
11. On French field fortifications, Duffy, *The Fortress in the Age of Vauban and Frederick the Great*, 36. On the defense in depth of the *pré carré*, Geoffrey Parker, *The Military Revolution: Military Innovation and the Rise of the West* (Cambridge: Cambridge University Press, 1996), 166.
12. Herbert Lüthy, *La Banque Protestante*, 229–230, 234–243.
13. On the arrival of Spanish and French treasure ships after 1710, see Kamen, *The War of Succession in Spain*, 187–195; On the establishment and significance of the *dixième*, see Guerre, *Nicolas Desmaretz*, 365–380; McCollim, *Louis XIV's Assault on Privilege*, 160–193; and Rowlands, *Financial Decline*, 64.
14. Rowlands, "The Stamina of the French Army," 334–341.
15. Jones, *Marlborough*, 187–188.
16. Lynn, *Wars of Louis XIV*, 337–338; Oury, *La Guerre de Succession d'Espagne*, 334–335; Villars, *Mémoires*, book 3, 80–85; El Hage, *Le maréchal de Villars*, 104–109; Jamel Ostwald, "Louis XIV aimait-il trop la bataille?" in *Les dernières guerres de Louis XIV, 1688–1715*, 112–113.

17. Ostwald, *Vauban under Siege*, 102–103.

18. "Instruction donnée au Sieur Marquis d'Huxelles, Maréchal de France, cheavalier des orders du roi, etc., at au Sieur Abbé de Polignac, conseiller ordinaire de Sa Majesté en son Conseil d'État, autidteur de la Rote, Revétus de ses pouvoirs pour traiter de la paix générale, [4 mars 1710]" in *Recueil des instructions données aux ambassadeurs et ministers de France: depuis les traités de Westphalie jusqu'à la Révolution francaise. XXI-XXII, Hollande*, book 2, ed. Emile Bourgeois (Paris: Fontemoing, 1922), 248–254; Torcy, *Mémoires*, book 1, 360–363.

19. Stork-Penning, "The Ordeal of the States," 126–129.

20. Torcy, *Journal*, 204–209; Torcy, *Mémoires*, book 1, 410–415.

21. Lynn, *Wars of Louis XIV*, 339; Oury, *La Guerre de Succession d'Espagne*, 337–338.

22. Francis, *First Peninsular War*, 313; Kamen, *The War of Succession in Spain*, 21–22.

23. Torcy, *Journal*, 126–127.

24. Lynn, *Wars of Louis XIV*, 340; Oury, *La Guerre de Succession d'Espagne*, 339–341.

25. Julian Hoppit, "Party Politics and War Weariness in the Reign of Queen Anne," in *Britain, Spain and the Treaty of Utrecht, 1713–2013*, eds. Trevor J. Dadson and J. H. Elliot (London: Legenda, 2014), 9–17.

26. Bély, *Espions et ambassadeurs*, 185–186.

27. G. M. Trevelyan, "The 'Jersey' Period of the Negotiations Leading to the Peace of Utrecht," *The English Historical Review* 49 (January 1934), 100–105.

28. Chaline, *L'année des quatre dauphins*, 24–32.

29. Torcy, *Mémoires*, book 2, 22; Legrelle, *La diplomatie francaise*, book 4, 588–590; Chaline, *L'année des quatre dauphins*, 143–149; Hattendorf, *England in the War of the Spanish Succession*, 238–245.

30. Jones, *Marlborough*, 191–196.

31. Villars, *Mémoires*, book 3, 111.

32. Lynn, *Wars of Louis XIV*, 342–344; Oury, *La Guerre de Succession d'Espagne*, 348–349.

33. Stork-Penning, "The Ordeal of the States," 135–137; B. W. Hill, "Oxford, Bolingbroke, and the Peace of Utrecht," *The Historical Journal* 16/2 (1973), 244–247.

34. On the negotiation and conclusion of the London Preliminaries, Torcy, *Mémoires*, book 2, 26–74; Legrelle, *La diplomatie francaise*, book 4, 595–610; Hill, "Oxford, Bolingbroke, and the Peace of Utrecht," 247–251. On Marlborough's dismissal, Jones, *Marlborough*, 219–222; Holmes, *Marlborough*, 273–275.

35. On the negotiations and intrigues that took place simultaneously with the 1712 Flanders campaign, see Bély, *Espions et ambassadeurs*, 658–666.

36. Gérard Lesage, *Denain (1712). Louis XIV sauve sa mise* (Paris: Economica, 1992), 49–61.

37. Chaline, *L'année des quatre dauphins*, 33–49.

38. Villars, *Mémoires*, book 3, 138–139.

39. Oury, *La Guerre de Succession d'Espagne*, 366–368; Lesage, *Denain*, 61–69.

40. Ostwald, "Louis XIV aimait-il trop la bataille?" 116; Lesage, *Denain*, 78–88; El Hage, *Le maréchal de Villars*, 125.

41. Lesage, *Denain*, 89–115; Oury, *La Guerre de Succession d'Espagne*, 369–370.
42. El Hage, *Le maréchal de Villars*, 137–140.
43. On the Treaties of Utrecht, Rastatt, and Baden, the best account is Pitt, "The Pacification of Utrecht," vol. 6, 461–479.

Bibliography

ARCHIVAL SOURCES

Service Historique de la Defense (SHD)

GR A¹ 2149 to 2153	Campaign of Flanders, December 1708 to December 1709.
GR A¹ 2154 to 2160	Intendancies of Flanders, Maritime Flanders, Hainault, Picardy, and Artois, December 1708 to December 1709.

Archives Nationales (AN)

G⁷ 14	Correspondence of the Controller General of Finances to the intendants, 1709.
G⁷ 90-91	Correspondence from the intendant of Artois and Picardy (Amiens), 1709.
G⁷ 263	Correspondence from the intendant of Flanders, 1709.
G⁷ 273	Correspondence from the intendant of Maritime Flanders (Dunkirk), 1709.
G⁷ 289	Correspondence from the intendant of Hainault, 1709.

Archives Diplomatiques du Ministère des Affaires Etrangères (AAE)

Hollande 215-221   Correspondence, Dutch Republic, July 1708 to December 1709.
Angleterre 227-229 Correspondence, Great Britain, January to December 1709.

Bibliothèque Nationale de France (BNF)

Manuscrits françaises 6257 *Traité de la guerre de campagne.*

PUBLISHED SOURCES

Allgemeine Deutsche Biographie. Volume 19 and Volume 32. Leipzig: Duncker & Humblot, 1884.

Atkinson, C. T. *Marlborough and the Rise of the British Army.* London: Putnam, 1921.

Baudrillart, Alfred. *Philippe V et la cour de France 1700–1715.* Paris: Bureau de la Revue, 1889.

Beckman, Steven A. "Sword of the Sun: Marshal Boufflers and the Experience of War in the Grand Siècle." PhD diss., The Ohio State University, 2022.

Beik, William. *Absolutism and Society in Seventeenth-Century France: State Power and Provincial Aristocracy in Languedoc.* Cambridge: Cambridge University Press, 1985.

_____. *Urban Protest in Seventeenth-Century France: The Culture of Retribution.* Cambridge: Cambridge University Press, 1997.

_____. *A Social and Cultural History of Early Modern France.* Cambridge: Cambridge University Press, 2009.

Belhomme, Victor. *Histoire de l'infanterie en France.* Volume 2. Paris: H. Charles-Lavauzelle, 1893–1902.

Bély, Lucien. *Espions et ambassadeurs au temps de Louis XIV.* Paris: Fayard, 1990.

_____. *L'art de la paix en Europe. Naissance de la diplomatie moderne XVIIe-XVIIIe siècle.* Paris: PUF, 2007.

Berkovich, Ilya. *Motivation in War: The Experience of Common Soldiers in Old-Regime Europe.* Cambridge: Cambridge University Press, 2017.

Bluche, François. *Louis XIV.* Paris: Fayard, 1986.

Boislisle, A. M. de, ed. *Correspondence des Contrôleurs Généraux des Finances avec les intendants des provinces.* Volume 3, *1708 à 1715.* Paris: Imprimerie Nationale, 1897.

Bouget, Boris. "'De peu d'effet.' Le fusil et le combat d'infanterie au XVIII siècle (1692–1791). Modèles tactique et efficacité." PhD diss., Université Paris-Sorbonne, 2013.

Brewer, John. *The Sinews of Power: War Money and the English State 1688–1783.* Cambridge, MA: Harvard University Press, 1990.

Brienne, Louis-Henri de Loménie, comte de. *Mémoires.* Edited by F. Barrière. Vol 1. Paris: Ponthieu, 1828.

Bryant, Mark. *Queen of Versailles: Madame de Maintenon, First Lady of Louis XIV's France*. Montréal and Kingston: McGill-Queen's University Press, 2020.

Burke, Peter. *The Fabrication of Louis XIV*. New Haven and London: Yale University Press, 1992.

Castelluccio, Stephane. *Marly. Art de vivre et pouvoir de Louis XIV à Louis XVI*. Montreuil: Gourcuff Gradenigo, 2014.

Cenat, Jean-Philippe. "Le ravage du Palatinat: politique de destruction stratégie de cabinet et propaganda au début de la guerre de la Ligue d'Augsbourg." *Revue historique* 633 (2005/1): 97–132.

———. *Le roi stratège: Louis XIV et la direction de la guerre 1661–1715*. Rennes: Presses universitaires de Rennes, 2010.

———. *Chamlay. Le stratège secret de Louis XIV*. Paris: Belin, 2011.

Chaline, Olivier. "La bataille comme objet d'histoire." *Francia—Forschungen zur westeuropäischen Geschichte* 34, no. 2 (2005): 1–14.

———. *L'année des quatre dauphins*. Paris: Flammarion, 2009.

———. *Le règne de Louis XIV*. 2 volumes. Paris: Champs histoire, 2009.

———. "Le sursaut Francais 1710–1712." *Revue historique des armées* 281 (4e trimestre 2015): 16–26.

———. *Les armées du Roi. Le grand chantier. XVIIe-XVIIIe siècle*. Paris: Armand Colin, 2016.

Chandler, David, ed. *John Marshall Deane: A Journal of Marlborough's Campaigns during the War of the Spanish Succession 1704–1711*. London: Society for Army Historical Research, 1984.

Chandler, David. *Marlborough as Military Commander*. New York: Charles Scribner's Sons, 1973.

———. *The Art of Warfare in the Age of Age of Marlborough*. New York: Hippocrene, 1976.

———, ed. *John Marshall Deane: A Journal of Marlborough's Campaigns during the War of the Spanish Succession 1704–1711*. London: Society for Army Historical Research, 1984.

Charrié, Pierre. *Drapeaux et étendards du roi*. Paris: Le Léopard d'or, 1989.

Childs, John. "The Scottish Brigade in the Service of the Dutch Republic 1688–1782." *Documentatieblad werkgroep Achttiende eeuw*. Jaargang 1984 (1984): 59–74.

———, *The British Army of William III 1689–1702*. Manchester: Manchester University Press, 1987.

Churchill, Winston. *Marlborough: His Life and Times*. 2 volumes. Chicago: University of Chicago Press, 2002.

Clément, Pierre. *La Police sous Louis XIV*. Paris: Didier, 1866.

A Collection of all the Treaties of Peace, Alliance, and Commerce, between Great Britain and Other Powers, From the Treaty Signed at Munster in 1648, to the Treaties signed at Paris in 1783. Volume 1. London: J. Debrett, 1785.

Collins, James. *The State in Early Modern France*. Second edition. Cambridge: Cambridge University Press, 2009.

Coombs, Douglas S. "The Augmentation of 1709: A Study in the Workings of the Anglo-Dutch Alliance." *The English Historical Review* 72, no. 285 (1957): 642–661.

Cornette, Joel. *Le roi de guerre: Essai sur la souveraineté dans la France du Grand Siècle*. Paris: Payot, 1993.

Corvisier, André. *L'armee francaise de la fin du XVIIe siècle au ministère de Choiseul. Le Soldat*. 2 volumes. Paris: Presses Universitaires de France, 1964.

———. *Armies and Societies in Europe, 1494–1789*. Translated by Abigail T. Siddall. Bloomington: University of Indiana Press, 1979.

———. *Louvois*. Paris: Fayard, 1983.

———. "La morale des combattants panique et enthousiasme: Malplaquet 11 septembre 1709." In *Les hommes, la guerre et la mort*, edited by André Corvisier, 289–314. Paris: Economica, 1985.

———. *La bataille de Malplaquet. L'effondrement de la France évité*. Second edition. Paris: Economica, 2013.

Cra'ster, H. H. E., ed. "Letters of the First Lord Orkney During Marlborough's Campaigns." *The English Historical Review* 19 (1904): 307–321.

Cruickshanks, Eveline. *The Glorious Revolution*. New York: St. Martin's, 2000.

Dahlgren, Erik W. *Les relations commerciales et maritimes entre la France et les côtes de l'Océan Pacifique (commencement du XVIIIe siècle)*. Paris: Honoré Champion, 1909.

Dangeau, Philippe de Courcillon, marquis de. *Journal du marquis de Dangeau avec les additions inédite du duc de Saint-Simon*. Edited by E. Soulié and L. Dussieux. Volume 12. Paris: Fermin Didot, 1857.

Da Vinha, Matthieu. *Les valets de chambre de Louis XIV*. Paris: Perrin, 2004.

Deane, John Marshall. *John Marshall Deane: A Journal of Marlborough's Campaigns during the War of the Spanish Succession 1704–1711*. Edited by David Chandler. London: Society for Army Historical Research, 1984.

Dee, Darryl. *Expansion and Crisis in Louis XIV's France*. Rochester: University of Rochester Press, 2009.

———. "The Survival of France: Logistics, Strategy and the Flanders Campaign of 1709." *Journal of Military History* 84/4 (October 2020): 1021–1050.

Dessert, Daniel. *Argent, pouvoir et société au Grand Siècle*. Paris: Fayard, 1984.

Doyle, William. *Venality: The Sale of Offices in Eighteenth-Century France*. Oxford: Oxford University Press, 1996.

Drake, Peter. *Amiable Renegade: The Memoirs of Capt. Peter Drake 1671–1753*. Stanford: Stanford University Press, 1960.

Drévillon, Hervé. *L'impot du sang: Le métier des arms sous Louis XIV*. Paris: Tallandier, 2005.

———. *Les rois absolus*. Paris: Belin 2011.

Drévillon, Hervé, Bertrand Fonck, and Jean-Philippe Cénat, eds. *Les dernières guerres de Louis XIV, 1698–1715*. Rennes: Presses universitaires de Rennes, 2017.

Duffy, Christopher. *The Fortress in the Age of Vauban and Frederick the Great*. London: Routledge and Kegan Paul, 1979.

———. *Fire and Stone: The Science of Fortress Warfare, 1660–1860*. London: Greenhill Books, 1996.

El Hage, Fadi. *Le maréchal de Villars: L'infatigable bonheur*. Paris: Belin, 2012.

———. "À propos d'une relation de la bataille de Malplaquet (1709) comme source de *L'histoire militaire du règne de Louis le grand* du Marquis de Quincy (1726)." *Revue du Nord* 395, no. 2 (2012): 457–471.

———. "Qui est l'auteur du 'Traité de la Guerre de Campagne' conservé à la Bibliothèque Nationale de France." *Annuaire—Bulletin de la Société de l'histoire de France* (2012–2013): 201–212.

Feldzüge des Prinzen Eugen von Savoyen. Spanischer Successions-Krieg. Feldzug 1709. Volume 11. Vienna: Verlag des K.K. Generalstabes, 1886.

Fénelon, François de Salignac de La Mothe. *Correspondance de Fénelon.* Edited by Jean Orcibal. Book 14, *Guerre, négociations, théologie 1708–1711.* Geneva: Droz, 1992.

Ferguson, James, ed. *Papers Illustrating the History of the Scots Brigade in the Service of the United Netherlands 1572–1782.* Volume 2, *1698–1782.* Edinburgh: University of Edinburgh Press, 1899.

Fonck, Bertrand. *Le maréchal général de Luxembourg et le commandement des armées sous Louis XIV.* Paris: Champ Vallon, 2014.

Fonck, Bertrand, and Nathalie Genet-Rouffiac. *Combattre et gouverner. Dynamiques de l'historie militaire de l'epoque moderne (XVIIe–XVIIIe siècles).* Rennes: Presses universitaires de Rennes, 2015.

Forster, Elborg, ed. *A Woman's Life in the Court of the Sun King: The Letters of Liselotte Von Der Pfalz 1652–1722.* Baltimore: The Johns Hopkins University Press, 1984.

Francis, Alan David. *The First Peninsular War 1702–1713.* London: Routledge, 1975.

Garnier, Emmanuel. *Les Dérangements du Temps. 500 ans de chaud et de froid en Europe.* Paris: Plon, 2010.

Geikie, Roderick, and Isabel A. Montgomery. *The Dutch Barrier 1705–1719.* New York: Greenwood, 1968.

Genet-Rouffiac, Nathalie. *Le Grand Exil: Les Jacobites en France 1688–1715.* Paris: Service historique de la Défense, 2007.

Girard, Georges. *Le service militaire en France à la fin du règne de Louis XIV: racolage et milice (1701–1715).* Paris: Plon, 1921.

———, ed. "Un soldat de Malplaquet: Lettres du capitaine de Saint-Mayme." In *Carnets de la Sabretache. Revue militaire retrospective,* troisième série. Paris: La Sabretache, 1922.

Girardot, Auguste Théodore Baron de, ed. *Correspondance de Louis XIV à M. Amelot son ambassadeur en Espagne 1705–1709.* Volume 2. Nantes: Merson, 1864.

Glete, Jan. *War and the State in Early Modern Europe: Spain, the Dutch Republic and Sweden as Fiscal-Military States, 1500–1660.* New York: Routledge, 2002.

Goslinga, Sicco van. *Mémoires relatifs à la Guerre de Succession d'Espagne de 1706–1709 et 1711.* Edited by U. A. Everetsz and G. H. M. Delprat. Leeuwarden: G. T. N. Suringar, 1857.

Gregg, Edward. *Queen Anne.* London: Routledge and Kegan Paul, 1980.

Guerre, Stéphane. *Nicolas Desmaretz. Le Colbert oublié du Roi-Soleil.* Paris: Champ Vallon, 2019.

Guignard, Pierre-Claude de. *L'école de Mars ou Mémoires instructifs sur toutes les parties qui composent le corps militaire en France.* Book 1. Paris: Simart, 1725.

Harris, Frances. *A Passion for Government: The Life of Sarah Duchess of Marlborough.* Oxford: Clarendon Press, 1991.

———. *The General in Winter: The Marlborough-Godolphin Friendship and the Reign of Queen Anne.* Oxford: Oxford University Press, 2017.

Harris, Tim. *Revolution: The Great Crisis of the British Monarchy 1685–1720.* London and New York: Allen Lane, 2006.

Hattendorf, John. *England in the War of the Spanish Succession: A Study of the English View and Conduct of Grand Strategy 1702–1712.* New York: Garland, 1987.

Henderson, Nicholas. *Prince Eugene of Savoy*. New York: Frederick Praeger, 1964.
Hill, B. W. "Oxford, Bolingbroke, and the Peace of Utrecht." *The Historical Journal* 16, no. 2 (1973): 241–263.
Hochdilinger, Michael. *Austria's Wars of National Emergence 1683–1797*. New York and London: Longman, 2003.
Holmes, Richard. *Marlborough: England's Fragile Genius*. New York: HarperCollins, 2008.
Hoppit, Julian. *A Land of Liberty? England, 1689–1727*. Oxford: Oxford University Press, 2000.
_____. "Party Politics and War Weariness in the Reign of Queen Anne." In *Britain, Spain, and the Treaty of Utrecht 1713–2013*, edited by Trevor J. Dadson and J. H. Elliot, 9–17. London: Legenda, 2014.
Houlding, J. A. *Fit for Service: The Training of the British Army 1715–1795*. Oxford: Clarendon Press, 1981.
Ingrao, Charles. *In Quest and Crisis: Emperor Joseph I and the Habsburg Monarchy*. West Lafayette: Purdue University Press, 1979.
Israel, Jonathan. *The Dutch Republic: Its Rise, Greatness, and Fall, 1477–1806*. Oxford: Clarendon Press, 1995.
Jones, J. R. *Marlborough*. Cambridge: Cambridge University Press, 1993.
Jongste, Jan A. F. de and Augustus J. Veenendaal Jr., eds. *Anthonie Heinsius and the Dutch Republic 1688–1720: Politics, War, and Finance*. The Hague: Institute of Netherlands History, 2002.
Kamen, Henry. *The War of Succession in Spain 1700–1715*. Bloomington: Indiana University Press, 1969.
_____. *Philip V of Spain: The King Who Reigned Twice*. New Haven: Yale University Press, 2001.
Karges, Caleb. "'So Perverse an Ally': Great Britain's Alliance with Austria in the War of the Spanish Succession." PhD diss., University of Saint Andrews, 2015.
Klaits, Joseph. *Printed Propaganda under Louis XIV*. Princeton: Princeton University Press, 1976.
Lachiver, Marcel. *Les années de misère: La famine au temps du Grand Roi*. Paris: Fayard, 1991.
La Colonie, Jean-Baptiste de. *The Chronicles of an Old Campaigner: M. de La Colonie 1692–1717*. Translated by Walter C. Horsley. London: John Murray, 1904.
Legrelle, Arsène. *La diplomatie française et la succession d'Espagne*. Volume 4, *La Solution (1700–1725)*. Paris: Cotillon, 1892.
_____. *Une negotiation inconnue entre Berwick et Marlborough, 1708–1709*. Paris: Cotillon, 1893.
Le Mao, Caroline. *Chronique du Bordelais au crepuscule du Grand Siècle: Le Mémorial de Savignac*. Bordeaux: Presses Universitaires de Bordeaux, 2004.
Lenihan, Pádraig. "Namur Citadel, 1695: A Case Study in Allied Siege Tactics." *War in History* 18, no. 3 (2011): 299–399.
Lesage, Gérard. *Denain (1712). Louis XIV sauve sa mise*. Paris: Economica, 1999.
The Life and Adventures of Christian Davies, Commonly called Mother Ross. London, 1741.
Lossky, Andrew. *Louis XIV and the French Monarchy*. New Brunswick: Rutgers University Press, 1994.

Lüthy, Herbert. *La banque protestante de la Révocation de l'édit de Nantes à la Révolution*. 2 volumes. Paris: SEVPEN, 1959–1960.
Lynn, John A. "The *trace italienne* and the Growth of Armies: The French Case." *Journal of Military History* 55, no. 3 (1991): 297–330.
_____. "Food, Funds, and Fortresses: Resource Mobilization and Positional Warfare in the Wars of Louis XIV." In *Feeding Mars: Logistics in Western Warfare from the Middle Ages to the Present*, edited by John A. Lynn, 137–160. Boulder: Westview, 1993.
_____. *Giant of the Grand Siècle: The French Army, 1610–1715*. Cambridge: Cambridge University Press, 1997.
———. *Wars of Louis XIV*. London: Routledge, 1999.
MacNeil, William H. *The Pursuit of Power: Technology Armed Force and Society since AD 1000*. Chicago: University of Chicago Press, 1982.
_____. *Keeping Together in Time: Dance and Drill in Human History*. Cambridge, MA: Harvard University Press, 1995.
Maintenon, Françoise d'Aubigné, marquise de. *Lettres à Madame de Maintenon*. Book 9, *1706–1709*. Edited by Hans Bots, Eugénie Bots-Estourgie, and Catherine Hémon-Fabre. Paris: Honoré Champion, 2009.
_____. *Lettres de Madame de Maintenon*. Book 4, *1707–1710*. Edited by Marcel Loyau. Paris: Honoré Champion, 2011.
Manning, Roger B. *An Apprenticeship in Arms: The Origins of the British Army, 1585–1702*. Oxford: Oxford University Press, 2006.
Mansel, Philip. *King of the World: The Life of Louis XIV*. Chicago: University of Chicago Press, 2019.
Marlborough, John Churchill, Duke of. *Letters and Dispatches of John Churchill First Duke of Marlborough from 1702 to 1712*. Edited by George Murray. Volume 4. London: John Murray, 1845.
_____. *The Correspondence 1701–1711 of John Churchill First Duke of Marlborough and Anthonie Heinsius Grand Pensionary of Holland*. Edited by Bert van 't Hoff. The Hague: M. Nijhoff, 1951.
McCollim, Gary. *Louis XIV's Assault on Privilege: Nicolas Desmaretz and the Tax on Wealth*. Rochester: University of Rochester Press, 2012.
McDowell, Simon. *Malplaquet 1709: Marlborough's Bloodiest Battle*. Oxford: Osprey, 2020.
McKay, Derek. *Prince Eugene of Savoy*. London: Thames and Hudson, 1977.
Mémoires de Louis XIV pour l'instruction du Dauphin. Edited by Charles Dreyss. Volume 2. Paris: Didier et Compagnie, 1860.
Monahan, W. Gregory. *Year of Sorrows: The Great Famine of 1709 in Lyon*. Columbus: The Ohio State University Press, 1993.
_____. *Let God Arise: The War and Rebellion of the Camisards*. Oxford: Oxford University Press, 2014.
The New Cambridge Modern History. Volume 6, *The Rise of Great Britain and Russia*. Edited by J. S. Bromley. Cambridge: Cambridge University Press, 1970.
Nicolas, Jean. *La Rébellion française. Mouvements populaires et conscience sociale (1661–1789)*. Paris: Seuil, 2002.
Nimwegen, Olaf van. *De subsistentie van het leger: logistiek en strategie van het Geallieerde en met name het Staatse leger tijdens de Spaanse Successieoorlog in de

Nederlanden en het Heilige Roomse Rijk (1701–1712). Amsterdam: De Bataafsche Leeuw 1995.

———. *The Dutch Army and the Military Revolutions*. Translated by Andrew May. Woodbridge: Boydell, 2010.

Nodot, François. *Le Munitionnaire des armées de France*. Paris: Imprimerie Royale, 1697.

Nosworthy, Brent. *The Anatomy of Victory: Battle Tactics 1689–1763*. New York: Hippocrene Books, 1990.

O'Malley, C. D. "The Medical History of Louis XIV: Intimations of Mortality." In *Louis XIV and the Craft of Kingship*, edited by John C. Rule, 132–154. Columbus: Ohio State University Press, 1969.

Ordonnances militaires du roi de France, reduites en pratique, et appliquées au detail du service. Ouvrage trés utile à tous les Gens de Guerre. Il contient l'explication des fonctions mlitaires, et un abregé des XV tomes d'ordonnances du roi, disposées, selon l'ordre des matières (Paris: André Chevalier, 1728).

Ostwald, Jamel. "The 'Decisive' Battle of Ramillies, 1706: Prerequisites for Decisiveness in Early Modern Warfare." *Journal of Military History* 64 (July 2000): 649–677.

———. *Vauban Under Siege: Engineering Efficiency and Martial Vigor in the War of the Spanish Succession*. Leiden: Brill, 2007.

Oury, Clément. "Les défaites françaises de la guerre de Succession d'Espagne, 1704–1708." PhD. diss., Université Paris-Sorbonne, 2011.

———. *La Guerre de Succession d'Espagne: La fin tragique du Grand Siècle*. Paris: Tallandier, 2020.

———. *Le Duc de Marlborough: John Churchill le plus redoutable ennemi de Louis XIV*. Paris: Perrin, 2022.

Oxford Dictionary of National Biography. Accessed July 2023. www.oxforddnb.com.

Pain, Stephanie. "The year that Europe Froze Solid." *New Scientist* 201, no. 2694 (February 2009): 46–47.

Paoletti, Ciro. "Prince Eugene of Savoy, the Toulon Expedition of 1707, and the English Historians—A Dissenting View." *Journal of Military History* 70, no. 4 (2006): 939–962.

Parker, Geoffrey. *The Military Revolution: Military Innovation and the Rise of the West*. Cambridge: Cambridge University Press, 1996.

Parrott, David. *Richelieu's Army: War, Government, and Society in France, 1624–1642*. Cambridge: Cambridge University Press, 2001.

———. *The Business of War: Military Enterprise and Military Revolution in Early Modern Europe*. Cambridge: Cambridge University Press, 2012.

Pénicaut, Emmanuel. *Faveur et pouvoir au tournant du Grand Siècle. Michel Chamillart Ministre et secretaire d'État de la guerre de Louis XIV*. Paris: École des Chartres, 2004.

Perjes, Geza. "Army Provisioning, Logistics, and Strategy in the Second Half of the Seventeenth Century." *Acta Academiae Scientiarum Hungarica* 16 (1970): 1–52.

Petitifils, Jean-Christian. *Le Régent*. Paris: Fayard, 1986.

Pincus, Steven. *1688: The First Modern Revolution*. London and New Haven: Yale University Press, 2009.

Plax, Julie-Anne. "The Meaning of War in Watteau's Recruë Allant Joindre Le Régiment." *Source: Notes in the History of Art* 16, no. 3 (Spring 1997): 17–23.
Praak, Maarten. *The Dutch Republic in the Seventeenth Century: The Golden Age.* Cambridge: Cambridge University Press, 2015.
Quincy, Joseph Sevin de. *Mémoires du Chevalier de Quincy.* Volume 2. Paris: Leon Lecestre, 1899.
Recueil des instructions données aux ambassadeurs et ministers de France: depuis les traités de Westphalie jusqu'à la Révolution française. XXI–XXII, Hollande. Edited by Emile Bourgeois. Book 2. Paris: Fontemoing, 1922.
Roumegou, Lenaig. "L'ordre du Saint-Esprit sous Louis XIV: un instrument au service du pouvoir (1643–1715)." Thesis, École nationale des chartes, 2017.
Rousset, Camille. *Histoire de Louvois.* 4 volumes. Paris: Didier, 1862.
Rowlands, Guy. "Louis XIV, Aristocratic Power, and the Elite Units of the French Army." *French History* 13, no. 3 (1999): 303–331.
_____. *The Dynastic State and the Army under Louis XIV: Royal Service and Private Interest, 1661–1701.* Cambridge: Cambridge University Press, 2002.
_____. "Moving Mars: The Logistical Geography of Louis XIV's France." *French History* 25, no. 4 (2011): 492–514.
———. *The Financial Decline of a Great Power: War, Influence and Money in Louis XIV's France.* Oxford: Oxford University Press, 2012.
———. *Dangerous and Dishonest Men: The International Bankers of Louis XIV's France.* London: Palgrave, 2015.
_____. "Royal Finances in the Third Reign of Louis XIV." In *The Third Reign of Louis XIV, c. 1682–1715,* edited by Julia Prest and Guy Rowlands, 38–52. London: Routledge, 2017.
_____. "Keep Right on to the End of the Road: The Stamina of the French Army during the War of the Spanish Succession." In *The War of the Spanish Succession: New Perspectives,* edited by Matthias Polig and Michael Schaich, 324–341 (Oxford: Oxford University Press, 2018).
Rule, John C. "King and Minister: Louis XIV and Colbert de Torcy." In *William III and Louis XIV: Essays 1680–1720 by and for Mark A. Thompson,* edited by Ragnhild Hatton and J. S. Bromley, 213–236. Liverpool: Liverpool University Press, 1968.
_____. "France and the Preliminaries to the Gertruydenberg Conference, September 1709 to March 1710." In *Studies in Diplomatic History: Essays in Memory of David Bayne Horn,* edited by Ragnhild Hatton and M. S. Anderson, 97–115. London: Longman, 1970.
Rule, John C., and Ben S. Trotter. *A World of Paper: Louis XIV, Colbert de Torcy, and the Rise of the Information State.* Montreal and Toronto: McGill-Queens University Press, 2014.
Saint-Germain, Jacques. *Samuel Bernard. Le banquier des rois.* Paris: Hachette, 1960.
Saint-Simon, Louis de Roucroy, duc de. *Mémoires complets et authentiques du duc de Saint- Simon sur le siècle de Louis XIV et la Régence.* Edited by Adolphe Chéruel. Twenty volumes. Paris: Hachette, 1856.
Sarmant, Thierry, ed. *Les Ministres de la guerre 1570–1792.* Paris: Belin, 2007.
_____. *Louis XIV. Homme et roi.* Paris: Tallandier, 2012.
Sarmant, Thierry, and Pierre Waksman. "The King and His Generals: the Military Correspondence of Louis XIV in 1696." *French History* 22, no. 2 (2008): 156–174.

Satterfield, George. *Princes, Posts, and Partisans: the Army of Louis XIV and Partisan Warfare in the Netherlands, 1673–1678*. Leiden: Brill, 2003.

Sautai, Maurice. *Le siege de la ville et de la citadelle de Lille en 1708*. Lille: Lefebvre-Ducrocq, 1899.

_____. *La Bataille de Malplaquet. D'après les correspondants du Duc du Maine à l'Armée de Flandre*. Paris: R. Chapelot, 1904.

Schama, Simon. *An Embarrassment of Riches: An Interpretation of Dutch Culture in the Golden Age*. New York: Knopf, 1987.

Schulenburg, Johann Matthias von der. *Leben und Denkwürdigkeiten Johann Mathias Reichsgrafen von der Schulenburg, Erbherrn auf Emden und Delitz, Feldmarschalls in Diensten der Republik Venedig: Aus Original-Quellen bearbeitet*. Volume 1. Leipzig: Weidmann, 1834.

Scouller, R. E. *The Armies of Queen Anne*. Oxford: Clarendon Press, 1966.

Snyder, Henry L. "The Duke of Marlborough's Request of His Captain-Generalcy for Life: A Re-examination." *Journal of the Society for Army Historical Research* 45, no. 182 (1967): 67–83.

_____, ed. *The Marlborough-Godolphin Correspondence*. Volume 2. Oxford: Clarendon Press, 1975.

Solnon, Jean-François. *La Cour de France*. Paris: Perrin, 2014.

Sourches, Louis François du, marquis de. *Mémoires du marquis de Sourches sur le règne de Louis XIV*. Edited by G. Cosnac and E. Pontal. Volume 11. Paris: Hachette, 1891.

Stansfield, Stewart. *Early Modern Systems of Command: Queen Anne's Generals, Staff Officers, and the Direction of Allied Warfare in the Low Countries and Germany*. Solihull: Helion and Company, 2015.

Stapleton, John. "Forging a Coalition Army: William III, the Grand Alliance, and the Confederate Army in the Spanish Netherlands 1688–1697." PhD diss., The Ohio State University, 2003.

Stork-Penning, J. G. "The Ordeal of the States: Some Remarks on Dutch Politics during the War of the Spanish Succession." *Acta Historiae Neerlandica* 2 (1967): 107–141.

Sturgill, Claude C. *Marshal Villars and the War of the Spanish Succession*. Lexington: University of Kentucky Press, 1965.

Sundstrom, Roy A. *Sidney Godolphin, Servant of the State*. Newark: University of Delaware Press, 1992.

Taté, Jean. *Chronique de Jean Taté greffier de l'hôtel-de-ville de Château-Porcien (1677–1748)*. Edited by Henri Jadart. Arcis-sur-Aube: L. Frémont, 1890.

Taylor, Frank. *The Wars of Marlborough 1702–1709*. 2 volumes. Oxford: Blackwell, 1921.

Torcy, Jean-Baptiste Colbert, marquis de. *Mémoires du marquis de Torcy pour server à l'histoire des négociations depuis le traité de Riswick jusqu'à la paix d'Utrecht*. Volumes 62 and 63 in *Collection des mémoires relatifs à l'histoire de France*. Edited by A. Petitot and L. Monmerque. Paris: Foucault, 1828.

_____. *Journal inédit de Jean-Baptiste Colbert Marquis de Torcy ministre et secrétaire d'état des affaires étrangéres pendant les années 1709, 1710 et 1711*. Edited by Frédéric Masson. Paris: Librairie Plon, 1881.

Trevelyan, G. M. "The 'Jersey' Period of the Negotiations Leading to the Peace of Utrecht." *The English Historical Review* 49 (January 1934): 100–105.

Vauban, Sébastien Le Prestre, marquis et maréchal de. *Vauban. Sa famille et ses écrits, ses "Oisivetés" et sa Correspondance.* Edited by Eugène Auguste Albert de Rochas d'Aiglun. Book 1. Paris: Berger-Levrault, 1910.

Vault, François-Eugene, and Jean-Jacques-Germain Pelet, eds. *Mémoires militaires relatifs à la Succession d'Espagne: extraits de la correspondance de la cour et des généraux.* Volume 9. Paris: Imprimerie Impériale, 1855.

Villars, Claude Louis-Hector, duc et maréchal de. *Mémoires du maréchal de Villars publiés d'après le manuscript original, pour la Société de l'histoire de France, et accompagnés de correspondances inédites.* Edited by Melchior de Vogüé. 6 volumes. Paris: Renouard, 1884–1904.

Vogüé, Melchior de. *Madame de Maintenon et le Maréchal de Villars. Correspondence inédite.* Paris: Jules Gervais, 1881.

Walton, Guy. *Louis XIV's Versailles.* Chicago: University of Chicago Press, 1986.

Whitman, James Q. *The Verdict of Battle: the Law of Victory and the Making of Modern War.* Cambridge, MA: Harvard University Press, 2012.

Wijn, Jan Willem. "Les troupes hollandaises à la bataille de Malplaquet." *Revue Internationale d'Histoire Militaire* 19 (1957): 344–371.

_____. *Het Staatsche Leger.* Part VIII. *Het Tijdperk van de Spaanse Successieoorlog 1702–1715.* Book II. *De Veldtochten Van 1706–1710.* The Hague: Martinus Nijhoff, 1959.

Wile, Aaron. *Watteau's Soldiers: Scenes of Military Life in Eighteenth-Century France.* New York: The Frick Collection, 2016.

Wilson, John. "The Journal of John Wilson an 'Old Flanderkin Serjeant' of the 15th Regiment and Later of the 2nd Troop of Life Guards who served 1694–1727." In *Military Miscellany II: Manuscripts from Marlborough's Wars, the American War of Independence, and the Boer War,* edited by David G. Chandler, Christopher L. Scott, Marianne M. Gilchrist, and Robin Jenkins. Gloucestershire: Society for Army Historical Research, 2005.

Wilson, Peter. *German Armies: War and German Society 1648–1806.* London: Routledge, 1998.

Wolf, John B. *Louis XIV.* New York: Norton, 1968.

Ziegler, François. *Villars. Le centurion de Louis XIV.* Paris: Perrin, 1996.

Index

Abbeville, 83, 143
Aguesseau, Henri d', 81
Aire, 36, 50, 84, 158, 159, 225, 224
Albemarle, Arnold Joost van Keppel, Earl of, 113, 136
Albergotti, Francois Zénobie Philippe, Comte d', 133, 174, 176, 182, 183, 184, 186, 194, 195, 197, 224
Alègre, Yves, Marquis d', 19–20, 112, 113
Almanza, battle of (1707), 24, 115
Alsace, 40, 69, 110, 113, 116
Amelot, Michel-Jean, 64, 152
Amsterdam, 4, 6, 17, 46, 86, 140
Anet, château of, 27, 53, 227
Angennes, Charles, Comte d', 190
Angoumois, 40
Anne, Queen of Great Britain, 19, 46, 86, 98, 99, 205, 228–29, 232
Annequin, 139
Antoing, 174
Antwerp, 4, 63, 86, 96, 204
Aragon, 212, 227

Argenson, Marc-René de Voyer, Marquis d', 162–63
Argyll, John Campbell, Duke of, 135–36, 189, 205
armies of the Allies: British army, 18–19, 72, 147; Confederate Army, 19, 23, 67, 133, 135, 141, 177, 207, 224; Danish army, 134, 135; Dutch States Army, 18–19, 72, 134, 136, 147, 184, 190, 191, 192, 198, 199; German auxiliaries and mercenaries, 67, 134, 135; Habsburg army, 18–19, 134–35; Imperial army, 55, 134–35, 141; logistics of, 140–41, 144, 222, 232; platoon firing, 72, 187, 190, 197, 199, 200; Swiss mercenaries, 134
Army of Flanders (French): campaign of 1709, 35, 37, 38, 51, 52, 57, 66, 82, 84, 102–6, 108, 109, 118, 125, 131–33, 138–40, 142, 145, 148, 150, 151, 159, 171, 172, 176, 177–78, 182, 194, 200, 201, 208–11; campaigns before 1709,

253

8, 22–24, 27, 28, 34, 47, 48; War of the Spanish Succession after 1709, 220, 221, 223, 224–25, 230, 233, 234, 235
Army of Germany (French), 53, 55–57
Arras, 36, 49, 50, 53, 102–5, 108, 138, 140, 148, 158–61, 172, 224, 225, 230, 231
Artois, 27, 35, 50, 52, 66, 67, 81–83, 104, 105, 122, 145, 207, 210
Asiento de negros, 17, 98, 230, 236
Ath, 38, 87
Austrian Habsburgs, 3, 9, 14, 15, 17, 18, 64, 85, 86, 97, 98, 100, 101, 110, 111, 115, 116, 134, 212, 213, 224, 228, 232, 235, 236; Hereditary Lands of, 6, 56, 134
Auvergne, François Egon de La Tour d'Auvergne, Prince d', 136, 177, 185, 200
Avesnes, 36

Barcelona, 13, 115, 228
Barrier (Dutch), 13, 17, 19, 21, 63, 85–88, 97, 98, 100, 110, 111, 114, 118, 173, 211, 235
Basville, Nicolas Lamoignon de, 81
Bavaria, 17, 19, 56, 57
Bavay, 176, 202, 204
Bay, Alexandre Maître, Marquis de, 64, 115
Beauce, 40
Beauvilliers, Paul de Beauvilliers, Duc de, 16, 89, 117, 118, 154
Benifontaine, 139
Bergeyck, Jean de Brouchoven, Comte de, 47, 63, 64, 207
Bergues, 36, 154, 226
Bernage, Louis de, 67, 78, 104–6, 108–9, 122, 148, 160, 209
Bernard, Samuel, 46–48, 77, 78, 106, 163, 221, 234
Bernières, Charles-Étienne Maignart de, 27, 63, 66, 106, 109, 145, 158
Berwick, James Fitz-James, Marshal, 24, 27, 53, 112, 113, 115, 210, 212, 224

Béthune, 36, 50, 84, 109, 118, 142, 158, 225
Blenheim, battle of (1704), 19, 72, 74, 76, 77, 99, 132, 135, 150, 172, 182, 201, 207
Bordeaux, 39, 40
Bouchain, 36, 151, 160, 161, 224, 231, 234, 235
Boufflers, Louis-Francois, Marshal, 12, 24, 27–28, 33–38, 49–53, 57, 103, 106–7, 108, 119–21, 145, 146, 162, 172, 182, 186, 192–94, 195, 199–202, 205, 208–11, 219–20, 224
Boulogne, 143, 224
Boulonnais, 84
Bourbon, house of, 3, 14, 15, 17, 22, 154, 225, 227, 228
Bourbon, Louise-Françoise de, 21
Bourgogne, Louis, Duc de, 21–24, 26, 52, 83, 89, 103, 117–19, 154, 233
Bourgogne, Marie-Adélaide de Savoie, Duchesse de, 27, 40, 103, 233
Brabant, 3, 4
Brändle, Jost, 192
Breisach, 13
brigades, French, 140; Bourbonnais, 182, 191; Brendlé, 182, 192; Bretagne, 160, 182, 188, 189, 194; Champagne, 161, 195–96; Charost, 182, 189; la Fere, 182; Gondrin, 182, 194; Guards (French and Swiss), 182; Guards of Bavaria and Cologne, 182, 195, 196; Irish, 140, 182, 195–96; Lannoy, 182, 192, 198; la Marine, 160; Navarre, 182; la Perche, 182, 191, 192, 193; Picardie, 174, 182, 192; Piémont, 182, 192, 198; Poitou, 182, 194; la Reine, 182, 197; le Roi, 140, 182, 188, 189, 197; Royal, 182, 192; la Sarre, 182, 189; Touraine, 182; Tourville, 182, 194
Brihuega, battle of (1710), 227
Brittany, 79, 81, 138, 148, 210
Bruges, 23, 27, 33
Brussels, 23, 53, 96, 145, 146, 204
Burgundy, 41
Buys, Willem, 86–88, 110, 221, 226

Cadogan, William, 135, 142, 144, 184, 186, 204
Calcinato, battle of (1706), 74
Cambrai, 36, 50, 122, 140, 204, 209, 224, 230, 231
Cambresis, 27, 207
Cambrin, 139, 158, 159, 161, 174
Camisards, 56
Campbell, James, 200
Campo Maior, battle of (1709), 115, 212
Cassano, battle of (1705), 22
Castan, Bertrand, 77, 78
Castano, Joshua, 141, 144
Castile, 64, 115, 212, 227
Catalonia, 115, 227
Catinat, Nicolas, Marshal, 55
Cavalier, Jean, 56
Ceberet, Claude, Marquis de, 193, 194
Ceva Grimaldi, Marcello, Marquis de, 209
Cevennes, 56
Chabert, Michel, 79, 223
Chamillart, Michel, 25–28, 37, 38, 43–52, 57, 65–67, 82, 83, 89, 103, 105, 108, 112, 119, 136
Chamlay, Jules-Louis Bolé, Marquis de, 5, 10, 11, 22, 145
Champagne, 83, 105, 233
Chanteloup-les-Vignes, vigneron of, 38, 80
Charlemont, 154, 226
Charleroi, 33, 87, 209, 211
Charles, Archduke, 15, 19–20, 85, 86, 97, 98, 101, 111, 226, 227, 228, 230, 231
Charles II, King of Spain, 4, 13, 16, 95, 118
Charles XII, King of Sweden, 136, 141
Charleville, 36
Chemerault, Jean-Noël de Barbesières, Comte de, 184, 197
Churchill, Arabella, 24, 112
Churchill, Sarah, Duchess of Marlborough, 19, 24, 99, 117, 120, 135, 177, 180, 201, 228
Churchill, Winston, 137, 193
Coehoorn, Menno van, 147

Colbert, Jean-Baptiste, 5, 43, 44, 95
Cologne, 17, 19, 34, 132
Condé, 36, 85, 86, 88, 148, 150, 151, 159–61, 173, 175, 210, 211, 234
contributions, 57, 83, 145, 159
Courtrai, 65, 84, 131, 133
Croissy, Charles Colbert, Marquis de, 95–96
Cuinchy, 84, 139

D'Artagnan, Pierre de Montesquiou, Comte, 133, 146, 147, 151, 176, 182, 184, 192, 199, 202, 206, 224, 234, 235
Dangeau, Philippe de Courcillon, Marquis de, 8, 40, 43–44, 107
Dangeau, Sophia von Löwenstein-Wertheim-Rochefort, Madame, 26
Dauphiné, 53, 69, 210, 212
Deane, John Marshall, 131, 196
Dedem, Coenraad Willem van, 174, 179
De la Colonie, Jean-François Martin, 125, 189, 196, 199
Denain, 151, 158, 159, 161, 174, 234; battle of (1712), 234–35
Dender, river, 23
Deshoulières, Guillaume de Lafon de Boisguérin, 145
Desmaretz, Nicolas, 27, 42, 43, 47, 48, 51, 67, 77–79, 81–83, 89, 103–6, 108, 109, 122, 154, 160, 163, 175, 204, 212–13, 220, 223, 237
Des Rocques, Guillaume, 147
Deûle, river, 140
Dinant, 36
Dopff, Daniel Wolf von, 142
Douai, 27, 28, 33, 36, 49, 65, 84, 104, 108, 110, 118, 139, 140, 142, 148, 154, 158–61, 173–75, 199, 224, 225, 226, 231, 235
Doujat, Jean-Charles, 106, 109, 176
Drake, Peter, 200, 204
Du Mée, Lucas, 147, 157
Dunkirk, 36, 37, 86, 111, 112, 224, 232, 233
Dutch Republic, 4, 10, 17, 18, 20–22, 46, 63, 85–87, 89, 96–100, 110, 112,

114–16, 118, 134, 136, 140, 141, 147, 204, 211, 213, 221, 223, 227, 228, 232, 235, 234; Council of State, 136, 137, 140, 141, 205; field deputies, 136–37, 143, 205; *stadtholder,* 6; States General, 17, 86, 87, 153, 213, 222, 233, 235; States Navy, 4

Dutch War (1672–1678), 4–6, 21, 53, 134, 136

Eckeren, battle of (1703), 34

Enghien, Louis Henri de Bourbon-Condé, Duc d', 21

English Channel, 35–37, 84, 138, 143, 222, 230

Estates of Artois, 109, 149

Estrées, Jean, Abbé d', 21

Eugene of Savoy, Prince, 54, 67, 96, 98, 103, 110, 118, 150, 161, 175, 176, 178, 200, 205, 206, 212, 237; character and career to 1709, 19, 20, 22–24, 27, 28, 100; conduct of campaign of 1709, 33, 38, 53, 134–35, 137, 142, 144, 147, 155, 157–58, 172–74, 208, 210–11; conduct of diplomacy and peace negotiations, 101, 113–16; generalship at Malplaquet, 177, 179, 184, 186–87, 189, 195, 197–98, 202, 206–7; War of the Spanish Succession after 1709, 220, 222, 224–25, 231, 233–36

Fagel, François Nicolas, Baron, 136, 147, 155, 190, 191

Fagon, Guy, 6

famine of 1693–1694, 11–12, 42

famine of 1709, 42–43, 52, 80–82, 162, 163, 236; "miracle of the barley", 81, 161, 237

Fargès, François-Marie, 52, 65, 105–6, 108, 148, 161

Fénelon, François, Archbishop of Cambrai, 22, 83

Flanders, 3, 4, 6, 8, 9, 11, 20, 22, 25–27, 33–37, 50, 52, 53, 57, 65, 67, 69, 82, 83, 87, 103, 104, 106, 108, 110, 113–16, 118, 120, 122, 138, 152, 160, 172, 175, 204, 209, 219, 220

Fleurus, battle of (1690), 11

Foix, 69

Folard, Jean-Charles, Chevalier de, 187–88

Fontainebleau, château of, 16

Fort Knocke, 36

Fouquet, Nicolas, 57

France, army, 5, 11, 18, 35l; artillery, 37, 76–77; battalions, organization of, 71; cavalry, 35, 74–76, 107; companies, organization of, 69, 71; dragoons, 35, 76, 107; drill, 69–71, 124; foreign troops, 132; honor of officers and soldiers, 122–25, 207–8; infantry, 35, 69–74, 107; Maison du Roi, 69, 74, 76, 105, 109, 132, 174, 182, 187, 192, 194, 200, 200–201; officers, 106–8, 122–23; regiments, organization of, 69, 71; size, 5, 11, 18; social origins of soldiers, 69, 123; squadrons, organization of, 75; tactics, 71–75, 77; uniforms, 35, 68, 124; *ustencile* (officers' supplementary allowance), 50; *vieux corps* and *petits vieux corps,* 69, 109, 132; wages of troops, 49–51; weapons, 70, 71, 73, 75, 76

France, finances, 12, 18, 22, 26, 44, 234, 235; bankers, 46–48; bills of exchange, 46–48, 78; borrowing and credit, 12, 46, 78, 79, 163; Caisse Legendre, 212, 223; *capitation* (tax), 12, 43, 44; debt, 12, 18, 46, 48, 79; *dixième* (tax), 223; *Extraordinaire des Guerres* (Royal Military Treasury), 46–51, 66, 106, 108; *gabelle* (tax), 44; General Farm, 44; indirect taxes, 44; mint bills, 45–46, 48, 77–80; mints, 79, 80, 108, 161; money, 45, 49, 50, 79–80; reformation of the currency, 45, 79; reminting of the currency, 79, 80, 108, 160, 163; *rentes* (bonds), 45; *taille* (tax), 44; venal officeholding, 45; War Bills, 46, 50

Index 257

France, government: *Conseil d'en haut* (Council of ministers), 16, 25, 27, 89, 96, 117, 154, 212, 219, 220, 221; intendants, provincial, 26, 42, 52, 66, 81, 83, 84, 103, 104, 209; *liasse* meetings, 25, 28, 103, 117, 219
France, navy, 11, 209
Franche-Comté, 6, 69, 101, 104, 111
Freiburg, 13, 235
Friedlingen, battle of (1702), 55
Furnes, 36, 86–88, 97, 110, 211, 236

Garonne, river, 40
Gaultier, François, Abbé, 229–30
Geneva, 48, 78, 79, 164
Germany, 10, 18, 19, 55–57, 76, 104, 113, 141, 150
Gertruydenberg, 221, 222, 226, 227, 234
Ghent, 23, 24, 27, 28, 33, 131, 133, 142, 148, 211
Ghlin, 210
Givet, 37
Glorious Revolution (1688), 10, 17, 132
Godolphin, Sidney, 98, 119, 142, 143, 157, 228
Goësbriand, Louis-Vincent, Marquis de, 133, 182, 186, 188, 190, 194, 225
Goslinga, Sicco van, 137, 144, 184, 192, 205
Grand Alliance (Nine Years' War), 10, 11
Grand Alliance (War of the Spanish Succession), 17, 63, 85, 95, 97, 98, 100, 114, 207, 211, 213, 220, 226, 229, 230, 235, 237; treaty of The Hague (1701), 17, 97
Gravelines, 36
Great Britain, 4, 10, 17, 18, 46, 86, 87, 97–100, 110, 111, 113–16, 120, 140, 141, 205, 211, 213, 227, 228–30, 237; Bank of England, 46; Parliament, 16, 97, 205, 226, 227; Protestant Succession, 87, 88, 97, 111, 210, 230; Royal Navy, 138, 143; Tories, 99, 204, 224, 227, 228, 231; Whigs, 97–99, 205, 211, 227, 228, 230

Great Winter of 1709, 38–42, 80, 101, 138, 163, 236
Guiche, Antoine de Gramont, Duc de, 133, 182, 198
Guinea Company (France), 17, 236

Hainault, 3, 4, 35, 82, 83, 104, 146, 207
Haine, river, 162, 174, 175
Hamilton, George, 191
Harcourt, Henri d', Marshal, 53, 103, 119, 138, 212, 225, 231
Harley, Robert, 99, 228–30, 232
Hautefort, François-Marie, Marquis de, 199
Havré, 175
Heinsius, Anthonie, 64, 88, 89, 96, 98, 99–100, 113–16, 119, 152–55, 158, 211–13, 220–21, 226, 230, 231–32, 237
Hélesmes, 151
Henry IV, King of France, 5, 22
Hepburn, James, 192
Hesse-Kassel, Frederick, Hereditary Prince of, 136, 174–75, 183, 184, 190, 200, 202
Heurtebise, 5, 6
Hogguer, Antoine, 164, 223
Hogneau, river, 175, 176, 202, 209
Holland, 5, 46
Holy Roman Empire, 6, 10, 18, 55, 86, 87, 101, 110, 111, 113, 235
Hooft, Willem, 137
Huguenots, 9, 46, 47, 56, 147, 157
Hulluch, 84, 139, 159
Hungary, 10, 18, 54, 135, 231
Huxelles, Nicolas du Blé, Marshal, 221, 225, 226, 227

Ile-de-France, 27, 40
Italy, 17, 18, 98, 101, 112, 113, 134, 150, 224, 231

Jacobites, 10, 17, 74
James II, King of Great Britain, 10, 17, 24
James III, Stuart Pretender. *See* Saint-Georges, Chevalier de

Jersey, Edward Villiers, Earl of, 227
Joseph Clemens, Archbishop of Cologne, 17–18, 84, 101
Joseph Ferdinand, Electoral Prince of Bavaria, 15
Joseph I, Holy Roman Emperor, 97, 98, 101, 114, 230
Jülich, 148

La Bassée, 52, 84, 109, 131, 138, 142, 144, 160; lines of, 52, 67, 85, 139, 144–46, 158, 159, 161, 222
La Cour, François Mauricet de, 52, 66, 103, 148
La Feuillade, Louis d'Aubusson, Duc de, 20
La Frézelière, Francois-Frézeau, Marquis de, 133, 182, 183, 191, 193, 194, 199
La Mothe-Houdancourt, Charles, Comte de, 33, 72
Landau, 13, 55, 235
Landrecies, 36, 230, 233, 234–35
Lannoy, château of, 65
La Reynie, Nicolas de, 12
La Trouille, stream, 162, 174, 175
Le Blanc, Claude, 106, 109, 146
Le Brun, Charles, 14, 102
Lens, 109, 145, 158
Leopold I, Holy Roman Emperor, 5, 6, 10, 14, 15, 17, 18, 19
Le Quesnoy, 36, 49, 50, 175, 202, 204, 206, 208, 209, 210, 220, 230, 231, 233, 234, 235
Lessines, 23
Leuze, battle of (1691), 11
Liège, 34, 148, 161
Lille, 4, 9, 23, 24, 27, 28, 36–39, 51, 52, 65–67, 84, 85, 88, 110, 111, 131, 140, 142, 143, 146, 159, 174, 211, 222, 223; siege of 1708, 24, 27, 34, 53, 63, 112, 133, 143, 145, 150
Limburg, 4
Lisbon, 97
logistics, French, 18, 37–38, 65, 85, 103, 148, 221; bread rations (*pain de munition*), 37, 51, 118, 138, 139, 149, 176, 209; fodder, 35, 37, 65, 108, 109, 138; grain supplies, 35, 37, 51, 52, 66, 104, 105, 138, 148, 208, 209; magazines, 35, 37, 51, 52, 65, 82, 103, 105, 138, 148, 158, 159, 208, 209, 220; mills and milling, 51, 105, 138, 139, 149; *munitionnaires* (French provisioners), 51, 52, 66, 82, 83, 103, 105–6, 138–39, 210, 223; supply trains (*equipage des vivres*), 51, 138–39, 149, 208, 209
Loire, river, 40
London, 17, 86, 229, 230
London Preliminaries (Seven Articles), 229–30, 231, 232
Lorraine, 83, 101, 105
Lottum, Carl Philipp, Graf von Wylich und, 136, 147, 155, 157, 186, 189–90, 194, 197, 198
Louis, Grand Dauphin, 15, 16, 21, 22, 40, 82, 89, 103, 117–19, 152, 229, 236
Louis XIII, King of France, 3
Louis XIV, King of France, *passim*; appeal of June 12, 120–22, 207, 238; appearance and health, 7, 111; *gloire*, attitude to, 3, 6, 8, 89, 220, 238; life and reign to 1709, 2–6, 8–22, 24–28; peace negotiations and diplomacy, 19, 21–22, 63–65, 85–90, 110–12, 117, 152–57, 211–13, 226–27, 230, 232; as *roi-bureaucrate* and conduct of government, 25, 89, 117, 154; as *roi de guerre* and conduct of war, 3, 5–6, 8–9, 11, 36, 70–71, 73–74, 103; strategy in Flanders, 28, 38, 49–53, 65, 84–85, 103, 118–19, 145–46, 149–52, 158–60, 176–77, 206, 209–10, 222–25, 228–29, 231–32, 235; War of the Spanish Succession after Malplaquet, 221–37
Louis XV, King of France, 44, 233
Louis-William, Margrave of Baden-Baden, 55
Louvois, François-Michel Le Tellier, Marquis de, 5, 6, 9, 10, 25, 37, 54, 100, 151

Low Countries, 36, 101, 115, 132, 147, 220
Lullin Frères, 48, 78
Lullin, Jean-Antoine, 78
Luxembourg, 4, 13
Luxembourg, Chrétien-Louis de Montmorency, Chevalier de, 133, 142, 174, 177, 182, 202, 204, 209
Luxembourg, François-Henri de Montmorency-Boutteville, Marshal, 11, 34
Lyon, 42, 48, 53, 77, 78, 164
Lys, river, 28, 35, 36, 52, 84, 85, 139, 140, 142, 144, 147, 160, 161, 173

Maastricht: siege of 1673, 54
Machado, Jakob Hiskia, 140, 141
Machado, Moses (Antonio Alvarez), 140
Madrid, 15, 16, 64, 95, 227, 226
Maillebois, château of, 43
Mailly, marquise de, 83
Maine, Louis, Duc du, 34
Maintenon, Françoise d'Aubigné, Marquise de, 16, 25–28, 33–34, 35, 40, 53–57, 65, 67, 77, 79, 81, 101, 111, 117, 119–21, 158, 162, 164, 176, 219–21, 235, 238
Malplaquet, battle of, 108, 209, 211, 220, 221, 224, 225, 237; battlefield and terrain, 176, 177, 181; battle plan, Allies, 184, 186–87; battle plan, French, 182–83; deployment of the Allied armies, 186; deployment of the Army of Flanders, 182–83; fighting during, 186–202; results and significance of, 203–7
Marchiennes, 160, 234, 235
maréchaussée, 149
Mareschal, Georges, 6, 204
Mariembourg, 36
Marie-Thérèse, Queen of France, 4, 14, 25
Maritime Powers. *See* Great Britain and the Dutch Republic

Marlborough, John Churchill, Duke of, 28, 34, 53, 56, 67, 75, 77, 103, 110, 137, 150, 161, 175, 176, 182, 205, 206, 232, 237; character and career to 1709, 19, 20, 22–24, 27, 99, 112; conduct of campaign of 1709, 33, 38, 133–35, 141–44, 147, 155, 157, 172–74, 208, 210–11; conduct of diplomacy and peace negotiations, 86, 89, 97, 98, 112–20, 153, 212, 213; generalship at the Battle of Malplaquet, 177–80, 184, 186–87, 193, 197–98, 200–201, 202, 203, 205, 206–7; War of the Spanish Succession after 1709, 220, 222, 224–25, 226, 230–31
Marly, château of, 47, 101–2, 111, 219, 233
Marseilles, 40
Marsin, Ferdinand, Marshal, 19
Martinet, Jean, 71
Masham, Abigail, 99
Massif Central, 41
Maubeuge, 36, 85, 86, 88, 97, 110, 111, 158, 160, 161, 173, 175, 176, 204, 209, 210, 211, 230
Maximilian Emmanuel, elector of Bavaria, 15, 17, 54, 56, 57, 65, 84, 101, 132, 173
Mazarin, Jules, Cardinal, 3
Medina, Solomon de, 140, 141
Menin, 36, 65, 85, 88, 97, 110, 142, 144–46, 211
Mesgrigny, Jean de, 145, 148, 156, 157, 171
Mesnager, Nicolas, 21–22, 232
Metz, 83
Meudon, château of, 16, 40, 82
Meuse, river, 9, 11, 22, 35, 37, 52, 86, 110, 118, 208, 210, 220, 229
Midi, 41
Milan, 15, 64
Milkau, Moritz Friedrich von, 188, 199
Moerdijk, 86, 219
Mohacs, battle of (1687), 54
Mongelas, Romain Dru de, 49, 50, 67

Mons, 13, 33, 50, 65, 87, 116, 140, 162, 173–76, 179, 206, 223; siege of 1691, 34, 37; siege of 1709, 208–11, 220
Montespan, Françoise-Athénaïs de Rouchechouart, Marquise de, 21, 25
Montpelier, 40
Morin, Louis, 39–41
Mormal, forest, 208
Mortagne, 36
Moselle, river, 23, 34, 56
mutinies, 49, 50, 106, 108, 236

Namur, 4, 49, 50, 87, 211; siege of 1692, 11; siege of 1695, 12–13, 34
Nangis, Louis-Armand de Brichanteau, Marquis de, 196, 206
Naples, 15, 85, 86, 88, 97, 110, 112, 224
Neerwinden, battle of (1693), 11
Ne Plus Ultra, Lines of, 230–31
Neuport, 211, 227
Nimes, 40
Nine Years' War (1688–1697), 10–13, 20, 34, 55, 76, 96, 133, 135, 142, 147
Noailles, Adrien Maurice, Duc de, 111, 162, 164
Normandy, 43, 138, 148
North Sea, 9, 10, 110
Notre Dame de Paris (cathedral), 11, 205

Obourg, 175
Orange, Johan Willem Friso, Prince of, 136, 155, 184, 190, 191–93, 198, 205
Orchies, 159, 174
Order of the Holy Spirit, 20, 21, 25, 219
Orkney, George Hamilton, Earl of, 135, 174, 185, 193, 198, 199, 200–201, 203
Orléans, Philippe, Duc d', brother of Louis XIV, 8
Orléans, Philippe, Duc d', nephew of Louis XIV and Regent of Louis XV, 20, 44, 64
Ormond, James Butler, Duke of, 232
Orry, Jean, 64
Orval, Jean-Robert Le Fèvre d', 234, 235
Ottoman Empire, 9, 76; Great Turkish War (1683–1699), 9–10, 19, 54, 234
Oudenarde, 23, 38, 87; battle of (1708), 23, 57, 63, 65, 73, 77, 99, 132, 135, 136, 143, 150, 172, 200, 207, 227
Oxenstiern, Bengt van, 136, 191

Palatinate, 10
Palatine, Elisabeth Charlotte, Princess, 8, 40
Pallandt, Johann Werner van, 174
Paris, 4, 12, 35, 36, 39–41, 80, 82, 84, 107, 111, 121, 142, 162–63, 202, 210, 220, 229, 231, 235
Parîs brothers, 148, 210, 221, 223
Parlement of Paris, 26, 81, 136
partition treaties, 15, 16, 17, 96
Peace of Nijmegen (1678), 6, 8, 9
Peace of the Pyrnees (1659), 3
Peace of Ryswick (1697), 13, 15, 17, 18, 87, 88, 96, 110, 235
Peace of Westphalia (1648), 110, 113
Petkum, Hermann, 63, 88, 152, 153, 155, 211, 213, 220–21
Philip, Duc d'Anjou. See Philip V, King of Spain
Philip IV, King of Spain, 3, 4
Philip V, King of Spain, 15–17, 19, 20, 24, 85, 97, 101, 110–12, 114, 115, 118, 152, 154, 211, 212, 220, 226, 228, 230, 236
Philippeville, 36
Philippsburg, 10, 13
Picardy, 27, 34, 35, 50, 52, 82–84, 104, 105, 122, 145, 210
Piedmont, 20
Polignac, Melchior, Abbé de, 221, 225, 226, 227
Pomponne, Simon Arnauld de, 96
Pontchartrain, Louis Phélypeaux, Comte de, 16, 43, 89, 154
Portugal, 10, 97, 115
pré carré, 9, 20, 36, 38, 52, 82, 84, 150, 206, 220, 223, 224, 231, 233, 235; fortresses of, 36
Preliminaries of The Hague, 116–18, 152, 154, 213, 226, 234; Article 4,

116; Article 37, 116, 121, 152–55, 157, 158, 212, 220, 221, 226, 236
Prior, Matthew, 232
Provence, 20, 69
Puységur, Jacques-François de Chastenet, Marquis de, 133, 182, 184, 201, 202

Quiévrain, 175, 176
Quincy, Joseph Sevin, Chevalier de, 39, 51, 107, 131, 178, 191, 194, 202, 206, 207–8

Raffy, François, 52, 66, 104
Rakozci, Ferenc, Prince of Transylvania, 17–18, 134
Ramillies, battle of (1706), 20, 22, 52, 72, 76, 99, 125, 132, 133, 135, 150, 182, 193, 205, 207
Randwyck, Jacob van, 137
Ravat, Louis, 42
regiments, British: Buffs, 133; Coldstream Guards, 133; Fifteenth of Foot, 194; First Foot Guards, 131, 133, 195; Green Howards, 133; Royal Scots, 133; Scots Greys, 133, 200
regiments, Dutch: Frisian Guards, 134; Holland or Blue Guards, 134, 191–92, 199, 203; May, 193; Prince of Orange's Regiment, 134; Scottish Brigade, 134, 190–92; Stürler, 193
regiments, French: Alsace, 192; Bombardiers du Roi, 77; Boufflers, 190; Bourbonnais, 69, 109, 191, 208; Bourgogne, 51, 107, 178; Bretagne, 190, 204, 208; carabineers, 75, 132, 174, 182, 198; Champagne, 109, 208; Charost, 190, 208; Chateauneuf, 191; Clare, 74; du Roi, 69, 109, 190, 196; Gardes du Corps, 34, 74, 177, 200, 201, 203; Gardes francaises, 69, 71, 107, 109, 162, 189, 198, 201, 208; Gardes suisses, 69, 109, 162, 198, 201; Gendarmes, 54, 74, 105, 109, 132, 174, 182, 187, 199, 200, 201, 204; Greder, 67; la Marck, 191; la Marine, 190; Lannoy, 192; la Reine, 190, 194; la Sarre, 190; May, 193, 208; Navarre, 69, 191, 193, 199, 208; Picardie, 109, 192; Piémont, 109, 191, 208; Provence, 189; Royal-Allemand, 201, 208; Royal-Artillerie, 76; Royal-Infanterie, 192, 193, 199, 204, 208; Royal-Piémont, 201, 208; Saintonge, 190, 208
Revocation of the Edict of Nantes (1685), 9, 47
Rhine, river, 9, 10, 40, 55, 57, 86, 101, 104, 113, 131, 212, 235, 236
Rhone, river, 40
Rhonelle, stream, 208, 209
Richelieu, Armand-Jean du Plessis, Cardinal, 3
riots and uprisings, 12, 80–81, 83–84, 105, 111, 163, 236
Rocroi, 36
Rotterdam, 96, 116
Rouillé, Pierre, 63, 65, 85–88, 110, 226
Roussillon, 69
Rozel, François, Chevalier du, 199, 202
Rumersheim, battle of (1709), 212

Sacheverell, Henry, 228
Sailly, marquise de, 83, 105
Saint-Contest, Dominique-Claude Barberie de, 83
Saint-Cyr, 26, 81, 119
Saint-Georges, James Francis Edward Stuart, Chevalier de, 17, 87, 88, 97, 110, 111, 200, 211
Saint-Germain, château of, 5, 10
Saint-Ghislain, 174, 175, 179
Saint-Hilaire, Armand de Mormès de, 133, 182–83, 189, 197, 198, 202
Saint-Mayme, Pierre de, 107–8
Saint-Omer, 36, 50, 140
Saintonge, 40
Saint-Simon, Louis de Rouvroy, Duc de, 43, 47, 76, 102, 136, 162
Saint-Valéry, 138, 143
Saint-Venant, 36, 85, 139, 142, 144–46, 158, 225

Sambre, river, 11, 35, 52, 110, 118, 161, 173, 206, 209, 210, 230, 233, 234
Sardinia, 86, 87, 224
Savignac, Joseph-François-Ignace de Labat de, 39–40, 120
Savoy, 10, 20, 228
Scarpe, river, 35, 84, 139, 151, 160, 231, 234
Scheldt, river, 22, 23, 28, 35, 135, 148, 150, 151, 159, 161, 174, 206, 209, 210, 231, 234, 235
Schulenburg, Johann Matthias, Graf von der, 136, 147, 155, 157, 186, 188, 190, 197, 198
Seine, river, 40, 231
Selle, river, 234
Sensée, river, 231
Seven Articles. *See* London Preliminaries
Sicily, 15, 85–88, 97, 110, 112, 224
Sinzendorf, Philippe von, 114, 154, 233
Soissonais, 83, 105, 161
Somme, river, 40, 83, 138, 143, 232, 233
Sourches, Louis du Bouchet, Marquis de, 107
Spain and the Spanish Monarchy, 3, 9, 10, 14, 15, 17, 18, 24, 64, 79, 85, 86, 96–101, 111, 112, 114, 115, 118, 152–55, 210–11, 226, 227, 228, 229, 231, 236
Spanish Habsburgs, 3, 14, 15, 96
Spanish Netherlands, 3, 6, 11, 13, 17, 18, 20, 34, 57, 63, 85, 96–98, 110, 114, 141, 143, 150, 173, 209, 211, 233
Sparre, Karel Willem van, 136, 191
St. John, Henry, 232
Stanhope, Alexander, 227–28
Starhemberg, Guido von, 227–28
Steenkerque, battle of (1692), 11, 34
Stollhofen, Lines of, 57
Strasbourg, 9, 10, 86, 101, 110, 112, 113
Surville, Louis-Charles de Hautefort, Marquis de, 122, 145, 148, 155–59, 171, 172
Sweden, 4

Tallard, Camille d'Hostun, Marshal, 19
Taté, Jean, 39
Templeuve, château of, 65
The Hague, 21–22, 85, 90, 96, 101, 103, 110, 112, 113, 143, 155, 211, 221, 224, 225, 234
Thirty Years' War (1618–1648), 3, 44, 86, 113
Tilly, Claude Frederic T'Serclaes, Count, 136, 142, 143, 160, 184
Tingry, Charles de Montmorency-Luxembourg, Prince de, 234–35
Torcy, Jean-Baptiste Colbert, Marquis de, 16, 21, 22, 63–65, 85–90, 95–98, 102, 103–4, 110–17, 120, 152–55, 211–13, 220–21, 226–27, 229–30, 232, 237
Toulon, siege of, 1707, 20, 143
Tournai, 13, 24, 36, 38, 50, 65, 84–86, 97, 106, 110, 111, 122, 138, 142–46, 158, 159, 173, 174, 211, 222, 223, 236; siege of 1709, 145–48, 155–58, 164, 171–72, 177, 179
Townshend, Charles, 154
Treaties of Rastatt and Baden (1714), 236
Treaty of Aix-la-Chapelle (1668), 4
Treaty of Succession and the Barrier (1709), 211, 231, 235
Treaty of Utrecht (1713), 235, 236
Trianon, château of, 40
Truce of Ratisbon (1684), 9, 10
Trudaine, Charles, 78
Tullibardine, James Murray, Marquess of, 192, 203
Turenne, Henri de La Tour d'Auvergne, Vicomte de, 53, 136
Turin, 20; battle of (1706), 20, 99, 150, 172, 207
Tuscany and Tuscan presidios, 85–87

universal monarchy, 6, 9, 10, 15, 99, 100
Ursins, Marie Anne de la Trémoille, Princesse des, 35, 64, 65, 81, 121

Index

Valenciennes, 5, 36, 50, 68, 122, 140, 150, 151, 159–61, 173, 175, 204, 208, 209, 210, 211, 225, 230, 234, 235
Van der Dussen, Bruno, 64, 86–88, 110, 221, 226
Vauban, Sebastien Le Prestre de, 5, 8, 9, 11, 14, 20, 36, 52, 73, 133, 147, 223
Vaux, château of, 57
Vegelin van Claerbergen, Philip Frederik, 137, 141, 144, 199
Vendôme, Louis-Joseph de Bourbon, Duc de, 22–24, 26, 27, 53, 72–74, 135, 227–28
Verdun, 104
Versailles, château of, 1–2, 5–8, 13–14, 20–21, 28, 33, 39, 40, 44, 57, 63–65, 78, 79, 89, 95, 101, 102, 107, 110, 116, 117, 145, 164, 204, 211–12, 219, 220, 222, 227, 230, 234
Victor Amadeus, Duke of Savoy, 17, 20, 53, 210
Vienna, 9–10, 56, 100
Villars, Armand, Comte de, 196
Villars, Claude-Louis Hector, Marshal, 75, 77, 79, 102, 110, 111, 120, 125, 131, 132–33, 142–44, 147, 148, 171, 186, 202, 204–6, 220, 235, 237, 238; early life and career up to 1709, 53–57; given command of the Army of Flanders, 57; logistical and financial challenges of the Army of Flanders, 65–67, 85, 103–6, 108–9, 138–39, 148–49, 158, 161; strategy during Flanders campaign, 65, 67, 84–85, 103, 118–19, 138–40, 145–46, 149–51, 158–62, 175–76; tactics and generalship at the Battle of Malplaquet, 178–79, 180–84, 195–97, 199, 201, 204, 205, 206–7; War of the Spanish Succession after Malplaquet, 222–25, 230–31, 233–36
Villa Viciosa, battle of (1710), 227
Villeroy, François de Neufville, Marshal, 20, 134
Voltaire, François-Marie Arouet, 55, 235
Voysin, Daniel, 64, 119, 138, 139, 145, 149, 154, 158, 161, 172, 204, 209–10, 222, 223, 234

Wackerbarth, August Christoph von, 188, 190
Warneton, 146–47
War of Devolution (1667–1668), 4
War of the Reunions (1683–1684), 9, 10
War of the Spanish Succession, 44, 49, 55, 69, 70, 76, 125, 134, 136, 147, 172, 226, 234; causes of, 14–17; course to 1709 of, 17–25, 34; developments after 1709, 219–38
Watteau, Jean-Antoine, 67–69, 77
Webb, John, 72
William III, Prince of Orange, King of Great Britain and *Stadtholder* of the Dutch Republic, 6, 10, 13, 15–18, 37, 96, 100, 136, 142
Wilson, John, 194
winter quarters, 35, 50, 102, 105, 108, 164, 208, 209, 211
Withers, Henry, 179, 186, 193, 197, 199
Wittelsbach, house of, 17–19, 34, 84, 101, 150
Wynendale, battle of (1708), 72

Ypres, 36, 38, 53, 65, 84, 85, 88, 97, 110, 138, 142, 143, 146, 172–73, 211, 225, 236

About the Author

Darryl Dee is an expert on Louis XIV's France and early modern warfare. He is currently an associate professor of history at Wilfrid Laurier University.

www.ingramcontent.com/pod-product-compliance
Lightning Source LLC
Chambersburg PA
CBHW071246230426
43668CB00011B/1608